DOUBLE VISION

DOUBLE VISION

HOW THE PRESS DISTORTS AMERICA'S VIEW OF THE MIDDLE EAST

ZE'EV CHAFETS

WILLIAM MORROW AND COMPANY, INC.

New York

For

Samuel Jacob Chafets 1915–1964

Carol Stenbuck Chafets 1925–1981

Library of Congress Cataloging in Publication Data

Chafets, Ze'ev.
  Double vision.

  Includes bibliographical references and index.
  1. Jewish-Arab relations—1973–   —Public opinion.
2. Israel—Foreign opinion, American. 3. Near East—
Foreign opinion, American. 4. Public opinion—United
States. 5. Press—United States. I. Title.
DS119.7.C437 1984   956'.048   · 84-6742
ISBN 0-688-03977-4

Printed in the United States of America

First Edition

1 2 3 4 5 6 7 8 9 10

BOOK DESIGN BY BERNARD SCHLEIFER

ACKNOWLEDGMENTS

This book could not have been written without a great deal of help from a great many people. I wish to thank Marvin Josephson, Esther Newberg, Leora Nir, Kenneth Smilen, and Tatiana Mendoza for their support and encouragement in the initial phases of this project; Janice Ditchek, Gail Gans, Christine Rimon, Linda Rembaum, Steve Leibowitz, and Rivka Zipper for their indispensable research assistance; and Michael Elkins, Joseph Colten, Harry Wall, Daniel Syme, and once again, Leora Nir, who read the manuscript and gave me the benefit of their honest opinions. I am also indebted to Joseph and Betty Miller, Malcolm MacPherson, Abraham Foxman, and Herb Krosney who were there with advice and encouragement at crucial moments.

I am grateful to the Smith-Richardson Foundation whose generous grant helped make this book possible; and to the Anti-Defamation League of B'nai B'rith, *The Jerusalem Post*, *The New York Times*, and the American Cultural Center in Jerusalem, all of which made their research facilities available to me.

In 1983–84 I was a Special Research Fellow of the Lehr-

7

man Institute in New York. During the course of that year the institute sponsored three seminars on the material contained in this book. The participants included some of America's leading media experts, and their comments and criticisms were invaluable. I wish to thank all those who took part in the seminars, and Professors Nicholas Risopolis and Michael Mandelbaum for organizing them.

Naturally, the conclusions reached in this book are mine alone and do not necessarily reflect the views of any of those who gave me the benefit of their help and guidance.

I am particularly indebted to Bruce Lee of William Morrow who explained to me how books are born, and to his assistant, Elizabeth Terhune.

Finally, my greatest thanks and love to my wife, Miri, my daughter, Michal, and my son, Shmuel, for putting up with a preoccupied and often absent husband and father, and for their warm support and encouragement in this project.

CONTENTS

10 CONTENTS

PERSONAL NOTE

When Anwar Sadat announced, with only four days' notice, that he was coming to Jerusalem, a handful of Israeli officials was called to an emergency meeting to discuss arrangements for the unprecedented, and still unbelievable, event. I was one of those officials, barely thirty years old, less than two months in my job as director of Israel's Government Press Office. My assignment was to be the liaison officer between the Israeli government and the international press.

It would be badly understating the case to say that nothing in the previous two months in the job—indeed nothing in my experience in Israel, which had begun ten years earlier, when I moved to Jerusalem from my hometown of Pontiac, Michigan—remotely prepared me for the Sadat visit. I suddenly found myself in charge of press arrangements for one of the most spectacular media events of the century, and when the visit got under way, with a ringside seat at one of the most frenetic and exciting political meetings in modern times.

The Sadat visit was my initiation into the wild world of Middle East diplomacy and international press coverage. Less

than a month later I became one of the first Israelis ever to
visit Egypt when I went to Cairo as a delegate to the Mena
House Conference. During the next five years, as we established press relations with Egypt and the diplomatic process
unfolded, I spent so much time there that Cairo began to
seem like a second home.

I also wound up spending a good deal of time in another neighboring state—Lebanon. During the 1978 Litani
operation I traveled throughout southern Lebanon with the
foreign press corps; and a little more than four years later
I found myself in Beirut at the height of the War in Lebanon and the controversy that accompanied its press coverage. Beirut, like Cairo, had once seemed a million miles from
Jerusalem, yet during those months in the summer of 1982
I was practically a commuter to the Lebanese capital.

Despite the time I spent in Egypt and Lebanon—and in
the United States and Western Europe where I often went
for talks with journalists and government officials—most of
my work was in Jerusalem where, during those years, there
was, in Menachem Begin's words, "never a dull moment."
There are more than two hundred resident foreign correspondents in Israel—one of the largest resident foreign press
contingents in the world—and as many as twenty-five
hundred more visit the country every year. When it comes
to generating news, Israel is a superpower, and just about
every important American editor and foreign correspondent turns up in Jerusalem eventually. In my years at the
Press Office I met and worked with some of the greatest,
and some of the worst, American journalists. Part of my job
was to explain Israel and its policies to them; they recipro-
cated by providing me with an education on how the American press works.

That education wasn't limited to the press coverage of
Israel. Nineteen seventy-seven to 1982 were tumultuous years
in the entire Middle East—from the overthrow of the Shah
of Iran and the American hostage crisis to the seizure of the
Grand Mosque in Saudi Arabia; and from the assassination
of Anwar Sadat to the outbreak of the Iran-Iraq war. Many
of these events were covered by Jerusalem-based correspon-

dents dispatched to the scene, or by journalists who passed through the Israeli capital on the way. Almost without exception they returned to Israel with stories—some funny, some terrifyingly serious—about the difficulties and dangers of reporting in the Middle East.

The five years I spent working with and observing American and other Western journalists, and the conclusions I reached about their work are, therefore, at the center of this book. Readers are cautioned, however, that it is neither a memoir nor an official statement of Israeli thinking. It presents my own view of America's Middle East reporting. The ideas and conclusions expressed are mine alone and emphatically not those of the government of Israel.

On the other hand, I don't claim to be an impartial scholar (if any such animal exists) or an objective and dispassionate journalist (an equally rare species). I am an Israeli veteran of the Middle East's press wars, and if I am sometimes critical of my country's policies, I am generally sympathetic to its point of view. I have tried my best to write a fair-minded book, but I do not pretend that it is a neutral one.

In the course of working on this book, I have discovered that writing a critique of the press contains an inherent and paradoxical danger—you are apt to commit many of the same transgressions that you criticize in others. The critic, no less than the journalist, is bound to make selections, to prefer the interesting to the mundane, and to concentrate on the weaknesses of the superior journalists and ambitious news organizations, while often ignoring the far more serious deficiencies of the mediocrities. This discovery has tempered my judgment of the motives behind many of the journalistic failures that this book chronicles; it has also reinforced my belief that the only antidote to the tyranny of technique is candor about its existence and about the distortions it inevitably causes.

It was the nature of my work at the Government Press Office that much of what I was told by correspondents (and much of what I said to them) was off the record and confidential. I have, therefore, refrained from recounting conversations I had with journalists during the course of our work together except when I have had specific approval from them to do so. On the other hand, once it became known that I was writing this book, I contacted and interviewed more than a hundred American journalists, many of whom were old friends or old foes. I was delighted to find that almost without exception, friend and foe alike were cooperative, helpful, and willing to put their views on the record—a happy indication that when it comes to the First Amendment, most American journalists practice what they preach.

Over the years I came to have a high regard for many of the journalists I worked with, and I have some very fond memories of them. I recall, for example, the *Chicago Sun-Times*'s Jay Bushinsky sitting in the lobby of the Mena House Hotel in Cairo, dressed in a trench coat in true foreign-correspondent style, bent over a portable typewriter, and pounding out a story about a Sabbath eve ceremony that a group of Israelis had just conducted in the hotel's El Nawas Room. Suddenly he spotted Anan Safadi, an Israeli-Arab journalist, and hollered, "Hey, Safadi, who the hell was Nawas?"

"A medieval Arabic poet," came the answer.

Bushinsky returned to his typing, then raised his head again. "Hey, Safadi," he demanded. "Gimme a century."

I remember when John Bierman, an imposing Englishman who worked for the *Boston Globe* was chosen as the pool correspondent for the funeral of Golda Meir. Before boarding the bus to the cemetery, he underwent a routine security check by a nineteen-year-old Israeli soldier who came up to the correspondent's shoulder. The boy asked him a list of stock security questions, the last of which was, "Are you carrying a weapon?" Bierman peered down at the young soldier and, in an arch, incredulous tone, asked, "My dear fellow, do I look the sort of journalist who would bring a *pistol* to a *funeral*?"

Reporters are supposed to be hard-boiled and cynical, but I vividly recall the joy with which the press corps greeted President Sadat's visit to Jerusalem; and as the peace process unfolded, it had strong supporters among the American journalists in Egypt and Israel.

When Israel's first ambassador to Egypt, Eliahu Ben-Elissar, arrived in Cairo to take up his post, I went with him to help with press arrangements. The day after we arrived I was invited, along with other Israeli officials, to a *Time* magazine reception, at the Nile Hilton Hotel, in honor of *Time*'s new bureau chief. The entire foreign diplomatic corps of Cairo had been invited, along with hundreds of the members of the Egyptian political and social elite. When I arrived at the reception, however, there were only about a hundred people in the enormous ballroom—and only two of them were Egyptians. Word had got out that Israelis had been invited, and Egyptian society had boycotted the event. I felt terrible, both for *Time* and for what the boycott augured for Israeli-Egyptian relations. After such a public display of anti-Israeli solidarity by the Egyptian establishment, I thought, no one in Cairo will dare have anything to do with the Israeli Embassy.

A few days after the *Time* fiasco, Don Schanche of the *Los Angeles Times,* the senior American correspondent in the Egyptian capital, and his wife, invited Ambassador and Mrs. Ben-Elissar to dinner at their home. Schanche knew of the boycott, and he also knew that he was risking his own standing and connections in Cairo. He asked sixteen Egyptian friends to attend the dinner party—and all sixteen turned him down. The American reporter proceeded to publish the entire story and made a point of letting people in Cairo know that he was friendly with Ben-Elissar whom, in fact, he hardly knew. Schanche's instinctive generosity and sense of fair play were emulated by many of his American colleagues in Cairo, who demonstrated a friendliness and respect for the Israelis, which was at least partially an expression of their support for the peace process and a quiet protest against the Egyptians' behavior.

I came to my job at the Government Press Office as an admirer of the American press, and by and large, I still am one. The great press critic A. J. Liebling once wrote that newsmen, whatever their weaknesses, are addicted to the truth. "A newspaperman may lie to hold his job," Liebling wrote, "but he won't believe it and the necessity outrages him

so that he craves truth all the more thereafter. A few newspapermen lie to get on in the world, but it outrages them
too, and I have never known a dishonest journalist who wasn't
a patently unhappy bastard."[1]

I have met a few of these "unhappy bastards" in my time
(and some of them figure prominently in this book), but most
of the American journalists I know are honest men and
women who are faced with a difficult, often dangerous job.
Their basic integrity makes this book both possible and, I
hope, worthwhile. Whatever the faults and failures of
American media coverage of the Middle East—and they are
deplorably many, and serious—there remains, I believe, a
hope for improvement, and for a more clear-sighted and
balanced approach to the Middle East, its peoples and conflicts.

INTRODUCTION

During the past decade no region in the world has been more important to the United States than the Middle East. From the 1973 Arab oil embargo through the Tehran hostage crisis to the dispatch of U.S. Marines and warships to Beirut, events in the area have had a direct, often personal effect on Americans.

Not surprisingly, American media interest in the region has grown along with U.S. involvement. Middle East leaders such as Begin, Sadat, Khaddafi, Khomeini, Arafat, and Assad have become household names; and the Middle East's perpetual drama—the Israeli rescue mission at Entebbe, the fall of the Shah and the rise of the Ayatollah, Anwar Sadat's visit to Israel and the Camp David peace process, Israel's destruction of the Iraqi nuclear reactor, the antics of Libya's Colonel Khaddafi, and the terrorist murder of American marines in Beirut—has caught the imagination and held the interest of the American press.

And yet, despite the torrent of media coverage and commentary, surprisingly little is actually *known* about the region. Unanticipated wars break out, supposedly secure national leaders are toppled by previously invisible rivals, mass religious movements spring up seemingly overnight, American allies inexplicably oppose American policy, and leaders who are customarily described as "moderate" speak of liquidating their neighbors. News from the Middle East often has a kind of Alice-in-Wonderland quality that stems from the obvious inability of the press to construct and convey a clear picture of events and developments there.

What accounts for this inability? A. J. Liebling once wrote, "A good reporter, if he chooses the right approach, can understand a cat or an Arab. The choice is the problem, and if he chooses wrong he will come away scratched or baffled."[1] The choices that have shaped the American press's approach to the Middle East in recent years have been influenced by a complex mixture of inexperience, parochialism, radical chic, economic self-interest, U.S. government manipulation, and the strong-arm news-management techniques of the Arab world. Often their result has been to leave the American public both scratched *and* baffled.

The Middle East is an enormous region, roughly the size of Europe, which, except for Israel, is "covered" by a tiny handful of American journalists—fewer, in fact, than the number of sportswriters at the New York *Daily News*. Most of these reporters can't speak the local languages or even read the newspapers, and they usually bring little or no background to the complex events that they are expected to cover. Even under ideal circumstances it would be physically impossible for such a small band of journalists, most of whom concentrate on the same stories, to simultaneously cover more than twenty countries in a region and milieu they do not fully understand; and the conditions under which foreign journalists are forced to work in the Arab world are far from ideal.

Most of the countries in the Middle East are closed societies that admit journalists on a selective basis and allow them only brief and carefully supervised visits. Reporters are made to understand that their future access to the country may well depend on the acceptability of their work. Even correspondents who are undeterred by this condition are usually hard pressed to find any real news in places that have no free press, no political debate, and few citizens who are prepared to speak candidly about public affairs. When American journalists were banned from Grenada during the first few days of the American operation there, the press was quick to point out the patent impossibility of gaining independent, reliable news from an area to which there is no access. Yet most of the Arab world (with the partial exceptions of Egypt and Lebanon) has denied any real access to the American press for years. The results have been predictable.

Worse still, American journalists in some parts of the Arab world have been the victims not only of exclusion but of physical intimidation. The Syrians, the Palestine Liberation Organization, and to a lesser extent, some other Arab regimes have practiced terror as a tool of news management. They have subjected "unfriendly" reporters to threats, harassment, assault, and even murder. Such techniques have sometimes forced journalists in the Middle East to practice self-censorship and restraint, to ignore certain dangerous subjects and to pull their punches in some situations. This self-censorship pollutes the flow of information, and it is compounded when news organizations hide the truth about the conditions under which their journalists are forced to work, thus preventing the public from making an informed assessment of the limitations and reliability of the reporting from and about the region.

While most of the Middle East is shrouded in self-imposed secrecy, few nations on earth are as open—and as closely scrutinized by outsiders—as Israel. A small army of foreign correspondents resides in Jerusalem and Tel Aviv, far more than are stationed in the entire Arab world, and they provide an enormous amount of media coverage on the Jewish state. During the past ten years no other foreign nation, with the exception of the Soviet Union, has been the subject of so much American air time and newsprint.

One obvious reason is that Israel is an easy country to cover. It is not only an open society, but a contentious one, and foreign correspondents can rely on its own hypercritical press and rough-and-tumble internal political debate to supply both controversy and information. As a key actor on the Middle East stage, a major American ally and recipient of U.S. aid, and as a country whose biblical associations and Jewish population make it familiar and evocative to millions of Americans, Israel is an eminently newsworthy place, one the American press has both the motive and the opportunity to cover thoroughly, not to say obsessively.

When it comes to the closed societies of the Arab world, however, the press has been forced to seek alternative means of reporting. "When information is available, the expert comes into his own,"[2] Liebling once warned, and the modern Middle East is a prime example of that dictum. Long-distance analysis—of the Iran-Iraq War, the stability of the Saudi regime, or of Hafez Assad's war against Syrian dissidents—has increasingly been substituted for actual eyewitness reporting. American "experts," have been used to fill the information vacuum, and all too often their judgments and assessments have proven anything but expert. Long-distance punditry portrayed the Shah of Iran as an invincibly secure monarch, declared Saddam Hussein's Iraq the sure winner in the Gulf War, and convinced many that the sale of AWACs to Saudi Arabia would secure its support for the Camp David peace process. The inaccuracy of these and other "expert analyses" is obvious and explains why reporters often refer to them as "thumb suckers."

The inability to do much serious, independent reporting in the Middle East provides the U.S. government with the means to significantly influence the media's agenda and perceptions about the region. The administration—any administration—is able to use what Walter Lippmann once referred to as a "searchlight"[3] to illuminate previously obscure places, situations, and developments, and by emphasizing America's interest in them, to make them the focus of press attention. In the case of closed societies, the media are often unable to check the accuracy and reliability of U.S. government claims and assessments. Officials have information that is unavailable to journalists, and this gives them an inestimable advantage in shaping not only the "what" but also the "how" of press coverage.

The opinions and interests of the American government are not the only outside influences that affect the coverage of the Middle East. The 1973 Arab oil boycott gave rise to a train of logic that put good relations with the Arab world at the center of America's regional interests—and saw the solution of the Palestine issue as the key condition for those good relations. For those who accepted this line of reasoning, Israel's refusal to allow a Palestinian entity to be created in the West Bank and Gaza appeared to be the primary impediment to the golden solution. This analysis became prevalent during the Carter administration and was adopted by the American economic establishment, which includes the people who own and control the American press. The Arabs never "bought out" the American media as some of their more emotional critics have claimed, but they were able to make the people who own and run news organizations more sensitive to the need for "greater balance" in the treatment of Middle East news.

Ironically, this petro-centered, essentially conservative analysis has been paralleled by a growth in sympathy and support for the PLO on the American left which, after the war in Vietnam, found itself in search of a new issue. A good many journalists, both at home and in the field, shared the general feeling that the Palestinians had become the new underdog, and that their demands for "self-determination" were both just and reasonable. The decade after Vietnam and the oil embargo saw the emergence of a rather incongruous pro-Arab coalition that extended from Jesse Helms on the right to Jesse Jackson on the left, and that found its journalistic expression in the alliance between Anthony Lewis and Evans and Novak.

Anthony Lewis also represented another influence on the coverage of the Middle East—its "Jewish component." Lewis, who considers himself a Zionist, is also one of Israel's most consistent detractors. Much of his criticism is based on his feelings, as a Jew, that Israeli policy does not represent Jewish moral and ethical values. There are a great many Jews at every level of American journalism, and they add a personal dimension to the coverage and commentary on the

Middle East. For years the Arabs have claimed that this dimension is essentially pro-Israel, while many Jews have argued that it causes the press to bend over backward to prove its objectivity. There is probably an element of truth in both these charges, as well as considerable validity to the counterargument that most American Jewish journalists are able to neutralize whatever personal feelings they may have about Israel. Certainly the sensitivity of the Arab-Israel conflict and the large number of Jews involved in its press coverage have given American Middle East press coverage a more self-conscious and emotional tone than is found in most foreign reporting and commentary.

If this "Jewish component" is unique to the Middle East, the other factors that influence media coverage of the area are not. Exclusion, censorship, and even intimidation of journalists are common in much of the Third World and in the Soviet bloc; the U.S. government exerts a considerable influence on foreign news selection from many places, most notably Central America; and the interests and ideas of the people who own and work in the media are always influential. These factors are particularly significant in the coverage of the Middle East, however, because the region is exceptional in two ways: It is extraordinarily important, strategically and economically, to the United States; and it is normally presented by the press in the context of the Arab-Israel conflict. The American public is called upon both to debate general American policy in the region, where political unrest and superpower competition have combined to create a particularly volatile and dangerous situation, and to decide the merits of the more narrow Arab-Israel struggle, one of whose key elements is the battle for American public opinion.

The current state of reporting on and from the Middle East makes this an extraordinarily difficult task. Most of the influences on the selection and presentation of news about the region are all but invisible to the public, which seldom stops to ask what news it is *not* getting. No American newspaper has ever run a blank column with the heading: "This is where we would put the news from Saudi Arabia if we could get a reporter in there," and remarkably few have been candid about the effects of dangers and pressures their reporters face in the Arab world. In the same way, not many news organizations have been forthcoming about the other hidden influences on their work, and they often act as if these were none of the public's business. As NBC spokeswoman Mary Lou O'Callaghan put it: "As for the questions pertaining to NBC's relations with the State Department or NBC News's handling of sensitive situations concerning its correspondents, it is NBC policy not to discuss these areas. If we were to have a public response in any way, it would come in the text of the *NBC Nightly News*."[4]

There is delicious irony in a news organization taking this position, and more than a little arrogance. NBC and its sister media giants argue for special prerogatives under the First Amendment, but it is not unusual for them to take the Fifth when it comes to their own affairs. They often justify this attitude by emphasizing their right, as privately owned corporations, to privacy—thus abandoning "the public's right to know" for the more businesslike slogan of "caveat emptor."

The Middle East is far too important, and American public opinion much too influential, for the national debate on the region to take place in the dark. Americans have the need and the right to know what news and commentary they are getting from the Middle East, and why; and to form their opinions about the region and U.S. policy there on the basis of a clear understanding of the reliability, comprehensiveness, and balance of the information they receive from the American press.

DOUBLE VISION

1

THE ARC OF
SILENCE

John Foster Dulles was once asked how peace could
be achieved in the Middle East. "Well," said the American
Secretary of State, "what we need is for the Jews and the
Arabs to start treating each other in a Christian manner."
The story is perhaps apocryphal, but it illustrates an important truth—many foreign observers find it exceedingly difficult to grasp the Middle East's complexity, its sheer
"differentness."

At first glance, the region is deceptively homogeneous.
Most of its inhabitants are Moslems who speak Arabic and
call themselves Arabs. The countries in the area have, for
the most part, a common Islamic tradition and a shared experience of recent European domination followed by post-
colonial independence. Moreover, this apparent uniformity
is fortified by some one-dimensional but remarkably enduring stereotypes—the noble nomad, the wily bazaar mer-
chant, the sultry belly dancer, the religious fanatic—that
inhabit the mindscapes of even sophisticated Westerners.

In fact, the Middle East is a remarkably heterogeneous
place, marked by regional and communal distinctions that
often seem minute to outsiders but are a cherished and nur-

tured source of identity to the area's inhabitants. Arabic is widely spoken, but to be conversant in all of the Middle East's languages, one would have to know Hebrew, Persian, Berber, Armenian, Aramaic, Turkish, and half a dozen dialects of Arabic, some as different from each other as Spanish is from French. Islam is the dominant religion, but there are sizable communities of Maronite, Coptic, Greek, and Armenian Christians, Druze, Bahais, and, of course, Jews. Moreover, within Islam itself there are deeply competitive schools of worship, from the orthodox Sunni Islam of Saudi Arabia to the Alawite sect of Syria and the resurgent Shi'a symbolized by Iran's Ayatollah Khomeini. In a region in which religion is not merely a set of beliefs and rituals but the basis of communal identity and life style, these differences can be crucial.

Much of the Middle East traces its history to common beginnings—the Moslem conquerors who swept out of the Arabian peninsula in the seventh and eighth centuries—and most of its people call themselves Arabs. But millions of others are not Arabs at all; they are Berbers, Persians, Kurds, Nubians, Jews, Armenians, and so forth. They trace their histories not to the Arab conquest, but to traditions and cultures that often predate the arrival of the Arabs by hundreds or even thousands of years.

The countries in the area, excepting only Israel, are united in the framework of the Arab League or the larger Islamic family of nations. Yet it would be hard to find a more fractious and divided group of neighbors anywhere in the world. Since the 1960s, full-scale wars have been fought between Iran and Iraq, in Yemen (with Egypt and Saudi Arabia backing different sides), and in Lebanon, where civil war claimed an estimated one hundred thousand lives. Syria has invaded Jordan, Algeria and Morocco have fought bloody and protracted border skirmishes, Egypt and Libya have exchanged gunfire and accusations, and, of course, Israel and the Arabs have fought more or less continuously.

The Middle East sometimes seems a region of established nation states, but there is hardly a single country without a significant ethnic minority engaged in a struggle for independence, or at least for greater autonomy. For decades the Kurds have fought both Iran and Iraq; Shi'ites in Saudi Arabia's Eastern Province have rioted against the central government; the Copts in Egypt have been a restive and sometimes violent minority; the Alawite regime in Syria has slaughtered thousands of Sunni Moslem Brothers in the last few years; recently the Iranian government has carried out bloody purges against the Bahai community; for years there was a prolonged tribal civil war in the Sudan; and in 1970, King Hussein's Bedouin troops killed thousands of Palestinians in what amounted to a civil war in Jordan.

There are also significant differences of internal organization and styles of government. Saudi Arabia is a kingdom ruled by a large extended clan that wields absolute power; Jordan is a monarchy controlled by one man and a small band of Bedouin loyalists; Iran under Khomeini is a theocracy; Syria is a dictatorship whose power rests on the Ba'ath political party, the army, and the loyal Alawite clansmen of President Assad; Iraq, controlled by a rival faction of the Ba'ath party, has a secular, totalitarian regime. No two states in the region have precisely the same form of government, although with the exception of Israel, all of them are, to one degree or another, authoritarian.

Finally, there is the fact that Middle Easterners, view the world differently from Westerners. Divided in much else, they are united in their fierce commitment to history, their integrated religious-communal-ethnic identities, their rejection of many of the secular, individualistic values of the West. The idea, once expressed to me in all seriousness at the height of the Iranian revolution by a West Coast newspaper editor, that what "these people" want is what everyone wants—"Cokes and T-shirts and Mustangs," is simply wrong.

A great Orientalist once remarked that Western reporters' descriptions of the Middle East sometimes read like those of an American baseball writer describing a cricket match. And in truth, American correspondents in the Middle East labor under severe handicaps in understanding and reporting on the people, developments, and issues at stake there. They—and through them, the American public—are con-

stantly surprised by unexpected developments. Unanticipated wars break out, seemingly stable regimes collapse,
beloved national leaders are assassinated, friendly governments refuse to cooperate, irrational religious movements
emerge where none had been known to exist.

The Middle East has always been an unpredictable region, but until recently it was of no special importance to
Americans. For much of its modern history, it was merely
another remote place inhabited by Wogs (the disparaging
British colonial term for "Wily Oriental Gentlemen"), of interest for its religious importance, but little else. During the
1950s and 1960s, the Arab world was covered by a tiny
handful of American reporters, mostly based in Beirut, whose
stories, if they got into the paper at all, were often found
among the lingerie ads. Even Israel, whose dramatic birth,
biblical connection, and Jewish population made it more familiar, and hence more interesting, to Americans, was covered, except for special events, mostly by the wire services
and only a few stringers. Not many American reporters were
assigned to the Middle East on a full-time basis.

But in 1973 things began to change. From a media backwater, the Middle East became the most newsworthy area of
the world. What brought about this change? Most American
journalists would agree with CBS foreign editor Peter Larkin: "Oil. I'd start with oil. I mean, what else? Everything
else is secondary, everything else is a variation on the theme."[1]

The 1973 Arab oil embargo that accompanied the Egyptian and Syrian invasion of Israel, and that has had a decade-long effect on the West's psychology and economy, was
truly a watershed for news interest in the Middle East.
Americans were suddenly waiting in lines at gas stations, and
they wanted to know why. The answer seemed to be found
in the board rooms and oil fields of Saudi Arabia, Iraq, Iran,
and the other OPEC giants. The great denominator of foreign news—perceived self-interest—was now applied to the
area with a vengeance.

At first, the media attention focused on the region after
1973 was a function of oil; as Larkin says, "everything else
was secondary. . . ." The Israeli-Arab conflict took on a new,

urgent dimension because of the once-and-future linkage of Western oil supplies with Arab political demands. Western governments, always a powerful influence on the agenda and perceptions of their nations' news organizations, proved sensitive to the Arab concern over the Palestine question, and this was reflected in the press. Later, the fall of the Shah of Iran and the rise of the Khomeini were watched microscopically for their effect on oil supplies; the Iran-Iraq war, to the extent that the West was able to penetrate it, was also seen as vital, because of its impact on the price and availability of fuel. Crises that only a few years before would have been considered parochial and even quaint—such as the 1979 seizure of the Grand Mosque in Mecca by Saudi rebels—were suddenly being followed with apprehension in the United States and Europe. Reporters crisscrossed the region attending Arab summit conferences that would have been ignored in the past, or accompanying Western officials on shuttles to capitals they would have been unable to find on a map only a few years before. New names and initials became common in the West—OPEC and PLO; Yamani and Khaddafi; the West Bank and the Persian Gulf.

As time went by, many foreign reporters and their audiences became caught up not only in the oil story and its implications, but in the intense drama of the modern Middle East: the Israeli raid on Entebbe; Sadat's mission to Jerusalem; the Camp David peace process; Islamic multitudes in the streets of Teheran and the American hostages in the embassy; the destruction of the atomic reactor in Baghdad; Israel's war against the PLO and Syria in 1982; and the American involvement in Lebanon. Each of these events grabbed the attention of the Western public. Middle Eastern leaders—Begin, Sadat, Arafat, the Shah, Khaddafi, King Hussein, and Hafez Assad—became as well known to Americans as presidential candidates during primary season.

Since 1977, events in the Middle East have dominated foreign news in the United States. That year *CBS Evening News* devoted ten percent of its total airtime to the region, and the other networks weren't far behind. Amazingly, this percentage continued to rise each year, and reached a peak in 1980, when the three networks gave almost one fifth of their combined evening news time to the events in the area.[2]

The new demand for news from the Middle East raised certain questions. Who would report the news? How would it be gathered? America's long involvement in Vietnam had produced a generation of newspeople who knew a great deal about Southeast Asia and covering an American war there. Decades of relative disinterest in the Middle East had created no comparable cadre of Middle East reporters. Nor was there a large pool of trained foreign correspondents to draw on from other parts of the world.* The number of foreign correspondents has been steadily declining since World War II, partially because of the exorbitant cost of keeping a staff reporter and his family abroad—estimated at $250,000 per year—and partially because fewer newspapers insist on gathering their own foreign news; most are content to accept the offerings of AP, UPI, Reuters, and the syndicated feature services.

In the absence of proven area experts or seasoned foreign correspondents, many editors assigned (and continue to assign) reporters with little or no background on the region. Some consider this a virtue and claim that a truly competent reporter is equally at home covering an American political rally, a stock car race, or, say, the Iranian revolution. In practice, however, this has produced rather mixed results.

In *Covering Islam,* Professor Edward Said comments on the work of American reporters in Iran during the revolution. "Not knowing the language is only part of a much greater ignorance, for often enough the reporter is sent to a strange country with no preparation or experience, just because he or she is canny at picking up things quickly or happens already to be in the general vicinity of where front page news is happening. So instead of trying to find out more about the country, the reporter takes hold of what is nearest at hand, usually a cliché or some bit of journalistic wisdom

---

*According to various surveys, the number of correspondents abroad declined by half from 1963 to 1975, and there is every indication that it has kept on declining since then.[3]

which readers at home are unlikely to challenge."[4]

Professor Said, who takes a dim view of almost all American journalists, hardly overstates the problems created by inexperience, and particularly the inability of most American reporters to speak the area's languages. Not more than a handful know Arabic, for example, and often they themselves are unaware of what a limitation this imposes on their work. According to media critic and journalist Mort Rosenblum, "The language problem far transcends the inability to read the local press. If a correspondent cannot speak the language of the country he is in, his sources are mainly fellow Americans or a small elite who have learned English for a particular reason. These sources are likely to give him an atypical point of view and a distorted idea of the society."[5] This is a special problem in the Middle East, where there is a pronounced tendency on the part of many Arab leaders and officials to say one, usually more moderate-sounding, thing in English for foreign consumption and something a bit more militant for the locals. Yasser Arafat and the PLO have dined out for years on this trick, and it is also a favorite of the Saudis. Often Arab leaders simply revise or retract ill-considered remarks by claiming that they have been mistranslated.

Even in Israel, where comparatively more people speak English, not knowing Hebrew can be a disadvantage. Throughout the first years of the Begin government, for example, visiting foreign correspondents consistently underestimated the Israeli prime minister's support, frequently (and incorrectly) predicting his imminent political collapse. This was largely due to the fact that many correspondents came into contact primarily with college-educated Israelis fluent in English, most of whom opposed Begin and his policies. These correspondents had little real contact with or understanding of the Hebrew- and French-speaking Oriental Jewish communities of Israel that provided the bulk of the Likud's support.

The question of language is, as Edward Said points out, not unrelated to an overall lack of background and experience. There are some Western reporters in the Middle East who know a great deal about the area. They have lived there, read its history, studied its folklore and temperament, and are acquainted with its major political personalities; there are others, often journalists who come for only a brief visit, who know virtually nothing. I was once asked by a reporter for a major U.S. daily newspaper whom I met on a flight from London to Israel if Jerusalem is located on the Mediterranean or the Red Sea (it's nowhere near either one). Four days later, the same man wrote a major article on the future of Jerusalem, one of the most controversial and complex issues in the Middle East. This kind of superficiality is not necessarily the fault of the reporter himself. Many newspapers simply make impossible demands on their personnel, who are unable to keep abreast of developments in fifteen or twenty countries simultaneously and still produce a story every day.

The problem with this disparity of expertise is that the average person in the West has no idea which reporter is which. Most Americans would have little difficulty detecting a sportswriter who didn't know much about football or a movie critic who had never heard of Paul Newman or a police reporter who got the name of the local police chief backward; but comparatively few Americans, even the well informed, are able to distinguish between the pros and the amateurs in Middle East reporting. In most newspapers their by-lines look the same.

Sometimes even the pros find covering the entire Middle East singlehandedly to be somewhat daunting. I remember visiting Jonathan Broder, the *Chicago Tribune*'s regional correspondent, only minutes after he had received an urgent request from his foreign editor to leave immediately for Turkey to cover the imposition of martial law there. Broder, who had never been to Turkey, didn't speak Turkish, and didn't know a soul there, was expected to get off the plane, spend a few hours in the capital city, and then file an authoritative account of a situation that was, after all, part of an ongoing political process. Unfortunately, he had spent the previous months traveling and was not quite caught up on his filing. When he turned to the dossier marked TURKEY, all he found were some six-month-old clippings. Half a year's worth of unmarked and uncut newspapers were stacked precariously against one wall. We divided up the pile into four smaller stacks, and the four of us—he and his wife, I and mine—started frantically leafing through the papers in search of stories about the country. Time was running out, and in desperation he turned to my daughter—seven years old at the time and just learning to read—wrote the word *TURKEY* on a piece of paper, and handed her a stack of newspapers to peruse. Six hours later he was on a plane, and the next day almost a million readers read his account of the situation in Ankara.

As the American appetite for Middle Eastern news has grown, American news organizations have sought to establish a presence in the region. Their operations tend to fall into one of three general patterns.

First, there are the three-bureau setups: full-time staff correspondents located in three Middle East cities—Beirut, Cairo, and Jerusalem.* These correspondents are backed up by local assistants—stringers (usually local journalists who moonlight by helping prepare stories and articles), tipsters, secretaries, and translators and, in the case of television, producers, camera crews (sometimes staffers from the States, sometimes locals), and the rest of the auxiliary helpers required by the medium. These organizations divide their regional coverage among the three bureaus, which are supplemented on major stories by "visiting firemen," correspondents from other places who fly in, work for brief stretches, and then fly back out. AP, UPI, and Reuters all maintain three-bureau set-ups (recently AP has added a correspondent in Bahrain to cover Gulf affairs); so do the networks, *Time* and *Newsweek* (*U.S. News and World Report* covers the area with a single roaming reporter who lives in Cyprus), and *The New York Times, The Washington Post,* and the *Los Angeles Times.*

The second mode of operation is the "one-man" Middle East bureau. The *Chicago Tribune, Baltimore Sun, Miami Her-*

* In the case of U.S. networks and wire services, partly in Jerusalem and partly in Tel Aviv.

ald, Christian Science Monitor, and a few other papers keep one staffer in the area, usually based in Israel. Often he or she is backed up by stringers in other cities and by occasional help from visiting reporters on big stories. A variation on this theme is *The Wall Street Journal's* practice of stationing its regional correspondents in London and flying them out to the Middle East as the need arises.

The third approach to covering the Middle East is common to almost all the rest of the American press: as a rule, they let others do it for them. Major American newspapers and chains—the New York *Daily News,* the *Detroit News,* the *Cleveland Plain Dealer,* the *San Francisco Chronicle,* to name only a few—have no full-time reporter stationed in the Middle East. Some of them do have semipermanent arrangements with stringers who write occasional special pieces; most rely almost exclusively on wire-service reports and on the offerings of *The New York Times* and *The Washington Post-L.A. Times* feature services. Occasionally, newspapers send journalists to visit the Middle East in order to write a few articles, but they are usually sent abroad more as a reward for good work or as a morale booster than to actually gather news.

Altogether, there are not normally more than thirty American staff reporters resident in the entire Moslem Middle East on a full-time basis. Moreover, they don't divide up the region in order to provide thirty different news items each day; rather, they tend to compete with each other in the same places for the same daily story. It is striking, for example, how consistently similar the Middle East coverage of the three networks is. They share the same conventions of what constitutes news and go after the same stories; they also live in dread of being scooped by the competition, and in foreign situations that means that they tend to keep a close eye on each other. Often they cooperate, share information and, in doing so, reduce the risk of missing a story—but also the possibility of discovering one.

"Scoops" by foreign correspondents are rare; usually they are simply stretched too thin to do more than report what the local media, with their greater resources and contacts, have already revealed, adding an American angle if possible. When a scoop does present itself, foreign editors, who stay close to the "news" as defined by the wire-service material ticking into their news rooms, are sometimes reluctant to accept it. More than one correspondent has been exasperated by the question "If this is true, why haven't I seen it on the AP wire?" Some reporters circumvent this by filing their own stories and then sharing them with the wire services, whose own reports then "confirm" the accuracy of the exclusive. Others can be very touchy about their editors' lack of confidence in them.

On the first day of the Six Day War in June 1967, CBS correspondent Michael Elkins somehow learned that Israel had attacked and destroyed virtually the entire Egyptian air force in a series of lightning strikes. Elkins, a former military man, understood the meaning of total air superiority in desert warfare—Israel had essentially won the war; the rest would be just mopping up. To this day Elkins refuses to reveal the source of his scoop, which obviously came from the highest levels of the Israeli army or government, but it was clearly one of the great journalistic coups of recent years.

His bosses at CBS didn't see it that way. He was too far ahead of the competition for his own good, and they hesitated to use the story at all. When they finally did, they sent him a cable saying, "You had better be right." Elkins, who had been with CBS for more than ten years, was deeply offended and quit on the spot. He also gave the story to the BBC, for which he worked as a stringer. The British network hesitated, then went ahead. Its report scooped the entire world by hours.[6]

The tiny band of American correspondents in the Middle East would find it difficult to produce an intelligible picture of such a huge area under the best of conditions. Given the political realities in the region, their job is virtually impossible. For aside from language barriers and the problems inherent in trying to cover such a dizzying multiplicity of countries, cultures, and issues, journalists in the Arab world face an insuperable limitation—they are not free to enter and work in many of the countries on their beat.

With the exception of Israel, and to some extent Lebanon, the countries of the Middle East are ruled by dictators, elected by no one, and answerable only to themselves. Some of these regimes are relatively open and benign—Tunisia, Kuwait, and Egypt are examples—while others, like Iran, Iraq, Syria, Algeria, and Libya, are closed, totalitarian systems where dissent is put down by torture and murder. None, however, may be called an open society in the Western sense, and taken together they constitute a virtual "arc of silence."

Naturally, such regimes do not encourage, indeed do not permit, freedom of the press, and for them repression begins at home. Foreign correspondents and the public they represent are a secondary problem for Arab rulers; their first priority is to control the information that reaches their own citizens. A good summary of the situation of the Arab press is provided by the 1982 edition of the *World Press Encyclopedia:*

IRAQ:

"The Iraqi press is described as a 'mobilization press,' that is, a press designed solely to promote the interests of the ruling group. It functions within an environment that is generally described as revolutionary but in many respects is reactionary. Although passive toward the regime in power, its tone is strident and contentious toward all others. Finally, because it reflects accurately a society in which there is no public dissent, debate or opposition, the Iraqi press is politically inert and dormant."

SYRIA:

"The press, like the nation, speaks with one voice . . . a de facto state mobilized press exists, and the Assad government has shown in recent years that it can be heavy-handed in dealing with its critics. Through constant intimidation, the press has been reduced to the status of an agent of the regime."

SAUDI ARABIA:

"The press's ownership is private, its communications functions are closely monitored by the government through the Director-General of Broadcast, Press and Publications. While there is no formal censorship, newspapers face suppression and their editors dismissal if they print anything deemed offensive by the government. In a recent demonstration of state power over the media, on March 16, 1980, the authorities "ordered" the dismissal of Turki Abd-Allah al Sudari, chief editor of the pro-government and privately owned Al-Riydah, and banned him from writing in the future.

"The State and the media thus have an excellent understanding of the needs and tolerances of the other. So long as the wishes of the royal family are met and the demands of the religious leaders are not ignored, the state prefers not to interfere overtly in actual media operations."

JORDAN:

"The press of Jordan has been characterized as loyalist. It displays some of the characteristics of a free press, such as private ownership, but the government has never tried to hide its whip, and numerous press casualties during the past two decades provide effective testimony to state control. Weak and passive, the press reflects the state of the country today; it supports a traditional system which views the media as an engine of modernization and therefore deeply suspect, and in which the very word 'opposition' is taboo."

ALGERIA:

"Even among educated Algerians, the press has only a limited influence because newspapers function primarily as government gazettes . . . Algerians maintain the fiction that the press speaks for the party and not for the state; the dis-

tinction is immaterial, party and state are one and the same
. . . While all of the printed and electronic media are controlled and monitored by the government, there are no specific agencies designated as censors."[7]

It is unnecessary to continue. The state of the press in
Khomeini's Iran or Khaddafi's Libya or in Afghanistan under Soviet occupation requires little elaboration. Quasi-state
control is exercised in Morocco and Tunisia, while much of
the rest of the Arab world—countries like Sudan and South
Yemen—have no press at all to speak of.

The two partial exceptions to this bleak picture are, not
surprisingly, the two Arab countries where foreign correspondents are resident in any numbers—Egypt and Lebanon. Neither is an open society in the American or Israeli
sense, but both allow considerably more freedom of the press
than exists elsewhere in the Moslem Middle East.

Lebanon, before the 1975 civil war, had a tradition of
journalistic variety. Virtually every Arab regime owned or
controlled a newspaper in the Lebanese capital, and these
papers, when read all together, could provide a fairly comprehensive picture of trends and events in the Arab world.
Adversaries published each other's bad news, and by making allowances for exaggeration, it was possible to read them
and keep abreast of most developments.

This began to change in 1975, when the civil war erupted.
Journalists were killed and threatened, newspaper offices
were attacked and pillaged, and many newspapers forced to
close or move their operations abroad. In January 1977, the
Lebanese government, acting under orders from the Syrian
occupation forces, declared official censorship. When this
failed to silence critical journalists, the Syrians resorted, as
we shall see, to intimidation and assassination. By the end
of 1980, the once lively Lebanese press was largely (but not
totally) cowed into silence. Even an-*Nahar,* long considered
the best and most reliable of the Lebanese newspapers, was
often forced to practice self-censorship for fear of reprisal.

In Egypt, the situation is somewhat different. Until the
mid-1970s the Egyptian press was as passive and servile as

the media in other Arab countries. The dictatorial Gamal Abdul Nasser allowed no criticism of his regime; he nationalized the newspapers in 1960, and even before that they had been little more than tools of the government.[8] In the first years of his regime, Anwar Sadat, who himself had been the government-appointed publisher and editor-in-chief of al-*Gomhouriya* early in his career and who liked to refer to himself as a journalist, continued Nasser's press policy. This began to change, like much else in Egypt, after the 1973 October War.

In 1974, President Sadat carried out a purge of the Egyptian newspaper scene. His most dramatic move was to fire Mohammed Hassanein Heikal, the editor of Egypt's most prestigious daily, al-*Ahram*. Heikal had been an intimate adviser of President Nasser, and as such, perhaps the most influential journalist in the Arab world. Sadat also removed other Nasserist editors and correspondents, replacing them with his own supporters; at the same time, he lifted some of the censorship restrictions that had hemmed in the press under his predecessor. Mild criticism, especially of Nasser and his regime, but also of many of the daily inconveniences caused by Egyptian bureaucracy, was allowed. Even veiled criticism of government figures (although almost never of President Sadat himself) was permitted. By the harsh standards of the Arab world, all this amounted to a liberality bordering on license. Still, the Egyptian press under Sadat and now under President Hosni Mubarak is far from free. Television and radio, the latter Egypt's most important medium, are totally controlled by the government and offer a rich diet of presidential doings and very little news. Newspapers, too, remain under government ownership, allowing the authorities to exercise decisive control over personnel and editorial decisions.

In fact, the Egyptian government regards local journalists as something akin to government employees. During the Israel-Egyptian peace process, the Egyptians insisted that their reporters be housed in Israeli hotels along with other Egyptian officials and that the government pay the journalists' bills. In January 1978, at the time of the Hilton Hotel peace talks

in Jerusalem, the head of the Egyptian Government Press
Office officially requested that the West Bank be placed off
limits to the Egyptian press; and when we refused to do so,
he imposed such a limitation himself.

At that same conference, I hosted a dinner for a senior
Egyptian official. During the course of the evening one of
the guests, Anan Safadi, at that time the Middle East editor
of the English language *Jerusalem Post,* asked about press
freedom in Egypt. The official asserted that the Egyptian
press was independent and unfettered. Safadi was skeptical
and mentioned several recent cases of government interfer-
ence. In rebuttal, the Egyptian official, in all seriousness, said
that his point was proved by the fact that President Sadat
had allowed Mohammed Hassanein Heikal to criticize his
government for months before firing him.

In July 1980, the Egyptian government promulgated a
new press law which made it illegal for newspapers to print
unconstructive criticism, defamation, libel, sensational sex or
crime news, indecency, sedition, and treason.[9] This period
also saw the beginning of an increasingly bitter relationship
between Sadat and the foreign correspondents in Cairo,
which culminated in a presidential tirade against their irre-
sponsibility, only weeks before the Egyptian leader was assassinated.*

During the Egyptian-Israeli peace talks, the Egyptian press
was often used by the government as a negotiating tool. In
a variation of the "good cop-bad cop" technique, the Egyptian newspapers savaged Israel and its government, often
employing anti-Jewish terminology and caricatures; and when
Israel protested that such material was fostering hostility and
thus defeating one of the main goals of the peace process,
the Egyptian government would, as a concession, move to
temper criticism. This situation was complicated by the fact
that many Egyptian journalists were genuinely opposed to
the peace process almost from the outset. This was a matter
both of ideology—most had been avid Nasserites—and of self-

---

*At a meeting with the foreign press, Sadat told Paul Miller of NBC that his
question about recent political arrests in Egypt was impertinent. "In other times I
would have had him shot," Sadat later remarked.[10]

interest. The isolation of Egypt in the Arab world caused by the peace process weighed most heavily on the Egyptian middle class, which had extensive business connections or personal involvements there. Lucrative job opportunities for journalists were endangered by the Egyptian-Israeli peace, and this was a major factor in the vituperative tone of the Egyptian press's treatment of Israel.*

Of course press repression is not unique to the Arab world. Throughout the Soviet bloc, China, and much of Africa, Asia, and Latin America, the situation is similar. An indigenous press exists only to convey news and views that fit the needs and goals of the government; all except a tiny handful of people are totally excluded from the circle of information; and no one is allowed to raise his voice in dissent or protest. Most Americans know about the absence of press freedom in the Soviet bloc and many are also dimly aware of the situation in the Third World. Such repression is often regarded as simply unfortunate for the people who are forced to endure it but of little practical interest for the citizens of the United States. This, however, is far from the case. The regimes of Eastern Europe, Africa, Asia, and Latin America—representing perhaps 75 percent of the world's population—are essentially closed not only to their own citizens, but to Western journalists. Simply put, much of the world, and virtually all of the Arab world, is immune to real reportorial scrutiny.

In 1978, Stanley Meisler, of the *Los Angeles Times* wrote: "The Third World creates problems for foreign correspondents never described by Hemingway and little understood by most American readers. Their difficulty comes from working in societies that have no understanding of the needs

---

*Actually, there was a great deal of editorializing in the Egyptian press about Israel, but very little coverage. Egyptian journalists have been discouraged by their government from visiting Israel except as members of official press parties accompanying Egyptian leaders, and only a handful of Egyptian reporters have visited Israel independently. When Israel opened its embassy in Cairo, the press, with the exception of *October* magazine, boycotted its activities. Israel's first ambassador, Eliahu Ben-Elissar, was never interviewed on Egyptian television or radio. This was in marked contrast to the hundreds of Israeli journalists who visited and reported on Egypt, and to the wide media exposure given Egypt's first ambassador to Israel, Sa'ad Murtada.

and demands of an unrestricted press. The national press in these countries never offends the government. As Third World leaders like to say, their press is enlisted in the battle for development. Rather than stand on the sidelines and snipe at government policies, editors and reporters help carry them out."[11] Meisler was writing primarily about Africa, but his description has an equal validity for the Arab world. The absence of a free press has a powerful, inhibiting effect on the free flow of information to the West.

In 1979, an international press seminar was convened in London on "The Arab Image in the Western Press." Its participants included Arab intellectuals like Edward Said, Mohammed Hassanein Heikal, and Hisham Shirabi, and pro-Arab Western journalists such as Eric Roleau of *Le Monde* and Robert Stephens, diplomatic editor of the British *Observer*. Stephens observed that, "The capacity to report fairly and accurately from the Middle East for the Western press depends to a very large extent on the help of the Arab press. If the Arab press itself is finding very great difficulty in surviving as an effective force in its own area and has such little access to its own bureaucracy, or when it does, gets very little out of it, I think this makes the task of Western journalists much more difficult. The reason is that in many cases foreign correspondents do rely in many parts of the world on reports given in the local press, or they copy such reports. I think that the existence of censorship in many Arab countries, and the general attitude to their own press of the Arab governments, does make it extremely difficult for Western journalists to operate."[12]

Stephens put his finger on one of the principal problems of reporting on the Arab world. One reporter, on his own, assigned an entire region to cover, finds the job exceedingly difficult under the best of conditions. He cannot go everywhere and see everything; he must select his story opportunities carefully. His primary tool for doing this is the local press, newspapers, radio, and television. They serve as the scouts for the foreign correspondent, turning up the stories which he then investigates and reports. But where the local journalists are, in the words of former *Time* chairman Andrew Heiskell, "really no more than government employees,"[13] they naturally produce really no more than the official government line—which does not usually coincide precisely with what the Western public might want or need to know.

The problem of covering closed Arab societies is compounded by another difficulty—a good part of the Arab world is physically off limits to most Western journalists. The most effective way, by far, of covering a foreign country is to establish a bureau there. These bureaus—such as exist in Israel, Egypt, and Lebanon—are able to accumulate files and clippings over a considerable period of time; to find trustworthy local employees who serve as tipsters and grease the way for journalists' contacts; to provide a base of operation for visiting correspondents on major stories; to gain a working knowledge of the country, its people, and its leading political figures; and to establish continuity of coverage by cultivating and passing on contacts, impressions, and files from one correspondent to the next. Such bureaus are staffed by resident correspondents, journalists who have time to develop comparative expertise. They are a necessary (if insufficient) condition for serious, informed reporting, which is precisely why most Arab nations wouldn't dream of allowing such bureaus to be established. At the start of 1984, no American news organization had a resident staff correspondent in Saudi Arabia, Algeria, the Sudan, Syria, or Yemen, just to name some.

In the absence of resident correspondents, many news organizations use local stringers, whose limitations A. J. Liebling once neatly summarized: "As to foreign stringers, since their necks are in imminent danger if they deviate from the government line in many countries and their livelihoods are in peril if they do in some others, it is the government line they stick to. This is one strong reason why the American press seems to foreigners always to be on the side of the party that is in."[14]

Andrew Heiskell of *Time* raised this issue in his 1977 testimony before the U.S. Senate. "The problem for stringers can be especially severe—they are even more vulnerable than foreign correspondents. They are subject to intimidation, dismissal, violence and frequently to indirect attack through harassment of their families."[15] Stringers may be useful in some situations, but they hardly make reliable reporters in the Arab world.

Without resident correspondents or credible stringers, most news organizations are forced to cover the Middle East by sending reporters for quick, sporadic visits to the region's various countries. There are more than twenty nations in the area, however, and even the best-staffed news organizations have only a few reporters in the region at any given time. Even worse, they are often unwelcome visitors. Iraq, Iran, Saudi Arabia, Libya, Yemen, and Algeria are difficult to get into for most correspondents most of the time. Visas are granted, if at all, on an individual basis and after careful consideration by the regimes of the correspondent in question. Reporters who do receive a visa are aware that unfavorable reporting may mean that they will not be allowed to return.

Edward Behr of *Newsweek,* one of the world's veteran foreign correspondents, relates a typical experience in his book *Anyone Here Been Raped and Speaks English?*

I took a plane to Algiers to report for *Newsweek* on Algeria's bid for leadership in the Arab world, and was held at the airport, made to remain in the transit lounge, and put on the first plane out of the country. In vain I begged to know the reason for such treatment. I had been blacklisted, I later found out, because of my book review of Ian Young's *The Private Life of Islam.*

Needless to say I protested, privately, to my old FLN friends—and was assured the whole thing had been an "unfortunate misunderstanding." So it was without any apprehension that four years later, in February 1978, I flew to Algeria to take part in a BBC-TV documentary film on Algeria. . . .

I arrived in Oran, where I was scheduled to interview some Algerian technocrats. To my horror the whole expulsion scene repeated itself. "You cannot enter Algeria," said a plainclothes inspector. I asked why. "We are unable to say," he replied. "We are just following orders."

I spent the night in the cold, stretched out on a couple of chairs in the airport lounge, hoping that word would come that it was all "an unfortunate misunderstanding." No word came. I also recalled that here was another instance of caricature imitating life. For all foreign correspondents know of the hoary cliché situation, involving their arrival in some Arab country, to the accompaniment of the police inspectors greeting: "Welcome. Welcome to my country. Why do you tell untrue facts about my country? You will please wait at airport. Welcome."

Even when access is granted, it is often difficult to find people who will talk freely to a foreign correspondent. The problem is compounded by government restrictions on the movements of reporters, including the necessity for government "guides" whose presence often has a dampening effect on their fellow citizens.

This, then, is the task that confronts a reporter in the Moslem Middle East—to cover, sometimes with one or two colleagues, often all alone, an area almost the size of Europe, where in most cases he cannot speak the language, knows little of the people, their history, geography, and culture, and cannot hope to get reliable and independent local helpers. Usually, he is unable to find citizens or officials who will speak to him frankly, and he has no access to any independent local media. There is no assurance that he will be able to get in to the country he wants to cover at the time he wants to cover it, and once he gets there, he may well be denied access to the area or individuals he wants to see. In certain places he can find himself the target of violence for unpopular reporting; and, if his story is too critical for the local authorities, may find himself permanently blackballed.

All these obstacles and difficulties have resulted in some extremely uneven coverage of the Middle East. Events in Israel, the only open society in the region, are intensely scrutinized and minutely reported. Lebanon and Egypt are accorded ongoing, if spotty, attention. But most Arab countries are hardly "reported" at all—and a good deal of what appears in the Western press about them is so superficial and uninformed as to be meaningless.

Given the great strategic and economic importance of the region, and the growing danger of a superpower confrontation there, the inability to obtain a steady and reliable flow of information poses a genuine danger. In 1977, *Los Angeles Times* publisher Otis Chandler told the U.S. Senate Subcommittee on International Relations: "The problem of obtaining pertinent information about Third World countries has assumed dimensions of such national importance that it should have the time and attention of everyone. This is because the energy crisis plus recognition that accommodation must be reached with the Third World have impelled the United States to formulate new policies toward nonaligned areas of the world." [16]

In those same hearings *Time* magazine's Andrew Heiskell summarized the real danger which press policies such as those of the Arab world pose for the United States. He told the Senators, "The American people [cannot] intelligently analyze or support your policymaking out of the depths of ignorance. The information we [the media] fail to get, they fail to get." [17]

In the years since Chandler's and Heiskell's testimony, the quality of information from most of the Middle East has decreased almost in proportion to the growing importance of the region. In those years Arab regimes have refined and honed their repressive news-management techniques and added new ones as well. One of the least known, but most effective, has been the use of intimidation and terror against Western reporters—a technique that, during the years of Syrian-PLO control of Beirut, sometimes forced the press to practice the most subtle form of suppression—self-censorship.

2

"A CROCODILE-INFESTED SWAMP"

On April 23, 1981, hundreds of Syria's elite special forces gathered in designated meeting places near the northern city of Hama. They were led by Syrian President Hafez Assad's brother, Rifat Assad, one of the most fearsome men in the Arab world, and they had come for a simple purpose—to teach the citizens of Hama a lesson.

For more than two years, the Assad government had been plagued with civil unrest and political dissent. Syrian military installations had been sabotaged, government buildings attacked, and even the president himself was no longer safe. The source of this turmoil was the mysterious Moslem Brotherhood, an organization of fanatical Sunni Moslems dedicated to the overthrow of the government. No one knew precisely where the Brotherhood was headquartered, but the city of Hama was widely considered one of its strongholds. The Assad brothers decided that the time had come to give its people a demonstration of good citizenship, Syrian-style.

Just before midnight, the troops were given the order to move. They streamed into the town and cut off several neighborhoods where Brotherhood sympathizers were believed to live. Then they systematically dragged hundreds of

49

civilians, many of them teenagers, from their beds, lined them
up against the walls of their own houses, and machine-
gunned them to death. At first they left the bodies bleeding
in the streets, for the edification of the townspeople; later,
municipal garbage trucks scooped up the corpses and
dumped them into open ditches. No official death toll was
published, of course, but later estimates put the number as
high as 350.*[1]

If you've never heard of this massacre, you're in good
company. The foreign editors of most of America's newspapers have never heard of it either. In fact, just about the
only Americans who are aware of the slaughter are those who
happened to read about it in an article on an inside page of
The Washington Post two months later.† There, under the
headline SYRIAN TROOPS MASSACRE SCORES OF ASSAD'S FOES,
the Post's Edward Cody, writing from Washington, D.C., told
the story of the mass murder. Cody, one of America's most
experienced Middle East reporters, noted that the first report on the massacre had been published abroad in the
French daily Le Monde on May 13, 1981, and that the Post
had delayed its own article until it had been able to gain independent confirmation of the story's veracity.[2]

The Washington Post's report was a considerable achievement—an American exclusive on a major political event in
an important Middle East country. But why, with so many
foreign correspondents in Beirut, all of them assigned to the
Syrian beat, did it take two months for the story to emerge?
And why did other news organizations—The New York Times,
Time, Newsweek, and the three networks, to name only some—
never report it at all? In the seventh paragraph of his story,
couched in diplomatic language, Cody gave the answer: "The
massacre reports, in trustworthy and untrustworthy variations, have been discussed in Damascus and Beirut in the
last two months. In an atmosphere created by the wounding
of Reuters correspondent Berndt Debusmann, shot in the

---

*Another, much greater, massacre took place in Hama in February 1982. For
a consideration of its treatment by the press, see Chapter 8.

†A few other American newspapers also gave terse descriptions of the massacre. The Christian Science Monitor alluded to it briefly, and Newsday ran eight lines
on the day after the Post's dispatch.

back by a gunman firing a silencer-equipped pistol, and threats against British Broadcasting Corp. correspondent Tim Llewellyn—both after stories considered by Damascus as unfriendly to Syria—*the Hama reports have not been widely published from the area.*" (emphasis added)[3]

Cody's phrase "have not been widely published" was a bow to journalistic professional courtesy by which reporters refrain from criticizing each other's work in print. His meaning, though, was unmistakable—the reporters stationed in Beirut must have heard the story circulating there and had chosen to ignore it. They had remained silent in response to recent Syrian violence against journalists. They had, in short, decided to censor themselves.

Self-censorship, the decision of journalists to ignore a story, or to tell less than they know, is an old phenomenon and not unique to the Beirut press corps.* Often self-censorship is simple prudence, usually it is perfectly human and understandable, and always, or nearly always, it is undetectable, like a fixed basketball game where no one really knows if a player is missing shots on purpose.

For obvious reasons, foreign correspondents customarily deny that they are being intimidated. They are brave people by definition—the simple act of being in the battle zone in a place like Beirut is evidence of that—and they pride themselves on their courage and independence. At the same time, as John Kifner of *The New York Times* once wrote: "To work here [in Beirut] as a journalist is to carry fear with you as faithfully as your notebook. It is the constant knowledge that there is nothing you can do to protect yourself, and nothing ever happened to any assassin. In this atmosphere a journalist must decide when, how, and even whether to record a story."[4] Kifner's newspaper never reported on the 1981 massacre in Hama.

The decision to practice self-censorship is often humiliating, and many reporters justify it to themselves by rationalization. "Faced with undefined threats," says Mort Rosenblum, "reporters may inadvertently withhold sensitive

---

*Following the 1973 coup in Chile, for example, journalists referred to the junta's press policy as "file now, die later."

information by convincing themselves that their perfectly reliable sources are not good enough."[5]

Doyle McManus of the *Los Angeles Times* left the Middle East only a few days before the April 1981 massacre at Hama, but he knows the kind of dilemma his colleagues must have faced. "You've got two problems," he says, "one is the question of whether people are intimidated. The other is the question of how many people have information that they think credible." Echoing Rosenblum, McManus adds, "The real maddening question—does the attempt at intimidation color the reporter's judgment on when the information is credible? . . ." His conclusion? "Yes, it probably does."[6]

The April 1981 attack on Hama was not the first case of collective restraint and self-censorship by the Beirut based press corps. Almost a year before, on June 27, 1980, shortly after the attempted assassination of President Hafez Assad, hundreds of Syrian political prisoners, most of them suspected members of the Moslem Brotherhood, were released from the Tadmor prison in the desert north of the Syrian capital of Damascus. The prison gates were opened and inmates streamed into the desert, heading on foot toward the nearest highway. They didn't get far before Syrian attack helicopters appeared overhead, opening fire with machine guns. The Syrian dissidents were mowed down as they scrambled frantically for safety through the sands.[7]

News of the desert slaughter spread like wildfire through Syria and Lebanon, but for weeks it went virtually unreported in the West. Then, on August 5, 1980, in an act of singular courage, Joseph Fitchett published an account of it in the *International Herald Tribune,* a newspaper sure to be seen by the Syrian authorities. Writing from Beirut, Fitchett reported on the Syrian reign of terror against foreign correspondents in Lebanon, and then recounted in detail the events at the prison.

"Reports of the massacre gradually filtered out via the Syrian grapevine and embassies," he wrote, but "Western media were cautious about reporting [the massacre]." This was a euphemistic way of saying that almost none of Fitchett's colleagues had been ready to touch the story with a ten-foot pole. Nor did Fitchett believe that they would be more reliable in the future. He concluded by noting that because of press intimidation in Lebanon, "Western media are gradually adjusting to the need for sources outside Beirut to follow events in Syria."[8]

It is hard to blame the correspondents in Beirut for being cautious. Moslem West Beirut, where most of them lived and worked, had been a battlefield since the Lebanese civil war of 1975–76. Following the intervention of Syria in 1976, much of Lebanon came under military occupation and Beirut became an urban nightmare of random violence, terrorism, and repression. Critics of the Syrian regime were often assassinated, and even the foreign press corps was not exempt.

It hadn't always been that way. In the 1960s and early 1970s, before the PLO arrived in Lebanon, destroyed the country's political and social equilibrium, and plunged it into chaos, Beirut had been one of the most sophisticated cities in the Middle East. It had been a place of nightclubs and casinos, smart shops and Mediterranean beach clubs, a city where the old colonial French influence was still strong. In contrast to the closed societies of the Arab world, Beirut was an oasis of tolerance and information. Salim Lawzi, the Lebanese-born editor of al-*Hawadess* and a man who was himself subsequently assassinated in Beirut, put it this way: "International journalists in the 50's and 60's who were responsible for covering the Middle East knew that Beirut was the best news source. A journalist frequenting the Beirut hotels could get more news about Iraq than in Baghdad. The secrets of Damascus, Cairo or Jedda could be gathered more efficiently in the sidewalk cafes of Hamra Street than in their own cities."[9]

During the sixties, Beirut became a magnet for a small band of Western correspondents whose assignment was to cover the Arab world at a time when editors in the United States and Europe displayed little interest in the area. One of the correspondents was John Cooley of the *Christian Science Monitor*. Writing from Athens in early 1977, after the imposition of Syrian-inspired press censorship in Beirut,

Cooley recalled the way the city had once been. "With all its faults, fears, and rivalries Beirut, Lebanon, in its golden years as the link between the West and the Arab world's business, intellectual and artistic life was a good place to live and work."[10] Cooley described the Lebanese press of the sixties as "free and easy . . ." but far more open than any other in the Arab world. Journalists could be bought, perhaps, but they weren't murdered.

The PLO, as we shall see in the following chapter, was the first to upset the tolerant Beirut press tradition, and to introduce terror as a technique of press management in the Lebanese capital. But it was the Syrians who, during the early eighties, turned censorship by terror into a way of life in Beirut.

Today, Doyle McManus lives in the U.S. and works for the *Los Angeles Times,* but when the Syrians came to Beirut, he was a reporter in UPI's Lebanon bureau. He and his fellow journalists had a pretty clear idea of the kind of relations they could expect with the Syrians. He recalls: "There were attempts at intimidation. In fact, the day the Syrians came into West Beirut, one of the first things they did was march down to the UPI office where I was working at the time, look around and see if there was anybody handy to arrest." McManus remembers that he and his fellow UPI staffers had laboriously practiced the phrase "long live Syrian-American friendship" in Arabic. "We thought that as a precaution it might be good if we could offer a few Ba'athist slogans when they came in the door," he laughs.[11]

Syria's first move against the press in Beirut was directed against the local Lebanese media, and it was carried out with the cooperation of the Lebanese government of Prime Minister Salim al-Hoss and the approval of President Elias Sarkis, both of whom were widely regarded as Syrian puppets. On January 4, 1977, the government imposed a state of national emergency, and with it, new and, for Lebanon, unprecedented curbs on freedom of expression, including a ban on the right of assembly and the institution of press censorship. Syrian forces also shut down seven local newspapers, including the relatively independent an-*Nahar,* through the simple expedient of seizing the printing presses and locking their employees out of the buildings.[12]

Syria's move against the Lebanese press was aimed at silencing the critics of its occupation. At this stage of the war, that meant the PLO-Moslem alliance. (Later, when the Syrians switched sides and re-joined the PLO, they attempted to silence Christian and centrist opponents.) Besides, Syria had about thirty thousand troops in Lebanon and had no interest in exposing them to the lively debate that characterized the Lebanese press. As the British *Economist* put it at the time: "Press freedom is an alien concept to Syria . . . for Syria's army officers, press freedom is intolerable impudence."[13]

Censorship of the foreign (but not the local) press was lifted on January 25, 1977. Foreign reporters were, however, still required to submit copies of their stories within twenty-four hours of filing them. Zehi Boustani, the chief censor and a senior official of the Lebanese security police, explained to the correspondents that this requirement was intended to provide the authorities with "a view of your work in Lebanon" and that no reprisals would be taken against reporters whose dispatches displeased the government. He urged the foreign correspondents to "let your conscience be your guide" in dealing with Lebanon.[14] Naturally, this engendered a certain unease in some members of the foreign press corps.

Throughout 1977, as the civil war subsided and the Syrians consolidated their hold on most of Lebanon, pressure on the press continued. On July 5, 1977, the Lebanese government once again tightened restrictions on freedom of expression. The Lebanese Press Association's protests had no effect and publishers began to leave the Lebanese capital to relocate in Europe.[15]

By 1978, the Syrian domination was a fact of life, and Beirut was divided between the Christian East and Moslem West. Syria abandoned its alliance with the Christian forces; Damascus was now cooperating with the PLO, and together they controlled West Beirut. Armed "fighters," some of them not more than fifteen or sixteen years old, roamed the streets,

brandishing Russian-made assault rifles. Almost every journalist stationed in Beirut had a close scrape or two. Most regarded these incidents as a kind of occupational hazard,
random and unpleasant, but not derived from any particular anti-press policy. The wave of PLO and leftist terror that
had been directed against the journalists during the civil war
period of 1975–76 was a receding memory, recalled at the
bar of Beirut's Commodore Hotel in boozy anecdotes by a
few of the old-timers. Occasionally something unpleasant
happened—in March 1978, for example, Agence France
Presse Middle East correspondent Georges Herbouze was
expelled from Beirut on the grounds that "he had not written a story favorable to Lebanon in the past three
months"[16]—but by the standards of the mid-seventies, it was
a relatively safe period for foreign reporters in Beirut.

And then Salim Lawzi was murdered.

Lawzi was a Lebanese, a Sunni Moslem from the northern city of Tripoli. During the 1970s he had built a reputation as a moderate and thoughtful journalist, a Lebanese
patriot and critic of the Syrian regime of Hafez Assad and
of the spreading influence of the Palestine Liberation Organization. In 1977, in a bid to retain his editorial freedom,
he moved his journal, al-*Hawadess,* to London, where the fifty-
eight-year-old editor's hard-hitting articles made it one of the
most widely read publications in the Arabic language. He
printed interviews with President Sadat of Egypt, with whom
he was personally friendly, and other Arab moderates, and
opened his pages to bitter attacks on Syrian political figures,
particularly Rifat Assad, the brother and strong-arm enfor-
cer of Syrian president Hafez Assad. These attacks made
Lawzi a marked man, and he knew it. He had once written
in an editorial about the treatment of Lebanese journalists
by various Arab governments: "Physical and moral pressures were used, threats and the severing of relations . . .
On other occasions, journalists were kidnapped and liquidated . . . Journalists were attacked and disfigured as a
warning that liquidation might follow."[17] These were portentous words.

It was his mother's death that took Salim Lawzi back to

Lebanon. On February 24, 1980, he was driving to the Beirut International Airport, on his way back to London from the funeral, when he was stopped and kidnapped within yards of a Syrian army checkpost.[18] For more than a week he was missing. Then on March 6, 1980, *The New York Times* reported, "The tortured body of one of the Arab world's most influential editors, who had been kidnapped by unidentified gunmen ten days ago, was discovered by a shepherd in a wooded area near here last night . . .

"Mr. Lawzi had been critical of the leadership of a number of Arab countries, notably Syria and Libya . . .

"Officials said that an autopsy showed that he had been shot twice in the head and subjected to torture by his captors. They said his *face was smashed and his fingers black from burning.*" (emphasis added)[19]

The *Times* article cautiously refrained from speculating on the identity of the "gunmen" who had abducted and mutilated Lawzi, but at the bar of the Commodore Hotel, the foreign correspondents' gathering place in Beirut, various theories, most of them related to the dread hit teams of Rifat Assad, were propounded. Needless to say, the murderers were never caught.*

On July 23, 1980, Beirut was shocked once again to learn of the assassination of Riad Taha, the longtime president of the Lebanese Publishers Association. Taha was on his way to a meeting with Prime Minister Salim al-Hoss when, according to the Lebanese police, his chauffeur-driven car was attacked by four gunmen. The driver made a frantic effort to outspeed the attackers, who sprayed the car with machine-gun bullets in gang-land style. Both the fifty-three-year-old publisher and his chauffeur were killed as the car went careening out of control on a West Beirut street. Despite the fact that the assassination had taken place in broad daylight, the police were, as usual, unable to find any clue regarding the identity of the murderers, who were rumored to be terrorists working for the Iraqis or the Syrians.[21] No one really

---

*The 1982 edition of the *World Press Encyclopedia* says: ". . . Salim Al Lawzi was murdered as he was leaving Lebanon, possibly because of his outspoken articles against the Syrians and the Palestine Liberation Organization."[20]

knew. That same day Charles Rizk, the Christian head of Lebanese television, resigned his post after having been kidnapped and held for four hours by "unidentified gunmen,"[22] and the publisher and editor of al-*Nahar* fled Beirut.[23] The terror had become an epidemic. Lebanese journalists declared a two-day strike to protest the murder of Taha, and the Lebanese Press Association issued a statement: "With Taha, press freedom and democracy were executed in Lebanon."[24] Everyone wondered who would be next.

With the Lebanese press largely terrorized into silence, the Syrians turned their attention to the last remaining independent journalists in West Beirut—the foreign press corps. Syria itself was in the throes of a brutal crackdown on dissent; thousands of Syrian civilians were being arrested and hundreds murdered. The regime in Damascus totally censored the news within the country, and by carefully controlling the entry of foreign correspondents, it tried to keep the word of its shaky position and bloody reprisals from reaching the outside world. But Beirut, as a listening post next to Syria, was a threat. Enemies of the Assad regime smuggled out information to foreign reporters, who in turn published it and even beamed it back to Syria via the BBC or Voice of America.

At first, the Syrians used threats. One American correspondent who was stationed in Beirut at the time, and who has asked to remain anonymous because he fears Syrian reprisal, recalls that shortly after he arrived to take up his post in Beirut he published a story the Syrians didn't like. "I was called in by the nominal head of the Arab deterrent forces, Sami al-Khatib, and I was told, as he put it, 'Some of my friends are upset,' meaning Damascus. Then he said, 'It's only fair to tell you that I can no longer guarantee your safety here. I suggest you make a correction. You're playing with fire. I strongly advise that you cooperate.' I checked with local sources and they told me—take the threats seriously; if you were called in, don't mess around. I ultimately 'moved' a denial, not a correction; it was very early in my tenure, and I was still very gung-ho, very First Amendmentish. Two years later, after what happened to Debusmann and Llewelyn, I wondered how wise I had been."

Debusmann was Berndt Debusmann, Beirut bureau chief for the British news agency Reuters. What happened to him was that he was shot, and almost killed, by Syrian assassins.

German-born thirty-seven-year-old Berndt Debusmann was considered somewhat reckless by many of his fellow correspondents. He had been in Beirut since 1976, had covered much of the civil war, and in September 1976 was wounded in the hand and leg by submachine gun fire. Undeterred, Debusmann remained an aggressive reporter, and as if the dangers of Lebanon were not enough, pursued his hobby—free-fall parachuting—in his spare time. His dogged insistence on reporting what he knew about the Syrian government was to prove more dangerous than jumping out of airplanes.

In the spring of 1980, the unrest in Syria was reaching a peak. Most correspondents, unable to get an eyewitness view of the fighting, were forced to rely on secondhand accounts and diplomatic leaks. Somehow, Debusmann got a line into the story of near insurrection against the Assad regime in the northern port city of Lattakia. "Berndt Debusmann had someone bringing him reports from Lattakia," says Doyle McManus, who knew him well. "He had better information than everybody else. Once he got ahead on the story, he hammered away on it. He was running stories daily on every development. I happen to believe that that's the reason he got shot."[25]

On June 5, 1980, Debusmann and his wife, Sue, were leaving a dinner party at the home of a fellow correspondent in West Beirut shortly after midnight. As they were getting into the car, another automobile with several men in it pulled up. His wife watched in horror as they fired five shots with silenced pistols and then sped away. The Reuters bureau chief, who was shot in the back, was rushed to the American University hospital. Later, he was transferred to the RAF hospital in Cyprus and subsequently relocated by Reuters.

The attempted murder of Debusmann did not come as a complete surprise. After his reports on Assad's difficulties began to appear, Debusmann had been visited by an officer of the Lebanese security police, which under the Syrian occupation was a toothless but sometimes well-informed organization. According to the British *Observer*,[26] Debusmann was warned that two armed Syrians were looking for him. This incident was followed by repeated telephone calls to the Reuters office in Beirut attempting to ascertain Debusmann's whereabouts and on one occasion a visit to the office by a Syrian "journalist" who asked for a recent photo of Berndt Debusmann. Friends advised Debusmann to leave Beirut, but he stubbornly refused.

Following the shooting of Debusmann, Reuters, for reasons of its own, sent out a story that stated, "There was no known reason for the shooting."[27] Reuters, which must have known about the repeated Syrian threats to Debusmann, chose to cover them up. But Debusmann's colleagues in Beirut and throughout the Middle East were perfectly well aware that he had been shot and almost killed by the Syrians. Later that summer, Joseph Fitchett, writing from Beirut, stated that ". . . Debusmann was warned with Mafia style techniques of intimidation that his coverage of Syrian developments could endanger him. Employees of the official Syrian news agency phoned his office to warn that 'the spontaneous anger of the Syrian masses is becoming uncontrollable.' "[28]

The party Debusmann had been attending on the night he was shot was held at the home of his friend BBC correspondent Tim Llewelyn. It was the last party Debusmann ever attended in Beirut; it was also the last one that Llewelyn ever gave there. For the BBC correspondent, who had watched the shooting of Berndt Debusmann from his upstairs balcony, would within weeks himself be forced to flee from Beirut ahead of the Syrian assassins. His crime was not that of having witnessed the attack on Debusmann—Beirut was far too lawless, and the Syrians much too powerful for concern over legal niceties—but that he, like his Reuters colleague, knew too much about Syria and, worse, reported it.

The threats against Tim Llewelyn and his back-up correspondent, Jim Muir, came after they had persistently reported on internal unrest in Syria. Llewelyn, an experienced and well-liked reporter in the Arab world, knew the chance he was taking; but he considered such risks to be part of the job. Indeed, he had reported sensitive stories about Damascus in the past.

Doyle McManus: "I was in my office in the an-*Nahar* building one day and I was gossiping with one of the Lebanese journalists there, a man who in my experience had very good Syrian sources. He took me aside and said, 'I've got a story we can't possibly print, but maybe you can do something with it. We've got a very solid report that Assad was at a going away reception for an African leader in Damascus and somebody rolled a grenade at him.'

"Well, that sounded like a pretty good story, so I made some calls and then I went to a cocktail party. Tim Llewelyn was at the party and David Hirst [Beirut correspondent for the British *Guardian*]. Hirst had heard the story from an entirely different source, which he felt was credible. He was doubly interested that I had heard it from a separate source. We got on the phone to another person who believed it was credible and at that point we had a story. . . . Then the question was—do we use it? We discussed the fact that this was not the kind of story that would make us popular with Hafez Assad or his brother. We were all quite aware of that problem. We all used the story, but we were all apprehensive."[29]

Nothing happened that time, but in July 1980, the BBC correspondent's luck ran out. A well-known Syrian go-between informed several diplomats in Damascus that Llewelyn and Jim Muir were going to be killed. They, in turn, got the message, "devious but unmistakable information from Damascus that because of our reporting of internal problems in Syria, our continued stay in Beirut would end in our assassination," in Llewelyn's words.[30] The British Embassy protested to the Syrian authorities, but were told, with what the British weekly *Economist* described as "laughable cynicism," that security in Beirut was the responsibility of the Lebanese government. That was enough. Llewelyn and Muir sought refuge in Cyprus, where they waited for several weeks while the BBC reportedly tried to negotiate the terms of their return to Lebanon. It was a lost cause. Llewelyn, like Debusmann, was reassigned to East Africa. Muir remained in Nicosia. And the BBC's new Middle East correspondent, Gordon Leach, took up resident in Cyprus. The BBC's Beirut operation had been closed down.

The reign of terror did not end there. Later that month, a *Figaro* correspondent was, in the words of *New York Times* Beirut correspondent John Kifner, "suddenly pulled out [of Lebanon] and word about town was that he, too, had received a warning from the Syrians."[31]

Reporters in Beirut clearly recognized the organized, explicit threat posed by the Syrian government, but they found it difficult to respond directly. In the summer of 1980, a group of them held a secret meeting to discuss what might be done. They agreed, as one later wrote, that their "only protection lies in achieving maximum publicity"[32] in order to show the Syrians that attacks on journalists would be counterproductive. They feared, however, that articles on the situation written from Beirut might lead to further harassment and violence. They decided instead to ask their home offices to print editorials and columns on the subject. For reasons that will be examined later, very few news organizations actually published such articles, but the ones that did were very clearly speaking the minds of the foreign correspondents in Lebanon. In an editorial entitled "Publish and Perish in Syria's Front Yard," the *Economist* of London forthrightly noted that Syria's campaign to silence reporters was succeeding: "By using the crudest forms of terror against journalists working in Lebanon—threats of death, attempted killings and actual murder—the Syrian government has just about succeeded in drawing a damask curtain around its increasingly perilous condition."[33]

The editorial went on to note that, ". . . the killings of Mr. [Salim] Lawzi and Mr. [Riad] Taha have made Lebanese journalists extremely wary of reporting on Syria; and what happened to Mr. [Tim] Llewelyn and Mr. [Berndt]

Debusmann has had the same effect on foreign correspondents."

Shortly after his narrow escape from Beirut, the BBC's Tim Llewelyn himself commented on the Syrian campaign: "So, four foreign correspondents have gone; the remainder are cowed in a city beyond Syria's borders but certainly not beyond its penetration. It's easy to die violently in Beirut; no one will, or even can, prove anything. The guilty agent, if accused, can easily take cover in the impenetrable lawlessness . . .

"What will the results be? Life will go on—I don't want arrogantly to over-estimate the role of the newsman—but there will be little or no news about Syria—which for now suits Syria fine."[34]

The atmosphere of intimidation and fear among Western journalists in Beirut was by now so pervasive that the merest hint of violence was taken seriously. Such a hint sent CBS correspondent Larry Pintak scurrying for safety in the winter of 1980.

Pintak's bosses at CBS headquarters claim not to know who wanted to murder him. In December 1980, Pintak, stationed in Beirut, received an anonymous telephone call; according to John Lane, vice president, director of news coverage at CBS, and Peter Larkin, CBS foreign editor, one call was enough. "We don't know who was behind it," says Lane. "There was some talk that it could be the Syrians, that it could be the PLO . . . we don't know." Larkin, who calls PLO and Syrian-run West Beirut "a zoo," downplays the possibility that Pintak was threatened for political or professional reasons. "Some guy comes up to you and says, 'Hey, I don't like the way you look,' and he's carrying an AK-47— who the hell does he represent? I mean, is he talking for Yasser Arafat or is he representing his girlfriend or the guy you bought the car from who thought he got a lousy price?"[35]

Some of Pintak's fellow correspondents in Beirut were more certain. The British *Observer*'s service, for example, reported that Pintak's departure came as a result of a threat from the Syrians, supposedly for having reported on their connection with CIA gun runner and mercenary Frank Terpil.[36] Only a few days before Pintak's life was threatened, CBS had reported that Frank Terpil had been snatched by Syrian military intelligence. Pintak was out of Lebanon when the report was broadcast; he was back in Beirut only briefly before he was informed that he was now a target. Pintak left Beirut immediately and didn't go back until the Syrians and PLO had been thrown out by Israel in the summer of 1982.

Damascus never took "credit" for driving Larry Pintak out of Lebanon, but by that time its reputation for intimidation was so well established that the press corps simply assumed that it was the Syrians who were behind the threat. There were plenty of other possibilities in a place like Beirut—which one journalist called "a crocodile-infested swamp"[37]—but many journalists preferred not to think about them. The Syrians were fearsome, but at least they were a known quantity. With a little prudence and some self-censorship, most felt that they were safe enough.

Not that the Beirut press corps was cowardly; on the contrary, its members were living examples of H. R. Knickerbocker's adage: "Whenever you find hundreds of thousands of sane people trying to get out of a place and a little bunch of madmen struggling to get in, you know the latter are newspapermen."[38] But even the bravest person can take just so much uncertainty. To cross the swamp one had to step somewhere, and the trick was to step on the rocks and not on the crocodile's back. The journalists needed to believe that there *were* rocks—and for many, they took the form of the Palestine Liberation Organization.

3

SEE NO EVIL

Sean Toolan's friends say he was a happy man on the night he was murdered. The forty-three-year-old journalist had just returned to Beirut from a six-week visit to the United States, and now he was back among his buddies at the bar of the Commodore Hotel. He and a couple of other reporters entertained the crowd with some Irish songs, accompanied on the guitar; earlier, over dinner, he had been filled in on the gossip and political news he had missed during his vacation, news he needed to know to resume his duties as ABC radio reporter in the Lebanese capital.

July 14, 1981, was Toolan's second night back in Beirut, and it was also his second night at the bar of the Commodore, the Palestinian-run hotel that served as a home-away-from-home for the American press corps. It was a unique institution, an island of efficiency and safety amid the chaos and violence of civil war-ridden Beirut. The hotel's management provided its guests with well-prepared meals even during times of scarcity, reliable telecommunications, and a well-stocked bar which was the center for political talk in Palestinian-controlled West Beirut. Here, almost every night, Beirut's resident foreign correspondents and visiting journalists could meet a shifting assortment of characters with information to sell or a story to tell. The correspondents reckoned themselves lucky to have such a hospitable base, and the extra surcharge added to their bills for PLO protection from the violent world outside the hotel was considered money well spent.

Among the foreign reporters who frequented the Commodore, Sean Toolan was a favorite. He was an Irishman, born in County Mayo, a former paratrooper, and something of an adventurer. In the past, Toolan had lived in the United States, and one of his reasons for going there in the spring of 1981 was to make final arrangements for his application for American citizenship. He was, his colleagues recall, a good man to socialize with, a storyteller, a drinker, and a ladies' man. Just before he left for the U.S., the management of the Commodore had thrown him an extravagant forty-third birthday party.

Sean Toolan had first come to Beirut less than a year earlier, at a time when Western reporters were being harassed and sometimes even assaulted in the Lebanese capital. Milt Fullerton, the man Toolan replaced as ABC radio correspondent, recalls a telephone call from Toolan shortly before he left the U.S. to take up his new post. The Irishman had heard the reports of violence, and he was concerned. Fullerton filled him in on the situation in Beirut, assured him that with a moderate degree of caution he would be relatively safe, and wished him good luck in his new assignment. Later on, when Fullerton heard of Toolan's murder, he would remember that conversation.[1]

It was past one A.M. when Toolan left the bar of the Commodore. He had been drinking but wasn't drunk. Many of his colleagues lived at the hotel, but Toolan had his own apartment a few blocks away. Bill Farrell of *The New York Times,* asked him how he was getting home. "I'll walk," Toolan said. "I always walk."[2]

When they found Sean Toolan's body, hours later, it was in a downtown Beirut alley. He had been shot in the back, badly beaten, and stabbed repeatedly, probably, from the look of the wounds, with an icepick. His wallet, with 120 Lebanese pounds, was still in his pocket. His bag, containing a camera and an expensive radio, was found lying near the body. Whoever murdered Sean Toolan had clearly not been intent on robbery.

The Lebanese authorities carried out a perfunctory investigation and then closed the case. During the civil war, which had begun in 1975 and was still sputtering along, tens of thousands of civilians had been killed, and the overburdened Lebanese police had long since ceased to get excited over one more dead body, even that of an American journalist. More important, the Moslem, western, sector of the town, where Toolan was murdered, was under only nominal Lebanese control. Its actual masters were the Syrian occupation forces and the PLO. Political assassinations were not uncommon, and journalists were sometimes the targets. In the previous three years alone, three newsmen had been murdered, and a fourth shot and badly wounded. Syrian intelligence and the PLO were widely rumored to have been behind these killings, and the Lebanese police knew that it was unhealthy to ask too many questions. The day after the murder, Camille Jaja, Lebanon's prosecutor general, told the press that "there is no clue yet if the murder was political or an ordinary crime," and that was the last public statement recorded by a Lebanese official regarding the murder. Toolan's body was shipped home, and the case remained unsolved.

Toolan's colleagues at the Commodore were badly shaken by his murder. Nick Tatro, AP bureau chief in Beirut at the time, summed it up: "Sean's death was a blow to us all. If there was any good in it, it was to remind us that no matter how expert we think we are, this place is dangerous as hell."[3]

Like so much else in Lebanon, the once-idyllic life of the Beirut-based foreign correspondents began to change with the arrival of the Palestine Liberation Organization in the early 1970s. In 1970 the PLO, whose armed presence in the kingdom of Jordan had already become an acute threat to the government there, lost a bitter, bloody war against King Hussein's troops. In the months following "Black Septem-

ber" of 1970, almost the entire leadership structure of
the PLO fled Jordan and relocated in Beirut. For decades
Lebanon had been a precariously balanced society whose
various religious and ethnic communities maintained a tenuous, suspicious equilibrium. Now the PLO brought its
armed, militant presence to bear on the side of the Lebanese Moslems, much to the displeasure of the dominant
middle-class Christians. It also brought a new method for
dealing with Western journalists that was both direct and
brutal. In those early days foreign reporters were considered enemies unless they proved otherwise; and certain
subjects were off limits to all journalists, friends and enemies alike.

This approach began during the period that the PLO was
still headquartered in Amman. In the late sixties, Milan Kubic covered the Middle East for *Newsweek*. On a visit to Amman, Jordan, in 1969, Kubic noticed a group of German
young people on the campus of the university. He struck up
a conversation with several of the Germans, who told him
that they were in Jordan as guests of the PLO. This was at
a time when the PLO's relations with the European new left
were just beginning to surface, and Kubic realized that he
had stumbled on to an interesting story. He filed a report
about PLO-European contacts, which *Newsweek* printed. The
following week Kubic returned to Amman, and he was informed that an official of the PLO wanted to meet with him.
As Kubic recalls: "I was taken to the office of the PLO's chief
spokesman in Amman. When I got there he pulled a gun
on me, brandished a copy of my article in *Newsweek*, and
threatened to kill me. 'The revolution knows how to deal with
people like you,' he said. 'Get out of Amman and never come
back!' " Kubic, one of *Newsweek*'s most experienced correspondents, knew a real threat when he heard one and left
Jordan. To "report" on the PLO he hired two part-time correspondents, one the son of the legendary British leader of
the Jordanian army, Glubb Pasha, the other Mark (Abdullah) Schleifer, a Jewish convert to Islam and anti-Israel prop-
agandist. Both stringers were presumably closer to what the
Palestinian revolution had in mind.[4]

After its expulsion from Jordan, the PLO began expanding its power in Lebanon. Its base was the hundreds of thousands of Palestinian refugees in the country, and it joined forces with radical Moslem groups in a rough alliance against the Christians. By 1973, there was sporadic violence throughout the country, and in the spring of 1975, full-scale civil war erupted. The small community of foreign journalists in Lebanon was reinforced to cover the fighting in a nation traditionally considered to be a key Western outpost in the Middle East. The PLO was particularly sensitive to the fact that its policies and methods were now under the scrutiny of a comparatively large group of Western reporters, and it undertook some of the same tactics that it had employed in Jordan in order to ensure that its "enemies" in the Western press remained at arm's length.

Even today, Bill Marmon has no idea how *he* got on the enemies list. Marmon, a tall, bearded man in his early forties, began working for *Time* magazine in 1966. After several domestic assignments and a stint in Vietnam, he was sent to Israel in 1973, as *Time*'s bureau chief. He soon established himself as one of the Jerusalem-based journalists most critical of Israel and sympathetic to the Palestinian cause. His wife got a job teaching at Beir Zeit University, near Ramallah on the West Bank, a Palestinian college that was a hotbed of anti-Israel sentiment and a thorn in the side of the Israeli authorities. On several occasions, he recalls, he angered Israeli press officials with his reporting on the West Bank. All this would, he assumed, stand him in good stead when, in 1975, *Time* transferred him from Jerusalem to Beirut.

During his stint in Jerusalem, Marmon had visited the Lebanese capital several times. Once, at a regional meeting of *Time* correspondents, he had been excluded from a group interview with Yasser Arafat; his superiors feared that the presence of an Israel-based correspondent might offend the PLO leader. Still, despite the fact that Marmon was perhaps the first American correspondent ever to be stationed in Beirut after having lived in Israel, he anticipated no particular problems. Not only did he have a "good record" on the Palestinian issue, but *Time* magazine was in the process of adopting a new Middle East policy. "There was a feeling in New York that Israel was getting too good a deal in the Western press, and that this needed correction," says Marmon. The explicit message from New York was—more sympathetic coverage of the Arab position. "It was part of my charter to enable the Arab story to emerge in a convincing way."[5]

The first indication that Marmon's Israeli connection might be a problem in Beirut came less than a week after he and his wife and infant arrived in Lebanon. "It had been spring vacation at the American University of Beirut, and one of the American students went to visit Israel during the break. Somehow, a group of Palestinian students found out about it. She was grabbed and the words *Jew Lover* were carved on her stomach with a knife. It made us a bit uneasy," he recalls.

During the summer of 1975, Marmon went on assignment to Egypt. One day Lebanese security officers came to his office. When they learned that he was in Cairo, they spoke to his local assistant, Abu Said. They told him that they had received reports that Palestinian intelligence had learned about Marmon's Jerusalem years, and that they were planning to kill him. Abu Said, himself a Palestinian, used his considerable contacts to investigate and informed Marmon when he returned that the threat had come from the PFLP faction of the PLO. The *Time* bureau chief contacted the American embassy in Beirut. There he was told that they had no specific information regarding the threat against him, but that in the past similar threats had been made against the lives of American diplomats in Beirut. The embassy's policy was to take these threats very seriously and to transfer the diplomats immediately.

Despite this warning, Marmon decided to stay on in Beirut. He sent Abu Said to mediate, and his assistant was apparently able to convince the Palestinian terrorists to drop the threat. "The whole thing didn't have much reality for me at the time," he recalls.

Marmon remained in Beirut throughout the fall of 1975, a period in which *Time*'s office was shelled and the civilian slaughter in the city was, in Marmon's words, "the worst I have ever seen." On New Year's Eve, Abu Said came to see him. He had word that PLO gunmen had been looking for the *Time* correspondent the night before but had gone to the wrong apartment. This time the message got through—the PLO intended to murder William Marmon.

"I had had enough," Marmon says. "I drove to the Beirut airport, got on the first flight out, and landed in Amman, Jordan. Ironically, I was working at the time on a story on terrorism." When he arrived in Jordan, Marmon contacted Dick Duncan, then deputy chief of correspondents for *Time,* and reported what had happened. Marmon never returned to an area under the control of the PLO.

As the civil war progressed, the fighting in Beirut intensified. In November 1975, Ray Vickers, veteran correspondent of *The Wall Street Journal,* described the situation this way: "No street is safe. Any block may see kidnappings, looting and murders. Mail is undelivered. Telephone service is breaking down. Garbage goes uncollected. Sections of the city lack water. Food shops open briefly if at all. Banks are closed. Bills go unpaid. Pay of most workers has stopped. Most bureaucrats are absent from offices and welfare services have collapsed. Hospitals are jammed. Morgues are overloaded. Old personal scores are being settled with guns under cover of civil strife."[6] Some of those personal scores were with members of the American press.

Today, Philip Caputo lives in Florida and leads the life of a successful novelist. In 1975, though, he was the Beirut correspondent of the *Chicago Tribune.* Caputo, a short, aggressive man who some of his colleagues remember as a hothead, had been a marine officer in Vietnam. His first run-in with the PLO came in May 1973. Caputo had been detained by the terrorists in Beirut on charges of "spying" and held for five days. Upon his release, he wrote a six-part first-person account of his ordeal described by the *Tribune* as "an agonizing alternation between suicidal urges and the certainty that he would die." As often happens with the PLO, Caputo received profuse apologies from the organization when, after scaring him out of his wits, they finally released him.[7]

But Caputo's problems with Beirut's armed thugs were not over. On October 26, 1975, he filed a report to the *Tribune* and then left his office. He hadn't gone far when he was stopped at a checkpoint by "leftist militiamen." As Caputo later described the incident: "They checked my credentials and told me to walk down to Hamra Street, a distance of about one hundred yards. I had gone about thirty yards when one of them fired a shot at me. I shouted at them to stop, but then another joined in and fired a burst of bullets, one of which literally went through my hair. I ran zigzagging and rolling low, and was grazed across the back and arms by flying bullets. Then one hit me in the right ankle and just as I reached the corner another one got me in the left ankle. I crawled down Hamra Street toward the Central Bank, and a householder took me in."[8] Caputo was taken in an armored car to a nearby hospital; later, he was evacuated to the United States. When the *Chicago Tribune* reopened its Middle East office, it was in Tel Aviv.

Shortly after Caputo was shot, Gamma Press photographer Claude Salhani was crossing into Moslem West Beirut from the Christian side of town. Salhani was stopped at a PLO checkpoint near the national museum and asked to identify himself. He produced his PLO press card, which was seized along with his cameras, and he was told to stand against the wall and raise his hands. It was then that the PLO men discovered that Salhani was wearing a bullet-proof vest, standard apparel for combat photographers in Beirut but enough to cause them to accuse him of being a spy. For a few terrifying moments, Salhani was certain that the PLO gunmen were going to shoot him there in the street.

The photographer was taken to a building near the American University where, for the next nine hours, he was beaten and interrogated. Two questioners demanded to know his real identity and allegiance. Salhani, who is half-Lebanese, begged them to contact the PLO's spokesman, Mahmud Labadi. Finally he was taken not to the PLO's press center but to the organization's main headquarters. There, he was received by Yasser Arafat's deputy, who apologized effusively and ordered his release. Seven years have passed, and Salhani still works in Beirut but he has never forgotten the beating he received at the hands of the PLO, nor the relief he felt when he was finally set free.[9]

Not only foreign correspondents were drawn into the cycle of PLO violence. As the civil war progressed, local reporters became a primary target of the gunmen. On January 31, 1976, Palestinians from the pro-Syrian al-Saiqa wing of the PLO attacked the Arabic newspaper al-*Moharrer* and the adjacent *Beirut*, both located in the Moslem suburb of Chiyah. Approximately one hundred men opened fire on the two newspaper buildings with rockets and 106 millimeter guns. Seven journalists were killed, including Nayef Chitlak, the deputy editor of al-*Moharrer,* seven were wounded, and five employees of the two newspapers were kidnapped.*[10]

By the summer of 1976 Beirut had become, in the words of James Markham of *The New York Times,* "the most savage and uncivilized place on earth."[12] Tens of thousands of civilians had already died in the fighting and the Moslem-PLO alliance seemed to be winning. Syria, which has traditionally considered itself the dominant power in Lebanese affairs, feared that a Moslem-PLO victory might upset the Lebanese balance of power and weaken Damascus' influence over the country. Accordingly, at the ostensible invitation of the hapless and almost fictional Lebanese government, Syrian forces entered the country and began to intervene in the fighting on the side of the Christians. This marked the beginning of the Syrian occupation of Lebanon. Their presence brought a new stage in the civil war, and with it new rules and dangers for journalists in Beirut. The already em-

*Among those who died in the attack on al-*Moharrer* was Ibrahim Amer, one of the most famous journalists in the Arab world. Amer was an Egyptian who had been expelled from Egypt in 1973 during one of President Sadat's press purges. A prominent figure on the Lebanese journalistic scene, Amer served as a foreign correspondent for the well-known Yugoslavian journal *Politika* as well as various Arabic publications.[11]

battled press corps* now had a new threat to contend with.

The Syrian violence against the press was intended to silence criticism, but it had another, perhaps unintended effect—it made the PLO look good by comparison. From the time the Syrians arrived, most of the Commodore Hotel crowd believed that, at least in terms of its dealings with the press, the PLO could be counted among the "good guys"—helpful, and somehow even protective. John Yemma of the *Christian Science Monitor,* writing about violence against foreign correspondents in Beirut, said: "the PLO is certainly not above suspicion, but most journalists in Beirut contend that the PLO is not the greatest of their problems."[15] Or as Ed Cody of *The Washington Post* put it, "You do not have to fear the PLO when you write about Palestinian affairs."[16]

Many of the Beirut veterans considered the PLO enlightened in its press relations—able to cultivate foreign journalists, willing to frame its goals in moderate language, and eager to facilitate the work of friendly reporters. They took as a proof of the organization's tolerance the fact that it accepted occasional unfavorable press stories, and they contrasted this apparent sophistication with the rigid intolerance and bloody-mindedness of the Syrians.

What many of the correspondents failed to see was that the PLO's tolerance was hardly more than the willingness of a violent, powerful group to establish ground rules and then to allow the reporters to play by them. Journalists were free to write—as long as they avoided certain "sensitive" subjects: Western reporters were welcome in Beirut—provided that they were not considered "hostile" to the Palestine revolution. This resulted in what *The New York Times* corre-

*During the pre-Syrian phase of the civil war, twelve journalists—nine Lebanese and three foreigners—died in Beirut. Perhaps the most gruesome death was that of the Christian Telex operator of UPI, who was kidnapped by Moslem leftists and literally hacked to death.[13] In August 1976, in an article entitled "Beirut's Thin Green Line," *Newsweek* magazine summed up the situation. "Among the fifty-odd foreign reporters covering the war in Lebanon, there is widespread agreement—even among the veterans—that combat reportage has never been so fraught with discomfort, difficulty and danger." *Newsweek* noted that many journalists had been forced to travel in packs to reduce their vulnerability, with obvious consequences for their ability to do independent work.[14]

spondent Thomas Friedman has referred to as the PLO's "often uncritical" press coverage.[17]

Under these circumstances, the PLO did not usually need to resort to the kind of heavyhanded tactics that characterized the Syrians. Hafez Assad was almost universally hated by the press; Arafat and his followers were, by and large, admired. Most of the Beirut press corps never saw the PLO's stick—they were too busy munching on its carrot. That carrot was the permission the PLO gave them to work in the Lebanese capital and its assistance in covering the secret, semi-underground activities of the organization.

Still, in the backs of their minds, even the most obtuse journalists knew that the stick existed. The PLO was, after all, a terrorist organization with a history of murdering its enemies and then proudly justifying the murders in the name of the Palestinian revolution. Nor did it confine itself to Israeli targets. The PLO had attacked supporters of Israel around the world, assassinated Arab "collaborators" in the West Bank and Gaza, massacred Lebanese Christians at Damur, and often conducted its own internal politics at the point of a gun. This violence was a part of the Palestinian mystique—Yasser Arafat himself had appeared in the UN General Assembly with a pistol strapped to his hip—and it worked for the PLO in the same way that the Mafia's reputation for strong-arm tactics often makes them unnecessary.

Thus, the Beirut press corps was aware that the PLO could get violent with its enemies, although many were reluctant to say as much. Doyle McManus reflected this reluctance when he said, "I've always felt that the question of PLO intimidation was misplaced. Frankly, I don't think there was any . . . well, obviously when I say there wasn't *any* I speak within certain limits, because I think that the PFLP killed Bob Pfeffer."[18]

In May of 1979 Robert Pfeffer of *Stern* magazine was murdered in Beirut. The thirty-eight-year-old German was on a leave of absence from *Stern* and was working on a book about contacts between the PLO and the Baader-Meinhof gang and other European terrorist groups. Pfeffer, a balding, intense, and introverted man, had a deep commitment to the Third World; he had spent much of his youth in Pakistan, where his father taught at the Lahore University, spoke some Arabic, and was generally considered one of the most sympathetic and best-informed Western journalists about Third World issues.

Pfeffer was not one of the regulars at the bar of the Commodore. He was a bit standoffish, and some of his fellow reporters considered him rather timid, at least by the demanding macho standards of the Beirut press corps. Still, in the tiny community of foreign reporters, he was well known.

On May 24, he was driving home; when he reached the parking lot of his building, a car pulled up next to him and someone shot and killed Robert Pfeffer. As usual in Beirut, the murderers escaped, and there was no serious investigation. But most of Pfeffer's colleagues guessed the identity of the murderers. Peter M. Ranke, the Middle East correspondent for Springer Publications, states flatly: "Robert Pfeffer was shot dead by two Palestinians belonging to one of the radical groups. Responsible for the killing was Brigitte Mohnhaupt from the Baader-Meinhof gang. [They murdered him] because Pfeffer told everybody in West Beirut that he was writing a book regarding the relations between Palestinians and the Red Army Faction."[19] Few members of the Beirut press corps doubted that Pfeffer's curiosity about the PLO's dealings with European terrorists had cost him his life.

Following Pfeffer's murder, the Beirut press corps stayed away from the subject of the PLO's contacts with European terrorist organizations. "Obviously Bob Pfeffer got killed, or at least most of us believe he got killed, for looking into the connection with Baader-Meinhof and the PFLP," says McManus. "I never raised the subject with anyone I knew in the PLO as to what would be going across the line. I didn't want to know what they would consider a reason for shooting a reporter."[20]

Were there circumstances under which reporters believed that the PLO might do such a thing again? "I imagine that there might be, sure," says McManus. "They are, in some measure, a gang of thugs." Milt Fullerton, who worked for ABC in Beirut, agrees. "If I heard that the PLO was threatening journalists, I wouldn't have been surprised at all,"[21] he says. This thought, in the backs of the minds of Fullerton, McManus, and their colleagues in Beirut, was in itself the essence of elegant intimidation.

Having established the limits of its tolerance, the PLO was then free to cultivate and befriend individual journalists. In the lawless atmosphere of Beirut, the organization portrayed itself as the guardian of the press—presumably from the Syrians and free-lance thugs. John Kifner of *The New York Times:* "In the chaos of predominantly Moslem, leftist Beirut the Palestine Liberation Organization, perhaps because it serves its political best interests, has functioned more as a protector of journalists than as an intimidator."[22]

It is ironic and rather puzzling that the PLO was regarded by many journalists as a guardian from the Syrians. During much of this time, Syria and the PLO were allied and often cooperated closely in the occupation of West Beirut. The Syrians, who exercised overall control, were content to allow the PLO to run day-to-day affairs in the western part of the Lebanese capital, and some of the PLO's constituent groups were either directly or indirectly controlled by Syria. Given the Arab propensity for dissension, there were, of course, bitter feuds and disagreements between the two, but on the whole the PLO and the Assad regime had a client-patron relationship. Still, even the illusion of protection from the dreaded Syrians was welcome, and in a Levantine variation of the old "good cop-bad cop" routine, the PLO was glad to provide it.

In conformity with the PLO-dependent security system, Western reporters ghettoized themselves and became, in effect accomplices to their own isolation and supervision. They clustered around the Palestinian-run Commodore, where they knew their movements, contacts, and outgoing communication would be monitored. Some of those with separate offices in the city found that they needed local Palestinian employees in order to establish contacts and guide them through the complexities of life in Beirut. These assistants were, in many cases, subject to the discipline of the PLO; and if the organization was circumspect in its dealing with most of the foreign reporters, it could afford to be far less so in its demands on its fellow Palestinians or Lebanese Moslems. Even reporters aware of the fact that their local employees might be a conduit to PLO intelligence were loath to give them up; in many cases such people were an invaluable buffer.

To work in Beirut one needed the help and sponsorship of the PLO. Bill Marmon put it this way: "The PLO was able to play on the willingness of journalists to meet it more than halfway. Generally in the Arab world it is necessary, to an extent unknown in Israel or the West, to prove you are a friend, and you try to do this to the extent possible without totally sacrificing your integrity—I did it myself. Often you must have a patron. He's crucial, and sometimes that relationship comes at the expense of hard hitting journalism." After a while, though, the pretense of friendship and sympathy can ripen into the real thing. "There is a sort of contract you make with organizations like the PLO—and they are skillful at extracting a good price from the press. One way it's done is through the 'I'm a friend, you should talk to me' kind of arrangement. You know, you tell the guy, I'm pro-PLO and anti-Israel, that sort of thing. The problem is that once you start that, some people really begin to believe it."[23]

Even in their own homes, some journalists were "protected" by the PLO. Peter Ranke, Mideast correspondent for Springer Publications, recalls a visit he paid to a colleague, Armin Reinartz of the German press agency DPA, at his apartment in West Beirut. During the evening, Reinartz told Ranke that he didn't dare report on Syrian affairs or the inside story of the PLO for fear of reprisal. Reinartz claimed that he was being watched by a PLO guard who lived in the basement of his building, ostensibly to protect Palestinian stores of beer and coffee, but actually to spy on the foreign residents of the apartment house. Ranke was skeptical until, as if on cue, the Palestinian guard appeared at the German journalist's door. As Ranke watched, astonished, the PLO man looked around the apartment, asked for a cold beer, and then left.*[24]

Many of the Beirut press corps came to feel that they had a special obligation to help the PLO make its case in the West. Vincent Schodolski, former bureau chief of the UPI in Beirut, once told an interviewer, "I think people here try to keep a balance, but you're here and have daily access to the Palestinians. You see the people, you see the refugee camps, you're bound to tell the story as you see it." Schodolski described a kind of competition between the Beirut and Israel-based journalists. "The job of the guys in Dixie [the code word for Israel] is to tell *their* side of the story." (emphasis added)[25]

Tim Llewelyn of the BBC was even more explicit. "The newsmen covering the Arab side of life began to feel in recent years that they were nearing a more equal battle—for battle it is—with their Israeli side colleagues trying to bring more 'balance' to the West's view of the Middle East."[26] This sentiment, shared by a good many of the American and British correspondents in Beirut during the years of PLO domination, goes a long way toward explaining why most of them, in Edward Cody's words, felt that "there was nothing to fear from the PLO in covering Palestinian affairs."[27]

This sympathetic view of the PLO colored the press corps's relations with Lebanon's Christians. During the civil war Beirut had become a divided city, the west under the control of the Syrians and the PLO, the east run by various Christian militias. Yet despite the fact that half the Lebanese story was on the Christian side, few foreign reporters visited that sector with any frequency, and virtually none lived there.†

---

*Sometimes PLO "protection" was totally shameless. After the murder of Robert Pfeffer, the PLO put out the word that *it* was conducting an investigation. Similarly, after the death of ABC's Sean Toolan, the PLO let it be known that *it* was looking into the matter. These investigative efforts by the suspects themselves were, apparently, taken at face value by a number of journalists in Beirut, who by that time had adopted an unquestioning belief in the PLO's role as their benefactor.

†When the PLO was driven out of Beirut in 1982, and the city was temporarily re-united, supporters of the Christian Phalangist Party proved that they, too, were not above intimidation of journalists. *Washington Post* reporter Loren Jenkins and

Some even encouraged their visiting colleagues to keep away from the Christian part of town. Former ABC *20/20* producer Barbara Newman, who came to Lebanon in 1980 to film part of a documentary, remembers the surprise and dismay at the ABC bureau in Beirut when it was learned that she was planning to stay at the Christian-run Alexandre Hotel and not at the Commodore.[29] Their reaction caused the documentary's correspondent, Geraldo Rivera, to book rooms in both places and to ferry from one side to the other. "I've often thought that the story of the media coverage of Beirut should be called 'A Tale of Two Hotels: the Commodore and the Alexandre,' " says Rivera, who is highly critical of the Beirut press corps's failure to cover the Christian side of the story in Lebanon. "The vast majority, including North American newsmen, got most of their leads, their tips, their sources, at the bar of the Commodore Hotel. That's why you had this terrible skewing, this real uneven view of things." Rivera, who did a full-scale interview with Bashir Gemayel in 1980, was told by the late Lebanese leader that he was the first American television reporter to stay overnight in East Beirut.[30]

The isolation of the Beirut regulars from the Christian point of view also bothered Peter Ranke, who claimed that in the early 1980s, "Some German, American, and English correspondents regularly reporting from Beirut, or staying there frequently, *have never* visited the Phalange party's headquarters . . . they can indeed have only one-sided information." Ranke noted that many Western reporters did attend Christian press conferences, but that was about it. "Last spring [1981] I was with the Lebanese forces in East Beirut during the heavy bombardment by the Syrian army. Nobody of all the permanent correspondents came over to [the Christian] side. They all stayed at the bar of the PLO's Commodore Hotel." Ranke's bitter conclusion: "Beirut [un-

The New York Times's Colin Campbell were reportedly threatened and forced to leave Lebanon after reporting on the Phalangist massacres at the Sabra and Shatilla refugee camps in September 1982. It was months before Jenkins returned to the Lebanese capital.[28]

der the PLO] is no working place for an honest journalist anymore. Sorry."[31]

But of course not all, or even most, of the reporters in Beirut were dishonest. Some, like Vincent Schodolski, believed that it was their job to tell "their" side of the story. Others were deeply committed to the Third World view of national liberation and wished the Palestinian revolution well (this group included both serious ideologues and thrill-seeking groupies). Some reporters in Beirut were influenced by the "hostage syndrome," the tendency of people under pressure to identify with those in a similar position, while others responded to the PLO's carrot-and-stick approach to press management. And since few professions are as vulnerable to the herd instinct as journalism, once attitudes in the Beirut press corps were struck, they stuck: newcomers were routinely initiated into the conventional wisdom of the Commodore bar. Simply put, the PLO did not have much need to practice intimidation on its supporters in the Beirut press corps.*

When it came to dealing with visiting journalists, however, the PLO had less reason to pull its punches. Correspondents who worked outside of Lebanon were subject to none of the influences that shaped the perceptions of their Beirut-based colleagues; nor could they be relied upon to respect, or even be aware of, PLO sensibilities. Many of these journalists became targets of PLO threats or were simply not allowed to come to West Beirut at all.

Hans Benedict found himself a victim of "preventive intimidation" when he applied for a Lebanese visa in 1980.

---

*Although it could when it felt the need to. The *Christian Science Monitor*'s Ned Temko received a death threat from the PLO after marrying an Israeli-American woman, according to the *Columbia Journalism Review*. (Temko himself says that the threat came not from the PLO but from a "Palestinian activist" who merely threatened to seize and hold his wife in order to exchange her for PLO prisoners held in Israel).[32] A few months after the threat to Temko, in September 1980, Graziella DePalo, a free-lance Italian correspondent, disappeared while on a PLO-sponsored trip to Lebanon. DePalo was apparently looking for information about Italian arms sales to various warring factions in Lebanon. She left Beirut for south Lebanon with a PLO guide on the morning of September 2, 1980—and was never seen or heard from again.[33]

Benedict, one of the most senior and widely respected European journalists, is the former chief editor of Austrian national television, and since 1979 he has been its diplomatic correspondent in the Middle East. Part of Benedict's job is to report on the PLO, and accordingly, early in his tenure, he applied to the Lebanese embassy in Vienna for a visa. The answer, Benedict was astounded to learn, was no. Even more amazing, a senior Lebanese diplomat told him that the decision had in fact been made not by the Lebanese government, but by the PLO.

Benedict became unpopular with the PLO when he interviewed its Austrian representative, Gazi Hussein, in the fall of 1978. It was during the PLO's diplomatic push to achieve a new, moderate image, and he had asked the PLO representative about the Coastal Road massacre of Israeli civilians, which his organization had carried out near Tel Aviv the previous spring. Hussein answered forthrightly that terrorism against Israelis, including women and children, was a legitimate tool of the Palestinian revolution and that the PLO would continue to use it as it saw fit. When the interview was aired, it caused a stir in Austria and was a major public-relations setback for the Palestinians. Despite the fact that Benedict's interview had been broadcast complete and unedited, the PLO considered showing it at all to be an unfriendly act.

The Lebanese diplomat who returned Benedict's visa application was apologetic. "We would welcome you," he told the Austrian newsman, "but we cannot guarantee your safety. We have information that your life is in danger from the PLO." Benedict was told that applications for Lebanese press visas had to be authorized by PLO headquarters and, "if we ask them for a visa for you, they'll be on the lookout for you at the airport." Hans Benedict, who first started covering the Arab world in 1946 and served as a correspondent for AP behind the Iron Curtain for more than fifteen years, knew a death threat when he heard one. He didn't get to the Lebanese capital until the PLO departed in August 1982.[34]

Another correspondent who had trouble with PLO intimidation was Peter Meyer Ranke. Ranke is something of a maverick in the Middle East press corps, an outspoken critic of both the PLO and its coddling by many of his colleagues. He began working in the region in 1960, first as resident Cairo correspondent for the German newspaper *Die Welt* and later as the Middle East correspondent for the Springer chain. Ranke covered the civil war in the Yemen and the Six Day War, wrote a book about Egyptian President Gamal Abdul Nasser, and spent 1965–66 as resident correspondent in Beirut. After serving as an editor and columnist back home, he returned to Lebanon in 1975 and lived in Beirut throughout the civil war. Since then he has lived in Athens where, as chief Middle East correspondent for Springer Publications, he travels throughout the Arab world and Israel and visits Lebanon two or three times a year.

"Once, in West Beirut, I was threatened by the PLO spokesman [Mahmud] Labadi—who speaks German and was trained in East Germany as a student," he recalls. Labadi let him know that he was considered an enemy, that he could expect no help, and that he would be watched. "I understood this as a clear warning," says Ranke, who had no doubt that Labadi was threatening his life.[35]

Perhaps the most blatant PLO threat was directed against Geraldo Rivera. It started when he and *20/20* producer, Barbara Newman, decided to do a documentary on the origins of Palestinian terror and its contacts with the USSR and European groups such as Baader-Meinhof and the Italian Red Brigades. It was a brave decision. Rivera knew about the murder of Robert Pfeffer and was aware of the Palestinian taboo on the subject. But he also saw that it was a terrific story and one that had gone largely unreported in the United States.

In the beginning of 1981, after meeting with Israeli experts on the PLO and interviewing PLO terrorists in an Israeli prison, Rivera flew to Beirut via Rome. The next day, he and Newman were taken by ABC's Beirut correspondent, Jerry King, to a meeting with PLO spokesman Mahmud Labadi. Several armed men were in the room when the three arrived, and they remained there throughout the meeting. "It was," recalls Rivera, "like going to see the right-hand man of some tin-pot dictator.

"The atmosphere was ominous. Somehow Labadi already knew almost our entire itinerary in Israel, and he refused us any real cooperation. He said right away that we were going to do a Zionist hatchet job and demanded to know if I was Jewish. I told him I was.

"There was a great deal of tension during our stay in Beirut," says Rivera. "I had the sense of being watched, American correspondents told me that the PLO didn't like the fact that I was there. It was an ominous feeling. I'm not a paranoid person, I've been in very tight scrapes in my professional life and those red flags don't get hoisted very often, but I definitely had a feeling that there were warnings implicit in almost everything Labadi said, in his entire attitude."

During the time Rivera worked on the documentary in Beirut, the warnings remained implicit. But when it was broadcast, the PLO's reaction crystallized. "Once it aired, I was definitely on the shit list," says the ABC correspondent.

Rivera's colleagues in Beirut passed along the PLO's message: "Don't come back to West Beirut, or else . . ." He received telephone death threats at his home in California, but they didn't bother him much at the time, particularly since he had no special interest in returning to Lebanon. Later, during the 1982 war, it was different. Rivera, like hundreds of other Western newsmen, found himself in the Lebanese capital, in his case to do an exclusive interview with Lebanon's president-elect, Bashir Gemayel. He checked with contacts and colleagues on the west side of the city to make sure that he could cross the border and do some reporting there. "I was told point-blank, and by more than one source, never to come back to West Beirut, to Palestinian territory. I was told that I had a death warrant out for me. The word was passed to me, unmistakably and very specifically."[36] Rivera believed the warnings; and the PLO was successful in keeping another "hostile" reporter off its turf.

* * *

The spring of 1981 was a time of considerable tension in Lebanon. Israel and Syria were faced off over the introduction of Syria's Russian-made SAM missile system in Lebanon's eastern Be'ka region, and Israel was aggressively pursuing a policy of preemptive strikes against PLO concentrations in the southwestern coastal area. The Beirut press corps was overworked and tense, expecting a major Israeli assault. One day late in May, less than two months before Sean Toolan was murdered, three American correspondents, Jonathan Randal of *The Washington Post* and William Farrell and John Kifner of *The New York Times,* decided to take some time off and have what Farrell later described as "a civilized dinner party, a dinner-jackets-in-the-jungle kind of evening" at Kifner's home in West Beirut.[37] Kifner cooked a chicken, and the three newsmen relaxed over drinks and swapped stories about previous assignments and absent colleagues. At about 11:30 their dinner party was interrupted by a telephone call. Someone informed Kifner that the long-anticipated Israeli raid on PLO bases in the Damur area was taking place. Despite the late hour, the three decided to investigate. Their first stop was the Commodore Hotel, always a fertile source of information. The consensus at the bar was that if there was a raid, it was probably a limited one, but Randal, Kifner, and Farrell decided that the tip was worth checking into. Julian Nundy of *Newsweek* and William Foley, an Associated Press photographer, asked to come along and the five piled into Kifner's car and headed toward Damur, about fifteen miles south of Beirut.

They never got there. At the outskirts of the city they were cut off and pulled over by, of all things, a Red Crescent ambulance belonging to the PLO's first aid and medical organization. Gunmen armed with assault rifles pulled them out of the car and demanded to see their identification papers, which they produced.* The armed men, members of

* "The situation was complicated by the fact that several of the group had been at a dinner party earlier in the evening given by this correspondent and wore jackets and neckties," John Kifner later wrote. "As a result, various cards, passes and pieces of identification normally buttoned into work clothes had been left be-

the PFLP-GC faction of the PLO examined the reporters' credentials, and decided to haul them in.

Bill Farrell later recalled: "They booked us, police style, put our belongings in envelopes and took us to an area with narrow, high-ceilinged, almost coffinlike cells, about six and a half feet long by three and a half wide. They had steel doors with a little hatch you couldn't see out of at all. There were no toilets, just a foam rubber pallet on the floor. It was hot as hell inside." After about two hours, the reporters were stripped and searched and then returned to their cells. They were fed bread, cheese, and cucumbers and given water to drink. "I tried to think about green pastures," says Farrell. "From time to time you could hear gunshots, and I wondered if someone else was being executed."

After a considerable time, the correspondents were taken, one at a time, into an interrogation room, where they were questioned by two men. "These guys knew what they were doing. It was all very organized, Moscow-style," says Farrell. "They asked what countries I'd worked in and I named them, including Israel. One of them said, 'Palestine,' and I said, 'Sure, anything you say, pal.'"[40] The PLO men then took four pictures, put them in his dossier, and sent him back to the lock-up.

Not everyone got the same treatment. Randal says flatly, "My life was not threatened."[41] At least two of the others, though, feared that their lives were in danger.[42] So, apparently, did their colleagues in town, who engaged in a frantic search throughout Beirut for the five journalists, contacting, in the process, senior officials of the PLO. The fact that these senior officials were contacted lends weight to Farrell's supposition that the PFLP-GC men were aware of the journalists' identities early on. "My feeling is that they knew very early in the day who we were and they just decided to put us through the hoops. Otherwise, I don't know why they

hind."[38] This, however, does not seem to have been the case. Both Farrell and Randal had all their credentials with them. Jonathan Randal, in a letter to the author, stated: "I can only speak for myself about press credentials and identification. I had both on my person."[39] Farrell, in an interview, said, "I had a press card; we all had our credentials with us." Presumably Nundy and Foley, who had not attended the dinner party and were still wearing their "work clothes," had their credentials as well.

would have held us after they knew we were hacks. Randal had some phone numbers of high-ranking PLO guys in his phone book, but they refused to call."[43]

At about five P.M., the five were reunited for the first time in fifteen hours. They were taken to another building, where they received profuse apologies, and were then released. When they were freed, Kifner raised the question of whether the story should be reported. *Time* later quoted one of the journalists as saying: " 'We made an informal agreement that we would not write about the incident. The stories would have just embarrassed everyone involved.' "[44] Especially the PLO.

Geraldo Rivera does not agree with Ed Cody that "you do not have to fear the PLO when you write about Palestinian affairs," although he might agree that there is nothing to fear if you write about them the way the boys at the Commodore did; Hans Benedict, Peter Ranke, Bill Marmon, and others may well wonder what their Beirut-based colleagues mean when they talk about the PLO as a guardian of the press. Robert Pfeffer is dead, and he can't wonder at all . . .

The story of Palestinian-Syrian-controlled West Beirut between 1975 and 1982 is one of terror against journalists— Syrian terror wielded, like a baseball bat, with crude, broad strokes; Palestinian terror, a scalpel used with discrimination and subtlety. Some resisted and paid with their lives, their careers, or their access to Beirut; others succumbed, wholly or partially, to the threats, the pressure, and the inducements to "get on the team." And in the case of the PLO, many journalists didn't need much encouragement.

Much of what went on in Lebanon and neighboring Syria was only partially reported or rarely mentioned—the excesses of the Assad regime, the PLO mini-state in south Lebanon, Palestinian links with international terrorists, and so forth. As in all cases of self-censorship, it is impossible to know *what* was being covered up; and in Beirut, the problem was compounded by an even greater omission—the failure of Western news organizations to tell the truth about what was going on.

COVER-UP

Bill Marmon works in an office building in downtown Washington, D.C., now. Years have passed since the PLO drove him out of Beirut at gunpoint, years that have brought changes to the Middle East and changes in his life as well. The PLO is no longer headquartered in Beirut; Marmon no longer makes his living as a journalist. But he hasn't forgotten the events of January 1976, when he fled Beirut to escape the PLO's gunmen.

"When I got to Amman, Jordan, I immediately contacted Dick Duncan, who at that time was the acting head of correspondents. I reported that I had been essentially expelled from Beirut by the PLO and that my life would be in danger if I tried to return. At the time Duncan was noncommittal, but as time went on I realized that New York was upset with *me*, not with them. There was a sense there that the PLO had to be cultivated, not alienated, and that somehow I was responsible for spoiling relations with them."[1]

Marmon was especially surprised, and dismayed, by the fact that *Time* magazine chose to keep his expulsion a secret. *Time*'s normal practice—indeed, standard operating procedure for American news organizations—is to loudly protest

89

any mistreatment or expulsion of its personnel. But, according to Marmon, it was six years before *Time* finally alluded to the incident in print, then saying only, "A *Time* correspondent [in Beirut] was once threatened with death,"[2] in the context of an article on violence against reporters in the Lebanese capital. When it happened, though, the magazine did not print a word about the incident.

"I felt at the time, well, this is all wrong, this isn't the way expulsions are supposed to be dealt with," says Marmon. "The special status of the PLO was underscored by *Time*'s approach. If this had happened in Russia, say, it sure would have been a story. In this case I felt that I had to justify having offended the Palestinians. It was backwards."

Marmon, who had been considered a rising star at *Time* magazine, was reassigned to the Los Angeles bureau, where he worked for a year and a half before deciding to quit. He sensed that the executives at *Time* had never quite forgiven him for inspiring the threats to his life. "Let's just say it wasn't helpful to my career at *Time*," he remarks dryly. When he left the magazine, he decided to quit journalism altogether. He enrolled in law school, and today he is a successful Washington attorney. Did *Time*'s treatment of him and its handling of the expulsion story affect his decision to quit the news business? Marmon shrugs. "Subliminally, I guess it must have."[3]

The death of Bill Marmon's journalistic career was an isolated personal tragedy, but it illustrates a strange, recurring phenomenon—the refusal of many news organizations to tell the truth about pressures and threats directed against their journalists in the Arab world. This refusal is at variance with normal journalistic practice; more importantly, it means the public cannot properly evaluate the credibility of news reports from much of the Middle East. Readers and viewers who were unaware of the atmosphere of intimidation and violence that existed in Beirut, for example, could not know that much of the news from there between 1975–82 was filtered through a veil of fear, caution, and self-censorship; nor did they have any idea that there was news they weren't getting at all, because some reporters had been driven out of the Lebanese capital. Censorship in Lebanon was accomplished by terror, exclusion, and expulsion—yet, remarkably, most news organizations acted as if the public had no right to know that it was going on.

There were, of course, exceptions. The PLO's abduction of Philip Caputo in 1973 was given considerable publicity by his paper, the *Chicago Tribune*.[4] Three years later *Newsweek* printed a page-long story on the violence against foreign correspondents, including two of its own reporters, in Beirut.[5] The imposition of Syrian-inspired censorship in early 1977 elicited a few critical articles in the Western press. But as the civil war dragged on and the Beirut-based correspondents got used to the situation and made their accommodations with it, less and less was mentioned about the pressure they faced. From mid-1976 until the summer of 1980, a four-year period in which a number of journalists were killed or harassed and the Lebanese press was effectively muted, almost nothing was reported by the American media about the situation in Lebanon. The murder of Robert Pfeffer, a politically motivated assassination, was barely noticed;* while the abduction and killing of Salim Lawzi, which shocked and frightened the Beirut press corps, was briefly noted in the major newspapers and ignored by almost everyone else.

News organizations whose own personnel were under attack often tried to play down the incidents. When the two BBC correspondents, Tim Llewelyn and Jim Muir, were driven out of Beirut in 1980, the BBC at first said nothing, in the apparent hope that it could negotiate their return. When that failed, it made a belated and terse announcement about the situation and continued to "report" on Lebanon from Nicosia, Cyprus. From time to time it sent in a special correspondent, but he was unfamiliar with the complexities of the Lebanon situation and obliged to keep in mind the penalty for reporting that the armed gunmen of Beirut disliked. The BBC's public, which included not only Great Britain but millions around the world who depend on the

---

The New York Times gave Pfeffer's murder ten lines on page A-9 in its "World Briefs" column on May 25, 1979. Almost all the other news organizations ignored it.

World Service for independent and comprehensive news, was effectively shut out of the Lebanese capital. What's worse, most of them had no idea that this was so.

Reuters, the world's largest news agency, was no more forthright when Berndt Debusmann was shot. It reported the incident but made no mention of the previous Syrian threats to the correspondent, and compounded omission with distortion by saying that "there was no known reason for the shooting."[6]

Most of the reporters in Beirut were afraid to write about the situation there for fear of further reprisal, and when they turned to their editors at home for help, they were, with few exceptions, met with indifference. Only a handful of newspapers addressed the issue editorially, among them the British *Economist* and the *Manchester Guardian*. The *Guardian* noted: "Although the BBC and Reuters were well aware that Syria was responsible for the intimidation of their reporters, neither organization felt able to publicise the fact."[7] The *Economist* was even more specific:

It was a week later [after their flight from Beirut] that the BBC broke the news that Mr. Llewelyn, Mr. Muir, and Mr. Stocklin had been forced to leave Beirut under threat of death. It made no reference to the Syrian connection, though it is hard to see how pressmen can be protected against attack unless their attackers are identified . . . at present there is no direct BBC reporting in either country.

"The Syrians have thus forced the representatives of the BBC and Reuters out of Lebanon by terrorism and have got away with it without even being named. Foreign and local pressmen in Beirut were all in favour of a concerted exposure of the Syrian role, but when the two leading British news organizations declined to name any names, the protest collapsed.[8]

Throughout the next two years, this pattern continued. Sean Toolan's murder was given a single 30-second mention on ABC, while the other two networks ignored it completely. *The New York Times* and *The Washington Post* reported it briefly, and among the major U.S. newspapers only the

Los Angeles Times gave the murder serious attention. Other outrages against newsmen in Beirut went wholly unreported.

The primary victim of this silence was, of course, the public, whose right to know was being subverted by a combination of Arab terror and journalistic acquiescence or indifference. But there were serious consequences for Israel as well, which was engaged in a struggle with both the PLO and Syria. If the press in Beirut was not reporting fully out of a fear of Arab reprisal, then Israel was being forced to fight the war for Western public opinion with one hand tied behind its back. People who knew little about the PLO's operations in southern Lebanon or its connections with international terrorist groups or about the internal situation in Syria often found Israel's concern about these matters "paranoid" and its attempts to deal with them overreactive. Moreover, when Israel tried to point out what was happening in Lebanon or Syria, its arguments had little credibility—after all, people reasoned, there were plenty of American and European reporters in Beirut who would surely be aware of a Palestinian "mini-state" in south Lebanon if one existed, or of large-scale massacres in Syria.

The notion that the intimidation of Western journalists in Beirut was working—to Israel's detriment—began to sink in after the murder of Salim Lawzi in early 1980. As the director of Israel's Government Press Office I was in close contact with many of the foreign correspondents in the Middle East. Some of them who visited Jerusalem told hair-raising stories about personal experiences they had had; many admitted that there were now subjects that they wouldn't report. For months I waited for the barrage of angry articles on how the press was being abused in Lebanon. Finally, in February 1982, I decided to raise the question myself.*

The immediate stimulus was an ABC documentary about the West Bank entitled "Under the Israeli Thumb," which

---

*It is especially interesting that *Time* and *Newsweek*—both of which have "Press" sections—ignored the situation in Beirut and reported nothing about the events of the summer of 1980, in which two journalists were murdered, two disappeared one was shot, and three more were forced to flee.

was shown on February 4, 1982. The program, which will
be considered in detail in the next chapter, was exceptional
in the harsh accusations it made about the occupation of the
West Bank and in its absolute indifference to Israel's point
of view. I knew that ABC had recently had difficulties with
the PLO in Beirut, and I wondered if there might be some
connection between the two. I couldn't prove it, of course,
but I wanted to give the public a chance to judge for themselves.

Having decided to go public, the next question was, where
and how. Anyone who has ever been interviewed knows the
feeling of dismay that can come from reading one's own
words in print—they frequently get mangled, even by the
best-intentioned reporters. I didn't want that to happen. The
subject—intimidation and its effect on Western news organizations—was very complex and sensitive. I wanted to be
sure that my message came through—that the reporters in
the field were mainly victims, not culprits, and that the real
villains were the armed groups in Beirut, primarily the Syrians and the PLO, who had been using force and threats
against them. I wanted to make it clear that this was not an
indictment of the press as anti-Israel or inherently unfair,
but rather an attempt to point out a specific problem that
was largely unknown in the United States and Europe. Finally, I intended to suggest that given the special problems
facing reporters in the Middle East, and especially in Lebanon, readers and viewers in the West should make allowances for possible self-censorship on certain kinds of stories.

I had been working with American and European journalists for five years, and I knew that they were hypersen-
sitive to criticism of the press in general and themselves in
particular. Not every correspondent would want to be involved in such a potentially unpopular interview. There was
also the question of getting the interview published. Many
news organizations are strangely reluctant to print criticism
of themselves. I remembered A. J. Liebling's adage: "Newspapers write about other newspapers with circumspection.
The two surviving press associations [AP and UPI], whose
customers are newspapers, write about newspapers with

deference. Newspapers write about themselves with awe, and only after mature reflection."[9] I decided to call David Shipler of *The New York Times*.

Shipler is a man in his early forties, a former officer in the U.S. Navy who has spent most of the past decade working for the *Times* overseas, first in Vietnam, later in Moscow, and from 1979 to 1984, as bureau chief in Jerusalem. He has an unkempt brown beard, soft brown eyes, and slightly rounded shoulders—he looks, in fact, like a Protestant rabbinical student. Shipler, who has broken new ground in his reporting on Israel's administration of the West Bank and the relations between Jews and Arabs there, is widely admired for his ability to understand and convey the feelings of all the sides in the complex Arab-Israeli equation. More important for me, I knew him to be meticulously accurate and totally fearless.

If Shipler was the right man for such an interview, the *Times* was, I thought, the right place. Despite its many failings, some of which come in for lavish examination in this book, the *Times* is, I think, the greatest newspaper in the world, the standard by which others measure themselves. I was confident that, more than any other newspaper, the *Times* would be willing to print the kind of charges I intended to make.

When I called Shipler he was interested, and he suggested we meet in his office in downtown Jerusalem. I outlined what I wanted to say. Shipler had two questions—first: could I base my thesis on concrete examples? The answer to that was yes. Second: was I prepared to go completely on the record, not to use the "Israeli official" dodge, but my own name? Yes again. Shipler nodded and reached for his notebook.

The interview lasted about an hour and was reprinted two days later in the *International Herald Tribune*. The *Tribune* is published as a cooperative venture of *The New York Times* and *The Washington Post,* and most of their foreign stories are sent, by prior arrangement, to the Paris-based paper. The *Tribune* is distributed widely in Israel, and it was there, on February 10, that I first read my interview, under

the headline ISRAELI ACCUSES MEDIA OF BOWING TO TERROR.
I was relieved to see that Shipler had done his usual accurate job. He began by setting forth my central contention—
that terrorism was being used against correspondents in
Beirut—along with my qualification: "I don't think it is always, or even usually, the newsmen on the spot who are
necessarily intimidated, although they have every right to be
afraid as well. But very often organizations acting in the interests of their personnel, which is legitimate, make decisions not to publish a certain thing because it would get
somebody in trouble or get somebody shot at. . . ."[10] This
was, if anything, understating the case. My caution was dictated both by a desire to avoid some Agnewesque-sounding
attack on journalists and also by the more practical consideration that I might have to work with some of these guys
in the future.

The interview then went on to my suspicion that ABC
had been trying to ingratiate itself with the PLO by doing
puff pieces on the organization. I also mentioned, as further examples of Beirut's dangerous ambience, the shooting
of Berndt Debusmann of Reuters and the warning to BBC
reporter Tim Llewelyn, and noted that the BBC had tried
to cover up the latter incident and that it still had no regular correspondent in the Lebanese capital.

Did I have any other examples of unpublished harassment of journalists? I hesitated, and I imagined Shipler knew
why. Both of us, indeed the entire foreign press community
in the Middle East, had heard the story of the five American reporters who were detained and threatened by the PLO
in May of the previous year. The problem was, two of them
were from the *Times*. Oh, what the hell, I thought. It's fit to
print. In the *Herald Tribune* it came out this way:

"Mr. Chafets, who is American born and has close
friendships with many foreign correspondents in Jerusalem, made explicit criticisms of *The New York Times*, *The
Washington Post*, The British Broadcasting Corp., and
ABC-TV. . . .

"Last summer, several American reporters in Beirut, including those from *The New York Times* and *The Washington*

Post, were seized by a left-wing faction of the PLO, 'held for a number of hours and threatened and frightened, and this didn't get any coverage," complained Chafets."[11] Did I care to name the reporters involved? No, although I knew who they were. I thought the publication of their names might get them in trouble in Beirut. Moreover, I knew several of them well and had no desire to embarrass them. After all, my real quarrel was with the terrorists and, secondarily, editors abroad who hadn't spoken out against them. Shipler didn't press the point. He didn't need the names to confirm the accuracy of my charges, because he knew the story, and the identities of most of the journalists involved, independently. He closed his notebook.

When the interview appeared in the *Tribune* I called New York to see if it was in the *Times* as well. It wasn't. I checked the next day, February 11, and again on the twelfth. Still no interview. I called Shipler. "Don't worry," he said. "They probably have a space problem." On the thirteenth, it still hadn't appeared. I called Shipler again. "They're afraid to print it," I said. "Look," Shipler replied. "I've been with the paper for a long time. They just don't do things like that."

On February 14 I called New York again. "Good news," I was told. "They published your interview today." I was relieved, both because what I had to say was now being read by hundreds of thousands of influential Americans and, strangely, for the *Times* as well. Five years in my job had made me cynical about the press, but I wanted to believe in the basic honesty of *The New York Times.* "What a newspaper," I said to my friend in New York. "How many other papers in America would be prepared to print charges that they themselves were guilty of a cover-up?"

"What are you talking about?" he asked.

"You know, the stuff about the correspondents who were picked up and threatened by the PLO."

"There's nothing in here about that," he said.

"Of course there is, read it again."

He read the entire article out loud. Everything else was there, the stories about the BBC and ABC, the complaints about Syrian and PLO intimidation. All that was missing were the two paragraphs about *The New York Times* correspondents and the paper's decision to keep their detention a secret.

I was furious. How could the *Times, The New York Times,* have committed such a sordid little offense against its own standards of fairness? I was so angry that I almost didn't realize that the *Times* had provided the greatest possible confirmation of my original charge—that news organizations in the U.S. and elsewhere, even the best of them, were committing acts of self-censorship to protect their own interests.

I called William Claiborne of *The Washington Post* and asked him to stop by my office. When he got there I showed him the two interviews, the first in the *Herald Tribune,* the second from the *Times* as I had copied it over the phone. They spoke for themselves, of course, and Claiborne was, to put it mildly, interested. The *Post,* which has a permanent (and well-founded) inferiority complex, had recently taken a drubbing over its phony Janet Cooke Pulitzer Prize story. Claiborne said he would check with his foreign editor, Jim Hoagland, and get back to me. When he did, he sounded disappointed. The *Post,* it seemed, wasn't interested.

"Newspapers write about each other with circumspection," Liebling had said. Norman Kempster of the *Los Angeles Times* thought it was a good story, but his foreign editor apparently didn't, and the *LA Times* declined to run it. I then called Tim McNulty of the *Chicago Tribune,* who had arrived from China that week to take up his post as Jerusalem correspondent. By that time I was pretty agitated, and McNulty, who didn't know me well, probably thought I was crazy. Still, he could recognize a good story when he saw one. Three days later, the *Chicago Tribune* was one of the first American newspapers to report on the *Times*'s censorship of my charge that it had committed, well, self-censorship.

The Israeli media seized on the story. *The Jerusalem Post* carried a front-page article, several Hebrew papers gave it headline treatment, and the national radio led its morning news bulletins with the incident. Now, I thought, the word is out. I was certain that the wire services, AP and UPI, would pick it up and send it out to their thousands of clients. They are intensely competitive and have insatiable news appetites; I would have bet anything that they would pounce on the story of official Israeli allegations of terrorist intimidation of journalists and self-censorship.

I'm glad I didn't bet. "The two remaining press associations, whose clients are newspapers, write about newspapers with deference." I had forgotten my Liebling. Neither wire service would touch it. Day after day the Israeli papers were full of the story—*The Jerusalem Post* ran an editorial about it, and the prestigious Hebrew daily *Ha'aretz* did a two-part series—while AP and UPI continued to maintain that it wasn't news. In fact, the two wire services first mentioned the entire affair *ten days later,* after both *Time* and *Newsweek* had devoted full pages to it in their media sections—surely one of the rare times that the wire services were scooped by weekly magazines.

During this long period of silence the wire services weren't inactive, however. The AP in Israel found the time for truly important news—on February 17 it sent out a story on Israeli broadcaster Abbie Nathan's decision to take his "Peace Ship" to Ireland; on the nineteenth, it ran a story about a Galilee kibbutz for the mentally ill; and on the twenty-second, it carried the news that a woman named Leah Supporta was involved in some interesting litigation over the adoption of a baby. When I wondered out loud about the AP's news criteria, I was told by one of its staffers in Israel that "we've got to be careful; we've got people in Beirut, too." UPI sent a reporter to talk to me, but never ran the story, although it too had plenty of space for trivia that week.

I was furious about the attempted blackout, and I began to telephone editors in the United States. "What do you think about this self-censorship story from Jerusalem?" I asked.

"What story?"

I then proceeded to give them the details.

"Is this public?" they asked.

"Public? It's all over the local press."

"Then why haven't we seen anything here on the wires?"

Pause.

The *Times* began to receive inquiries from around the

country. On February 18, four days after the sanitized interview had appeared, it published a follow-up entitled OFFICIAL IN ISRAEL ASSAILS THE TIMES. It said in part:

"Zev Chafets, the director of Israel's Government Press Office, has criticized the New York Times for deleting from an interview published with him on Sunday his criticisms of the paper for not reporting the detention last summer of two of its correspondents by a Palestinian faction in Lebanon . . .

"The interview containing his criticisms of the paper was published on February 10 in the *International Herald Tribune*. The references to the *Times*, however, were not included in the article as published in the *Times*."

The article went on to say that I had photocopied the two articles and was showing them to correspondents in Jerusalem, (which was true—they didn't know about the calls to the editors, I guess). The *Times* also quoted my indignant (and somewhat overwrought) statement that "from a journalistic standpoint this is one of the strangest and most incomprehensible things in recent years."

Well, I thought, this is more like it. It takes a big paper to apologize and set the record straight. And then I read:

"THE POLICY OF THE TIMES: Craig H. Whitney, deputy foreign editor of the New York Times, said . . . 'It is the policy of the Times to report difficulties encountered by its correspondents in the course of reporting only if the difficulties themselves become news and we did not consider this such a case, then or now.' "[12]

This was apparently a new policy. I recalled a recent piece in *The New York Times*[13] by Youssof M. Ibrahim entitled AT JORDAN BRIDGE, A TOUGH CHECK ON ARABS, in which Ibrahim, an Egyptian who then worked for the *Times*, described his crossing from Jordan into Israel by way of the Allenby Bridge. He had arrived at the bridge unannounced with tapes of conversations with leaders of the PLO and correspondence between various PLO officials, and these aroused the interest of Israeli security officials. Ibrahim was questioned for about five hours and then allowed to drive to Jerusalem. Some of his notebooks were examined and returned a day later. In the shuffle, a pair of pants got lost. I remembered meeting with Ibrahim the day after he arrived in Jerusalem. I had tried to explain that the unannounced appearance of a young man at the Jordanian border with PLO documents and a *Times* press card had created suspicion at the sensitive crossing point between two countries in a state of war. Ibrahim was understandably agitated, especially about the five-hour delay, and proved it by writing a tough piece on the incident. But he had never been locked up in a cell or threatened by gunmen, nor was he held overnight. I wondered why his experience was more newsworthy than that of his colleagues in Beirut.

And then there was the story written by Martin Tolchin, a *Times* correspondent, about his vacation in the Middle East. On Sunday, February 3, 1980, the *Times* headlined its travel section with A HARD CROSSING FROM JORDAN TO ISRAEL, in which Tolchin told of his experience trying to get permission to cross into Israel via the Allenby Bridge. He described his feeling that he and his family had been treated rudely and hassled unnecessarily because they are Jewish and that this treatment at the hands of the Jordanian bureaucracy was a matter of policy. Certainly Tolchin's experience was unpleasant and aggravating, but it was a far cry from twenty hours in a PLO slammer. If the *Times* had a policy about not printing stories about difficulties encountered by its journalists, "unless the difficulties themselves became news," it was a rather selective one.*

On February 22, twelve days after the interview had first run in the *Herald Tribune,* the *Times* made an effort to rectify things. It ran a piece entitled REPORTER'S NOTEBOOK—FEAR IS PART OF THE JOB IN BEIRUT, in which John Kifner, the *Times*'s Beirut correspondent, described the conditions under which he and his colleagues were forced to work and

---

*The *Times* also printed stories on the difficulties of journalists in other countries. In 1981 alone, it carried seven articles on the working conditions of journalists in China, several reports on Egyptian press restrictions, and a story on the expulsion of CBS-TV correspondent George Natanson from Guatemala. It gave prominent treatment to the limitations of press freedom for foreign correspondents in Poland, reported on the expulsion of seven Belgian journalists from Zaire, and even carried the news that press censorship had been imposed in Sri Lanka.[14]

the possible implications for the reader who expected full and comprehensive information. In Beirut, Kifner admitted, "a journalist must often weigh when, how and even whether to record a story." The piece was somewhat bland and defensive in tone, but it confirmed the existence of serious harassment of journalists in Beirut. It was the first such article that Kifner had ever done and one of the few ever written by any resident correspondent from Beirut about the dangers and pressures they were subjected to in the Lebanese capital.

Although Kifner didn't say so in his article, he was very nervous about having had to write it. He made an unusual request—that the *Times* run the article in New York but keep it out of the *International Herald Tribune,* the reverse of what the paper had attempted to do with my interview with Shipler. The *Times*—once again bowing to the fear of Arab violence against its reporter—agreed.

But the comedy of errors was not yet over. Through a mistake, the *Tribune* published Kifner's article. At this point, according to Craig Whitney, the Beirut-based correspondent, decided "it would be a good time to go and update his reporting elsewhere in the Middle East for a few days." Of course the *Times* never mentioned this in print.[15]

Kifner's hurried departure from Beirut might have gone unnoticed but for an article on Arab terror against journalists published by the London *Observer*'s Service.[16] It stated that Kifner had left Lebanon because of threats he had received after his story had been published in the *Tribune.* The *Observer* article was written by its Beirut correspondent, Colin Smith, who did not ask to be anonymous. However, the *Observer,* in an effort to protect him, left his name off the story and by-lined it only "A Special Correspondent," a designation that greatly concerned Smith's local stringer in Beirut, who feared that he, and not Smith, might be held accountable by local gunmen.

If *The New York Times* at least tried to deal with the story, other American news organizations were less forthcoming. *Newsweek,* for example, published WHO'S AFRAID OF THE PLO?[17] written in part by Julian Nundy, the Beirut *Newsweek* correspondent who had been one of the five detainees. The article didn't explain why Nundy had failed at the time to report on his detention, and sought to minimize the whole event by noting that the correspondents had been held and then released "with profuse apologies" by the Palestinians. Missing from the *Newsweek* account (but included in *Time's* article on the incident that same week) was the fact that the reporters had been abducted at gunpoint, and that at least two of them had felt that their lives were in danger.

On February 23, the charges of press intimidation in Lebanon and the effort of much of the American press to hush them up led to a discussion of the issue in the Israeli Knesset. Even the wire services couldn't ignore this, and they sent out brief reports on the parliamentary debate. Other major papers—the *Miami Herald, Los Angeles Times, Chicago Sun-Times,* and a few more—also carried accounts of the Knesset proceedings and mentioned, for the first time, the controversy that had been so widely reported in Israel during the previous two weeks.

Throughout the controversy, only one of the American news organizations whose reporter had been involved in the PLO abduction managed to keep the whole matter blacked out of its news pages—*The Washington Post.* From February 10 until early March, for almost a month, the *Post's* editors apparently thought that the paper's readers would be best served by being kept unaware of what the readers of *The New York Times, Los Angeles Times, Chicago Tribune, Miami Herald, Time,* and *Newsweek* already knew—that a debate was going on in Israel over charges of journalistic self-censorship and that one of the *Post's* own correspondents had been accused of practicing it. The *Post* ignored the entire matter until the liberal weekly *New Republic* wrote about its stonewalling in A JOURNALISTIC COVER-UP. The article, written by the magazine's editor, Martin Peretz, noted that *"The Washington Post* hasn't given the story an inch," and revealed, for the first time, the names of the as yet unnamed abducted reporters.[18]

The *Post's* vehicle for addressing the controversy was an op-ed article by Jim Hoagland, the paper's assistant managing editor for foreign news, who, presumably, was the man who had decided to maintain the *Post*'s blackout of the story for almost a month. Hoagland was thus a well-informed, if somewhat subjective, commentator on the issue.[19]

Writing on March 4, Hoagland conceded that "there is something in what Chafets said," at least in regard to the Syrians. As to the PLO, however, he described it as a benevolent force, which "tacitly provides protection for the American embassy and [has] as often pulled correspondents out of scrapes as imperiled them." To buttress his point, Hoagland quoted *Post* correspondent Edward Cody on the exquisite symmetry of the threat to journalists. "You know that you can get picked up by Palestinian kids with guns anytime you do your job. Or you know you may be bombed by Israeli jets. That does not mean you write any differently." Probably even Cody didn't intend to say that Israel was carrying out air raids on journalists in order to intimidate them. Yet Hoagland was trying to make it seem as if Israeli jets posed the same threat to press freedom as the "Palestinian kids" who had murdered Robert Pfeffer, threatened Geraldo Rivera and Hans Bendict, and driven Kubic and Marmon out at gunpoint.

Regarding the failure of Jonathan Randal to report on his detention by the PLO, Hoagland admitted that, "in retrospect Randal was probably a bit too phlegmatic in dismissing so lightly his arrest by Palestinians on a day when Israel had bombed into Lebanon and the Palestinians were on full alert because of rumors of an Israeli invasion." He then presented a long anecdotal defense of the *Post* correspondent's physical courage, which is undoubted, but wholly beside the point.

There was a lot wrong with Hoagland's article: the fact that it had taken him almost a month to write it; his effort to trivialize the problem of intimidation in Beirut; and his transparent attempt to "balance" threats by PLO terrorists against journalists with Israeli air attacks on PLO targets. Worst by far, however, was Hoagland's version of how the entire incident of the five reporters' abduction had first come to light. He wrote: "Chafets also cited an incident that occurred last May, when a *Washington Post* correspondent, two *Times* reporters, a *Newsweek* correspondent and an Associated Press photographer were stopped at a Palestinian roadblock outside of Beirut, detained for questioning for about 20 hours, and then released. *Chafets said that one of the reporters, William Farrell, formerly Jerusalem correspondent for the Times and now based in Cairo, had subsequently told him the five were 'held for a number of hours and threatened and frightened.'* " (emphasis added)

What was he talking about? I had never mentioned Farrell's name at all, never mentioned any names, in fact, and certainly hadn't said what my source for the story was. I couldn't believe that Hoagland could have made such a sloppy mistake. He had publicly named Bill Farrell, who was still stationed in the Middle East, as a source of information for an Israeli official, a charge that could get the *New York Times* reporter into serious trouble in the Arab world. I imagined that the *Post* editor had simply assumed that Farrell was my source, without checking. Damnit, I thought, the man had an entire month to ask me. Later, I was astonished to find that not only had Hoagland never contacted me, he never bothered to contact Farrell, either.

Farrell, I subsequently learned, was badly frightened by Hoagland's article, and I was, as I said, very upset. I immediately sent a letter to the *Post* to set the record straight. It took the paper *six weeks* to publish that letter, which appeared on April 17 and said in part:

"Mr. Hoagland states in his article that I have named William Farrell of *The New York Times* as the source of this story. This is a figment of Mr. Hoagland's imagination. At no time have I ever publicly named the source of my information. . . ."

The letter continued: "I challenge Mr. Hoagland to produce any public statement saying, as he claims I have said, that Mr. Farrell told me of this incident. When he cannot, he will owe Mr. Farrell an apology and one to me as well."

The *Post* hadn't wanted to print this letter; it took a month and a half and three transoceanic telephone calls to get them to do it. When they finally did, they appended an editor's note, which said:

"Mr. Hoagland replies: 'In July 1981, Mr. Chafets told William Claiborne, *The Washington Post*'s Jerusalem correspondent, that Mr. Farrell had recounted the Damur incident to him that month, and Mr. Chafets confirmed that fact *in an on the record interview* [emphasis added] with Mr. Claiborne on Feb. 15, 1982.' "[20]

I couldn't believe my eyes. This was a plain lie. There had never been any interview by Claiborne in which I mentioned my source. In fact there had been no interview at all, just a private conversation in which I had tried to interest the *Post* in the self-censorship issue. Farrell's name hadn't figured in that at all.

I asked Claiborne to come see me and showed him Hoagland's reply. We had known each other for almost four years, and nothing like this had ever happened before. We had a short conversation:

"Did you and I have an on the record interview on February 15?"

"No."

"Did I ever name Farrell as my source for the story on or off the record?"

"No."

"What's this all about?"

"I don't really know," Clairborne answered, and blushed.

On April 28, *The Washington Post* published the following:

"CORRECTION: On April 17, the *Post* published a letter from Zev Chafets denying that he had publicly said that William Farrell of *The New York Times* had told him of the detention of five Western reporters in Beirut in 1981 by Palestinian guerrillas. Through an error it was stated in a response that my conversation with Mr. Chafets on this point on February 15 was on the record. Mr. Chafets did not address that point on the record during the February 15 conversation, and continues to refuse to say for the record if he has discussed the incident with Mr. Farrell."

It was signed William Claiborne, Washington Post Foreign Service, Jerusalem.[21]

The *Post*'s behavior in this matter sheds some light, I think, on the paper's recurrent troubles with false stories—from Janet Cooke's invented Pulitzer exposé, to the bogus tale of Reagan administration wire tapping of the Blair House during a visit by President Carter. The formula is one part carelessness, one part arrogance, with a big touch of bias thrown in. In this case it was perhaps compounded by the fact that the good name of the PLO, whose cause the *Post*, under Hoagland's guidance, has adopted with the fervor of a fresh air camp fund, was called into question.

And what of the real issue—that of self-censorship? Was *Post*man Jonathan Randal practicing it when he decided not to file a report on his experience at the hands of the PLO gunmen, and was the *Post* following its normal policy when it accepted Randal's decision? To answer these questions it is only necessary to see how the *Post,* and Randal, have dealt with similar issues in the past when the perpetrator was not the PLO.*

A cursory look through the *Post*'s back issues reveals that it often publicizes the difficulties its reporters encounter in the line of duty; and very often these difficulties are considerably less serious than abduction at gunpoint by a group that *The Washington Post* had been touting as moderate and responsible. There was, for example, ROMANIAN AGENTS BLUNDER AFTER VISITING NEWSMAN,[22] by correspondent Mi-

---

*There was an interesting postscript to the cover-up of the May 1981 abduction story. A little more than a year later, during the war in Lebanon, five American reporters—David Ottoway of *The Washington Post*, Tim McNulty of the *Chicago Tribune*, Dan Williams, then with the *Miami Herald*, David Lamb of the *Los Angeles Times*, and the luckless Bill Farrell—were stopped at an impromptu checkpoint in West Beirut. The five were hauled out of their taxi by Palestinian gunmen and taken to an abandoned office building where they were detained and questioned. Later they were transferred to a deserted apartment house near PLO headquarters and held for several hours until a representative of al-Fatah arrived and ordered their release.

Although they had been detained for only a few hours, and their lives had not been directly threatened, the five decided that the incident was newsworthy. "It told a great deal about the working conditions and general atmosphere in Beirut," one of them later told me. "And besides, while we were discussing it somebody said, 'Hell, if we *don't* write it, Chafets will find out and raise hell.' "

chael Dobbs, a seventeen-paragraph article on Dobbs's
problems, which in fact amounted to no more than being
followed throughout his visit to Romania; or INTERROGA-
TION—POST REPORTER RUNS AFOUL OF BOLIVIAN ARMY,[23] by
Charles A. Krause of the Washington Post Foreign Service,
twenty-four paragraphs devoted to Krause's arrest and interrogation by "five army intelligence agents, one of them
armed with a submachine gun." The whole episode lasted,
according to Krause, nearly three hours, and he was never
threatened physically. Other stories in recent years included
a report of September 10, 1980, that Indonesian authorities
had refused to renew the visa of *Post* stringer Paul Zach; a
long article on February 7, 1981, on reporters' working conditions in Poland, written by Michael Dobbs; and a report,
on February 12, 1981, stating that *Post* correspondent in
Moscow, Kevin Klose, had been called in by Soviet authorities for a fifteen-minute meeting in which he was "rebuked"
for some allegedly "slanderous assertions" about the USSR.

Nor did the *Post* restrict itself to reporting the difficulties of its own correspondents abroad. On October 4, 1980,
it carried news of the expulsion of left-wing journalist Simon Malley from France; on October 16, the expulsion of
Reuters's Jeremy Clift from Basra, Iraq, and on August 21,
1981, the expulsion of *Mother Jones* magazine correspondent
Lawrence T. Johnson from Colombia for a visa violation.
Later that year, the *Post* also ran stories about problems encountered by UPI's South African bureau chief Nat Gib-
son,[24] the banning of AP reporter Tina Chou by Taiwan,[25]
and the expulsion of AP reporter Cynthia Stevens from South
Africa.[26] The list goes on and on: AMERICAN CORRESPONDENT
LEAVES AFGHANISTAN,[27] BRITISH JOURNALIST WOUNDED IN AN-
GOLA,[28] BOLIVIA TO PUT REPORTER ON TRIAL,[29] and so forth.
I do not mean to imply that these stories should not have
been printed. On the contrary, an important duty of the press
is to monitor and publicize infractions of its freedom, and
to appraise readers of the conditions under which their news
is being gathered. This deluge of "press hassled abroad"
stories does, however, raise the question of why the PLO
should be exempted from the list of noteworthy hasslers.

Part of Hoagland's explanation was that Jonathan Randal, a seasoned reporter, was simply "too phlegmatic" to have taken the twenty-hour detention seriously. But Randal has not always been so phlegmatic when he has come under attack in Beirut, and on at least one occasion his phlegmaticism turned into verbosity. That was in 1975, in a stirring first-person account entitled MORNING IN REBEL HANDS, in which Randal recounted how, just after dawn, armed men had burst into his room, arrested him, and taken him and some of his belongings, including a typewriter, into headquarters.[30] The detention that time lasted not twenty hours, but only a couple. Randal was not locked up, merely questioned and then taken to the home of his old friend, the Algerian ambassador. It was a gripping article in which the reader learns that Randal has worked in Vietnam, that Randal has worked in Algeria, that Randal speaks French, that Randal is extremely cool in tight situations (we have his word for it), and that Randal sleeps in boxer shorts and a black T-shirt. The article was published, presumably, to convey a sense of the situation in Beirut. It is hard to see why what happened to the *Post* correspondent in May 1981 at the hands of the PLO should be less revealing of the prevailing Beirut climate or any less informative to the *Post*'s readers. But that, perhaps, was the point. In October 1975, Randal's abductors were "members of two Lebanese Communist outfits" and not members of the PLO. Randal is not considered a supporter of the Lebanese Communist Party.

Probably none of the incidents mentioned here is of earth-shattering importance. Taken together, though, they add up to a depressing chapter in Western journalism—the willingness of important news organizations to bow to Arab terror and to play an active part in hiding it from the public. At one time or another Reuters, *Time, Newsweek, The New York Times, The Washington Post,* CBS, ABC, the Associated Press—to name only some—were subjected to intimidation and violence by the Syrians or the PLO. Many of these organizations made changes of personnel as a result of intimidation, and others made accommodations about which we can only speculate.

Nor do these organizations have the right to protest against such speculation. The essence of journalistic credibility is candor, both in what is reported and about what restrictions and constraints limit or influence that reporting. News organizations that tell less than the full story become suspect. It is never quite possible to know what is being withheld and who is being protected.

5

ABC UNDER
THE THUMB

On February 4, 1982, Hugh Downs, former quiz-show host turned moral philosopher, capped an ABC *20/20* segment with this observation: "You know, military occupation by its nature tends to be oppressive, even though it starts out as temporary. I think it raises the question again of whether if freedom and dignity are denied anywhere, they're not likely to be undermined everywhere."[1] With that oblique warning about the universal danger posed by Israeli oppression, ABC ended one of the most extraordinary documentaries ever shown on American television, an examination of the lives of Palestinians "Under the Israeli Thumb" on the West Bank. The documentary and the events and decisions that led up to it form a special chapter in the history of American television coverage of the Middle East; as such, they deserve a close look.

The seed of "Under the Thumb" was planted on April 2, 1981, almost a year earlier, when ABC aired its "Unholy War" documentary on Palestinian terrorism. That program, which was a stark exposé of the PLO and its connections with other world terrorist organizations, brought forth howls of protest from PLO supporters in the United States. ABC, like the other American networks, is used to such reactions, which occur whenever a controversial program is shown; indeed, previous, critical documentaries on Israel had triggered similar outpourings from Israeli supporters in the U.S. Such viewer response, whether spontaneous or organized, is accepted as a legitimate part of the game and is not usually taken too seriously by network executives. But this time the offended party was the PLO and it had additional means of making its displeasure known. The American Broadcasting Company, in April 1981, was about to find that out.

Barbara Newman, who produced "The Unholy War," was a journalist at National Public Radio when, in 1976, she published an article in *Rolling Stone* about the Israeli nuclear program. Newman charged Israel with having diverted uranium from an American concern in order to further its production of nuclear weapons. Her accusation, which was hotly denied and bitterly denounced by Israel, won Newman national attention, an appearance on some network talk shows, and a job as a producer for ABC's *20/20* news magazine.

In late 1980, when she and Geraldo Rivera first considered doing a Middle East documentary, Newman, who had never been to Israel, had wanted to do a show on the Mossad, Israel's intelligence agency. She took her request to the Israeli Consulate in New York, which informed her that the Mossad does not cooperate in journalistic projects and would not be open to her inspection. Undeterred, she visited Israel in December 1980 to look around for herself. Newman soon realized that the Mossad story would be impossible—no visuals, for one thing—but another subject began to interest her, PLO terror and its links to the USSR and European terror organizations. She received permission to meet with convicted terrorists in Israeli prisons. She now recalls:

"What convinced me about the Palestinian angle was meeting the prisoners themselves and talking to them. They told me that they were glad they had killed Israelis, that it was their country and they'd do it again. They were absolutely unrepentant. I realized that there was a very savage hatred, a savage animosity. That's how the whole thing started."[2]

The program, when it was aired the following April, reflected that savage hatred and the complex ways in which the PLO operated to give it expression. Although it was a well-researched and technically polished look at one aspect of the Israeli-Arab conflict, many of Newman's colleagues at ABC hated it. She came under attack at the network and the rumor spread that she was an Israeli agent—a rumor that she believes may, in part, have cost the producer her job.

"You see, in my piece we didn't go into the West Bank issue, we were dealing with the issue of terrorism," says Newman, who is herself a critic of the Israeli occupation. "The criticism of my piece was that it didn't talk about Israeli acts of terrorism during the 1948 War of Independence, but it didn't talk about the Arab terrorism in that war, either. We were dealing with current events."[3]

The storm of criticism in the United States was more than matched by the reaction in Lebanon. Geraldo Rivera, the correspondent on "The Unholy War," recalls: "I know that there was a high degree of displeasure with the story in Beirut. The PLO hierarchy had seen a cassette of it and some of the more radical elements, like the PFLP-GC, were extremely angry. I got definite feedback about that. I was told never to come back to the Commodore, to West Beirut."[4]

Newman, too, was warned not to return to Lebanon. While on assignment to the Sudan, she met an ABC camera crew from Beirut. "They told me never to go back there, that it was dangerous," she says. "One guy said he and his wife had had to stay inside their house for ten days after 'The Unholy War' aired. They were afraid they'd get killed because of the anger in Beirut over our piece. He told me, 'You can't imagine what it was like.' "[5]

When Newman and Rivera had first come to Beirut to work on "The Unholy War," they were taken to meet the PLO spokesman Mahmud Labadi by ABC bureau chief Jerry King. Geraldo Rivera, recalling that meeting, says, "My only regret is about the ABC reporter who attended, Jerry King.

At one time in the meeting he was put on the spot by Labadi, he was asked point-blank—'Do you back this man?' and
Labadi made a big flourishing point at me. King said, 'Yes,
I believe he is sincere and fair.' And of course King never
went back to Beirut after that. He was called out immediately after to go to Poland, and once the piece aired, he considered himself persona non grata. At least that was the
feeling around here, that Jerry wasn't going back to Beirut
because of that incident and the risk to himself . . ."

King himself denies that his transfer was anything more
than a routine change of posts after five and a half years in
Beirut. The timing, according to him, was coincidental.[6] This
is a matter of some controversy, however. On March 6, 1982,
TV Guide's John Weisman noted, "It is rumored, but not
confirmed, that ABC's Jerry King left Beirut for the same
reason [threats on his life]."[7] The *New Republic* looked into
the rumors and later reported that "it turns out—at least according to ABC staffers in New York and Washington—that
not only were there threats made against ABC personnel in
the Middle East [by the PLO], but that its Beirut correspondent Jerry King was shifted to Warsaw because of those
threats."*[8]

Shortly after King left Beirut, ABC's Beirut radio correspondent, Sean Toolan, was murdered. His murderers were
never caught, and the case was never solved. To this day no
one knows who killed the ABC reporter or why. But at the
time of his death, speculation was rife that it had been in
reprisal for "The Unholy War." Reports by the AP and the
Los Angeles Times at the time made it clear they did not consider Toolan's murder an isolated incident but rather one in
the string of violent acts against foreign correspondents in
the Lebanese capital.[9] The Canadian weekly *MacLeans*, for
which Toolan also worked, included his name in a list of reporters who had been murdered for political reasons.[10] And
one of Toolan's best friends, NBC's Beirut correspondent

---

*During the 1982 war in Lebanon, King, who was stationed in Poland at the
time, was brought into Syria to help with coverage from there. But despite his five
and a half years in Lebanon, he did not go back to Beirut. This, of course, lends
weight to the speculation that he could not go back because the city was still under
PLO control.

Vic Aiken, told a visiting American colleague that Toolan had felt threatened because of "The Unholy War," over which, according to Aiken, the PLO had gone "berserk."[11]

At ABC in New York, there was also speculation about Toolan's murder. Some of the network's Beirut personnel blamed the documentary and said so to their superiors. "Everyone was talking about it, and certainly there were people who had that immediate reaction," says Geraldo Rivera, of the feeling at ABC headquarters. "I have no evidence that Toolan was murdered because of displeasure with ABC over 'The Unholy War,' " Rivera says, but he concedes that "the fact that he was murdered and the timing of the murder indicate that there was at least some connection. . . . He had been there prior to that and had never had any trouble."[12]

For the record, ABC believes, as anchorman Peter Jennings put it, that "Mr. Toolan sadly was killed, largely, we believe, as the result of a personal grudge."*[13]

On July 26, 1981, less than two weeks after Sean Toolan was buried, ABC invited PLO chairman Yasser Arafat to appear on *Issues and Answers*. The two ABC interviewers, Chris Harper and John McKenzie, treated the PLO leader with such deference that the show's producer, Peggy Whedon, actually apologized for their performance. In a letter to an irate viewer, Whedon said that the regularly scheduled correspondents had been unable to get to Beirut in time for the program, which she conceded had been a disaster. She blamed the whole thing on the incompetence of Harper and McKenzie: "I have produced several significant inter-

---

*Many of Toolan's colleagues at the Commodore are "certain" that he was murdered for personal reasons. It is curious, though, that every one of them has a different inside story on the motive behind the murder. I have been told that he was murdered by a foreign diplomat who was then recalled, a PLO officer bent on jealous revenge, a Lebanese husband, the son of a jilted Lebanese woman, and paid assassins for the sum of $125, for unspecified reasons.

It is hard to escape the conclusion that the Beirut press corps preferred to believe that Toolan was murdered for personal reasons that were, presumably, not applicable to them, and not for professional ones. Less understandable is why experienced reporters should be so certain (and so adamant) about the motive behind a totally unsolved murder. Precedent, after all, is on the side of the "PLO theory." No other journalists in Beirut had been murdered in recent years for personal reasons, but several had been killed for unpopular reporting.

views with Arafat in the past where our correspondents have pinned him down. And I hope to be able to do so again in the future. This one was just bad luck all around. I hope our audience, like you, could see through the man's un-challenged answers. . . ."[14]

Whedon's explanation—that the correspondents had been unable to cope with Arafat—was rather strange. Harper, ABC's Cairo bureau chief, was an experienced Middle East hand and former Beirut correspondent for *Newsweek*, and he had dealt with Arafat and the PLO before. McKenzie was temporarily stationed in Beirut. Their failure to challenge Arafat's transparently false answers could not possibly have been due to inexperience. Furthermore, the suspicion that ABC was now playing softball with the PLO deepened when, in early September, *ABC World News Tonight* did a two-part mini-series on the organization, which Peter Jennings him-self called "unusual."[15]

The series was reported by Mike Lee, who had come to Beirut especially to do it. Lee portrayed the PLO as a be-nevolent group dedicated to peaceful struggle and welfare programs and pointed out, "Yasser Arafat's military and political machine ironically has the same basic components as the Israeli government—a parliament, a cabinet, an army, police, and social services."[16] To reinforce this irony, Lee failed to note that the "parliament" was unelected, the "cab-inet" was guided by a constitution that calls for Israel's de-struction, and the "police" operated in violation of Lebanese sovereignty. Lee also mentioned the PLO's Red Crescent, which he called "the equivalent of the American Red Cross," without mentioning that it is a highly politicized organiza-tion run by Yasser Arafat's brother, and told how "thou-sands of Lebanese civilians" were treated in PLO hospitals. This was his only mention of Lebanese-PLO relations (less than a year later, when Israel drove the PLO out of Beirut and south Lebanon, it became evident that the Lebanese in fact despised the PLO for trampling on their sovereignty and oppressing whole areas of the country).

On the first day of the two-part series, correspondent Lee asserted that "terrorism as Palestinian policy has been re-

placed by mainstream, high-powered politics." At the time
of this astonishing assertion (and to this day), terrorism was
precisely PLO policy, enshrined in its Covenant, ratified at its
biannual National Councils, and proclaimed by its leaders.
Moreover, it was also PLO practice. In the six weeks preceding Lee's report, Palestinian terrorists carried out eight terrorist attacks in Israel, including an assault on a civilian bus
in which a pregnant woman, a twelve-year-old boy, and a
seventeen-year-old girl were wounded. On September 12,
four days after Lee's report that the PLO had abandoned
terrorism, two Italian pilgrims were killed and twenty-seven
civilians (including twenty-two pilgrims) injured, in a terrorist attack in Jerusalem.

ABC's correspondent Lee had an interesting way of re-
solving this contradiction: "Even today," he said, "PLO leader
Yasser Arafat, a *moderate who denounces most operations outside
Israel, is still labeled by many as a terrorist.*" (emphasis added)
This cleared everything up. Obviously, Lee didn't consider
attacks on civilians to be immoderate—provided, of course,
the civilians were Israelis.

Meanwhile, back at *20/20,* network officials were looking
for additional ways to present the Palestinian issue. Barbara
Newman attended a meeting in *20/20* executive producer Av
Westin's office in which the problem was discussed, and
Westin suggested that they do a piece on the West Bank.
According to Geraldo Rivera: "That piece ['Under the Israeli Thumb'] was, in my opinion, related to the pressure
that followed my piece. Anyone who says that 'Under the
Israeli Thumb' was not related to 'The Unholy War' is not
being candid."*[18] Correspondent Tom Jarriel, who knew
almost nothing about the subject, was assigned to do the report.

"It's curious that I was not the person to do the West Bank
story," says Rivera, who was not even told about the project

---

*In its February 1982 newsletter, the Arab Association of University Graduates
boasted: "The idea for this program ['Under the Israeli Thumb'] was advanced by
the AAUG, the American-Arab Anti-Discrimination Committee, and the Palestine
Congress in an April 1981 meeting with *20/20* producers to protest . . . a previous
20/20 program, 'The Unholy War.' "[17]

until it was under way. "Given the fact that I had the experience, that I'd been in the West Bank ten times, and that I had so much video shot already, I thought I should be the one to do it."[19] But Rivera was a part of ABC's Palestinian problem, not a part of the solution—and Jarriel was selected instead.

But Jarriel came later. First to arrive in Israel, in early September, was researcher Jay Lamonica. In any television documentary the researcher is crucial. These projects are normally far too expensive to waste the reporter's time on reporting. By the time a television documentary team shows up at your door, they usually know what they are looking for. Lamonica's job was to prepare the information which Jarriel would then use on the air.

Lamonica met with Israeli officials, including me, and raised a series of questions: "What is the economic situation of the Arabs in the West Bank?" (greatly improved since 1967); "Is it true that there are no written laws in the area?" (he was provided with a set of the legal code); "What is the status of women?" (given the vote for the first time by Israel); and so forth. Each positive aspect of life in the West Bank was crossed off his mental checklist of possible Israeli abuses.

After a few weeks of research, Lamonica headed home, but he continued to pepper the staff of the Government Press Office with long-distance questions about life in the West Bank—the infant mortality rate, the number of administrative detainees in Israeli jails, the health budget for the area, and so on. It was clear from the questions, and from his obvious lack of interest in those aspects of life "under the Israeli thumb" that had improved since 1967, that the program would be not only negative, but one-sided.

Later, Lamonica returned with producer Stanhope Gould and correspondent Tom Jarriel, who went to the West Bank mostly to be photographed on location. During these shooting sessions, the ABC camera team worked without the usual ABC stickers plastered on its equipment, and Steve Leibowitz of the government press office wondered why. He was told that recently ABC crews in the Middle East had been ordered to remove the stickers for fear of Palestinian reprisals.

When "Under the Israeli Thumb" aired in February 4, 1982, it began with a lie.

Tom Jarriel: "Hugh [Downs], the first thing we must stress is that despite repeated requests from *20/20,* the Israeli government refused to provide an official to appear on camera and talk about the issues this report raises. . . ." This was a crucial matter for ABC; it was about to accuse Israel of serious crimes—including encouraging Arab infant deaths—without a word of Israeli explanation or rebuttal. This, of course, ran counter to ABC's own professional standards, as well as common sense and fairness. So important was this point that Jarriel returned to it at the end of his report: "Again, we must remind you that the Israeli government would not provide an official spokesperson to address the issues on camera." Who could doubt that such an unambiguous statement was true?

In fact, Defense Minister Ariel Sharon had met with Jarriel and his crew in his Tel Aviv office in late October 1981 for almost two hours and agreed to ABC's request that he appear on the program. It was a nervy request—there aren't many foreign countries where newsmen can even meet with the defense minister, much less ask him to appear as a participant on what everyone clearly understood by this time was to be a hostile documentary; but Sharon was willing. He had one condition, though; no editing on his remarks. ABC could say whatever it liked on the documentary, of course, but Sharon wanted his own words to be uncut and unchanged by editors in New York. He didn't trust the program's producers, and as it turned out, for good reason. Jarriel made no mention of Sharon's conditional willingness to appear on the program, however; and he also largely ignored the information he had received from him during their meeting.

When Sharon refused to submit to editing, ABC demanded that he designate a general to appear on the show. Sharon declined on the grounds that the West Bank, although under the daily administration of the army, is a political issue, and he didn't want Israeli military figures discussing it on American TV.

This was the basis for ABC's contention that Israel was not prepared to provide an official spokesperson. In fact, ABC simply refused to allow Israel to provide one. When Sharon's condition was turned down, the Government Press Office (Israel's official agency for dealing with the international press) suggested a number of alternatives: Foreign Minister Itzhak Shamir; the director-general of the Prime Minister's Office, or of the Foreign Ministry; a justice of the Supreme Court who had dealt with Arab land claims; a senior Member of Knesset (MK) from the governing Likud faction; and so forth. ABC turned them all down. In addition to various senior officials, we also proposed a long list of Israeli experts on the West Bank. Professor Amnon Cohen of the Hebrew University; Professor Moshe Sharon, also of the Hebrew University and a former adviser to Prime Minister Begin on Arab affairs; and other academic and legal experts were all suggested—and all rejected. We had never encountered a situation in which a network wanted to dictate *our* spokesman.

Lamonica explained that ABC wanted someone who could speak with authority. "But surely you realize that the foreign minister would be speaking authoritatively," he was told.

"Perhaps," said Lamonica, "but he has no expertise on the West Bank."

"Don't worry, Lamonica," we assured him, "he'll bone up on the subject." But ABC wasn't interested.

ABC's "Sharon, a general, or nothing" attitude was even less reasonable in view of the Palestinian spokesmen the network chose. There is a rough rule of thumb in television news that the spokesmen on two sides of an issue should be of approximately the same rank or status. The West Bank Arabs interviewed were not well-known political figures or officials, but a doctor, a scientist, a health expert, an economist, a farmer, and a couple of men on the street. It would have been incongruous for the defense minister to appear in this company, even if ABC had let him.

It is hard to avoid the conclusion that ABC's position—

that senior Israeli officials were not official enough and Israeli experts not expert enough—was simply a device intended to prevent any Israeli response to the charges that Tom Jarriel leveled.

"To take one Israeli farmer speaking heavily accented English [the only Israeli to appear, briefly, in the entire segment] is almost to set up the Israelis for a fall," says Geraldo Rivera. "You can manipulate by editing the same way you can manipulate by distortion—and I don't claim this was distortion at all—but you can manipulate by whom you interview. . . . I would have liked to have seen an articulate Israeli spokesman, a hard-working Israeli doctor talking about how he had saved Palestinian babies, for example. I'm sure they exist, because I've interviewed them myself." [20]

Even without Israeli spokesmen, ABC sometimes had to do some fancy footwork to keep from being tripped up by the facts. The show began with an argument between a Jew and an Arab over the possession of some disputed land. The Arab says, "This is my property, my life. I have titles to prove this land is mine." The Israeli replies, "Every ground which we are building on are property of the Israeli government [sic]." Jarriel neutrally noted that "regardless of who is right about the land, this settlement has plans to triple its size."

But Jarriel knew who was right. The status of the disputed property was explained to him by another Israeli settler on the scene, whose English was apparently too good for inclusion in the program. The land had indeed been confiscated by the government—but it was by the *Jordanian government in 1966.* Jordan had intended to turn the site into a military air base. The former owners had been paid compensation and the Jordanians had declared the land to be state owned. Their titles had been invalid since 1966. ABC was thus informed (and could easily have confirmed) who was right in that particular dispute. But it chose to include the scene anyway.

Jarriel also noted that in the dispute between the Israelis and the Arab over the land, "Under military occupation, the Arab farmer will lose." The implication was that the Arab would lose not on the merits of the case, but because under military occupation all Arab claims are doomed. Jarriel must have known that Israeli courts had previously ruled in favor of West Bank Arabs in land cases against the Israeli government, the most famous being the Alon Moreh dispute in October 1979 which was widely reported in the U.S.

Sometimes, in the absence of any Israeli spokesman, Jarriel assumed the role himself. At one point, he stated that "the Israelis say that because of continuing violence, democratic freedoms taken for granted in Israel cannot exist in the West Bank." Jarriel was mistaken; no Israeli spokesmen say, or have ever said, anything of the kind. The West Bank is under military occupation and is not a part of Israel. The democratic freedoms of Israel can be extended to it only if it is annexed and made an integral part of Israel; their absence has nothing whatever to do with violence or the lack of it, but with the territory's political status. It was a case of the ABC correspondent putting incriminating and dishonest-sounding words in Israel's mouth.

But the worst was yet to come. Jarriel visited Ramallah hospital and met with Palestinian political activist Dr. Shawki Harb. Like fellow Palestinian physicians Fathi Arafat (brother of Yasser) and Dr. George Habash (leader of the PFLP), Harb is a doctor who knows how to resolve any possible conflict between his professional ethics and his patriotic duty. Jarriel, for his part, was hardly less patriotic in the service of ABC's interests. Here is how they collaborated:

Jarriel: "The infant mortality rate is going down almost everywhere in the world, but on the West Bank, say Palestinian doctors, it's actually going up. The Israelis had figures to dispute this, but at Ramallah hospital, Dr. Harb claims there's a shocking situation."

Dr. Harb: "Well, I'll tell you something. All babies who need respirators in this hospital, they die, because we don't have simply baby respirators. And these are locked."

Jarriel: "You've seen it?"

Dr. Harb: "Of course, it's almost a daily occurrence."

Jarriel: "The Israelis say there is one baby respirator at the Ramallah hospital, but that's not nearly enough, according to independent medical experts. At Hadassah, for example, an Israeli hospital serving about the same size population, there are ten baby respirators."

There were almost as many distortions in the Harb-Jarriel accusation as there are baby respirators at Hadassah Hospital.

First: The "Palestinian doctors" (other than Dr. Harb) who say the infant mortality rate is going up were unnamed, perhaps because no reputable physician would have his name associated with such a demonstrable lie.

Second: Jarriel stated that "the Israelis have their own statistics to dispute this," as if Israeli government statistics, which are accepted as authentic by the World Health Organization (WHO), can be compared to the anonymous and perhaps nonexistent physicians Mr. Jarriel cited.

Third: Between 1968 (the first year of Israeli occupation) and 1980, the infant mortality rate in the West Bank declined from 33.6 per 1000 live births to 28.3 deaths per 1000 live births. These official figures are, as I have said, accepted by WHO.*

Fourth: "All babies who need respirators in this hospital, they die . . ." Dr. Harb maintained. He might as well have said that all patients who need complicated brain surgery in the Ramallah hospital die. In fact, complex medical problems are treated at Hadassah Hospital, about twelve miles away. If babies die in Ramallah hospital for lack of respirators, it is through the negligence of its staff, who do not diagnose their cases correctly and refer them to the proper medical facility. This arrangement of regional medical centers is intended to avoid redundancy in equipment and is practiced not only in the West Bank, but throughout Israel. At the time of the documentary, Tel Aviv's Ichilov Hospital also had no respirators and sent patients who required them to the Tel Hashomer medical center. This arrangement was not intended, presumably, to encourage Jewish infant mortality in Tel Aviv.

*In the period preceding the 1967 occupation, Jordan did not compute official infant mortality statistics for the West Bank.

Fifth: "The Israelis say there is only one baby respirator at Ramallah hospital," says Jarriel. In fact, Israeli authorities said that there were two, and there were.

Sixth: "And this is not nearly enough, according to independent medical experts." ABC's implication is that Israeli medical experts (who contended that the respirator situation was satisfactory) are perhaps less independent than Dr. Harb, something which must make even Dr. Harb blush.

Seventh: "At Hadassah, for example, a hospital serving about the same size population . . ." Ramallah is included in the area served by Hadassah Hospital. According to the American Hadassah Organization, approximately one third of the patients in its pediatrics department at any given time are Arabs from the West Bank, Gaza, and Israel itself.[21]

Last (and worst): ABC knew all of this *before* it made its assertions. All the statistics were forwarded to ABC, and it was explained that Ramallah hospital—like other local hospitals in Israel—and the West Bank—is meant to handle simple cases, with more complicated ones being referred to regional medical centers.

As to Dr. Harb's contention that the Israeli-inspired infant deaths are "almost a daily occurrence," one wonders about the imagination of a physician who could invent something like that, or the gullibility of a reporter who could believe it.

In case anyone missed the point, Jarriel added: "The Palestinians insist it's part of a subtle Israeli policy with a very specific aim," which is, according to Dr. Harb, to throttle the once great medical institutions of the West Bank and thereby "practically killing, destroying the population."

This is a charge of infanticide, plain and simple, based on the word of one Palestinian doctor with an obvious political bias. And, of course, the word of ABC's correspondent, who ignored a UN statistic, the hundreds of Arab children in Israeli medical centers, and simple common sense. Mr. Jarriel may have found all this trivial, but for Israelis, the descendants of two thousand years of well-poisoning slanders and "drain-the-baby's-blood-for-matzoh" inspired pogroms, the falseness of ABC's effort was eclipsed only by its evocative ugliness.*

What would have happened if ABC had decided to do an honest documentary on the West Bank? It would no doubt have included many of the negative aspects of life under the occupation that appeared in "Under the Israeli Thumb"—not the charges of infanticide, certainly, but questions of land appropriation, water rights, military justice, the behavior of some of the Israeli settlers toward the Arabs, and so on, as well as an examination of the political aspirations of the Palestinians. It would also have included an Israeli or two, and might have noted that life under Israel had not been all bad. A serious look at the question would have mentioned the open bridges between the West Bank and Jordan; the fact that Israel has helped raise the local standard of living, allowed universities to open, provided West Bank Arabs recourse to the Israeli courts, and permitted more personal freedom for local residents even within the context of military rule than they ever had under Jordanian control. It would also have noted that one area in which life in the West Bank has unquestionably improved is medical treatment, which under Jordan was primitive and elitist and is now available, at a high standard and low cost, to everyone.

This is not to argue that the occupation is a positive thing for the Arabs of the West Bank or that they do not suffer injustices and hardships; it is merely to say that this issue, like most, has two sides. This is the normal assumption of television news; its suspension in the case of "Under the Israeli Thumb," along with the documentary's melodramatic misrepresentations, raises serious questions about ABC's motive for producing it.

---

*There is an ironic, and disturbing, counterpoint to the anti-Jewish theme on which Jarriel and Harb collaborated. In a panel discussion on the media and the Middle East held by the New York Media Forum on May 3, 1982, the show's producer, Stanhope Gould, acknowledged that the program had been controversial and "even my mother was upset with me." The message was that if Mrs. Gould's nice little Jewish boy Stanhope was involved, the program couldn't really have been so bad.

6

CHAIRMAN YASSER'S
BEST BATTALION

Late in 1983, during the siege of Tripoli, Chairman Yasser Arafat called one of his almost daily press conferences. For days Arafat's supporters has been cut off in the Lebanese port city, battered by Syrian-sponsored Palestinian rebels led by Abu Mussa, and no one knew how much longer Arafat would be able to hold out. The PLO chief was facing both an irreparable split in his organization and a military defeat that would rob him of his last foothold in Lebanon.

And yet, as the press conference began, Arafat seemed in a mellow mood. Looking out over the assembled journalists, some of whom he had known for years, he nostalgically recalled the siege of Beirut sixteen months earlier. "I still remember the most important battalion I had with me then," he told them. "It was the battalion from the Commodore"—a reference to the foreign press corps and its headquarters in West Beirut.

"Yes," Arafat's spokesman chimed in, "and now they are here."[1]

The PLO's warm, almost proprietary attitude toward the foreign press corps did not begin in the summer of 1982.

For almost a decade the Western press had been one of Arafat's most formidable allies. During that time the "Commodore Battalion" provided the PLO with "often uncritical" press coverage in the gentle phrase of *The New York Times*'s Thomas Friedman.[2] Meanwhile, a gaggle of pundits and commentators in the United States and Western Europe encouraged and propagated the notion that the PLO is a legitimate political movement whose only goal is a Palestinian state next door to Israel. Many journalists believed this as an article of faith, a self-deception that enabled the PLO to conduct its activities and retain its program for the liquidation of Israel while, at the same time, nurturing a positive, moderate image abroad.

The PLO's special relationship with the press first began after the 1973 Arab-Israeli War. Until then it had been known largely as a radical terrorist organization whose members carried out attacks on innocent civilians. Founded in the mid-1960s as an umbrella group for a number of Palestinian terrorist factions, in its early years it was a political football, kicked back and forth by various Arab patrons.

Then, as now, its largest and most important member was al-Fatah; now, as then, the organization's goals are defined in its constitution, the Palestine National Covenant. The covenant sets forth, in clear and specific terms, the aim of the PLO—the destruction of the state of Israel and its replacement with a Palestinian Arab state.

The covenant is too long to be reprinted here in full. The relevant articles—19, 20, 21, 22, and 23—are as follows:

Article 19: The partition of Palestine in 1947 and the establishment of the state of Israel are entirely illegal, regardless of the passage of time, because they were contrary to the will of the Palestinian people and to their natural right in their homeland, and inconsistent with the principles embodied in the Charter of the United Nations, particularly the right of self-determination.

Article 20: The Balfour Declaration, the mandate for Palestine and everything that has been based upon them, are deemed null and void. Claims of historical or religious ties of Jews with Palestine are incompatible with the facts of history and the true conception of what constitutes statehood. Judaism, being a religion, is not an independent nationality. Nor do Jews constitute a single nation with an identity of its own.

Article 21: The Arab Palestinian people, expressing themselves by the armed Palestinian revolution, reject all solutions which are substitutes for the total liberation of Palestine and reject all proposals aiming at the liquidation of the Palestinian problem, or its internationalization.

Article 22: Zionism is a political movement economically associated with international imperialism and antagonistic to all action for liberation and to progressive movements in the world. It is racist and fanatic in its nature, aggressive, expansionist and colonial in its aims, and fascist in its methods. Israel is the instrument of the Zionist movement, and a geographical base for world imperialism placed strategically in the midst of the Arab homeland to combat the hopes of the Arab nation for liberation, unity and progress. Israel is a constant source of threat vis-à-vis peace in the Middle East and the whole world. Since the Liberation of Palestine will destroy the Zionist and imperialist presence and will contribute to the establishment of peace in the Middle East, the Palestinian people look for the support of all the progressive and peaceful forces and urge them all, irrespective of their affiliations and belief, to offer the Palestinian people all aid and support in their just struggle for the liberation of their homeland.

Article 23: The demands of security and peace, as well as the demands of right and justice, require all states to consider Zionism an illegitimate movement, to outlaw its existence, and to ban its operations, in order that friendly relations among peoples may be preserved, and the loyalty of citizens to their respective homelands safeguarded.[3]

Following the 1967 Six Day War, the buffoonish Ahmed Shukieri was replaced as head of the PLO by al-Fatah's Yasser Arafat. Arafat announced that he would focus his efforts on waging guerilla warfare against the Israeli occupation in the West Bank and Gaza Strip, but this proved beyond the PLO's operational capacity, and by 1968 it had moved its activities across the Jordan River, to the East Bank, from which it launched terrorist forays into Israel. As these were met with increasingly effective Israeli responses, the PLO gradually moved eastward, away from the Israeli lines and into large Jordanian cities and towns. Here, their armed presence and hostility toward Jordanian authority precipitated a crisis. In September 1970, King Hussein's armed forces administered a bloody defeat to the Palestinian terrorists and drove them out of Jordan into Lebanon, the only country in the region weak enough to accept them.

Once in Lebanon, the PLO embarked on a campaign against civilians—Israeli and foreign, Jewish and non-Jewish—that earned it worldwide notoriety. Airline hijackings, the slaughter of Israeli athletes at the Munich Olympics, the ambush and murder of a school bus full of Israeli schoolchildren at Avivim on the northern border of Galilee—these and other operations became the PLO's trademark.

In 1973, the West was suddenly made aware of the economic power of the Arab world, which let it be known that the steady flow of oil would, from now on, be hostage to the satisfaction of Arab political aspirations—and first on the agenda was the Palestinian grievance. The following year, the Arab summit meeting at Rabat, Morocco, decreed the Palestine Liberation Organization to be the "sole legitimate representative of the Palestinian people." As such, the PLO was now an important factor in the Middle East political equation—*the* representative of *the* problem whose solution was considered vital for the continued flow of oil to the West. Radical or not, the PLO would have to be taken into account.

The leadership of the PLO clearly saw the golden opportunity that the Arab oil weapon had provided, an opportunity to raise the Palestinian issue to the forefront of international concern, force the Israelis on to the defensive, and gain European, perhaps even American, support. There was, however, a hitch. It soon became clear that even the most craven European leaders, the greediest Western oil barons or the trendiest Third World enthusiasts, could not publicly support the PLO's explicit demand for the destruction of the state of Israel. On the other hand they could, and would, go along with any formula that smacked of compromise with the Jewish state—certainly one that called for a Palestinian state *next* to Israel, in the West Bank and Gaza. By late 1974, Arafat and his fellow PLO chiefs knew that massive international support and pressure for such a state could be mobilized, at the cost of abandoning the ultimate goal of Israel's liquidation.

This, however, was impossible. The PLO, formed in order to abolish Israel, could no more accept a compromise with the Jewish state than the KKK could elect a Black Grand Wizard. A great many PLO loyalists (and much of the group's leadership) had originally come from *Israel proper*, pre-1967 Israel. For them, the West Bank and Gaza were unfamiliar places, no more "home" than Lebanon or Jordan; their dream of national liberation focused on Haifa, Jaffa, Lod, Ashkelon, and the Galilee. A compromise on the Palestinian demand for a total return of their lost lands would be traitorous. It would rob its advocates of their nationalist legitimacy, not to mention endanger their lives. For the PLO's leadership such a compromise was out of the question.

This created a real dilemma—how to appear moderate enough to get Western support without forsaking the unforsakable goal. The answer: the creation of a smokescreen that would obscure the PLO's intentions, convince the gullible, and satisfy the cynical. The vehicle for this was the PLO's "Ten Point Program," adopted in 1974, which became the basis for the assertion that the PLO had given up its intention to destroy Israel and would be prepared for a "Two-State Solution," i.e., the creation of a Palestinian state *next* to Israel, on the West Bank and Gaza—two nations, one Jewish and one Arab, living side by side in the territory from the Mediterranean Sea to the Jordan River.

This contention was based on Article 2 of the Ten-Point Program:

"The PLO will struggle by every means, the foremost of which is armed struggle, to liberate Palestinian land and to

establish the people's national, independent and fighting
authority *on every part of Palestinian land to be liberated.* [emphasis added] This requires making more changes in the
balance of power in favor of our people and their struggle."[4] The phrase "on every part of Palestinian land to be
liberated" was seized on and interpreted by the PLO's supporters in the West as proof of the group's willingness to
accept a state in part (not necessarily all) of Palestine. But
those who honestly believed that this was its meaning simply
didn't keep on reading.

Article 3 stated:

"The PLO will struggle against any plan for the establishment of a Palestinian entity, the price of which is recognition [of Israel], conciliation [with Israel], secure borders [for
Israel], renunciation of the national right, and our people's
deprivation of their right to return and their right to determine their fate on their national soil."[5]

Article 4 made this even clearer:

*"Any liberation step that is achieved constitutes a step for continuing [the efforts] to achieve the PLO strategy for the establishment of the Palestinian democratic state that is stipulated in the
resolutions of the previous national councils."*[6] (emphasis added)

In other words, the PLO was willing to accept a part of
Palestine as a stage in the overall struggle to get it all. Even
the framers of the plan must have been amazed at the willingness of so many newsmen and "experts" to accept this
exterminationist formula as proof that this PLO would settle for something less than all of Palestine.

In the PLO of the mid-1970s there were those who rejected even this phased plan, on the grounds that a tactical
political solution was illegitimate and that all action should
be military. These people, who came to be called "rejectionists," were either primitives, unable to grasp the sophistication of Arafat's approach, or stalking horses for Arab
governments who opposed Arafat's leadership of the PLO
and sought to maintain internal divisions in order to keep a
degree of influence within its councils. Their importance to
Arafat's strategy of appearing moderate without abandoning terrorism and the goal of destroying Israel is hard to

overstate; it was in comparison with these "rejectionists" that he could seem reasonable and pragmatic. Moreover, they provided him with the most plausible excuses for outrageous action. Did the PLO launch a raid on Israeli schoolchildren in Ma'alot? The regrettable act of an extremist faction not under the control of Chairman Arafat. Did Arafat himself order and then warmly praise the Coastal Road massacre near Tel Aviv in which thirty-five Israeli civilians were murdered? A necessity in order to keep his radical faction in line and prove his own revolutionary credentials. Did he continue to call for the destruction of Israel? A sop to the rejectionists, and not really representative of his thinking. Did the PLO refuse to amend its covenant, reject UN resolutions 242 and 338, decline to abandon terrorism? These were explained as the unfortunate influences of the rejectionist minority within the PLO, whose "mainstream" was, of course, reasonable and accommodating.

The PLO worked a number of variations on this theme. Its heterogenous makeup enabled it to speak to various audiences in different voices. Moderates, such as the late Dr. Issam Sartawi, were sent abroad to talk of peaceful coexistence with Israel following the establishment of a Palestinian state in the West Bank and Gaza, while the true PLO leaders spoke (in Arabic) about the strategic goal of Israel's destruction.

Another PLO public relations ploy was perfected by Arafat himself. It consisted of meeting with foreign dignitaries or journalists and coyly hinting in private, off-the-record discussions of his willingness to live in peace with Israel. The implication was that his public statements, the resolutions of the Palestine National Council, and even the organization's continued terrorist acts were less representative of its real mood and intent than these secret assurances.*

---

*As early as March 1976, Arafat victimized Senator Adlai Stevenson III of Illinois with this trick. Stevenson, who is a living refutation of political Darwinism apparently hadn't the wit to understand that he was being hoodwinked and spent an uncomfortable week or two trying to explain his way out of his own statements about PLO moderation after the PLO had officially denounced them as "false." Other politicians who have been taken in include Reverend Jesse Jackson and, during the 1982 war in Lebanon, Congressman Pete McCloskey.

Throughout the 1970s the PLO's moderate image was polished by an admiring Beirut press corps, assisted in the United States by an incongruous alliance of big oil, left-wing academics, and State Department Arabists, who found it expedient, each for different reasons, to promote the idea of PLO pragmatism and moderation. In 1977, they got a powerful ally—the President of the United States.

Less than two years before Jimmy Carter became President, Secretary of State Henry Kissinger had, in exchange for Israeli concessions to Egypt, given Jerusalem a written commitment that the United States would not recognize the PLO so long as it refused to accept Israel's existence. This seemed like a rather reasonable undertaking at the time— Israel was, after all, an American friend, and the PLO, a Soviet-sponsored terrorist organization bent on its destruction—but it soon came to be regarded as a major stumbling block by the Carter administration. President Carter and his advisers believed that the Palestinian issue was the key problem in the Middle East and that the PLO, as its sole representative, must somehow be brought into the political and diplomatic process.

Early in his administration Carter, apparently believing the PLO's PR, thought it possible to persuade Arafat to accept UN Resolution 242, which meant implicitly recognizing Israel. It seemed reasonable that a PLO that wanted only a mini-state of its own in the West Bank and Gaza would be only too glad to embrace the UN resolution in return for inclusion in the process that could bring about this goal. Accordingly, in early 1977, the administration began "the process of exploring whether the PLO was prepared to make the needed public commitment to UN 242, thereby opening the door to its involvement in the peace process," in the words of National Security Adviser Zbigniew Brzezinski.[7]

On March 12, 1977, only a few weeks after the Carter administration had begun exploring PLO readiness to accept UN Resolution 242, the Palestine National Council, the PLO's supreme deliberative body, met in Cairo. American press speculation was rampant that this meeting would at last see the PLO translate its true moderate views into policy. On March 7, for example, *The Washington Post* carried a front-page curtain-raiser in which it contrasted the Palestinian militant position of George Habash with the moderation of the Arafat-led forces, which it characterized as "doves." The article, written by a Reuters correspondent in Cairo, stated, "A majority of the PLO is believed to favor Palestinian attendance at a reconvened Geneva Peace Conference to seek creation of a Palestinian mini-state in the West Bank of the Jordan River and on the Gaza Strip.[8] Four days later, on the op-ed page of *The Washington Post,* Evans and Novak wrote that "the PLO may next change its formal Covenant and acknowledge Israel's right to exist" at its biennial meeting.[9]

Even after the closed-door meeting began in Cairo, American reporters still believed that it would end with a show of PLO accommodation. *New York Times* correspondent Henry Tanner thought the conference's keynote speaker "struck what observers regarded as a decidedly moderate note."[10] *The Washington Post*'s Thomas Lippman said, after three days of deliberations, that the PLO had clearly implied that it would attend a Geneva conference. He noted, too, that the PLO meeting was under the firm control of PLO chief Yasser Arafat.[11] This view was shared by UPI correspondent Maurice Gindi, who reported that the PLO's rejection front was demanding what "amounted in effect to a call for the destruction of the state of Israel," but that these rejectionists were only about one third of the delegates, the remaining two thirds being under the undisputed leadership of the PLO chairman.[12]

American reporters were in general agreement—the moderates were in control, they were no longer intent on destroying Israel, they were prepared to go to Geneva if asked, and they were willing to accept a Palestinian state in the West Bank and Gaza.

And then, mysteriously, the conference broke up, its resolutions and decisions were announced, and it appeared that something had gone wrong. According to a wire-service item buried on page 20-A of *The Washington Post,* "The Palestine National Council, termed a Parliament-in-Exile, [also] reaffirmed the strategic aim of dismantling Israel." [13] Other "moderate" decisions of the Arafat-dominated meeting included the outright rejection of Resolution 242 and a rejection of the Geneva conference participation "under the present terms of reference." [14] Needless to say, there was no mention of amending the Covenant or any talk about settling for a mini-state in the West Bank and Gaza. Moreover, the *Post*'s account omitted one very significant piece of information. The call for dismantling Israel was based on a resolution introduced not by the rejectionist primitives, but by Arafat's own followers. [15]

Just in case anyone missed the point, the PLO's Faruk Kaddoumi set out the group's strategy in an interview with *Newsweek:* "There are two initial phases to our return," he told the magazine. "The first phase to the 1967 lines, and the second to the 1948 lines. . . . The third stage is the democratic state of Palestine. So we are fighting for these three stages." [16]

The U.S. administration was undeterred by this frank talk. In August, Secretary of State Cyrus Vance visited the Middle East and was told by the Saudis (and in turn told the reporters traveling with him) that the PLO, at its Central Council meeting later that month, would now accept what it had rejected in March—UN Security Council Resolution 242. This so impressed *The Washington Post* that it led the paper with the headline PLO WILL SHIFT STAND ON ISRAEL, ARABS TELL U.S. [17] *Time* magazine was even more enthusiastic. On August 29, it reported that *"Time* has learned that after extensive negotiations . . . the so-called rejectionists have decided to end their defiant stand against peace on any terms with Israel and *agree with the larger Palestinian Liberation Organization on the goal of securing an independent state on the West Bank and Gaza.*" [18] (emphasis added) By the time the magazine was on the newsstands, the PLO had already met in Damascus, re-rejected Resolution 242, and published a scathing attack on Israel and the United States. As for *Time*'s report on the "rejectionists," it was based on a false premise— that the "larger PLO" had ever agreed to the goal of an independent state on the West Bank and Gaza.*

In May 1978, *New York Times* columnist Anthony Lewis visited the Middle East and had a chat with Yasser Arafat. He added a brick to the monument that was being built to the PLO's alleged moderation by writing: "The Palestine Liberation Organization originally took the position that all of what was Palestine before the establishment of Israel in 1948 should become the secular democratic state. Then, in 1974, the Palestine National Council called for the establishment of a Palestinian State on any territory recovered from Israel, presumably in the West Bank and Gaza."[20]

In fact, as we have seen, the Palestine National Council in 1974 had decided and explicitly stated that any entity established on the West Bank and Gaza would be the first step toward establishing a Palestinian state encompassing the entire country, including what is now Israel. Mr. Lewis quoted only Article 2 of the Ten-Point Program; he ignored Articles 3 and 4, a piece of intellectual trickery that ought to get him a life sentence of reading the collected works of Evans and Novak.

The *New York Times* columnist also offered an explanation for the puzzling failure of the PLO to recognize, even tacitly, Israel's right to exist: "Last year the Carter Administration tried to get the Palestine Liberation Organization to abandon language in its Covenant indicating that Israel should be replaced by a secular state and to endorse Resolution 242 adopted by the United Nations Security Council in 1967," he wrote. "The resolution calls on Israel to withdraw from occupied territory, but also speaks of assuring 'secure and recognized borders.'

Time's profound intellectual dishonesty regarding the PLO was displayed again in March 1978, when Arafat's own Fatah faction (the main group within the PLO) raided Israel and murdered 35 Israeli civilians and wounded tens more. This attack contradicted *Time*'s repeated assertions that the PLO had rejected terrorism in favor of politics. The magazine resolved the inconsistency by noting that the PLO had *returned* to a "policy of militancy" after "three and a half years of relative moderation."[19] *Time* failed to mention that during this halcyon period of moderation, Palestinian terrorists had conducted operations in Israel that killed 74 civilians and wounded 510 others, had carried out numerous attacks on civilians abroad, and had been active combatants in the Lebanese civil war. Only *Time*'s doctrinaire advocacy of the PLO could have enabled it to view this behavior as "relative moderation."

"The PLO refused in the end to make such statements. Privately its officials have said that recognition of Israel was a vital card for them to be played only when and if Israel is ready to deal with the liberation organization as the representative of Palestinians."[21] Since Chairman Arafat refused to say any such thing, Lewis accommodatingly served as his spokesman by assuring his readers that the PLO was, in fact, prepared to accept Israel and was only awaiting some reciprocal flexibility. In fact, in the coming years the PLO gave no indication whatsoever that it was prepared to play its "recognition of Israel card" or, indeed, that any such card exists as other than a public relations ace up its sleeve.

In January 1979, the Palestine National Council held another biennial meeting, this time in Damascus. Once again, the Arafat faction controlled the clear majority of the delegates, so much so that it succeeded in depriving George Habash, an Arafat rival, of a seat on the fifteen-man executive committee. The meeting, which was almost totally ignored by the American press, was a festival of mainline PLO radicalism. There was no talk of amending the Covenant or accepting Resolution 242; no mention of West Bank mini-states or peaceful coexistence. Arafat called for an increased guerrilla war against Israel,[22] and to demonstrate his sincerity, publicly claimed credit for an explosion in a Jerusalem open-air market that injured twenty-one civilians on January 17, while the conference was in session. None of this made any particular impression on *Time* magazine, however, which was just about the only American publication to pay any real attention to the secret, closed meetings. In its report on the council's deliberations, it noted that "the relatively moderate Yassir Arafat remains the dominant figure within the PLO . . ." Under his "moderate" leadership, ". . . [the delegates] rejected the Camp David Plan for creating an autonomous 'entity' on the West Bank and Gaza, and they insisted the PLO and not King Hussein should represent the Palestinians." And, consistent with *Time*'s view of PLO moderation, the magazine noted, "Moderates and militants alike remained committed to the use of terrorism against the Israelis, and in fact, a minor wave of violence continued throughout the week. In Jerusalem, for example, a grenade exploded in an open air market, injuring a score of Israeli shoppers . . ."[23]

In May 1979, PLO terrorists landed at the Israeli town of Nahariyah and murdered a father and his small children in cold blood. PLO information director Majed Abu Sherar told *Newsweek*, " 'Nahariyah was only a small sample. It will be repeated many, many times.' " This was echoed by Abu Iyyad, described by *Newsweek* as Arafat's "right-hand man," who said: " 'This so-called peace treaty [Camp David] didn't give us anything new. So we will escalate the armed struggle.' "[24]

The following month, *New York Times* correspondent Youssof M. Ibrahim visited Beirut and found a different PLO.[25] According to Ibrahim, "Leaders of the organization concede that the best they can do is form a state in the West Bank and Gaza; there is virtually no talk anymore of 'liberating all of Palestine.' The result is an emerging consensus on the ultimate objective." From this assertion—that the PLO had now decided to settle for a state in the occupied territories—Ibrahim went on to attribute it to a willingness to recognize Israel as well. "Spokesmen for the organization contend that negotiating a peaceful solution is only a matter of time," that "the leaders [of the PLO] and others said that the organization was not opposed to the principle of a peaceful settlement, and was basically in agreement with United Nations Resolution 242, as long as Palestinian rights were guaranteed."

Mr. Ibrahim quoted Sabri Girguis, whom he called "a principal ideologist for Al Fatah": "Rejectionists no longer have a moral basis in the Palestinian movement. All factions have accepted the establishment of a state [in the West Bank and Gaza only]. Besides, Al Fatah represents 85% of the PLO. A Fatah decision is a PLO decision."

Ibrahim was asserting that the PLO, adamantly rejectionist as recently as its National Council in January, had totally changed its basic positions. No longer did its leaders want to destroy Israel, to bring about a phased defeat of the Zionist entity; they agreed with UN Resolution 242 and were

prepared to recognize Israel. Ibrahim did quote one obligatory Israeli, who doubted the sincerity of these sentiments,
but the *Times* correspondent made it clear that he himself
had no such doubts.

Of course, by this time the PLO's rhetoric was so moderate that even its leader could hardly recall its true program. In September 1979, Yasser Arafat appeared on ABC's
Issues and Answers. Interviewer Barbara Walters read him a
clause from the Palestine National Covenant regarding the
necessity to destroy Israel:

Walters: "It does not call for the elimination of the state
of Israel?"

Arafat: "I did not remember that."[26]

In May 1980, al-Fatah held its first congress since 1971.
Four hundred fifty delegates met in Damascus to debate and
deliberate on the goals and strategy of the organization.

The Fatah Congress provided a forum for the true views
of Yasser Arafat and his followers. Fatah was Arafat's organization, the strongest single faction in the PLO and the
one most clearly under his control. It was here that the supposed "new Palestinian moderation" and willingness to compromise with Israel could be expressed, free of the inhibiting
rejectionism of the primitives who, according to the press,
had so often frustrated the statesmanlike instincts of Chairman Arafat.

The Congress held its deliberations in secret and passed
this resolution:

"Fatah is an independent patriotic revolutionary movement and its aim is to liberate Palestine and completely liquidate the Zionist entity. . . . Armed popular revolution is
the only way to liberate Palestine and armed struggle is a
strategic rather than a tactical goal."[27]

This unequivocal demand for the destruction of Israel
might well have puzzled Americans who had believed the
assurances of Anthony Lewis, Youssof Ibrahim, *Time* magazine, and the members of the Commodore Battalion that
all the PLO really wanted was a little country of its own right
next door to Israel. The press coverage of the congress and

its decisions reflected a commendable effort on the part of the American media to shield the public from any such unpleasant confusion.

Time magazine, for example, simply ignored the entire matter and made no mention whatever of the resolution.* *The Washington Post* buried the wire service report on the meeting far back in the paper, next to an ad for Magruder's Boneless Chicken.[28] Most American news organizations failed to report it at all.

The New York Times at first also ignored the outcome of the Fatah congress. In the first days after the meeting, readers of America's newspaper of record learned nothing about Fatah's renewed pledge to destroy the Jewish state and so could continue to believe that such a pledge was impossible—they had Youssof Ibrahim's word for it. Then on June 5, the *Times* did carry a story, entitled PLO SOFTENS STAND CHALLENGING ISRAEL: DEMAND FOR DESTRUCTION OF JEWISH NATION WAS MISUNDERSTOOD, A SPOKESMAN CONTENDS. Written by Nicholas Gage, it gave no explanation of why the *Times* had waited three days to report on the congress's resolution; presumably, if the PLO spokesman, who was trying after the fact to change the sense of the resolution, had kept silent, the *Times* would *never* have reported it. Readers who got nine paragraphs into the story saw Mr. Gage's assessment that the "contradiction" between the moderate explanations of the PLO spokesmen and the resolution itself was "an attempt to play to two audiences." But most readers, seeing the headline, and bereft of any previous information on the resolutions of the congress, were left with the impression that al-Fatah had *softened* rather than reaffirmed its commitment to liquidate Israel.[29]

No American newspaper was as disconcerted by the resolution as *The Washington Post*. A month after the congress, *Post* correspondent Edward Cody offered a retrospective

---

*On October 6, however, *Time* ran an article entitled, ARAFAT'S NUDGE: INCHING TOWARD RECOGNITION? about a meeting between Arafat and four Israeli Communists at a conference in Belgrade. *Time* found Arafat's meeting with the Israelis (all of whom were anti-Zionist) "conciliatory," lending credence to the impression that the PLO was ready to accept Israel. This, *Time* apparently felt, was the *real* Fatah—not some stuffy old congress.

explanation of the resolution in an article not labeled
ANALYSIS, entitled TOUGH RHETORIC MASKS PLO STRATEGY.[30]
Cody noted that the Fatah call "to liquidate the Zionist entity politically, economically, militarily, culturally and ideo-
logically," had, for some reason, been interpreted in Israel
and the United States as . . . a call to liquidate Israel. He,
on the other hand, found the language a "fuzzy enunciation
of Palestinian goals" because, as one of Yasser Arafat's aides
told him, the congress had also accepted the idea of a West
Bank state. The aide apparently didn't tell Cody, who didn't
tell his readers, that this West Bank State would, in Fatah's
view, serve as the base for the ongoing struggle to liquidate
Israel.

Another month passed, and *The Washington Post* came up
with a new explanation for the Fatah liquidation resolution.
Not only had it been "fuzzy," in Cody's words, but it also
had never existed. This curious argument was advanced in
an article by Joseph Fitchett. Fitchett is not a regular *Post*
reporter (he works for the *International Herald Tribune*), and
the use of his dispatch signaled that he was saying something that the *Post*'s editors wanted in the newspaper.

Fitchett quoted a statement by Chairman Arafat that the
offending resolution was merely a proposal and had never
been passed. Arafat claimed, and Fitchett did not in any way
contradict him, that the rumor that such a resolution had
been adopted was, in fact, an Israeli propaganda ploy.[31]

This theme was taken up by the *Post*'s sister publication,
Newsweek, which reported: "At a meeting last May of Fatah,
Arafat's own wing of the PLO, militants presented a resolution calling for the 'liquidation' of Israel, undercutting
Arafat's moderate image. Arafat had to dissociate himself
from the provocative measure. Last week he insisted that it
was 'only a draft resolution' and that 'it was not approved.' "[32]

Neither *Newsweek* nor the *Post* answered (or even addressed) the obvious question: If Arafat's current version was
true and Fatah had never adopted the resolution, why had
it been broadcast on Radio Falestin, the PLO's own official
radio, on June 2? And, given the conflicting versions being

offered by the PLO on what was, after all, a matter of some importance, why hadn't the *Newsweek* and *Post* Beirut correspondents found out definitively if the resolution had indeed been passed?

One journalist thought the controversy worth investigating. In November 1980, free-lance American reporter Robert Friedman visited Beirut and interviewed May Sayegh, Secretary-General of the PLO's Women's Union:

FRIEDMAN: "Since you were a delegate to the Fatah Congress in Damascus last summer, you'd know if a resolution was passed calling for the destruction of Israel. Yasser Arafat has denied it."

SAYEGH: "I'm not sure what Chairman Arafat told the press, but nothing new happened at the Congress. Our strategy was always to liberate Palestine. We have our democratic solution to the Palestinian problem. This does not mean two states. One state, comprising Palestinian Christians, Moslems and Jews is our solution. A resolution was passed supporting this view. Resolutions are laws. They are passed by majority vote."[33]

An insight into the PLO's "acceptance" of a Palestinian state next to Israel was provided by Abu Iyyad (Salah Khalaf), Arafat's chief lieutenant in Fatah, with whom Friedman also spoke.

FRIEDMAN: "You also wrote in your book [*A Palestinian Without a Country*] that terrorism will stop when we have a state to run. . . . As a state and a neighbor, you promised, Palestine would pose no threat to Israel."

KHALAF: "That translation is not correct. I mean that an independent state on the West Bank and Gaza Strip is the beginning of the final solution. That solution is to establish a democratic state in the whole of Palestine. Arms, however, will not be the only means we use to achieve this end."[34]

On September 24, 1981, in *The New York Times* and in hundreds of newspapers around the country, syndicated columnist Anthony Lewis, undaunted by the PLO's policy returned to the question of its *true* intentions: "In recent years the PLO has moved away from the original position stated in its charter, that all of Palestine should be a 'secular, democratic state'—a goal that would mean the end of Israel. Since 1974 the Palestine National Council has called for a Palestinian state on any territory from which Israel has withdrawn or been expelled. The implication was that the state would consist of the West Bank and East Jerusalem, freed from Israeli occupation, and would co-exist with Israel."[35]

With this, Mr. Lewis, who back in 1978 had committed the intellectual crime of trying to sell Article 2 of the Ten-Point Program as if there were no Articles 3 and 4, became a recidivist. By this time, however, he had a lot of company. One of the most prominent was *Washington Post* correspondent Jonathan Randal, who during the 1982 War in Lebanon asserted, "The PLO insists on the Palestinian people's right to a homeland, although over the years it has dropped its original claims to Israel proper in favor of setting up an independent state on any land relinquished by Israel— meaning the West Bank and Gaza Strip, both occupied by the Jewish state since 1967."[36]

Randal's assertion was made despite, not because of, the PLO's own public statements and actions. Chairman Arafat himself, even under the pressure of the Israeli siege of Beirut, remained unwilling to go beyond the ambivalent slogans that made up his PR repertoire. And yet, the question was crucial—was the PLO really prepared to come to terms with Israel, or not?

Michael Elkins, the BBC's correspondent in Jerusalem, was determined to get the definitive answer to that question. During the 1982 war, Elkins, who is both a Zionist and a harsh critic of Israeli policies since 1977, approached the PLO via a third party in Europe and requested an interview with Arafat. His proposal was simple—he would turn on his tape recorder and ask the PLO leader three straightforward questions about his willingness to accept Israel's existence in return for a West Bank state. If Arafat answered directly, Elkins would broadcast the interview to the BBC's tens of millions of listeners; but if the PLO chief evaded the questions, or equivocated, Elkins would say so on the air. To his surprise, Arafat agreed to these terms.

One day at the height of the siege, Elkins drove to East Beirut, ditched his Israeli Army escort officer, and slipped into West Beirut where he was met by then PLO spokesman Mahmud Labadi. He was taken to a nearby apartment where, he was assured, Yasser Arafat would meet him. While they were waiting, Labadi asked him about the interview he intended to conduct. Elkins reiterated his conditions, and his determination to get the PLO leader on the record, once and for all, on the key question of his organization's intentions toward Israel. Labadi left the room for a few moments and then returned to announce that Chairman Arafat had been delayed, and that the interview would have to be postponed. It was—indefinitely.

During his long wait for the PLO leader, Elkins struck up a conversation with some PLO officials. One began to berate him for his Zionist sympathies and activities. What right, the PLO man demanded, did Israel have to exist?

"That kind of extremism makes it very hard for people like me who are critics of the Begin government," Elkins told the Palestinian. "Why don't you have a dovish opposition? Where is your Peace Now Movement?"[37]

Mahmud Labadi piped up, "Our Peace Now? That's Sartawi," and he and the other men burst into laughter.

For years Dr. Issam Sartawi was the darling of the "PLO-can't-really-mean-all-those-terrible-things" apologists. Back in early 1982 Anthony Lewis wrote a two-column series on him entitled "A PLO Voice for Peace."[38] He described Sartawi as a leading advocate of the "two-state" solution, and noted that his position as a genuine Palestinian moderate was a precarious one. This evaluation proved prescient. Dr. Sartawi was so isolated in the PLO, his belief in coexistence with Israel so incongruous, that he was prevented by the ever-moderate Chairman Arafat of all people from addressing the Palestine National Council meeting in Algiers in 1983. Shortly thereafter, Sartawi was assassinated in Portugal by Arab gunmen while attending a meeting of the Socialist Internationale. Dr. Sartawi paid the price of real (as opposed to PR) Palestinian moderation: his life.

When Israel invaded southern Lebanon in the summer of 1982, a new kind of information about the Palestine Liberation Organization began to surface. Great stockpiles of weapons were found throughout the areas controlled by the PLO, giving credence to the Israeli charge that far from having abandoned its military or terrorist objectives, the organization was expending a growing amount of its energy and treasure on the creation of a serious military force. There were also revelations regarding the behavior of the PLO toward both Lebanese and Palestinian civilians in Lebanon and the role the organization had played in destroying Lebanese sovereignty throughout the south of the country.

David Shipler, in a major, ground-breaking article in *The New York Times* on July 25, 1982, entitled LEBANESE TELL OF ANGUISH OF LIVING UNDER THE PLO, gave details of the PLO's behavior in the south: "For about six years, until Israel invaded southern Lebanon on June 6, the Palestinians had something closely approaching an independent state.

"Those who lived within its rough boundaries said they were too terrified then to describe it to outsiders. Now, for the first time, they are describing what it was like, telling of theft, intimidation and violence."

Shipler described the reign of terror perpetrated by the PLO, which included the theft of homes, land, and property, the forced conscription of children into the terrorist group, the destruction of Lebanese sovereignty in the southern part of the country and, in some cases, murder. "The major tool of persuasion was the gun, according to those who lived through it," said Shipler.

The *New York Times* correspondent's findings were corroborated by other journalists. The British *Economist*, for example, reported that the PLO had previously set up "people's committees" to dispense PLO-style justice, supplanted the Lebanese authorities, and were accused by some south Lebanese residents of arbitrary murder.[39] Even Israel's long-time critic Rowland Evans, of Evans and Novak, visited the area and reported: "Israel's accusation that the PLO was a rogue elephant whose arms and swagger created resentment and fear in Lebanon's largest cities was no fabrication." Evans went on to detail the PLO's reign of terror in the southern part of the country.[40]

Which raised one rather embarrassing question. Why was it left to journalists like Shipler and Evans—outsiders who had not lived in Lebanon during the preceeding six years—to reveal this aspect of the PLO? Where were the dozens of American correspondents stationed in Beirut? Why had they, with few exceptions, ignored this situation, an obvious contradiction to the notion that the PLO was really a moderate political organization?

There are various explanations, of course. Some of the Beirut-based reporters claim that they were unaware of the situation in the south because the frightened Lebanese civilians had been unwilling to disclose it before the Israelis arrived. This explanation would be more plausible were it not for the fact that several members of the Beirut press corps, such as David Hirst of the *Guardian,* had previously discerned and reported on the PLO mini-state in the area south of Damur.[41]

Some critics charge that the PLO's terrorism deterred journalists from writing about the situation in the south. This is a difficult claim to evaluate. The journalists themselves deny that they were intimidated, although it is unlikely, given the nature of self-censorship, that they would be willing to admit that they had been forced to practice it. On the other hand, by the late 1970s, a good many of the Beirut correspondents had been more or less co-opted by the PLO, and there was little need to frighten them away from a story that didn't accord with their sympathetic view of the organization and its behavior.

The most likely explanation for the press's indifference to the situation in the Lebanese south is the feeling that most reporters had that they were in Beirut in order to report on the Palestinian revolution and not Lebanese affairs. Their brief, as they saw it, was to cover one of the sides in the Israeli-Arab conflict. The persecution of Lebanese peasants, or even Palestinian refugees, by the PLO was simply outside the scope of their interests. In journalistic terms, it was not part of the "story."

On the few occasions when the American press corps in Lebanon took notice of the situation in the south, their support for the PLO and tendency to blame Israel for everything blinded them to the PLO's behavior. In mid-March 1981, for example, *The Washington Post* did a major, four-part series on southern Lebanon. The articles made a couple of brief mentions of Palestinian unpopularity among the Lebanese, but blamed it as much on Israeli policy as on PLO behavior. For the most part, the series concentrated on the supposed sins of the pro-Israel southern Lebanese militia leader Major Saad Haddad and the brutality of Israel's responses to PLO activity.[42]

The *Post*'s series was exceptional in its length and anti-Israel tone (at one point it even quoted Professor Israel Shahak, an obscure member of Israel's anti-Zionist lunatic fringe known only to connoisseurs of anti-Israel propaganda);[43] but it was typical in its near silence about the behavior of the PLO in south Lebanon, and what that behavior implied about the organization's aims.

Many in the American press reacted negatively to the revelations regarding the PLO's activities in the south. NBC president for news, Reuven Frank, went so far as to slyly hint to *Jerusalem Post* correspondent Leon Hadar that Shipler's piece had been ordered "by somebody in New York" in response to pressure from the Israel lobby.*[45] The *Times* correspondent was especially unpopular around the bar at the Commodore. Most of the angry and embarrassed journalists in Beirut did not (indeed could not) deny the truth of Shipler's article, but they had become so thoroughly identified with the Palestinian cause that they resented its publication.

On September 1, 1982, with the PLO dispersed, the U.S.

---

*Shipler had, in fact, been working on the story for days before he informed New York about it. He calls Reuven Frank's assertion "unprofessional," especially since it was made without checking with him first.[44] I had hoped to ask Mr. Frank about this, but he declined to be interviewed.

issued the Reagan Plan, which called for a joint Jordanian-Palestinian negotiating team to discuss the future of the West Bank and the Gaza Strip. The plan advocated the establishment of some sort of Palestinian entity in these areas, to be connected in an unspecified way with Jordan. It failed, to be sure, to offer an independent Palestinian state and assigned no role to the PLO as an organization, but it was, by all odds, the most far-reaching American initiative ever offered the Palestinians. The Begin government, aware of its potential for wresting the West Bank and Gaza from Israeli control, rejected it immediately. Undeterred, the American government decided to press ahead.

Most foreign observers believed that the PLO would jump at the plan. The organization was scattered and demoralized, deprived of its territorial base in Lebanon, and desperate for some political movement. Moreover, since it supposedly had long since abandoned its demand for the liquidation of Israel and had embraced the "two-state" formula, it was only *logical* that the PLO would seize the opportunity to establish an "entity" in the coveted territory.

Just four days after the announcement of the Reagan Plan, Henry Tanner of *The New York Times* reported from Jordan, "Initial signals given by Palestinian spokesmen during the last few days make it seem that the PLO will give a favorable, if guarded response to the American proposals . . ." He added that "most Arab experts are convinced that Mr. Arafat is looking for a peaceful solution of the Middle East conflict."[46] When, two months later, the Palestine Central Council met in Damascus and rejected the plan, Mr. Tanner's newspaper noted editorially, ". . . The PLO's Central Council still refuses to recognize the reality of Israel and lays claim to all its land for a state that the PLO would run alone."[47] But, as usual, the PLO, having rejected coexistence, began to double-talk immediately. On December 1, Chairman Arafat said that the PCC had not actually rejected anything. "We merely had some reservations because the American proposals do not satisfy Palestinian aspirations."[48]

At this point, Arafat and the PLO undertook a round of

talks with the Jordanians and left the distinct impression that they would indeed accept the Reagan Plan. David Ignatius of *The Wall Street Journal,* for example, wrote a lengthy article citing a PLO diplomat in Jordan who offered "a surprisingly forthright acceptance of two key premises of the Reagan Plan; a joint Jordanian-Palestinian negotiating team and an eventual Jordanian-Palestinian federation."[49]

Throughout late December, January, and early February the American press was confident of two things: that the PLO, led by Yasser Arafat, would accept the Reagan Plan at its meeting in Algiers in mid-February 1983; and that King Hussein of Jordan would then join the process, agree to negotiate with Israel, and enlist American support in gaining control of the West Bank for a Palestinian entity. Some reports even went so far as to state that should the PLO turn down the U.S. initiative, King Hussein would then be prepared to go it alone, and to turn to the leaders of the West Bank and Gaza as negotiating partners, thus bypassing the PLO. This, however, was considered only a remote possibility. Arafat and his organization were now routinely referred to as "moderate" (just as Begin was automatically "hawkish") and logic was all on the side of such a moderate leader choosing what was, after all, a giant step toward his supposed goal—a West Bank and Gaza entity for his people.

It didn't work out that way at all. The Palestine National Council met in mid-February 1983 in Algiers, Arafat was greeted with wild applause, and the press duly noted that he was in firm control of his organization (later in the week he was reelected chairman, and all his candidates for the executive committee were elected too). As usual, the council meeting was presented as a struggle between the moderate Arafat and the radical rejectionists, but in the opening days of the conference there was confidence in the press gallery that the moderates would win.

Yet, on February 22, after eight days of deliberations, the media reported that the PLO had reached a disappointing compromise—neither to accept nor reject the Reagan Plan. *The New York Times* headline read PLO COUNCIL SAYS REAGAN'S PROPOSAL IS NOT ACCEPTABLE—NO MANDATE FOR JOR-

DAN—PALESTINIANS DO NOT REJECT THE US PLAN OUTRIGHT, GIVING ARAFAT ROOM TO MOVE.[50] *New York Times* correspondent Thomas Friedman predicted out that this decision of the council's political subcommittee would be formally approved by the entire council that evening; that the council's failure to reject the Reagan Plan was a victory for Arafat; and that "neither the PLO moderates nor radicals seemed particularly pleased with the compromise." The networks and most American newspapers reported in the same vein—no acceptance of the Reagan Plan, but no outright rejection either; a minor victory for the dovish Arafat, whose week-long control of the conference had seemed to evaporate, as usual, during the hour or two when decisions were made.

But when the political sub-committee reported to the plenum, there was another surprise in store. The compromise language had been discarded in favor of a "radical" amendment—that the PLO "rejects considering the Reagan Plan."[51] *The New York Times* (and the rest of the press) scrambled to explain this unanticipated "marginal" toughening of the language won by the radicals, but conceded, "The Council refused . . . to either accept the plan or grant any kind of mandate to Jordan or non-PLO Palestinians to negotiate with Washington on its behalf."[52] In short, the PLO had flatly rejected the Reagan Plan.

If the Algiers meeting was not exactly a triumph for PLO moderation, it was the occasion for some notable journalism by *The Washington Post*'s Jonathan Randal, by now the unofficial Commander of the Commodore Battalion-in-exile. Upon arriving in Algiers, Randal discovered that the council's official booklet, prepared by the PLO itself, described the organization as the representatives of "various heavily armed desperado groups." Randal admonished the PLO for this self-portrait which was, he noted, not different from the usual Israeli descriptions of the group. To clear up any possible misunderstanding, he explained to his readers that the pamphlet had been mistranslated.[53]

Then on February 16, Randal helped the PLO with a little revisionist history. He quoted Khalid Fahoum, chairman of the PNC, as saying: "We don't want to drive anyone into the sea," and explained to his readers that the PLO leader was "paraphrasing traditional Israeli accusations that the PLO was determined to throw the Jews into the sea." By this simple device, the *Post* correspondent transformed almost twenty years of PLO official doctrine and declarations into an Israeli "accusation."[54]

As a veteran observer of the PLO, Randal must have understood that the organization was apt to reject the Reagan Plan. This, of course, would tarnish its image as a moderate group and lend credence to the belief that the PLO, even in its darkest hour, would not (or could not) settle for less than the liquidation of Israel. Randal began preparing the groundwork for such an eventuality even before the National Council convened. On February 7, he wrote, "Diplomatic sources stressed that the success of the whole process depended on American forcefulness in bringing about the withdrawal of Israeli troops from Lebanon by mid-February [the date of the Palestine National Council meeting]."[55] Here was the fallback position—(known in some quarters as an alibi) if the organization failed to accept the Reagan Plan, it would not be because of its own unregenerate radicalism, but because of the Israelis. This rather spectacular inversion of reality became the major theme of all Randal's reporting from Algeria:

February 14: "U.S. inability to persuade Israel to withdraw its troops from Lebanon has confirmed Palestinian pessimism and has convinced key PLO officials that Hussein would not dare to enter negotiations without their blessing."

February 15: "But with the U.S. unable to persuade Israeli troops to leave Lebanon, Arafat apparently felt he was in no position to ask the radicals to accept a compromise. . . . King Hussein of Jordan is not believed ready to enter such talks under the Reagan Plan formula—consistently rejected by Israel—without proof of American determination in Lebanon."

February 17: "American failure to persuade or force the Israeli army to leave Lebanon was also reported to have discouraged King Hussein from joining peace talks with Israel as desired by the United States."

February 22 [the day the PNC finally rejected the Reagan Peace Plan]: "Israel has rejected the U.S. plan from the start, and Washington's failure to persuade Israel to withdraw its army from Lebanon is said to have moderated King Hussein's enthusiasm for it."[56]

Randal's relentless repetition of this assessment was not duplicated by his less committed colleagues. *The New York Times,* for instance, only once mentioned a possible connection between Israel's presence in Lebanon and the PLO's attitude toward the Reagan Plan—and when it did, it made it clear that this was a PLO spokesman's argument.[57] But by this time it was hard to know where the PLO spokesmen left off and the *Washington Post* reporter began.

And yet, it was in Algiers that Jonathan Randal and the other members of the Commodore Battalion discovered that the wages of virtue can be ingratitude. During the course of the week-long council session, the PLO decided to take the assembled journalists on a visit to a Palestinian training camp, located in an isolated region near the Algerian-Tunisian border. A large contingent of reporters was flown by Hercules transport to an airstrip near the camp; the PLO brass followed in a private Lear jet.

At the airstrip the reporters were greeted by PLO public-relations officers who provided each of them with an inflatable Arafat balloon bearing a picture of the chairman, and then bused them to the nearby training camp, where they witnessed a surrealistic scene—PLO "fighters" practicing mortar fire using imaginary mortars against imaginary targets. This bizarre activity naturally aroused the reporters' curiosity, and they asked to interview some of the men. Their request, however, was turned down; they were informed that they could meet with and interview senior PLO officials but not the troops. A couple of the American reporters were incensed They requested, they *demanded* the run of the camp.

One became so livid that a British journalist who witnessed the scene told me later that he feared the man might burst like an Arafat balloon. "How can you do this to us," he recalls the American journalist screaming indignantly. "How the hell can you treat us this way! After we saved you in Beirut! After all we've done for you."

7

THE SAUDIS WANT
TO BE ALONE

It was the first day of the Islamic year 1400 (November 20, 1979). Although it was well past midnight, some fifty thousand devout Moslems were crowded into the Great Mosque of Mecca to celebrate at Islam's holiest shrine. There was an atmosphere of high expectation—1400 had long been regarded by many Moslem mystics as an especially portentous date—and it was rumored that the Saudi king and his entourage would be arriving shortly to commemorate the New Year.

Shortly after 4:00 A.M., the worshipers were astonished to see armed men rushing through the mosque compound carrying Soviet-made assault rifles. Pandemonium broke out as shots were fired in the air, and most of the crowd rushed into the streets of Mecca to escape. One of the armed men seized the mosque's sound system and proclaimed Muhammed ibn-Abdullah al-Qahtani, a former divinity student from the Qhatan tribe, as Mahdi, the long-awaited spiritual messenger of Islam. At the same time, the more than seven hundred attackers fanned out in the mosque compound and seized strategic positions at the order of military commander Juhayman ibn-Sayf, brother-in-law of the newly proclaimed Mahdi. The mosque, Islam's most venerated shrine, was in the hands of rebels.[1]

The news spread through the kingdom like wildfire, but it was almost a day before word first reached the outside world. The Saudi leaders, charged with the sacred duty of protecting Mecca and its holy places, were not anxious to have the world learn about the seizure of the mosque. They cut Telex and telephone lines to Europe and the United States, erected roadblocks at the approaches to Mecca, and declared the mosque and the entire city off limits to newsmen. After some twelve hours,[2] telecommunications were restored, and the first reports began to filter out. The roadblocks stayed, however; no reporters were to get anywhere near the mosque until the Saudis liberated it.

The first fragmentary reports on the mosque situation, broadcast in the United States on the networks' evening news programs on November 20, 1979, sent shock waves through the political and financial world. Ever since the fall of the Shah of Iran, speculation had been rampant that the Saudi monarchy might be vulnerable to the same sort of Islamic revolutionary fervor that had brought the Ayatollah Khomeini to power. Now, it seemed, the nightmare could be coming true, with the area's biggest petro-power in the throes of rebellion. It was a potential catastrophe.

When the news first broke, reporters from all over the Middle East and Europe began frantically trying to get in to Saudi Arabia. Most of them never made it. Typical was the experience of Milt Fullerton, then with ABC, who was in Tunis when he heard about the seizure of the mosque. He made an immediate request for a Saudi visa, just as his colleagues were doing in Washington, in European capitals, and in the Arab world. Neither he nor anyone else from ABC was given a visa, and the network, like most other American news organizations, was forced to "cover" the mosque crisis from the studio.[3]

NBC's James Compton happened to be in Saudi Arabia when the mosque was taken, although this wasn't quite the stroke of luck that NBC hoped it would be. The day after the mosque was seized, John Chancellor laconically noted,

"We have an NBC crew in Saudi Arabia, but its equipment was impounded. Nevertheless, we do have an audio report from correspondent James Compton." Compton's report originated from the Saudi capital, hundreds of miles from the scene of the rebellion.[4]

In fact, throughout the crisis the few reporters who were allowed into the country were kept in Riyadh. This fact, coupled with the total absence of any independent Saudi press, enabled the Saudi rulers to manipulate and control the coverage of the incident from the very beginning. The technique was simple: having totally cut off access to the area, they then established their own version of the events (which was subsequently proved wrong in almost every particular) and made sure that all the senior Saudi officials stuck to it. The press was thus denied even the most elementary information: Who had seized the mosque? Why? When was it liberated? By whom? And perhaps most important, was this an isolated outbreak of religious fanaticism or an attempt to overthrow the Saudi government?

Faced with censorship-by-exclusion, the press had little choice but to parrot the official Saudi answers to these questions. The result was that the American public was kept in the dark for two weeks while the fate of one of the United States' most valued allies hung in the balance. Here is the way it was, day by day:

DAY ONE (NOVEMBER 20):

Terse, thirty-second reports on all three networks about trouble at the mosque.

DAY TWO (NOVEMBER 21):

The New York Times reported, from Washington, MECCA MOSQUE SEIZED BY GUNMEN BELIEVED TO BE MILITANTS FROM IRAN. This belief, which was totally wrong, came from "American intelligence sources," which also told reporter

Philip Taubman that there were no Shi'ite Moslems in Saudi
Arabia. In fact, there are between 150,000 and 250,000, and
they are concentrated in the oil-producing Eastern Province. Taubman's sources, like many others who surfaced in
Washington during the next two weeks, recalled Liebling's
famous maxim: "When information is unavailable the expert comes into his own."[5]

The Washington Post, reporting from Washington, published the official Saudi statement that "the incident was over,"
a whopper that the Saudis repeated with the religiosity of
daily prayers for the next two weeks.

The *Detroit News,* America's ninth largest newspaper, and
one that serves the city with the largest Arab population
in America, had no correspondent in the Middle East.
Throughout the crisis, it made prominent use of wire-service
stories, however. On November 21, it ran an AP dispatch
on page one which strongly suggested that most of the
mosque had already been liberated and that the attack had
been an aberration carried out by a group of religious fanatics. Throughout the U.S., hundreds of newspapers carried this story or its UPI equivalent.

DAY THREE (NOVEMBER 22):

The Washington Post's Edward Cody arrived in Riyadh, the
Saudi capital, and produced a long-distance "thumbsucker"
on the revolt. "The takeover of the sacred Mosque," he said,
"reportedly by Shi'ite Moslems, constituted an unprecedented affront to this conservative Islamic kingdom." According to Cody, it "brought home with brutal intensity to
the Saudi royal family the potential for turmoil in the revolutionary brand of Shi'ite Moslem fundamentalism that has
surged to power in nearby Iran and whose influence is being
felt in several wealthy Persian Gulf countries." It was a good
guess, reflecting the conventional wisdom of the American
State Department and diplomats on the scene, but as it later
turned out, totally wrong. The gunmen were not Shi'ites, had

no connection with Iran, and were motivated by strictly internal Saudi considerations.

CBS News announced on its evening news that the mosque had been liberated. Walter Cronkite read the twenty-second announcement from the studio ("The armed occupation of Islam's holiest shrine, the Great Mosque at Mecca, is over"), thus becoming one of the first American newsmen—but by no means the last—to "liberate" the mosque during the next fortnight.

DAY FOUR (NOVEMBER 23):

The Washington Post headlined its story SAUDIS CAPTURE MOST OF GUNMEN HOLDING MOSQUE, and quoted Saudi officials who said that they had arrested "most of the Moslem extremists who had occupied the shrine," and that "the incident is totally removed from any political motives." Correspondent Cody backtracked on his Shi'ite theory and called the rebels "Madhists" instead.

The *Times* headline, SAUDIS SAY GUNMEN STILL HOLD MOSQUE, was much more cautious (and accurate) than the *Post*'s. The *Times* also reported that there had been gun battles at the Prophet's Mosque in Medina. This was the first hint that the incident in Mecca might have wider implications.

The *Detroit News* published a wire service round-up which assumed that the mosque had already been liberated. Headlined SAUDIS VOW DARK FATE FOR MOSQUE REBELS, it quoted, without comment, the Saudi information minister, who stated that "Saudi troops gained full control of the Grand Mosque of Mecca and were pursuing the last of the Moslem extremists who had seized the building last Tuesday and taken hostages."

At the networks, ABC reported that the Saudis had apparently gained control of the mosque, NBC noted that "some fanatics" still occupied the shrine, and Walter Cronkite on CBS, perhaps embarrassed by his premature evacuation of the day before, spoke sternly of the unreliability of information from Saudi Arabia.

DAY FIVE (NOVEMBER 24):

By now almost all the newspapers had accepted the official Saudi version of events. The mosque had been seized by religious fanatics acting for no political reason; the incident had been confined to Mecca; after three days the Saudis had freed the mosque; and now things were getting back to normal. The *Times* and *Post* both noted that a handful of gunmen were rumored to be still at large, but this was treated as a minor detail.

But the networks, with the advantage of a later deadline, reported that evening that somehow fighting in the "liberated mosque" seemed to be still going on.

DAY SIX (NOVEMBER 25):

The New York Times and *The Washington Post* made two interesting discoveries. One, their reports on the liberation of the mosque had been mistaken—it was still not in Saudi hands; and two, the assumption that the rebels were merely religious fanatics was also wrong—in the words of *Post* correspondent Cody, "their opposition to the Saudi leadership is political as well as religious."

These rather belated discoveries prompted the *Times* to explain the difficulties of covering the story from Saudi Arabia:

"The uprising has, at least temporarily, driven Saudi Arabia back to its reclusive ways, with government officials unavailable to provide information except optimistic remarks about the situation and occasional denials by the Saudi press agency of rumors . . .

"The country, which cut communications to the outside world for twelve hours after the attack, has refused to allow the importation and distribution of English language news publications since then, and has apparently tightened its visa requirements. An English language newspaper, the Arab News, was told it would be closed if its correspondents continued to send dispatches to American newspapers."

Nor, said the *Times,* was this the first time the Saudis had exploited their closed society to hide internal difficulties. "According to various reports the seizure of the Mosque is the most serious in a series of recent problems in Saudi Arabia arising from the tensions over rapid social changes. Diplomatic officials believe that the Saudis have hushed up smaller incidents in recent months."

The *Detroit News,* having freed the mosque two days earlier, ran a five-paragraph story on page 13 saying that Saudi forces were fighting to free it once again. The *News* made no explanation to its readers why the liberated mosque should be the scene of room-to-room fighting.

That evening the networks were once again ahead of their print competitors. This time it was ABC's Sam Donaldson who conveyed the Saudi assurances that now the mosque really had been retaken.

DAY SEVEN (NOVEMBER 26):

Today Edward Cody liberated the mosque for *The Washington Post:* "Saudi Arabian's Islamic religious leadership urged severe punishment today for the band of Moslem fanatics who occupied Mecca's Great Mosque for five days before being overcome early today by Saudi security forces." Only in the eighth paragraph did Cody note the possibility that gunmen were still in the mosque.

The *Times* story, headlined SAUDIS SAY MOSQUE HAS BEEN RETAKEN, agreed. And the *Detroit News* freed the mosque for the third time (SAUDIS ROUT REBELS IN MECCA). That evening the networks reported, once again, that the incident was finally over and the mosque in Saudi hands.

DAY EIGHT (NOVEMBER 27):

Nothing on the networks or in most of the press about the incident, now assumed to be over. The few reporters who had got into Saudi Arabia began to pull up stakes.

DAY NINE (NOVEMBER 28):

It was post-mortem time. *The Washington Post* editorialized that the attack could have an impact comparable to the fall of the Shah of Iran, while the *Times*'s Steven Rattner did an analysis from neighboring Kuwait in which he considered whether the Mecca incident would be good or bad for the United States (bad, he thought).

That night, CBS showed official Saudi film clips of the clean-up crews at the mosque (although it noted off-handedly that there were rumors about rebels still inside), while NBC ran a four-and-a-half minute special on Islam on its evening news program.

And then, silence. The story was over, the revolt had been put down, and there was nothing left to do but read the newsmagazine accounts.*

But the mosque rebellion was not dead—it had simply been buried alive by the press. And on December 1, twelve days after the shrine had been seized, the lid of the coffin slowly began to rise. From Bahrain, Reuters sent out a dispatch that indicated that there were still rebels in the mosque. This rather amazing development was discovered when the Saudis had been unable to hold the usual Friday prayer service. Then, for the next three days, there was more silence.

DAY SIXTEEN (DECEMBER 5):

The Washington Post headline said it all: 130 WERE KILLED AS SAUDIS RECAPTURE MOSQUE. The story was written by Mi-

---

*Newsmagazines, in A. J. Liebling's words, "perform the service of the waiter captain who meets you in front of the smorgasbord and says, 'let me help you make a selection.' Then he fills your plate with all the items the management particularly wants to get rid of. They specialize in réchauffés of newspaper dispatches, livened with sauces prepared on the premises."[6]

chael J. Hall (Edward Cody had long since left Saudi Arabia, perhaps on the theory that the mosque had already been recaptured several times, and that was enough for him), and it revealed that during the night the Saudis had finally managed to liberate the mosque. For more than a week, the American press had been unaware that hundreds of gunmen, along with hundreds more civilian hostages, had been holding out in the shrine. They had, in a word, missed the story.

Naturally, when this came to light, there were some rather embarrassed editors and reporters. *The New York Times* carried a brief wire-service report on page 18 about the battle. The networks gave the story the twenty-second treatment and then moved on to other things. The hapless *Detroit News* (and other papers throughout America that also had relied on the wire services throughout the crisis) ran the story on page 6— LAST OF MECCA FANATICS OUSTED.

It soon became apparent that not only had the press missed the mosque story, it had basically misunderstood the events in Saudi Arabia during the previous two weeks. What had in fact taken place was a concerted and coordinated effort to overthrow the Saudi government. The rebels were not simply religious fanatics (at least not more than the Saudi government itself), but highly motivated political activists, possibly trained in PLO camps in Soviet-controlled South Yemen.[7] Moreover, there were persistent rumors that the attack had been accompanied by simultaneous violence in Medina and Taif.[8]

The press had also been largely unaware of rioting in the strategic oil-producing Eastern Province, where as many as 20,000 Saudi troops had been sent to put down the mostly Shi'ite dissidents. These riots had a decidedly anti-American tone, lasted for several days, and were ended after considerable bloodshed.[9]

The performance of the Saudi armed forces at Mecca— a key question given the Saudi role in guarding its oil fields— was worse than anyone had imagined. On November 24, the Saudis attempted to storm the mosque with more than two thousand elite troops, tanks, and armored personnel carriers. The attack was a fiasco, and the Saudis lost more than five hundred soldiers without taking full control of the mosque. The Saudis apparently then asked for, and received, the assistance of French troops, who were able to enter Mecca and take part in the Saudi operation without being noticed by the press.*[10]

The performance of the elite American press during the siege of the mosque had its comic-opera aspects—the solemn analyses of experts who didn't know anything about Saudi Arabia; the straight-faced dissemination of the most improbable official communiques; the repeated journalistic "liberations" of the mosque; and perhaps most of all, the spectacle of American correspondents with their noses pressed up against the opaque window pane of the United States' "best friend," while American political and financial interests hung in the balance: It all seemed like something out of Evelyn Waugh's *Scoop*. But there was another, more sober, side to the mosque coverage. Far from being atypical, the Saudi behavior toward the American press was entirely in character. Unfortunately, the reaction of the press—its willingness to docilely accept the Saudi restrictions and make do with bogus expertise, and a large dash of local color, was also in character.

Over the past decade, as Saudi Arabia has become increasingly rich and influential, it has become correspondingly secretive. From time to time, when it suits their purpose, the Saudis open a flap of the tent and allow someone to peek

---

*Most of the American public never knew what happened to the surviving rebels, either. On December 3, 1979, former *Village Voice* press critic Alexander Cockburn predicted: "The Saudis have been handling the media with some severity but even their resources will no doubt be strained when the followers of the Madhi have to pay the penalty for their blasphemy by having their heads chopped off. There's nothing like a good beheading to bring the sports reporters out . . ." Cockburn underestimated the Saudis, though. On January 9, 1980, sixty-three rebels were publicly beheaded, as an object lesson, in the town squares of eight Saudi Arabian cities. Such a gory scene was deemed unfit for Western eyes. Heads rolling in the streets of the Kingdom might be misinterpreted by the squeamish as an evidence of Saudi primitivism. So, in a classic case of selective coverage, Western cameramen were simply excluded from the spectacle. Saudi Arabia's official news service released a laconic bulletin on the execution for foreign consumption, and that was that.

inside—and then they lower the flap. In an excellent (and rare) op-ed article in *The Washington Post,* deputy managing editor Richard Harwood once explained how this works:

"All Saudi newspapers were expropriated in 1966 (without compensation to the owners) and were handed over to reliable friends of the ruling family. They are published at the sufferance of the family. And they are subsidized, both directly and indirectly by the government. So they are careful about what they print. At least four broad subjects are off limits: *the Islamic religion; the status of women; military and defense affairs; and the royal family.*" (emphasis added)[11] What Harwood is saying is simple. There is no news in Saudi Arabia about the government (which is synonymous with the royal family), military matters, or significant social and religious issues. What, then, do the Saudi papers report? According to Robert Lacey, author of *The Kingdom,* "the local newspapers are rather like school magazines, complaining about the lunches or the library regulations but not really questioning the basis of the system."[12] Television and radio are, if anything, even more controlled than the print media. Peter Larkin, foreign editor of CBS News, remembers attending a broadcasting conference in Algeria where he met one of the heads of Saudi television. "We got into a long discussion about our problems of access to Saudi Arabia. . . . He looked me straight in the eyes, and this is a smart guy, he was educated at Princeton, and he said, 'You know, I have the same problem.' "[13]

With no local press to contend with, the second step in the Saudi news blackout is the prohibition on resident foreign correspondents. There are no permanent foreign news bureaus in the country, the implications of which became clear during the Mecca mosque incident. Those few reporters who got into Saudi Arabia had been there rarely or never; they had few contacts and lacked the resources resident reporters develop—tipsters who might have told them about the riots in the Eastern Province or the attempted uprisings in other parts of the country, a familiarity with recent social and political trends, or personal friendships with government officials and bureaucrats who could have informed them about the real situation at the mosque.*

The world's press is thus forced to resort to other measures to get the news from Saudi Arabia. One is the use of stringers, who supply stories to foreign news organizations. But the absence of free political discussion or a free press means that these stringers can rarely find out any real news, and even if they do, they are often not free to pass it along. As Harwood noted, "The same prohibitions [on stories about women, Islam, the royal family and military affairs] affect the news supplied to Western clients."[14]

The only way to gather news about Saudi Arabia is, therefore, for reporters to visit the country. And it is here that the Saudis demonstrate their true mastery of the tools of modern news management.

First, they are extremely careful about which reporters are allowed to visit. No one, and certainly not a newsman, is allowed simply to drop in on the Saudis; a visa is required. And these visas are not available to everyone. When I spoke with the foreign editor of *The New York Times*, Craig Whitney, in March 1983, he complained that the *Times* had been trying unsuccessfully for more than a year to get a political reporter into Saudi Arabia.

"It's outrageous," said Whitney. "For a country that is supposedly America's most important Arab ally, they treat reporters, at least from *The New York Times*, worse than the Soviets do.† We try to get visas and are turned down for the flimsiest reasons—I think it's really outrageous." Especially galling to Whitney was the Saudi refusal to allow *Times* Middle East correspondent Thomas Friedman to visit. "Their objection to Friedman is that he knows them too well, he knows and speaks Arabic, he's a student of Arab politics and culture. They know he'll write about things they perhaps don't want to see written about."[15]

---

*Such a situation is rare even for totalitarian states. The Soviet Union, for example, permits resident Western reporters in Moscow, albeit under controlled conditions, and in recent years China has allowed some American news organizations to open bureaus in Peking. Saudi Arabia is one of the few important nations in the world—and certainly the only "pro-Western" one—which enforces a total ban on resident journalists.

† Whitney is a former *Times* Moscow bureau chief.

Other newspapers have had similar experiences with the Saudis. One of them is the *Los Angeles Times.* Doyle McManus was its Middle East correspondent from 1978 to 1981, and Saudi Arabia was a part of his beat. He covered it without ever setting foot in the country.

"I never got a visa. No explanation, I haven't the faintest idea why not. I went to D.C., had lunch with the Saudi ambassador, had a long talk with Fred Dutton [Saudi PR consultant in Washington]. I did all the soft-soaping I would need to do . . . I never found out why I wasn't allowed in. As far as I know, between 1978 and 1981, no one from the *Los Angeles Times* got into Saudi Arabia."[16] McManus's colleague Don Schanche, then stationed in Egypt, was also kept out. "I'm convinced that there was a general Saudi exclusion of most Cairo-based correspondents," he says.[17]

When the Saudis do allow reporters into the country, it is often as members of the press party of some visiting official or as registered representatives to an international conference. These journalists are then sometimes allowed to remain briefly to "report" on approved subjects. A good deal of the news from Saudi Arabia is actually nothing more than a Saudi dateline for such international stories.

Sometimes not even an official visit is enough to get the Saudis to unbend on their restrictive approach to correspondents they don't care for. One such time was in 1975, when the Dutch foreign minister was scheduled to pay an official visit to Saudi Arabia. Jaap Van Wessel, a senior correspondent for the Dutch weekly *Vry Nederland,* asked to join the press contingent that would be accompanying the foreign minister and applied for a visa at the Saudi embassy in The Hague. The application included the question: "Religion?" and Van Wessel wrote, "Jewish." He was informed on the spot that his application had been denied. The incident caused a stir in Holland, and the foreign minister cancelled his scheduled visit in protest.*[18]

---

*During the 1975 visa controversy, Van Wessel asked Secretary of State Henry Kissinger, through one of the State Department correspondents, to raise the question of his exclusion with the Saudis. He never received a reply. Kissinger's own experience as a Jew in Saudi Arabia was summed up in his memoirs: "Oblivious to

It is an index of Saudi sophistication that their admissions policy is carried out in such a way that it has not become a topic in the American press. As McManus says: "There is a reticence to make yourself the center of news. For one thing, the Saudis always handled things very cleverly. They'd just say, 'Oh, no visa yet, sir. Come back next week.' They weren't dumb. One could never actually do a story that said TIMES REPORTER DENIED SAUDI VISA."[20]

Craig Whitney adds: "They don't refuse; it just never happens. They are very subtle that way. You don't apply unless you've already got approval for a visa. How do you get approval for a visa? Well, some member of the royal family invites you. Or once in a while they'll let in a correspondent who's clearly going to write about nothing but oil."[21]

The need to have the sponsorship of a leading Saudi official is one of the ways in which the Saudis influence the work of reporters they allow in. An implicit agreement about what will be written is often a condition of entry, and a deviation from that agreement is not simply an affront to some abstract foreign government, but to a personal contact.

The *Los Angeles Times*'s Otis Chandler, speaking of the Arab world in general put it this way: "As it is with most business and diplomatic endeavors in the Arab world, a journalist's fact gathering depends heavily on unofficial access to information, that is, close personal relationships and contacts. There are implicit dangers in this kind of news gathering, not the least of which is protective self-censorship."[22]

The reporter who does get into Saudi Arabia has been carefully screened and selected. "Usually the journalists they admit are people they consider to be favorable," explains Don Schanche. "In your letter for a visa you must note who you want to see and what you want to do. Then, all plans are made through the government information office."[23] A few

my ancestry—or delicately putting me into a special category—[King] Faisal insisted that an end had to be put, once and for all, to the dual conspiracy of Jews and Communists. . . . It was hard to know where to begin in answering such a line of reasoning. When Faisal went on to argue that the Jewish-Communist conspiracy was now trying to take over the American government, I decided the time had come to change the subject."[19]

reporters have been allowed to wander more or less freely in the country, but this doesn't happen often. And even when it does, the information available to them is very limited. The local press tells them almost nothing, there is no opposition party, and many local citizens, unused to reporters, or to foreigners for that matter, are unwilling to talk candidly. David Aikman, *Time*'s veteran correspondent, says, "You're totally cut off there. Access to Saudi citizens is either controlled or so difficult as to involve unacceptable risks."[24] The result of this is, of course, that Saudis quoted in the American press are almost always delighted with their country, its leaders and policies, and engagingly free of any but the most constructive criticism.

The inability to do serious journalistic work in Saudi Arabia eventually becomes an inhibition on press interest in the country. As Peter Larkin of CBS put it: "Being there isn't so crucial. . . . Our experience over time has been that going to Saudi Arabia doesn't necessarily mean you're going to get anything. It's a very closed society."[25]

The extent to which these restrictions have made Saudi Arabia impenetrable became clear in 1981—the year of the AWACs. Following the debacle at Mecca and the outbreak of the Iran-Iraq War in the Persian Gulf in September 1980, the Saudis were at pains to present themselves as a stable, cooperative, and moderate nation. They wanted to buy $8.5 billion worth of sophisticated military hardware from the United States, and they realized that a positive image would be necessary to get such a controversial arms sale through Congress. They knew, too, that the proposed arms sale would focus massive media attention on their stability and reliability, their attitude toward Arab-Israeli conflict, and the degree of their commitment to American and Western interests in the Persian Gulf.

The Saudis weren't wrong. During 1981, *The New York Times* carried more than 400 articles, editorials, and letters about Saudi Arabia, and *The Washington Post* more than 300. The three networks broadcast more than 300 items that mentioned the kingdom. But on close inspection, it became clear that most of the "reporting" was being done at long range: *The overwhelming majority of the newspaper articles (in most papers as many as 90 percent) were written from outside of Saudi Arabia,* and exactly seven of the television items originated from the country. Mountains of analyses were made from molehills of information, as myth, caricature, and "expertise" replaced firsthand investigation. As Liebling once said, "The expert . . . becomes a national menace when he is substituted for the reporter. This is like substituting whiskey for food—it gives the illusion without the nourishment."[26] Americans who were under the impression, in 1981, that they were being fed a rich Saudi diet woke up after the AWACs sale with a considerable hangover.

There were sound practical reasons for the Saudi press policy in 1981. The country's rulers, and their American advisers, realized that Saudi Arabia—which represses women, practices a kind of medieval feudalism, is crudely anti-Semitic,* and had only recently declared a *jihad* (holy war) against Israel—might suffer under careful inspection by American journalists. During the spring of 1981 they conducted a public relations drive, allowing selected reporters a very controlled and limited view of their country; then, at midyear, they virtually sealed themselves off and stayed that way allowing only one or two "friendly" journalists to enter until the AWACs sale passed the Senate in late October.

The Washington Post, The New York Times, and *Time* magazine, to mention only three, were all included in the spring PR offensive. By mid-March each had carried a major series or story on Saudi Arabia, all of them similar and all reflecting the tight supervision under which their reporters had

---

*In September 1981, shortly before the sale of the AWACs, the government-controlled newspaper al-*Jazira,* in an article entitled THE TORAH AS A SOURCE OF JEWISH WAR CRIMES, said: "The Jewish religion is nothing but a collection of criminal racist principles, sowing cruelty, bloodlust and killing in those who believe in it." Earlier that year, another controlled newspaper, al-*Nadwa,* asserted, "Treachery is the Jews' most prominent feature . . . the hatred of the Jews for the human race knows no bounds . . . in their hearts they seek to do evil, steal and injure others."[27] One can well imagine what would happen were an official Israeli organ to make similar observations about the Arabs; luckily for the Saudis, however, there were no American reporters around to notice these reflections on the Jews, six million of whom are American citizens.

been forced to work.* *The Washington Post* series was typical. Correspondent David Ottoway was unable to find many negative things to report about life in the desert dictatorship.[28] His first article, SAUDI CULTIVATE EUROPEAN LINK TO OFFSET U.S., simply set forth, uncritically, the Saudi warning to the U.S. that it had better sell the AWACs or else it would buy them in Europe. Ottoway based his article on the opinion of "one American diplomat" (obviously Ambassador John West) that "Israel as the arbiter of Saudi defense requirements is intolerable." There was no investigation of any of the relevant questions about the AWACs—Saudi Arabia's capacity to handle the equipment, why it needed such sophisticated weapons, or its degree of potential internal stability. No Saudi officials or leaders were interviewed on these or any other political questions.

The next article in the series was a wrap-up of the Gulf Cooperation Council, through which "Saudi Arabia is reaching out to assert power in the Persian Gulf." It dealt uncritically with the Saudi role in the Gulf and provided no information at all about the country itself, nor did it give any indication that Ottoway had as yet spoken to any Saudi political figures.

On March 4, SAUDIS CAST WARY EYE ON FOREIGN WORKERS dealt with a genuine problem—the potential restiveness of the almost two million foreign workers in the country— entirely from the Saudi point of view, treating as axiomatic the premise that foreigners are automatically a security threat. Ottoway made no mention of the severe discrimination against these workers, although in the fifth paragraph he noted offhandedly that as many as sixty thousand had been deported by the Saudis in the previous three months. The

*Occasionally, reporters have the temerity not only to get information about Saudi Arabia's forbidden subjects, but to print it. One such correspondent was David Ignatius of *The Wall Street Journal*. At the beginning of his tenure as the *Journal*'s Middle East correspondent, he put together a series on corruption in the royal family. The articles were a detailed, aggressive account of malfeasence on a grand scale by members of the ruling class of the country. The Saudi reaction was unequivocal; Ignatius was blackballed, and his recurrent visa applications turned down. The use of this threat, the denial of a visa next time in reprisal for an unwanted story this time, can be a powerful tool for keeping reporters within the confines of acceptable criticism.

only Saudi official with whom he spoke was Hisham Nazer, the economic planning minister, and most of the article was given over to Nazer's explanations of Saudi development plans.

The following day, March 5, Ottoway visited a Red Sea deep-water port to see, firsthand, a major Saudi development project. He wrote admiringly about what he had been shown, again quoting only one Saudi official—"Hisham Nazer, the Kingdom's highly articulate planning minister."

On March 6, Ottoway wrote about Saudi oil policy. He cited a six-week-old speech by oil minister Yamani, and quoted Ambassador West and "Hisham Nazer, the Minister of Planning." Ottoway accepted the Saudi argument that by producing more oil than they need, they are doing the West a favor. He also quoted without comment Nazer's veiled threat that production might have to be slowed down.

The last article, on March 10, RUSH INTO THE FUTURE TARNISHES THE PAST IN SAUDI PORT CITY, was simply a story about modernization and urban planning in the city of Jedda.

Ottoway thus had been forced to observe Harwood's list of restricted subjects and dealt only with topics the Saudi government wanted discussed: its development program, its problem with foreign workers, its moderate and reasonable oil production policies, its growing influence in the Persian Gulf, and its determination to buy American AWACs or take its business to Europe. It was a series that could have been written, in its entirety, by a Saudi government public relations officer. *The Washington Post*'s major series on Saudi Arabia in the crucial AWACs year contained no on-the-record discussions with government officials other than the minister of planning; ignored questions regarding the country's social fabric, politics, military preparedness, discrimination against women and minorities, or anti-Israel activities; and, perhaps most remarkably, made no acknowledgment that this selection of topics was, in any sense, imposed (that is, assuming that Ottoway didn't *prefer* to ignore all political and military issues).

Between March 23 and March 27, *The New York Times* did *its* series on the kingdom, reported by correspondent Pranay

B. Gupte. Those who had read Ottoway's pieces in the *Post* might have felt that they were seeing a rerun. The titles of the articles tell the story: SWEPT BY CHANGE, SAUDIS FEAR LOSS OF OLD VALUES, SAUDIS DON'T PLAN TO CUT OIL OUTPUT, YAMANI SAYS, SAUDI OIL REVENUES SEEM TO OUTSTRIP NATIONS CAPACITY TO PUT THEM TO USE, SAUDIS AIM FOR A HARMONIOUS SOCIETY OF NEW MACHINES AND OLD TRADITIONS, ON SAUDI ARABIA'S PATH TO PROSPERITY: LONG TRAIL OF ABANDONED AUTOMOBILES, AND SAUDI-IZED CITIBANK RETAINS STRENGTH. Their tone, like the *Post*'s, was admiring, uncritical, and respectful. The Saudi oil policy was presented as an altruistic "I'm-too-good-for-my-own-good" favor to the United States. U.S. Ambassador John West once again served as the Saudi spokesman and told Gupte: "I personally think the interests of the U.S. would be best served by not following the advice, counsel and exhortations that the friends of Israel provide so freely."* On the crucial issue of Saudi stability, West said: "Can Iran repeat itself here in the kingdom? My answer would be no." And that opinion, unchallenged by any eyewitness reporting or discussions with Saudis, is all the *Times*'s readers got.

The Saudi March 1981 PR drive was also taken up by *Time* magazine. On March 16 it provided what, with typical modesty, it termed a "comprehensive assessment" of the country by William Stewart. It was, in fact, an open-mouthed look at what the Saudis were selling—their need for AWACs, their nice-guy oil policy, and their growing influence in the Arab world. Stewart glossed over Saudi corruption, dealt with the status of women in half a paragraph, and noted that "Riyadh lately has also called for a *jihad*, or Holy Crusade, to liberate the occupied territories"—as if declaring a holy war on an American friend was normal occurrence. Stewart cast the "surprisingly popular King Khalid" and the "amia-

*West's own advice is not given freely, at least not since he left government service. In 1982, the *Miami Herald* reported that the ex-ambassador had become "a director of two U.S. companies that have substantial business connections to Saudi Arabia," and that he could earn as much as $40,000 for serving on the board of one of them. West has also not been above running errands for the Saudis; in April 1982, for example, he went to bat for a Saudi prince whose apartment was raided by Miami police—on suspicion of slaveholding.[29]

ble and energetic" Prince Fahd in the role of benevolent
desert democrats; had the mayor of Jedda boyishly confess
that "our biggest problem has been too rapid expansion";
and quoted the ubiquitous Hisham Nazer on the egalitarian
nature of Saudi society. The article ended by quoting a Saudi
technocrat who summed up his country as " 'What shall I
say—humble. The spirit, the core is still there.' "[30]

An American who had read the two series in the *Times*
and *Post* and the article in *Time* would be entitled to regard
himself as well informed about Saudi Arabia. This would be
so—provided he wasn't interested in the nature of the Saudi
political system, the existence of a special religious police force
to enforce public morality, the discrimination and second-
class status of Shi'ite Saudis in the Eastern Province, the internal politics and rivalries of the governing family, human
rights, freedom of the press, the preparedness of the Saudi
military and the quality of its armed forces, the Saudi role
in bankrolling the PLO, Saudi leadership of the economic
boycott against Israeli and Jewish business interests, and so
forth—subjects which understandably pale in importance
compared to the Jedda urban renewal plan or the deep-sea
port at Yanbu.

There were other journalistic highlights from Saudi
Arabia during the year of the AWACs. One came on May
13, when *The New York Times* carried an article on the status
of women in Saudi Arabia, with which, it became clear, Saudi
women themselves, are mightily pleased. Correspondent
Gupte quoted Samira al-Fawzan: " 'If a woman in Saudi
Arabia wants to work she can. The veil won't stop you. In
running a business I am contributing to the economic growth
of Saudi Arabia and I am doing so by observing all our Islamic traditions and practices.' " He also spoke to Wassa
Hakim, who said, " 'I don't think our women should go as
far as Western women do. We don't usually discuss things
like politics, for instance, but these are things that as women
don't concern us.' " Of course Gupte didn't ignore the fem-
inists. He spoke to one twenty-year-old who, while generally
satisfied, admitted she would like the freedom to drive a car

and to travel—which women are not allowed to do in the desert democracy.[31] It is not easy to imagine the *Times* (or any other American newspaper) publishing such a sympathetic article about the repression of women anywhere else in the world.

But if the Saudis had a Pulitzer Prize, it would undoubtedly have been awarded in 1981 to *Time* magazine for its handling of the Fahd peace plan. The plan was first advanced in August 1981 and, in the absence of correspondents in Riyadh, was reported off the radio from Beirut and Cairo.[32] The plan was couched in ambiguous language, calling for "recognition of the rights of all states (or peoples, as it later emerged in the Saudi official translation)[33] to live in peace." Israel immediately pointed out that if the term is *states,* then Saudi Arabia doesn't recognize Israel as one; whereas if it is *peoples,* it clearly would not imply recognition of the *state* of Israel. Either way, in the Israeli view, the Fahd plan was far from clear about whether Israel was included or not.

Some of the journalists in the region believed that the Saudis had indeed intended to include Israel, even though the Jewish state had not been directly mentioned in the plan. Their hunch was not good enough for *Time,* however, which, in a headline, flatly asserted CROWN PRINCE FAHD SPEAKS OF ISRAEL'S RIGHT TO "LIVE IN PEACE." In the story itself, *Time* again reported that "Fahd stated that Israel 'could live in peace' with its Arab neighbors."[34]

This venture of *Time*'s into creative journalism fooled a number of its readers, one of whom was apparently the Saudi ambassador to the UN, Gaafar M. Aliagany, who declared that the Fahd plan "recognized Israel and that recognition was the core of the proposal." If *Time* editor Henry Grunwald had been running Saudi Arabia, instead of the Saudi princes, the ambassador would have been on solid ground. As it was, the Saudi government published an official statement denying that the UN delegate knew what he was talking about.[35]

Time, of course, never mentioned this development, which didn't fit into its Middle East diplomacy.

* * *

At the end of October, the AWACs sale went through. Fittingly, *The New York Times* ran a story on its front page about the Saudi reaction to the sale—written by its correspondent in Beirut, while *The Washington Post*'s reaction story came from its reporter in Cairo. America's newsmen couldn't get into Saudi Arabia even to cover its victory celebration. The Saudis, as Edward Cody once wrote during the Grand Mosque crisis, "demonstrated for westerners the extent to which an absolute monarchy, particularly in the Saudi tradition of privacy, is free of the need to keep its subjects informed."[36] Other countries' subjects, too.

8

BEHIND THE DAMASK CURTAIN

In 1982, there were two bloody massacres in the Middle East. One was in Hama, Syria, in February; the other, at the Sabra and Shatilla refugee camps near Beirut, in September.

There were remarkable similarities between the two events. Both in Hama and at Sabra and Shatilla, armed men entered civilian areas and wantonly slaughtered innocent civilians, including women and children. In both cases the murders were acting on orders, but were also consumed with the dehumanizing hatred that rival religious and ethnic groups often feel for each other in the Arab Middle East. In Syria and in Lebanon, the death toll was awful. Hundreds of civilians were killed at the Sabra and Shatilla camps; thousands, perhaps tens of thousands, at Hama. And when it was over, the killers in both places tried to deny that any massacre had taken place.

Yet for all their similarity, there was one great difference between the two mass murders. The Sabra and Shatilla massacre instantly (and properly) became one of the most infamous events of recent times. Thousands of newspaper articles, television reports, and photographs documented the

177

atrocity. *Time* and *Newsweek* devoted cover stories to it, ABC did a special hour-long documentary. American newsmen won Pulitzer Prizes for their work there.

In Israel, a special judicial commission, headed by the Chief Justice of the Supreme Court, determined that Israel had no direct blame for what had happened—no Israelis had been in the camps, and none had participated in the killing—but bore a heavy measure of indirect responsibility. Defense Minister Ariel Sharon and the head of military intelligence were forced to resign. Hundreds more articles were written about the commission's work and its repercussions. Sabra and Shatilla became household words in the United States.

Things were different at Hama. For almost three weeks the Syrian army methodically destroyed a good part of Syria's third largest city. Whole neighborhoods the size of Sabra or Shatilla were simply leveled. Thousands were killed in what was, by all accounts, one of the biggest mass murders in the history of the modern Arab world.[1] And yet, unlike the massacre in Lebanon, it was carried out in almost total privacy, shielded from view by the Syrian government's censorship-by-exclusion and by the indifference of the American press. There were no eyewitness reports of the massacre in the Syrian city. No network produced a retrospective documentary about its victims. There were no cover stories in the national news magazines. And no one won a Pulitzer at Hama.

In fact, no American reporter got to Hama at all, not until the streets had been swept clean of debris. It was too late then to record the scattered corpses of children lying next to their mothers in the street or the awful wailing of the orphans. For most Americans, it was as if Hama had never happened at all. . . .

Among the violent and dictatorial regimes of the Arab world, the Ba'athist government of Hafez Assad has a special place. Assad has ruled Syria since he seized power in a coup in November 1970,* a record for longevity in a coun-

*He became president in 1971.

try not previously known for the life expectancy of its leaders. One of the Syrian president's first acts was to establish the special defense units, made up of fellow Alawites of unquestioned personal loyalty and commanded by his brother Rifat. These forces—a kind of Ba'athist "Tonton Macute"—keep order through repression and terror. In Syria, political arrests are common, and often, suspects simply disappear. This is, of course, perfectly legal, for under Assad a perpetual state of emergency is in force, and with it the suspension of all constitutional rights in matters of arrest and detention.[2] Nor is there any recourse. There is no free press in Syria, no parliamentary opposition, no elections—there is only Assad and his party.

And yet, despite the police-state tactics of the Syrian government, dissent began to grow in the late 1970s. Like much political activity in the Arab world, it was rooted in conflict between religious and ethnic groups. Hafez Assad is an Alawite, a breakaway sect of Islam which makes up about fifteen percent of Syria's population. Traditionally, Alawites have been despised by the Sunni Moslem majority, who consider them crude and rustic and look down on their religion as an off-brand form of Islam. Beginning in 1979, the fanatical and mysterious Sunni Moslem Brotherhood began to harass the Assad regime. Ba'athist officials came under attack, party and government buildings were sabotaged, and there was even an attempt on the life of the Syrian president. The ringleaders of this antigovernment agitation were believed to be in the Syrian cities of Homs, Aleppo, and especially Hama.

The regime responded with a series of mass arrests and executions. In January 1981, there was reportedly a police action in Aleppo in which two hundred suspected dissidents were shot to death in the town square;[3] in April of that year, hundreds more were killed in Hama.[4] Despite this stern response, the rebellion continued to simmer. In August, a bomb exploded in the Damascus office of the Syrian prime minister.[5] Two weeks later, a booby-trapped car exploded in front of the Syrian air force headquarters in Damascus, killing twenty and injuring fifty more.[6] Then, in November, the

Syrian capital was rocked by a car bomb, which killed more than ninety civilians and wounded 135.[7] Each of these incidents brought on a new wave of arrests and more government pressure.

In early January 1982, there was a coup attempt against Assad. It was caught in time, and its ringleaders, including a colonel, were executed. The Syrians tried to keep it a secret, but word began to filter out in early February.[8] It was then that Assad apparently decided to put an end, once and for all, to the dissent.

On the night of February 2, Hama was surrounded by eight thousand government troops, led by Rifat Assad. A raiding party began to comb the houses in the winding labyrinth in the center of Hama's open-air marketplace. According to a story that was widely reported but never confirmed, the Syrian scouts were ambushed in a dark alley by Moslem Brothers, who then seized the loudspeakers of the city's mosques and called for insurrection against the Alawite infidels. This was the provocation that the government troops have been waiting for. They opened fire on the city with artillery and tanks and began to level whole neighborhoods. The massacre of Hama had begun.

For nine days Syrian guns battered Hama, killing thousands of innocent civilians and leaving tens of thousands homeless. Yet during these nine days virtually no word of the massacre reached the West. As John Kifner of *The New York Times*, who first wrote about the incident on February 11, noted, "A strict blackout kept news of the uprising from circulating here [Damascus] until today."[9]

The Assads were able to keep the lid on the Hama massacre for more than a week, but even they couldn't hide it indefinitely. Rumors began to circulate in the Syrian underground, and some of them were picked up by diplomats, who forwarded them to their ministries abroad. Foreign editors got the word and informed their correspondents in the Middle East. No one had any doubt that if the rumors were true, something major was going on. As Seth Lipsky, foreign editor of *The Wall Street Journal*, later said: "It was a spectacularly important story, a really seminal story. It really told you a lot about the character of the government there and the size of the problem. I mean, imagine if the American government surrounded Cleveland, Ohio, or someplace and blew most of it away in an effort to put down some kind of domestic rebellion. It would be just mind-boggling." [10]

What happened in Hama *was* mind-boggling, and foreign reporters began to come to Syria to see it for themselves. The government allowed them into Damascus, and kept them there, more than one hundred miles from the scene of the fighting.

The Syrians weren't at all bashful about making their ground rules known. Reporters, who began arriving in Damascus on February 10, were called together by Minister of Information Ahmed Iskander and informed that a search for weapons was going on in Hama and that the city was off limits; [11] when they grumbled about the restriction, Syrian officials privately warned them that trying to visit the besieged city would be "life threatening." [12] This was confirmed by the few correspondents who made an effort to go to Hama. The *Philadelphia Inquirer* correspondent, Richard Ben Cramer, got as far as the city limits when he was stopped by Syrian soldiers. "If you want to die, go on," his driver was told by a soldier. "There's three thousand dead already." [13] The assembled journalists, many of whom remembered the Syrian attacks on their colleagues in Beirut, took the threat seriously. Some, like John Kifner, even conducted their telephone conversations with their editors in code. [14] And yet, despite the palpable danger of angering Syrian authorities, the journalists in Damascus wrote what they knew. It was a brave performance, but flawed by one basic fact—under the circumstances, they knew hardly anything at all.

No American newspaper tried harder than *The New York Times*. It sent Kifner to Damascus, and in his first dispatch, on February 11, he noted that the fighting had begun in Hama more than a week earlier, and according to evacuated Japanese businessmen and Western diplomats, the town was being bombarded and civilian deaths were estimated at "more than one thousand." Kifner stated that the identity of the rebels was "not immediately clear," although it was assumed that they were Moslem Brothers. He cited the strict news blackout on events in the city and said that U.S. State Department reports about the situation in Hama were being branded as lies by the Syrian government.[15]

It was a good beginning, setting forth the situation as it was known in Damascus on the day Kifner arrived. During the next week, however, the total lack of access to the scene of the fighting compelled the *Times* to print virtually the same story day after day. Kifner made an effort to get more information, talking to "a traveler near Hama on Wednesday," or to "Japanese evacuees," and of course, to "Western diplomats," but none of them could tell him very much.

On Sunday, February 14, the *Times*'s "Week in Review" section summed up what was known after two weeks: "A Syrian army raid February 2 on Moslem Brotherhood cells in the northern city of Hama mushroomed into a bloody embarrassment for the regime of President Hafez el-Assad."

"Not much more than that could be said with certainty last week about the fighting in Hama."

Five days later, on February 19, there was still no news. Kifner wrote of an unconfirmed rumor that the Syrian government was razing much of the city and that diplomats believed that thousands had been killed. The rest of his story was a simple rehearsal of the few facts and several rumors that he had been recycling all week. He noted once again that "the government has declined to give any details of the fighting" and that "Western journalists have been warned not to go to the area."[16] Fed up, Kifner left Damascus and returned to Beirut, and most of his colleagues, equally frustrated, did the same.

Between February 20 and the end of May, the *Times*'s coverage of Hama consisted of three reports. From Beirut, on February 24, Kifner filed the official Syrian version of the massacre, noting yet again that foreign correspondents had been kept out of the city; on March 8, a *Times* report on a Syrian accusation that the United States was supplying Syrian insurgents with weapons made a passing reference to Hama; and on March 24, Henry Tanner wrote a story from

Damascus in which he quoted a government official as saying that Hama was "more or less quiet," although Tanner himself was not allowed to visit the city. And that was all, until *Times* correspondent Thomas Friedman was allowed to visit Hama in late May, and write, retrospectively, the story of the massacre.

As fragmentary as the *Times*'s coverage was, it was far better than almost any other American news organization. *The Washington Post,* for example, didn't bother to send a reporter to Syria until February 15. The correspondent, Edward Cody, filed two dispatches from the Syrian capital and then turned around and went back to Beirut. Most of the *Post*'s coverage came from wire-service reports or radio monitoring, and the stories were run far back in the paper.* Throughout February, the massacre at Hama never made *The Washington Post*'s front page.

Most American newspapers relied on the wire services and paid the story little attention. The *Detroit News,* for example, carried only two reports. The first was an AP dispatch on February 11, headlined HUNDREDS DIE AS TWO SYRIAN SECTS CLASH—thus characterizing the government of Syria as a sect. The following day it ran a combined AP-UPI report saying that the U.S. State Department considered the situation in Hama serious and that as many as two thousand people had been killed in ten days of fighting. That apparently exhausted the attention span of the *News*'s editors, who never bothered their readers again with the unpleasant story. Nor was the *News* coverage atypical; most American papers did as little or less.

Time magazine covered Hama in two articles, on March 8 and March 29. In the first it simply repeated the few facts that were known to the press, although it significantly failed to mention that the Syrians had not allowed any reporters to visit the city. It was only in the second article, in which *Time* published some "exclusive photographs" from Hama, that the magazine emphasized that the city had been off limits to the press. It would be comforting to think that *Time* did

_____
*The *Post*'s initial article on Hama ran on page 36; Cody's reports were carried on pages 28 and 10.

so in order to help the reader evaluate information coming out of Hama, although it looked suspiciously as though *Time* was trying to point out what a great scoop the photographs were.

American television treated the massacre as a matter of little importance. In this regard, NBC was typical. On February 10, *NBC Nightly News* anchorman John Chancellor introduced the week-old mass murder this way: "An uprising has been reported in Syria, and it looks serious. The Syrian authorities have sealed off the city of Hama, north of Damascus. There have been rebellions against the government before in Syria, in 1979 and 1980. But the fighting this time has been going on for a week and apparently is not over."

The next *NBC Nightly News* report was on February 12: "Syria said today that its soldiers are continuing the battle against Moslem extremists in the city of Hama. The government said it has arrested scores of what it calls criminals and fugitives and has seized large quantities of weapons."

On February 13, NBC's *evening news broadcast* devoted another twenty seconds to the situation in Syria, and on the following day it had a report from correspondent Vic Aiken in Damascus. Aiken called the slaughter "an outbreak of violence," and spoke of "vicious battles being fought," but, like anchorman Chancellor, didn't mention civilian casualties at all. In the absence of film from the city, Aiken showed pictures of the bazaar in Damascus.

Throughout the Hama crisis, NBC, and especially John Chancellor, displayed a considerable equanimity. Lest this be misconstrued as indifference to the Middle East, however, Chancellor's news show did carry one major "Arab story" that week—an item on Arabian stallions, on February 12. NBC devoted two minutes to the training of Arab horses, approximately the same amount of time it had devoted throughout the week to the murder of thousands of Arab people.

ABC and CBS were not quite as crass as NBC, but neither of them treated the massacre as a major story. Their coverage began on February 10 and ended within a week. Almost all their reports were little more than brief wire-service items read from the studio, and despite efforts on their part, none got any footage from the city. CBS Vice-President John Lane, looking back on the incident, summed it up sadly: "I don't think we covered that story." [17]

There is a tendency at the networks to explain the failure to cover the massacre on technical grounds. The problem, American television executives say, is that television was prevented from getting into the city and thus was unable to get footage of the slaughter. And for a visual medium, this virtually guarantees the absence of more than superficial coverage.

This explanation is only superficially plausible for it fails to take into account previous stories that, despite the lack of "visuals," were given major attention in the United States. One recent example was the shooting down of a Korean airliner by the Soviet Union in September 1983. Needless to say, there was no footage of the airliner being shot down or even any film of the downed aircraft and its victims. Nevertheless, television (along with the newspapers) gave the incident massive attention.

Had they been concerned about the slaughter of thousands of civilians at Hama, the networks had a number of options. They might have interviewed Americans of Syrian origin who had once lived in the city or had relatives there; shown file footage of Hama and on the Moslem Brotherhood; interviewed State Department officials on the situation in Hama; offered commentary (as John Chancellor did, for instance, a few months later, during the war in Lebanon); blacked out their screens in protest over Syrian censorship by exclusion (as happened during the Lebanon war as a protest against Israel's military censorship); and so on. The fact that they did none of these things indicates that the networks' sparse coverage of the February massacre was, at least in large part, simple indifference.

Although there were persistent rumors about the civilian death toll in Hama, it took months for the true size of the tragedy to become evident. On April 1, 1982, the *Christian Science Monitor*'s John Yemma wrote, "Estimates of the number killed in the three weeks uprising and army coun-

terattack range from a conservative 5,000 to 13,000." To put
the latter figure in perspective, 13,000 is approximately the
number of Israelis who have been killed in all Israel's wars.
Yemma's article was the first indication that something truly
extraordinary had happened in the Syrian city.[18]

On May 3, Edward Cody visited Hama, one of the first
American journalists to do so, and reported: "The scale of
the retribution meted out by President Hafez Assad's government against Moslem Brotherhood rebels has become
clear only recently, as the city, for weeks closed to outsiders,
has been reopened. More than two months after the siege,
the scene is still one of widespread damage. . . .

"The cost of lives was also high. Diplomatic sources estimate that more than 5,000 civilians were killed. There are
an estimated 20,000 orphans."[19]

A few days later, *Wall Street Journal* correspondent David
Ignatius got a look at Hama. Unable to get permission from
the Syrian authorities to visit, he boarded a bus in Damascus
for Aleppo, and its route took him through the Syrian city.
According to Ignatius: "Up to ten thousand residents died
in the confrontation . . . yet little news of the battle or its
aftermath has reached the west."[20]

Perhaps the most ghastly account of what took place was
provided by the prestigious British weekly *Economist:* "Estimates of the numbers killed range up to more than 30,000
(including the army's own losses). The Brotherhood's estimate is 9,000 killed, but that is a hospital figure and does
not include people buried without being reported to hospitals. Neither mosques nor churches were spared (in Hama,
some 8,000 Christians of several different sects had long lived
peacefully among the Sunni Moslem majority). There was
widespread looting, and charges that the soldiers also perpetrated many rapes seem to be supported by the fact that
scores of Hama women have asked for abortions—something normally unheard of in this very conservative society."[21]

It is easy to sympathize with reporters and editors whose
efforts to get the news from Hama were stymied by the Syrian authorities. They at least tried (although some, like *The*

New York Times, tried harder than others). A few, such as Edward Cody of *The Washington Post,* Thomas Friedman of *The New York Times,* and David Ignatius of *The Wall Street Journal* did go to Hama when the city was reopened, for a retrospective view of what had happened there. Most news organizations, however, did not. Neither *Time* magazine nor the networks ever bothered to inform the public of the facts about Hama as they came to be known in May and early June, and this failure is one of the principal reasons that the massacre remains largely unknown in the United States.

Perhaps the most mysterious aspect of the American press's treatment of the massacre was the almost total apathy it evoked from the nation's opinion makers—columnists, commentators, and editorial writers. Unlike their colleagues on the news side, they do not need a firsthand view of events to practice their art. On the contrary, they sit at home and attempt to make sense of distant developments, to put them into perspective and explain their practical and moral significance.

In the case of Hama, the pundits had an additional role. In the face of the Syrian news blackout, they were the ones whose job it was to denounce the Assad government's brutality and censorship. And later, when the magnitude of the massacre became clear, it would have been natural for them to deplore the atrocities and examine the motives of the Syrians.

It didn't work out that way, however. During the actual massacre, in February, only a tiny handful of newspapers expressed any editorial opinion on what was going on in Hama. One that did (and, in doing so, demonstrated what a concerned newspaper *could* say) was the *Los Angeles Times,* which noted, on February 19, that the fighting, "so far has claimed an estimated 3,000 civilian casualties . . ."[22] Most other major newspapers, and virtually all the national commentators, simply ignored the entire affair.

Even later, Hama failed to excite the interest of America's opinion makers. *The New York Times* did publish one editorial, in June, but this was an isolated occurrence. The *Times* columnists were silent. Even Anthony Lewis, who has written passionately about the Middle East and often has been critical of Israel's mean-spirited refusal to conform to Mr. Lewis's own Olympian standards of morality, had nothing to say about the slaughter of thousands of innocent civilians.

The Washington Post did even less. It *never* published an editorial on Hama, and none of its regular columnists, not even the hawk-eyed Mary McGrory, wasted a single word on the massacre. In fact, the only article ever to appear on the *Post*'s op-ed page on this subject was a singular column written by *Post* assistant managing editor for foreign news, Jim Hoagland.

Considering the traditional separation of "church and state" that keeps newspeople at a distance from the opinion page, Hoagland's article was something of an event, signaling his desire to address a major issue. On closer inspection, however, it became apparent that Hoagland's column was not a denunciation of the Syrians for their brutality, but a spirited defense of, among other things, the *Post*'s coverage of the massacre. Hoagland felt that this coverage had, under his guidance, been pretty damn good, and that while the critics were carping about American journalistic shortcomings, "the *Post* and other Western organizations were in Damascus sending detailed accounts of the bloody fighting in Hama."[23]

Whether the *Post*'s correspondent Edward Cody had provided "detailed accounts" in his two articles from Damascus is a matter of opinion; Cody's, apparently, was that he had not. In late May, on his first visit to Hama, Cody wrote that "only recently" (two months after Hoagland's column) had "the scale of retribution meted out by President Hafez Assad's government . . . become clear."[24] But even if Hoagland had been correct, it still would have been curious that the only article concerning Hama ever to appear on *The Washington Post* op-ed page had to do not with the suffering of the victims, or the behavior of the Syrian government, but with the good work done by the *Post*.*

---

*The massacre at Hama was not without its admirers. On June 29, 1983, in an article labeled "News Analysis," *Post* correspondent Jonathan Randal argued, "What

It is striking how similar press coverage of Hama was to that of the Saudi Great Mosque incident two years before. In both cases the authorities calculated that the press would try to get the story, fail, and then let the entire matter fade away. And that is essentially what happened. Hama and Mecca were both victories for "censorship by exclusion" over the right of the public to know.

As in the case of Saudi Arabia, Syria could never have achieved such successful news management without years of systematic censorship. Damascus, like Riyadh, has no resident correspondents. Normally, it is "covered" from neighboring Lebanon, and with the help of a few local stringers who are generally understood to be agents or informers of Syrian military intelligence. Nor does Syria have an independent press of its own. Reporters who want information about Syria must make special arrangements to go there and look for themselves.

It is easier to get a Syrian visa than a Saudi one, and normally most Western journalists have no trouble getting into Syria.* But reporters find it is difficult to actually come up with any news, and even when things are "normal," there is little access. The first problem, most agree, is the sense that they are constantly under surveillance. "When you get there, they try to stick you with a car and an 'interpreter,' and presumably they follow you," says Don Schanche. "A condition for getting a room at the Semiramis Hotel is that you hire a particular driver, who is quite clearly there to watch you. Not only that—they go through your bags in the hotel and don't bother to hide it. It's quite chilling."[26] Jonathan Broder of the *Chicago Tribune* had the same experience. "I

emerged from the Hama rubble, according to local residents, was a respect for the government in large part born of fear but also of a feeling of avoiding even greater catastrophe. Some analysts have argued that the destruction of Hama, an anti-government center since the days of the Ottoman Empire, marked the birth of modern Syria and the triumph of centralized power."[25]

*Not all correspondents, however. In 1976, for example, the late Joe Alex Morris of the *Los Angeles Times,* who was later killed in Iran, saw and reported that Syrian troops were pouring across the border into Lebanon at a time when Syria was claiming that this was not taking place. The Syrians cancelled Morris's visa and kept him out of the country for more than a year. Similarly, Hans Benedict of Australian telelvision has persistently attempted to enter Syria—and has been turned down on more than twenty-five visa applications.

always assumed I was being watched by Syrian agents, and I *knew* they were going through my bags every night at the Sheraton; they didn't even put the things back in the same way. They *wanted* you to know."[27]

The close supervision of correspondents—indeed, of all foreigners—by the authorities is well known to the average Syrian, who is prudently unwilling to discuss the country's problems with outsiders. Douglas Watson, former regional correspondent of the *Baltimore Sun,* and today correspondent for *U.S. News and World Report,* visited Syria a number of times, but never really made any local contacts. "I met a couple of Syrians, but I was never quite sure who they were or what they were. Even with them, I needed to be extremely careful about where we met. There are secret police in all the hotels, and you're always under observation."[28]

The understandable inhibition of Syrians to talk freely is a considerable barrier to news gathering, especially in the absence of an independent local press. It means that the visiting journalist must deal primarily with Syrian officials. This is especially unfortunate, because most Syrian officials won't have anything to do with them.

"Usually you get to see only an official of the Ministry of Information," says Jonathan Broder, "and then they only say what they're supposed to say. You can't find anything out beyond the government line."[29]

"The more closed and restricted a place, the more you rely on the U.S. embassy," adds Douglas Watson. In fact, American diplomats and, to a lesser extent, other European envoys in Damascus, are the primary, and often, as in the case of Hama, almost the only sources of information about the country. This troubles some correspondents, who wonder how much the diplomats themselves really know; and worse, to what extent they influence coverage to reflect the institutional perceptions and interests of the American State Department.

It is not only hard to gather independent, reliable information in Syria; it can also be difficult, and sometimes dangerous, to send it.

"Once, I was staying at the new Sheraton Hotel in Damascus," recalls Douglas Watson, "and I did a piece on the anniversary of the October War. It wasn't political, mainly it was a history of the war itself, and naturally I mentioned Israel in the story.

"There was no sensitive information in the story at all. You're supposed to get clearance from the military censor, but I didn't. I filed the report from the hotel Telex, and went to my room.

"A while later, the manager of the hotel called me and told me to come to his office urgently. He greeted me by saying, 'You are in deep trouble. My whole hotel is in deep trouble, because of you. You don't mention things like Israel in cable dispatches from here!' "[30]

Watson debated whether to make a run for the airport, then decided to stick it out. Nothing happened to him, but he was keenly aware that the Syrians had, in the past, shot correspondents in Lebanon for stories they didn't like. He began to take notes and gather information in Syria and then to file his stories from outside the country. Even this technique, however, has its limitations, because articles in the American press may get back to the authorities in Damascus. Milt Fullerton of NBC says, "I simply assumed that the Syrians wouldn't let me return if I did a story they didn't like."[31] Syria's border with Israel and the fact that fighting can flare up at almost any time (as it did, for example, in June 1982) make it imperative for Middle East reporters to be able to get back into the country at short notice. The loss of a visa can be a serious professional problem.

The exceptional restrictions on the work of Western journalists and the obstacles to normal reporting that they face have given birth to some rather strange reportorial techniques. One of them is exemplified by the "news analysis" on Soviet-Syrian relations written by The Washington Post's Stuart Auerbach from Damascus on May 15, 1981. Auerbach, whose regular post was in India, knew very little about his subject—a difficult starting point for any analyst. His job was made even harder by the fact, obvious from the article itself, that he never got to speak with a single Syrian official. Accordingly, the *Post*'s "analysis" was sourced in the following way:

"According to Western and Asian diplomats here . . . diplomats here say . . . Syria is not a Soviet puppet, declared one West European diplomat . . . the Soviets were said to be angered . . . Moscow appears unable . . . the Soviets are seen . . . the current crisis is seen here . . . said one diplomat . . . an editorial this week in Al Ba'ath said . . . but in the view of these Asian and Western diplomats . . ." and so on.[32]

Another way in which Syria is "covered" is by substituting local official newspapers for contacts with government functionaries who are usually unavailable. *The Washington Post*'s Loren Jenkins did such an "interview" with the Syrian newspaper *Tishrin,* on December 6, 1981. His topic was Syrian anger with the United States during the visit of U.S. envoy Philip Habib to Damascus.

"In an editorial in the official Syrian newspaper Tishrin," Jenkins began his article, and went on to source it this way:

"In the editorial Syria also vowed . . . the editorial charged that the US-Israeli agreement . . . today's editorial accused the United States of involvement . . . Tishrin today termed it 'an American Zionist reactionary gift' . . . the newspaper said . . . the newspaper declared . . . the Syrian newspaper charged . . . " and so forth.[33] Jenkins was presenting the available information, but not the full picture. He was unable to determine whether the Syrian anger was simulated or real, a tactic or an expression of genuine bitterness, widely held in the government or associated with particular circles . . . in short, to provide the kind of information that would have made the subject understandable to the readers of *The Washington Post.*

Another instructive aspect of Jenkins's piece is its dateline—it was written from Beirut. A good deal of the reporting about Syria actually comes from Lebanon or some other third country. This is a circular process: because reporters are unwelcome in Syria and unable to find out much when they get there, they find more than infrequent visits to be unproductive; and because they visit so infrequently, they tend to know less about Syria than a reporter assigned to cover a country might be expected to. Furthermore, the ways in which reporters work in Damascus—speaking to Western diplomats and fellow journalists and monitoring the newspapers and state radio—can be done just as easily from Beirut.*

Syria's ability to restrict journalistic activity and to prevent serious press coverage became especially important following the 1982 war in Lebanon, from which Syria emerged as the Soviet's principal client in the Middle East. As U.S. Marines and other troops in the multinational force took up their positions in Beirut, the Syrians consolidated their hold over the Bekaa area of eastern Lebanon. It was widely reported—from afar—that Syrian-controlled Lebanon had become a base both for Soviet advisers and Iranian-inspired Shi'ite terrorists. These reports, pregnant with significance for the United States, remained unconfirmed, however, as Syria simply closed off the Bekaa region to inspection by the press.

In early June 1983, two American press photographers, Bill Pierce of *Time* magazine and William Foley of the AP, tried to get a close look at what was going on behind the lines in Syrian-controlled Lebanon. They drove from Beirut toward the Bekaa, but were stopped at a Syrian Army checkpoint. Despite the fact that both were carrying valid Lebanese press credentials, they were dragged from their car and had their hands tied behind their backs. The two photojournalists watched as their driver was severely beaten. Then, still handcuffed, they were taken at gunpoint to Tripoli

---

*When Western reporters do get to Damascus, sometimes they are able to do good work based on personal impressions and good luck. An example of this kind of piece was David Ottoway's DAMASCUS IS AN ARMED CAMP AFTER TWO AND ONE HALF YEARS OF TERRORISM, which appeared in *The Washington Post* on January 23, 1982. Ottoway himself had a brief run-in with what he describes as "Syria's omnipresent security forces," and he was able to use it as a springboard for a tough, incisive article on the atmosphere in the capital after several years of Moslem Brotherhood terrorism. It was the kind of story the Assad brothers are not happy to see. Writing it took both intuition and guts. Articles like this are rare—and Syrian press policy is calculated to keep it that way.

where they were interrogated and later released—with the customary profuse apologies.[34]

Foley and Pierce's experience may well have had a dampening effect on the journalistic enterprise of their colleagues in the Lebanese capital who, throughout the following months, continued to "report" on Syrian activity in Lebanon largely by monitoring the radio, or by using stringers who were wholly under the thumb of Syrian authorities. Naturally these stringers were somewhat less than reliable, a fact that was often insufficiently emphasized by frustrated American journalists.

This was precisely the case when, on January 5, 1984, the *New York Times* lead headline proclaimed that an Israeli air strike in the Bekaa had killed one hundred and wounded four hundred more—mostly civilians. The report was based on a monitored broadcast of Lebanese radio, which was, in turn, taken from the report of a local stringer. Naturally the report—which was a phony—went unverified; and the fact that the *Times* had the good grace and integrity to apologize on the following day for what it termed a "significant lapse" in having led the paper with this unconfirmed story only partially corrected the impression that the Syrian propagandists had been aiming for.[35]

During the tense months following the October 1983 terror bombing of marine headquarters in Beirut—for which the U.S. government held Syria partly responsible—most of the American media were denied access to Syria. Even when Washington and Damascus became involved in active hostilities, including the downing of American aircraft over Syrian-held territory, most of the American press reports on Syria actually emanated from Beirut.

Not that Syria went entirely uncovered during this period. When Jesse Jackson arrived in Damascus to negotiate for the return of navy flier Robert Goodman, he was accompanied by a party of American newsmen; and following Goodman's release, a few American reporters were allowed to visit Damascus to report on the new Syrian "flexibility" which it supposedly signaled. But they were the exceptions who proved the rule—that press coverage of Syria is a selective matter, and it is the Assad brothers who do the select-ing. Like their friends the Saudis, who have closed their tent flaps to the outside world, the Syrians want to be alone: free to shape their Ba'athist utopia, and to weave their schemes of radical anti-American and anti-Israel activity behind the damask curtain.

9

SADDAM HUSSEIN'S TYPEWRITER

At the end of September 1980, after months of escalating tension and border skirmishes, Iraq invaded its neighbor, Iran. It was a nightmare come true, two of the world's wealthiest oil-producing nations at war. It was also a bold move by Iraqi leader Saddam Hussein to overthrow the fanatical regime of Ayatollah Khomeini and to seize the role of strong man of the Persian Gulf.

Rarely in recent times has a foreign war been of such direct importance and interest to people in the United States. The mere threat of an oil boycott during the October 1973 Arab-Israeli war had plunged the West into a prolonged economic slump. All-out war in the Persian Gulf was a potential economic disaster, with personal repercussions for millions. To add to the drama, Iran was still holding the American hostages in the embassy in Teheran, and attention in the U.S. and Europe had been focused for months on the bizzare behavior and fierce anti-Americanism of the Ayatollah's government; now, many predicted that this despised but riveting figure was about to be toppled by the modern, efficient war machine of Iraq, the Middle East's ascendant power.

197

When the war broke out, Jonathan Broder was in his office in Tel Aviv. As regional correspondent for the *Chicago Tribune*, Broder had been aware for some weeks of the possibility of war and had been desperately trying to get an Iraqi visa; he had made application in Iraqi embassies throughout Europe and at their Interest Section in Washington, D.C., all without success. Now, with fighting raging between the two nations, he had to find a way to get in. He checked with other correspondents. What did they know, what were they doing, what did they suggest? One said that he had heard that it was still impossible to get in to Iraq via Baghdad, but the Iraqis were allowing reporters to enter at the southern town of Basra, across the border from Kuwait.

Broder threw a few shirts into his suitcase, grabbed his portable typewriter, and headed for the airport. He took a night flight to Athens, transferred to a Kuwait-bound plane the next afternoon, and by evening he was at the Iraqi-Kuwait border. There he received some good news and some bad news.

The good news was that he would be allowed in. The Iraqis, who normally do not permit foreign correspondents to reside there and allow precious few to visit, were confident of a military victory. The bad news was that Broder was welcome, but his typewriter wasn't. Unregistered typewriters are illegal in Iraq, he was told, at the personal order of President Saddam Hussein. The machine would have to stay at the border station.

Broder had heard stories about the ban on typewriters in Iraq, but he had never really believed them. He knew that Saddam's old upright model was in the Revolutionary Museum in Baghdad—a symbol of the power of the written word, and the Iraqi leader's respect for the potency of propaganda—but he had considered the stories about the illegality of owning a typewriter in Iraq to be apocryphal. Still, the guard seemed serious, and Broder didn't want to jeopardize his entry into the country. He left the machine behind.

Once in Basra, the *Tribune* correspondent decided to find an Iraqi official and protest. A few of the other correspondents who had arrived had been allowed to bring in type-writers; others had had theirs confiscated. There was no clear pattern. The Iraqi press official was sympathetic, but unable to help. He suggested that the correspondent apply for a permit, a matter that might take a few days. Jonathan Broder wrote his dispatches from Iraq in longhand and pondered over the method in this seeming madness.

Two weeks later, an English journalist and colleague of Broder's lost his typewriter to the authorities.[1] Outraged, he demanded to know where he could get a permit to buy a new one. He was sent to an office in Baghdad, which turned out to be the headquarters of one of Iraq's senior intelligence officers. He was invited to wait. While he did, he noticed that the chairs in the office had manacles on them. He left the office, and wrote his stories with a pen.

When Broder heard the story of the British reporter, he had mixed feelings. He was glad that he hadn't wasted time applying for a typewriter permit, of course, but chilled by the thought of those manacles. "Jesus," he thought. "These people aren't fooling around."[2]

Iraq lies to the east of Syria and the north of Saudi Arabia, and it shares some characteristics with each of them. Like Saudi Arabia, Iraq is oil rich—before the 1980 war, it was one of OPEC's largest producers. Like Syria, it is ruled by a wing of the militant, secularist Ba'ath Party. The two sister parties are bitter rivals, however, and their respective leaders, Hafez Assad of Syria and Saddam Hussein of Iraq, mortal enemies. Like Assad, Saddam Hussein is a dictator who uses repression and violence as the tools of his political control, but unlike the Syrian leader, he does not employ his brother to carry out his policies. He prefers to be his own executioner and is known as the Butcher of Baghdad, a nickname he reputedly cherishes.

In one thing Iraq is similar to both Syria *and* Saudi Arabia. It has no free press, no political debate, no resident foreign correspondents, and no tolerance for any kind of scrutiny by visiting journalists. Iraq has erected a barrier between itself and the outside world, and little is actually known about the regime, its behavior, and its policies. This has become manifestly clear during the years of the Iran-Iraq war, in which Baghdad has written a new chapter in how to manipulate, emasculate, and often eliminate press coverage. In Mecca and at Hama, the Western press had been kept at bay for weeks; during its protracted war with Iran, Iraq has controlled the access and limited the output of the world's news organizations for years. As *The New York Times*'s deputy managing editor Craig Whitney says, "The situation in Iraq is like watching a fight under a blanket. You hear the screams, you see the movement, but you never know who is doing what to whom."[3]

The story of the press coverage of the Iraq-Iran war—a saga of frustration and impotence in the face of repression and censorship—actually begins with the fall of the Shah of Iran. Until then, Iran and Saudi Arabia were the focal points of American concern and interest in the region; they were both considered strong friends of the United States and served as twin pillars of U.S. interests in the Persian Gulf. Iraq was a backwater—a radical Soviet client, so uncompromising in its hatred for Israel that it had never even accepted the Arab-Israel armistice agreements of 1949, so hostile to the United States that the two countries have no ambassadorial relations. Despite Iraq's radical posture, however, its distance from the Israeli border kept it from being a real front-line confrontation state, while its leader, the stodgy Ahmed Hassan al-Bakr, held the country on an even, totalitarian keel that created little interest in the West.

All this began to change in 1979. The fall of the Shah left a serious vacuum in the strategically vital Persian Gulf. Great potential power and prestige could accrue to the nation that replaced Iran as the regional leader. Al-Bakr was not a man to dream such dreams; but in July 1979, he was replaced in a bloodless coup by Saddam Hussein—young, dynamic, with ambitious goals which included extending his influence in the Arab world, and beyond.

He immediately set out to consolidate his power in Iraq, executing a group of senior Iraqi officials whom he deemed potential opponents ("twenty-one of his most intimate friends," Anwar Sadat later said, with evident distaste)[4] and at the same time, he began to lay the plans for the Iraqi invasion of Iran. He also strengthened the xenophobic and repressive press policies of his predeccesor.

"In 1979, I was invited to visit Iraq by the government," recalls Jonathan Broder, who, as an official guest, was allowed to keep his typewriter that time. "They met me at the airport and never let me out of their sight. I had to give them a list of whom I wanted to see and where I wanted to go; some they approved, and others they just turned down flat. No explanation at all.

"The requirement to have an official with me when I went outside of Baghdad was a serious problem. For example, we went to a Kurdish village in the north. The Iraqi government had just uprooted whole villages of Kurds, and I wanted to know how they felt about it and about their Kurdish identity. The people I spoke with there were obviously under strict control, however, and they wouldn't talk freely in front of my 'guide.' In fact, the entire time I was there, I saw only people they wanted me to see."[5]

Even in Baghdad, where reporters' movements are less supervised, there is always a pervasive sense of fear and repression. "You don't just wander around Baghdad with a camera," says Ted Stanger of *Newsweek*, a former Middle East correspondent of the *Miami Herald*. "No one will talk to reporters on the street, all the hotels are government owned and full of spies, who report on the reporters to the government."[6] In fact, it is illegal for Iraqis to talk with foreign reporters, and they are required by law to report all unavoidable conversations with foreigners to the Ministry of the Interior.[7] Even by Saudi Arabian and Syrian standards, such total repression is unusual.

Throughout the past decade, Iraqi press management has succeeded to a considerable extent in keeping the country an enigma to the West. Little news of what is actually happening gets out; and evaluations, even those written by the few correspondents who are able to visit the country, suffer from a lack of contact with ordinary Iraqis, a paucity of firsthand information, and the disproportionate influence of various Western diplomats, usually the only people with whom foreign journalists meet and talk freely. Even the most astute reporters are often unable to penetrate the wall of silence and propaganda that the Iraqis have built.

After the fall of the Shah of Iran, this vacuum of information provided a golden opportunity for "experts" in the American government to assert their views on Iraq. America missed the Shah, and some officials of the Carter administration began to tout Iraq's Hussein as a possible replacement. There were, of course, serious problems with this scenario, not the least of which was Iraq's tradition of strong hostility to the United States. But some, like National Security Adviser Zbigniew Brzezinski, thought that Baghdad might be coaxed out of the Soviet orbit and into the American in the same way that Kissinger had brought Egypt into America's sphere in the mid-seventies. By late 1979, the administration was already sending signals to Saddam Hussein.

In January 1980, Brzezinski told *The Wall Street Journal* that "the U.S. wishes friendly relations with all Moslem nations. This explicitly includes Iraq and Libya, countries with whom we don't have irreconcilable differences."[8] In April, he said on *The MacNeil-Lehrer report* that "we feel that Iraq desires to be independent, that Iraq desires a secure Persian Gulf. And we do not feel that American-Iraqi relations need to be frozen in antagonism."[9] Such statements made the American interest in a conciliation with the Iraqis plain—so plain, in fact, that in April 1980, the Iranians were condemning Iraq as an American puppet and threatened to kill the American hostages in the embassy if the Iraqis attacked in the Persian Gulf.[10]

Brzezinski's public signals to Iraq were just the tip of the iceberg. In private conversations and briefings American officials pointed to Iraq as the emerging power in the area; a power now mobilizing under the dictatorial but efficient Saddam Hussein to translate its oil riches into modernization, and regional influence. This assessment implied that the U.S. ought to find ways to encourage closer ties to the Iraqi dictator, ties that might require public support or Congressional approval. The Carter administration thus had a practical interest in seeing its opinion of Saddam Hussein reflected in the media.

In the year preceding the outbreak of the Iran-Iraq war, a concert of interest emerged between the government of Saddam Hussein and the Carter administration, each of which was interested in projecting an image of Iraq as a country of growing power and influence. This assessment was accepted readily enough by most of the press, which had no means of arriving at independent judgments, and most of them "discovered" what the administration was touting as the new conventional wisdom. In April, only a few months before Iraq invaded Iran, *The New York Times*'s Youssof Ibrahim wrote, "In the region, Iraq seems to be discarding its big stick, opting instead for a good neighbor policy . . . [it] has moved away from its former extremist positions. On most pan-Arab and international issues it is now in the Arab mainstream." Ibrahim concluded his look at Iraq (written with a London dateline) by characterizing Iraq as "a no-nonsense secular state." [11]

That same week *The Washington Post*'s Jonathan Randal visited Baghdad and reported on Iraq's new moderation. "Barring an unforseen accident," he wrote, "the border tension is not expected to expand into serious fighting, much less a full scale war, largely because of Iraqi restraint and power; in the event of war, the Iraqis would easily defeat their Iranian counterparts." [12] These assessments, which later proved totally mistaken, were just what the American administration wanted reported. Unfortunately, when war actually broke out, they formed the basis of some of the most uninformed press commentary in recent history.

In June 1980, Saddam Hussein held "elections" for the Iraqi National Assembly, a puppet parliament, in which only candidates approved by the president were allowed to run. These "elections" were called by the Iraqi leader to demonstrate his country's new, modern approach; and he threw open the normally closed gates of Iraq to hundreds of foreign journalists so they could witness the birth of Iraqi democracy. Reporters were herded from one polling place to another by special Iraqi guides; later, many wrote of the elections as if they were something more than a bogus public relations ploy. Few mentioned in their reports that the central instrument of Iraqi government was, and would remain, not the gavel but the rack. Typical was a report in *The Washington Post* headlined LARGE TURNOUT REPORTED FOR FIRST IRAQI VOTE SINCE 1958. A casual reader looking at the headline would have concluded that here was a rare case of a former dictatorship moving toward democracy. Only in the eighth paragraph of the story was it explained that "President Saddam Hussein will continue to make all key decisions." [13]

Not all American reporting about Iraq was naïve, of course. Bill Paul of *The Wall Street Journal* visited the country and was less impressed than some of his colleagues by its new PR front. "On the surface Saddam Hussein at-Takriti seems like a decent enough sort of chap," he wrote, but, "on the other hand, if [he] doesn't like you he is apt to have you shot or thrown into prison." [14] Paul's dark view of the Iraqi president was by no means typical, however, and the effects of America's greening of Saddam Hussein were widespread among U.S. journalists writing about the country in 1980.*

The cumulative impact of the Saddam Hussein media blitz, reinforced by the U.S. government assessments, was to paint a picture of Iraq as a dynamic, wealthy nation only now emerging from long years of radicalism and prepared to assert its power in the Middle East. Few doubted that if war came, the Ba'athist regime in Baghdad would make short work of its Iranian rival.

* * *

*And later. In April 1981, *The Washington Post*'s David Ottoway visited Iraq and noted, "Many Western and Asian diplomats are giving Saddam Hussein high marks for skillful handling of the war to consolidate both his personal authority and the unity of the nation rent in the past by its ethnic and religious divisions." He went on to compare Saddam Hussein with an "American politician on the election hustings," who "had been traveling tirelessly since the war broke out in September, meeting with peasants." [15] This "father of his country" approach was published just three days after Amnesty International reported that the Iraqi president was running Iraq through the use of widespread, systematic torture and murdering an average of one hundred political opponents annually—activities not necessarily associated with American politicians, on or off the hustings.

On September 22, 1980, Iraqi airplanes launched a co-ordinated attack on Iranian airfields, followed by an all-out invasion of the Iranian oil-producing province of Kuzistan. The ostensible reason for the attack was a border dispute involving territory at the head of the Persian Gulf, but this was a transparent pretext. Saddam Hussein was moving to establish primacy in the region, to deal a blow to his enemy the Ayatollah, and to catapult Iraq into the first rank of the "non-aligned" nations.

In a sense, Saddam Hussein's aims were both offensive and defensive. While clearly the aggressor, he was also moving to preempt the threat he perceived from the militant Shi'ite government of Iran. Saddam Hussein himself is a Sunni Moslem, while more than sixty percent of Iraqis are Shi'ites, and they were thought potentially susceptible to the inflammatory religious rhetoric of their Iranian neighbor. Nor were the Ayatollah's motives for proselytizing among the Iraqi Shi'ites simply ideological or religious. Khomeini had lived in exile in Iraq for fourteen years. In 1975, as part of an overall agreement with the government of the Shah, he had been expelled by the Iraqi authorities. One of the leading Iraqi advocates of his expulsion had been Saddam Hussein.

The Iraqi move against Iran came with apparently exquisite timing. Teheran was in political and economic turmoil following the overthrow of the Shah and the internal struggles brought on by the rise of the Khomeini government. Moreover, by holding American hostages in Teheran, the Iranians had foreclosed any possibility of obtaining American political or military assistance. Iran seemed isolated, chaotic, and altogether ready for a quick military defeat.

Such a defeat would have brought immediate benefits to Iraq. Egypt, the traditional leader of the Arab world, was in eclipse because of its unilateral dealings with Israel, and it appeared that an Iraqi triumph in the Gulf could make Saddam Hussein the leader of the Arab world. Moreover, the nonaligned nations were scheduled to meet in Baghdad,

and the Iraqi president hoped, by the time of the conference, to be the major force in the Persian Gulf, and thus a
Third World leader of substance and influence. Perhaps most
important, a victory over Iran would resonate throughout
Iraq—which has historically seen Iran as a threat—and assure Saddam Hussein a large measure of popular acclaim as
well as increased control over the army. For the Iranian-Iraqi
rivalry was a matter of deep historical significance. The Persians were despised *ajem,* non-Arab Eastern Moslems, who
had once ruled Iraq and had been defeated at the battle of
Qadusiyah, about twenty miles southeast of Baghdad, in 637.
In the Middle East, thirteen hundred years can be a short
time indeed; Saddam Hussein hoped to capitalize on this fact,
and to use it to mobilize domestic support for his war, which
his government's propaganda referred to as "Saddam's
Qadusiyah."

When the first word of the Iraqi invasion of Iran reached
the West, it came, typically, from the official Iraqi news
agency and was picked up and rebroadcast by monitors in
Beirut, Cyprus, and elsewhere. Almost no U.S. newsmen were
in Iraq, and the American press had long been excluded from
Iran, the other combatant. But even without reporters in the
country, the American media had no difficulty in appreci-
ating the potential disaster of war in the Persian Gulf. *Time*
magazine wrote: "Suddenly the nightmare, the conflict that
had been discussed only as a worst case scenario, was at
hand—war amid the oilfields and across the vital oil routes
of the Persian Gulf." [16] *The New York Times* editorialized:
"There is no American 'side' in the widening conflict between a resurgent Iraq and a vulnerable Iran. But American interests are plainly involved. . . . Any conflict in that
unstable region can jeopardize the West's oil supplies." [17]
    With so much at stake, the American press opened a two-
front campaign to cover the war. Hundreds of reporters
scrambled for entry into Iraq, and at the same time, a bat-
tery of Western "experts" on military and political matters
were pressed into service to explain what was going on and
what it might mean.

At first it seemed that despite past policy, it would be possible to cover the war from the battlefield. Reporters who, like Jonathan Broder, had come to the Iraqi border station hoping to talk (or bribe) their way into the country were pleasantly surprised to find that they were welcome.

In fact, Iraq, convinced that it was about to conclude a swift, historic military triumph, was determined to get as many journalists as possible to witness the campaign. On the first day of the war, its diplomatic representatives around the world began to telephone correspondents who had pending applications with the offer of immediate access to the country. Consular officials in Iraqi embassies and missions worked around the clock to issue visas; passengers were bumped off Baghdad-bound Iraqi planes to accommodate the press corps. Even when the Baghdad airport had to be closed to air traffic, the reporters kept coming. Many of them rented taxis in Jordan and drove to the Iraqi capital. Within a week after the beginning of the fighting, there were more than three hundred correspondents in Baghdad and another fifty in Basra, near, but by no means at, the scene of the actual fighting.

Yet despite their presence in Iraq, the news fare from Iraq was strangely thin. Little battle footage was shown on American television; few firsthand dispatches from the front appeared in the newspapers. As for the political story, always a major aspect of war coverage, the huge press corps in the capital seemed to know less than their colleagues who had stayed home in the United States and Western Europe. Something was evidently wrong with the journalistic efforts coming out of Iraq.

The problem, it soon emerged, was not with the correspondents, but with the Iraqi authorities. They had invited the press to witness the victorious thrust of the army of the New Iraq. But the battle plan was not working out, and the reporters were soon enmeshed in layers of "protective" Iraqi government censorship of the most effective kind—the censorship of exclusion and denied access.

During the first few days of the war, some of the more enterprising Basra-based journalists were able to rent taxis

and get an occasional glimpse of the front, although even
then much of the reporting was of the "Radio Baghdad said"
variety. Soon, however, even their relative freedom came
under strict supervision, as Jonathan Broder recalls: "After
the first few days of the war in Basra, the situation got very
tight. There were far fewer transports than reporters wanting to go to the front. Some of the reporters—I don't want
to mention their names, but we all knew who they were—
tried to ingratiate themselves with the Iraqi government and
passed along their official communiqués as if they were entirely credible, in order to make sure they got transportation to the front. A lot of us were upset about this, and once
it even led to a scuffle between an American wire-service reporter and a correspondent for a major U.S. newspaper.

"After the first week or so we were there, they finally realized that there were reporters in Basra not under any real
government control. They posted police to arrest reporters,
and eventually they rounded us up in the Hamdan Hotel
and ordered us to leave town. They said it was to rotate us
with correspondents who were waiting in Baghdad, but that
was bogus. It never happened."[18]

As to the reporters headquartered in Baghdad, *The
Washington Post*'s William Claiborne claimed that "since the
start of the war [they] have been tightly restricted in their
movements and have been provided with little more opportunity than to glean official statements and communiques,
interview Western diplomats who themselves are often isolated from official sources, and monitor radio reports and
dispatches of the official Iraqi News Agency."[19]

John Kifner of *The New York Times* reported that because
of the lack of access, most of what had been reported from
Iraq during the first few weeks of the war had not been based
on real information or firsthand knowledge. "The frustrated correspondents [in Iraq] complain that they have been
effectively prevented from covering the war. The [Ministry
of Information] officials, members of a rigidly closed society, find the journalists completely outside of any frame of
reference they can understand. They alternately threaten the

correspondents with expulsion and take them on tours that provide little or no information.

"The correspondents have almost no first hand or reliable information about what is happening on the battlefield. . . . The closest journalists have come to actual fighting, and to comparing the slow progress to the euphoric official announcements, has been when information people have blundered into the Iranian artillery fire while taking journalists into supposedly safe areas."[20]

According to Kifner, most of the foreign reporters in Iraq were actually getting their news about the war from listening to the BBC radio reports—a rather limited source, since the BBC correspondent was himself stuck along with everyone else. He also noted that Reuters reporter Jeremy Clift had been expelled from the country for allegedly "writing lies" about the war, an object lesson for the rest of the press corps.[21]

Just how inadequate the reporting from Iraq was, was illustrated in another story, related by Kifner, of a newly arrived colleague who brought a three-week-old *Times* of London with him. The newspaper was something of an attraction for the news-starved press corps (almost all foreign-language publications, except *Popular Mechanics,* are outlawed in Iraq). The reporters were in for a shock, however. "Spread across the front page," said Kifner, "was the story describing the Iraqi advance on the key oil refineries of Abadan. *It was virtually the same story that had been written with minor variations every day since.*"[22] (emphasis added)

Meanwhile, back in the States, the experts were busy trying to supply some answers to the questions that the war had raised. From the outset, they almost unanimously accepted the official U.S. assessments: that the Iraqis had the stronger army; that Iran was too disorganized to fight effectively; that the war would thus be short and end in a victory for Saddam Hussein; and that this would elevate the Iraqi leader to a new stature in the Arab world. *The New York Times*'s military expert, Drew Middleton, for example, wrote on September 23: "The seizure of American hostages and subsequent end to American aid to Iran has left the country virtually defenseless against an Iraqi army that has emerged as the dominant military power in the region."[23] *The Washington Post* cited expert opinion in the American capital to the effect that "overall . . . the Iraqi forces are considered far superior to the Iranian military."[24] The assessment of the *Times*'s State Department correspondent Bernard Gwertzman was similar: "Unless Iraq's military moves suffer an unexpected setback, President Saddam Hussein appears destined to become a powerful political and military force in the region . . . no indigenous force seems able to challenge Iraq."[25] *Time* considered the Iraqi victory certain and likely to be swift: "Most Western observers assume that the Gulf War . . . cannot go on for too long. . . . If Iraq chooses to prolong the conflict it will almost certainly be to inflict such punishment on the Iranian economy and military machine that they will not be a factor in the Gulf for some time to come."*[27]

Reporters on the scene warned that there was no independent confirmation of the Iraqi victory claims, but their caution was not emulated by many of the commentators at home. Often, in fact, it seemed that the two groups were writing about different wars. On October 3, for example, while a U.S.-based *New York Times* reporter was quoting defense experts in Washington on the ineffectiveness of the Iranian military, John Kifner reported major Iranian air strikes on Iraqi industrial targets from Kirkuk in the north to Basra in the south, and even on Saddam Hussein's hometown, Takrit. Similarly, many Washington reporters persisted in believing that Iraq's failure to capture Kuzistan province was a calculated military tactic. On October 7, Karen Elliot House, of *The Wall Street Journal,* noted that the "U.S. says that Iraq's slow advance is a deliberate decision and doesn't stem from Iranian resistance alone."[28] Two weeks

---

*Almost all American commentators relied heavily on "observers" or "analysts," and in doing so implicitly endorsed their views. As Mort Rosenblum, author of *Coups and Earthquakes,* has noted, "One rule of thumb for anonymous attribution is that no responsible reporter will relay information unless he believes it to be true."[26]

later, Drew Middleton opined: "Iraq's cautious, methodical tactics in the advance into Iran's Kuzistan Province seem to be paying off."[29] But most reporters on the scene, even with their limited view, were not so sure that the Iraqis' slow pace was the product of design. John Kifner spoke for many: ". . . there was a growing suspicion on the part of some of the journalists that this was a battle between rather inefficient Third World armies who were simply hurling the expensive weaponry bought from the great powers with their oil money into sand and marsh without any great effect."[30]

Nothing more clearly illustrated the reportorial difficulties of the first few months of the war than the question of the capture of the Iranian port of Khoramsharr. The port was the major goal of Iraq's initial drive, and like the Saudi government's false optimism during the Mecca Grand Mosque crisis, the Iraqi authorities announced the capture of Khoramsharr almost daily. The press, reporting from long distance, was repeatedly taken in by this official Iraqi optimism. As early as September 26, Henry Tanner wrote in *The New York Times,* from Beirut: "Iraqi ground forces reportedly fought their way into the Iranian oil port of Khoramsharr today . . . and advanced to points fifty miles inside Iran." Tanner noted that his information came from official Iraqi communiqués monitored from the radio and that little independent information was available, but he gave the clear impression that he accepted the accuracy of the Iraqi claim.[31]

Four days later, David Ottoway reported from Washington, D.C.: "Iraq appeared yesterday to be on the verge of finally seizing the besieged Shatt al Arab port of Khoramsharr."[32]

One week after that, Karen Elliot House, also in Washington, wrote in *The Wall Street Journal:* "Iraq appeared yesterday to have at last taken the Iranian port of Khoramsharr."[33] This "capture" of the Iranian port, announced first by one newspaper and then by another, went on for another two and a half weeks—until the port was actually taken, on October 24.

There was considerable confusion about other matters as well. *The New York Times,* on September 23, stated, "To reach the open sea, tankers must pass through the narrow Straits of Hormuz. No power could keep Iran from closing the Straits temporarily." Six days later, however, *The Wall Street Journal*'s Walter Mossberg reported from Washington, "US military and intelligence analysts say that it is their best guess that neither Iran nor Iraq is capable of blocking the Straits physically."[34] In the event, the Straits remained open; but the contradictory assessments revealed how little factual information was available.

This dearth of information did not, however, deter the more lion-hearted experts from making predictions not only about the war, but about its repercussions for the entire Middle East. Two such commentaries appeared in *The Washington Post* early in the war. The first, by Svetlana Godillo, the *Post*'s staff astrologer, described Saddam Hussein as "strong, dynamic, charismatic, perceptive, intuitive, optimistic, and, to top it all off, very lucky. Khomeini is now faced with an enemy who is much more ruthless than the Shah ever was. In fact, I will go so far as to say that Hussein will be the instrument of the Ayatollah's downfall."[35] The *Post*'s assistant managing editor for foreign news, Jim Hoagland, made a similar prediction: "But, with its initial ground successes," he wrote, "Iraq has hastened the dismemberment of the collapsing Persian empire, an accomplishment that will stir Arab national pride at the apparent beating the Aryans of Iran are being handed, bringing a new power equation to the region."[36] Eighteen months later, with the "Persian empire" far from collapsed or dismembered and the Ayatollah very much in power (and apparently winning the war), the Hoagland-Godillo theory was addressed in the *Post* by Professor Fouad Ajami, director of Mid-East studies at Johns Hopkins School of Advanced International Studies, in an article entitled IN IRAQ, YET ANOTHER ARAB DREAM OF GLORY BITES THE DUST. According to Professor Ajami, "Iraq's dreams of power have proven to be short-lived. The weaknesses that states hide from their frightened citizens and dazzled outsiders eventually assert themselves."[37]

Not all of the American journalistic experts were dazzled; a few saw, even from a distance, some of the possible twists and turns of a war between countries like Iraq and Iran. On September 29, 1980, one day after *The Washington Post* had awarded victory to Iraq and dismembered Iran, the *Christian Science Monitor*'s Ned Temko noted: "Iraq, the emerging 'winner' in the latest Middle East war, may soon be searching subtly for peace. Ironically the danger is that loser Iran may go right on fighting."[38] Which is, of course, precisely what happened.

While most of America's most prestigious newspapers and magazines were publishing the "it's-in-the-bag-for-Iraq" views of their military and political commentators, some minority opinions were being heard in the heartland. One was carried in the Lincoln, Nebraska, *Sunday Journal and Star*, under the headline FORMER NEBRASKA COLONEL SAYS IRAQ UNDERESTIMATED IRAN. "A former Nebraskan, who helped train the Imperial Corps twenty-five years ago, says he thinks Iraq miscalculated Iran's ability to respond to invasion.

"Retired army colonel Carl Beyers, an Omaha native, was in Lincoln last week to attend the Nebraska-Florida State football game.

" 'Even the United States misread their ability to put planes up,' Beyers said."[39] Colonel Beyers's analysis was, of course, exactly right; his advantage was not having "inside information" from Washington's analysts.

The fact is that by mid-November 1980, the Iraqi invasion was finished and the momentum that its invasion had produced had dissipated. From this point on the Iranians would gather strength, first gradually and invisibly, then with dramatic effect, as they drove the Iraqis out of their territory, menaced Iraq's own border areas, drained the Iraqi economy, and forced the Baghdad government into ruinous war debts. Not much of this would be reported firsthand, though.

In the late autumn of 1980, the foreign press corps in Iraq dwindled as it became apparent that reporters would be unable to get within viewing distance of the war or to gather any significant political news in the Iraqi capital. Most of the film being shown on U.S. television was official Iraqi footage, which was, naturally enough, sanitized of barbarity, failure, and defeat before being passed along for viewing in the West. Reporters in Iraq were reduced to writing mostly color stories, and even these were rather colorless because of their isolation and inability to travel freely. Frustrated and disappointed, foreign correspondents began leaving Iraq and by January 1981—less than four months after the outbreak of fighting—only a tiny handful remained. Many of those who left assumed that fighting was over for the winter and that they could always return if there were any new developments in the war. Both of these assumptions proved false. The fighting was about to enter a new stage, but few journalists would be allowed back to witness it. The Iraqi authorities had concluded that they no longer wanted foreign correspondents around. From the beginning of 1981, the opportunity to cover the war would be by invitation only.

The effect of this decision was obvious. Before, very little had been actually *known* about the war, but the very presence of so many reporters in Iraq had ensured a constant stream of articles full of speculation, rumor, color, details, and anecdotes; and this, in turn, had generated a flow of analytical pieces attempting to say "what it all meant." From now on, there would be far less written and broadcast about the war.*

In September 1981, a year after war had broken out, most American newspapers ran articles about what many referred to as the "forgotten war." *The Washington Post* noted dryly that "American journalists have been excluded from the battle zone for months,"[40] and John Yemma of the *Christian Science Monitor* explained "accounts of battles and casualties proved to be notoriously unreliable. The press lost interest. The conflict slipped out of the news."[41]

And that, more or less, is where it has stayed ever since.

---

*One obvious problem for the press was its inability to get into Iran, from which American reporters were excluded until December 1980. This led many journalists to underestimate Iranian internal unity, morale, and its capacity to wage war. Important developments, such as the cooperation between regular Iranian military officers and the fanatical "Revolutionary Guards," which produced new battlefield tactics of great originality, went unnoticed. Such attention as was focused on Iran during the fall of 1980 was given largely to the continuing hostage crisis. Later, both the Iranians and the Iraqis allowed journalists in on a selective basis—when it suited their purpose.

Reports of the fighting have been largely confined to wire-service copy based on monitoring the official battle communiqués of the two sides; an occasional assessment written from Cyprus, London, Washington, or New York; or, from time to time, articles by reporters allowed into one or the other of the warring countries for a supervised view of the battle. Under the circumstances, some extremely important developments have gone all but unreported.

In May 1982, for example, when the Iranians struck into Iraqi territory for the first time, the *Times* picked it up off the radio in Beirut. When Khoramsharr, the symbol of early Iraqi success in the war, was retaken by the Iranians, *The Washington Post* reported it from Kuwait, and *The Wall Street Journal* from London. Then, more than a year later, NBC's Edwin Newman, in a 9:00 P.M. news update, read a report by Iraq that it had killed eleven thousand Iranian soldiers during the previous two days.[42] The claim, if true, would have made this one of the largest battles in modern Middle Eastern history, but, of course, no one could verify it, and it was largely ignored by the American media.

Even more significant was an Associated Press dispatch in late January 1984 which quoted *Jane's Defense Weekly* as reporting that Iraq was now using mustard gas to repell Iranian attacks.[43] Iraq's use of the outlawed weapon would, if true, be a significant indication of its inability to contain Iran through conventional means, and an important illustration of Saddam Hussein's lack of restraint (as well as a retrospective proof to Israel that it did the right thing in destroying Iraq's nuclear facility in 1981). But once again, the report could not be verified by impartial observers on the scene.

Occasionally, an American news organization made a serious effort to get real information about the conflict, but none has been conspicuously successful. Occasionally, too, frustration has driven the press to rather unorthodox lengths. On March 22, 1982, for example, *Time* magazine carried what at first glance appeared to be a real exclusive—an eyewitness account of a battle between the Iraqis and the fanatical Islamic guards of Iran:

"Then, without waiting for orders, 500 Islamic guards and

militiamen leaped out of their trenches swinging West German G3 and Soviet Kalashnikov rifles and Soviet anti-tank rocket launchers. Screaming 'Allahu Akbar' ('God is great'), they charged the advancing Iraqis and were quickly locked in savage hand-to-hand combat. Meanwhile the Iranian army commander, startled by the untimely appearance of his fanatic countrymen, was obliged to re-direct his guns to the rear of the enemy formations in order to avoid killing fellow Iranians."[44]

This stirring passage would have done justice to the legendary Richard Harding Davis. There was only one problem—*Time* "reported" the story from New York.

American news organizations that were not prepared to adopt *Time*'s devil-may-care approach to news gathering have been able to give their public considerably less. The war, which is now one of the longer conflicts in this century, has exacted a terrible price. At the end of February 1984, the BBC estimated that two hundred thousand had been killed;[45] and hundreds of thousands (or millions, according to the Iranians) have become refugees. More, it has raised serious questions about the stability and future of the Persian Gulf and Western fuel supplies; about the position of Iraq in the Arab world; the role of Iran in the Middle East equation; and the role of resurgent Islamic militancy in the region. How much of this news has been, or will be, available to the American public? Craig Whitney, who, as foreign editor of *The New York Times,* had to contend with the problem of gathering news from the area, shakes his head sadly. "How much news? I think almost none."[46]

10

BAYONETS
AND ICBMS

Picture a map of the world on which the countries are drawn not according to their actual size, but proportional to the amount of attention they receive in the American press. The United States itself would be by far the largest, followed by its sister superpower the Soviet Union. A third superpower would be on this media map too, almost as large as the USSR, and far bigger than the next nearest nation. That country would be Israel.*

Although it has a population smaller than Los Angeles and occupies an area no larger than Massachusetts, Israel is

*Perhaps the most detailed study of this phenomenon was made by Professor James Larson of the University of Texas, who measured the frequency with which foreign countries were mentioned on network television's evening news programs during the period 1972–79. Professor Larson found that on all three networks the Soviet Union ranked first in the amount of coverage, Israel second, and South and North Vietnam, both largely out of the news since 1976, came third and fourth. It is extremely likely that this same proportion held true for the print media as well.

Since 1979, specific events have drawn periodic concentrated press attention to other nations: Iran during the hostage crisis, Afghanistan during the Soviet invasion, and Honduras and El Salvador in the summer of 1983 and again in 1984, are examples. But Israel, since Professor Larson's study, has also been in the news constantly—notably during the strike on Iraq's atomic reactor in June 1981, the many Begin-Sadat summit meetings, and especially during the Lebanese war, which dominated America's foreign news throughout much of 1982.[1]

one of the most prolific news centers in the world. More than two hundred full- and part-time resident Western foreign reporters and news personnel are stationed in Jerusalem and Tel Aviv—certainly the highest per-capita concentration of foreign correspondents permanently based anywhere. Moreover, they are augmented each year by as many as twenty-five hundred visiting correspondents who come to Israel on assignment for brief periods.

All this press attention is a relatively recent development. From its birth in 1948 until 1973, Israel was a comparative media backwater, covered mostly by stringers and part-time reporters, with wars and other special events, such as the visit of the Pope or the Eichmann trial, handled by visiting correspondents.

When the change came, it was as a result of the repercussions of the 1973 October War. For the first time, Americans began to perceive the Middle East as vital to their own economic interests and national security, and this created a demand for news from the area. Israel was a major factor in the Middle East conflict and, what's more, a safe and hospitable place for journalists to live and work. News organizations that could afford it established bureaus in both Israel and an Arab capital, either Beirut or Cairo (or both). Poorer organizations, with only one regional reporter, usually put him in Israel, especially after the Israel-Egyptian peace permitted free movement between the two countries.

In recent years the foreign press corps in Israel has come to read like a who's who of American journalism. *The New York Times, The Washington Post, Los Angeles Times, Baltimore Sun, Christian Science Monitor, Miami Herald, Chicago Tribune, Time, Newsweek,* AP, UPI, ABC, NBC, CBS, and CNN all have at least one full-time staff correspondent in Israel, and many have three or four; at least half a dozen other U.S. newspapers employ full-time stringers.

As the foreign press corps expanded, its demography changed. Until 1973, Israel was usually covered by stringers who were themselves Israelis, often immigrants from Western countries. Reporters like Moshe Brilliant of *The New York Times*, Michael Elkins of the BBC and *Newsweek*, Yuval Elizur of the *Boston Globe*, Andrew Meisels of ABC, the late Ruth Cale of the *Baltimore Sun*, and David Halevy of *Time*, to name only a few, were mainstays of the foreign press corps, and in many cases still are, and they bring a number of important advantages to their work. Most (but not all) speak and read Hebrew and thus have access to the Israeli press and other local sources of information. They know the country well and are able to put new events into historical perspective. They are also able to cultivate contacts and friendships within the governing circles of Israel, a rarity for foreign reporters, and thus to come up with information not normally available to outsiders.

There is, of course, one major problem for these Israeli reporters. Their intimate connection with Israel sometimes leads to a lack of detachment and to some highly opinionated reporting. This became especially true following the election of Menachem Begin in 1977. Arab critics of the still large number of Israelis in the foreign press corps in Israel sometimes argue that they give Israel an unfair propaganda advantage. These critics assume that Israeli journalists will act like their Arab counterparts—that is, will servilely parrot the government line; it is ironic that since 1977, the veteran "Israeli" foreign correspondents have been among the most vociferous (and, because of their contacts, the most effective) critics of the government of Israel.

Since 1973, the percentage of non-Israelis among foreign reporters has increased significantly. Most of them arrive in Israel with little preparation and with no knowledge of the language or history of the country. Some of the less sophisticated come expecting a kind of Brooklyn-by-the-Mediterranean and are shocked to find that Israel is a foreign country with its own mentality and customs. After a period of adjustment, a few have become superior reporters of the Israeli scene.

Most of the print journalists live in Jerusalem, while the networks and the Associated Press have their main operations in Tel Aviv, although they also station reporters in the capital. The foreign news operations in Tel Aviv are, to some extent, a hangover from the pre-1977 period, when most

Israeli government figures spent at least half the week there, a practice that ended when Prime Minister Begin established his residence in Jerusalem on a full-time basis. The Israeli Defense Ministry, the general staff of the army, and the foreign embassies—all important sources of news—are still in Tel Aviv, and this too has encouraged some correspondents to remain there. Others stay in Tel Aviv because of its night life and proximity to the Mediterranean beaches. Finally, some organizations, especially the Associated Press, have chosen Tel Aviv at least partially to avoid angering Arab clients.* Still, the trend in recent years has been to move from Tel Aviv to Jerusalem, which is the scene of the Israeli Knesset and government and is close to the West Bank.

Foreign correspondents usually consider Israel to be a highly desirable assignment. It is a modern, open society and offers considerable personal comfort to the reporter and his family. Fine schools, superior health services, a good deal of Western cultural activity, and a large, sophisticated English-(and French-) speaking population make Israel a pleasant place to spend a few years.

Even more important, Israel is constantly in the news. Americans are interested in it, both as a part of the Arab-Israel conflict and as a fascinating and evocative country in its own right. It is axiomatic that "Jews are news," mostly because of the large number of Jews in major American urban areas who have an abiding interest in Israel. *The New York Times,* perhaps the single most influential newspaper in the United States, has an extremely high percentage of Jewish readers, as do the *Los Angeles Times,* the *Chicago Tribune,* and the *Miami Herald.*

These factors and others, including the ongoing U.S.-Israeli relationship and the dramatic nature of the Arab-Israel conflict, are all part of the reason that Israel has such a

---

*Wire services, in addition to reporting the news, also sell their services to foreign newspapers, television, and radio. In the Arab world, with its government-controlled media, this means, in effect, doing business with the government. The sale of news and photos is an important source of income for UPI and AP, who have been loath to upset their Arab clients by setting up headquarters in Jerusalem. Still, the advantages of covering Israel from its capital are substantial, and in early 1984, United Press International moved its main Israeli bureau to Jerusalem.

disproportionately large foreign press contingent. The press corps in turn creates a dynamic of its own. Journalists are paid to report the news, and keeping a foreign correspondent abroad is an expensive proposition. There are times when events themselves dictate their output—the war in Lebanon, for example, or Israeli national elections. But during slow news periods, journalists are still expected to produce copy. This creates an interesting circular situation. Reporters are stationed in Israel because of the demand for news from there; but they report on the country even when nothing of any great international concern is happening. This means that Americans get much more exposure to and information about Israel than almost any other foreign country. Which, of course, further increases the demand for news and information. And so on.

This process is made possible by the fact that Israel is a country in which information is readily available. In this regard it is almost the exact opposite of its Arab neighbors. Foreign correspondents in Jerusalem and Tel Aviv have easy access to a variety of political parties, the government bureaucracy and the local Israeli press, each of which is an expression of the extreme diversity of opinion, not to say contentiousness, that characterizes the country. Moreover, Israel, which *The New York Times*'s David Shipler calls "a nation of op-ed article writers," is filled to overflowing with "men and women in the street" who are articulate in foreign languages and more than willing to give their opinions on topics of current interest. There are virtually no limitations on the work of reporters, and even Israel's military censorship is little more than an occasional annoyance.

Unlike most Arab countries, Israel doesn't require American journalists to obtain an entry permit; they simply arrive at the airport and get their passports stamped with a tourist visa. The Israeli authorities have no way of knowing that the tourist is a reporter; often they find out he has been in the country only weeks later, when they read his articles in the foreign press. Nor does Israel require journalists to obtain official press credentials. Those who want accreditation, however, get it automatically, provided only that they can demonstrate that they are bona fide correspondents on assignment.

Resident foreign correspondents, like visiting colleagues, are under no obligation to obtain press credentials, although they usually find them convenient. There are no restrictions on reporters' housing or the employment of local assistants. Some foreign correspondents live in Arab neighborhoods, but most prefer to live in the predominantly Jewish west side of Jerusalem. Almost all of them employ local assistants—some Jewish, some Arab—for translation, office management, or routine reportorial duties. Local stringers also receive press accreditation, and in the past the government has given press credentials to Palestinian newsmen such as Nafez Nazzal of *Time* magazine, free-lance journalist Jamil Hamad, and dozens of others.

The basic sources of information for foreign journalists in Israel are, more or less in order of importance, the Israeli press, including Palestinian media of East Jerusalem; Israeli and Palestinian political and government figures; foreign diplomats; and the Israeli public.

Although their "beats" are smaller than their colleagues' in the Arab world, who often have to cover an area the size of Western Europe, even a tiny country like Israel is too large for one or two (or even three or four) reporters to cover on an eyewitness basis. Their primary tool is the Israeli press itself, called by columnist Murray Kempton "the most trustworthy set of newspapers on earth."[2]

Israel has seven major Hebrew daily newspapers and a number of foreign language publications, most notably the English-language *Jerusalem Post,* as well as a vast array of weekly and monthly magazines. Three of the newspapers are controlled by political groups—al-*Hamishmar* by the left-wing Mapam faction of the Labor Alignment, *Davar* by the Labor Party-dominated General Federation of Labor (Histadrut), and *Hatzofe* by the Orthodox National Religious Party. The other four papers are independent and privately owned. *Ha'aretz,* a left-of-center morning paper, has been perhaps the bitterest critic of the Likud since 1977 but it has a long history of "troublemaking" for previous Labor governments as well. It was a report by *Ha'aretz* correspondent Dan Margalit about the illegal American bank account of Prime Minister Itzhak Rabin's wife that forced Rabin's resignation as Labor's candidate in the 1977 election.

The two veteran evening newspapers, *Ma'ariv* and *Yediot Achronot,* appeal to a mass audience. They are centrist or even right-centrist in their editorial policy, although *Ma'ariv* especially has been a sharp critic of the Likud. In 1984 *Ha'aretz* began publishing a new tabloid called *Chadashot. The Jerusalem Post,* which is widely read by the foreign press community, is also an opposition paper, partly owned by the Labor Federation and has been consistently and vocally opposed to the Likud.

The tenor of the domestic Israeli press criticism of the government tends to be brutal, and many new foreign correspondents in Israel are somewhat taken aback by its venomous tone, which stems largely from the intimate nature of Israeli society. In the U.S., administrations come and go and their key members—Kennedy's Boston mafia, Johnson's Texans, Nixon's Californians, or Carter's Georgians—are often regional figures who have had very little personal contact with the permanent Washington press corps before they arrive in the capital. It wasn't until 1975, for example, that Jimmy Carter began meeting national correspondents and columnists.[3] Israel, on the other hand, is so small and intimate that virtually all of the major political figures and important journalists have known each other for years. Israeli officials are among the most accessible in the world. They mingle with reporters in the dining room of the Knesset, answer their own phones at home, and very often socialize with journalists; and many reporters and politicians share family, school, or army ties. All this makes for a highly personal brand of journalism. Often, reporters are known as supporters of one or another political figure; just as often, they bear personal grudges or longstanding animosities toward various public personalities. In the U.S., battles between the press and the politicians are frequently fought with ICBMs fired across a gulf of mutual impersonality; in Israel, they tend to have the quality of a bayonet attack.

Naturally, the foreign press corps is a major beneficiary of this kind of Israeli journalism. Few secrets remain secret for long, and little that happens in the country—from a demonstration in the Galilee to a garbage strike in Eilat—goes unreported. Many journalists employ Israeli reporters as stringers or tipsters; others simply copy information from *The Jerusalem Post* or from translations of the Hebrew press, provided by the Government Press Office, rewrite it in their own style, and pass it along.

Another source of information is the electronic media. Until the 1960s, there was no television in Israel and the radio was under the control of the prime minister's office. Today, both television and radio are publicly run, along the lines of the BBC. Israel has only one television channel, and its daily half-hour news program is a potent factor in the national information equation. It has raised the hackles of every government since its inception in 1968 and continues to be a favorite target of official criticism for its "lack of objectivity."

In recent years much of the international press's attention has been focused on the West Bank as it relates to the overall Palestinian issue. The area is accessible to journalists, who are able to meet with its residents and usually to travel freely. Three Palestinian Arab newspapers are published in East Jerusalem—al-*Quds,* al-*Sha'ab,* and al-*Fajar.* The first is generally considered pro-Jordanian and reflects the opinions of the Hashamite government in Amman, while the other two are pro-PLO. All three are subject to censorship that is far more rigid than the military restrictions applied to the Hebrew press. The rationale for this political censorship is that the Arabic newspapers are primarily distributed and read in the West Bank and Gaza Strip, areas under Israeli military occupation. Israeli authorities maintain that incendiary articles could serve as a catalyst for violence and rebellion. Still, despite censorship, all three newspapers routinely print news and editorial opinion hostile to Israel's occupation and sometimes to the state itself. These newspapers have far less freedom of expression than their Israeli counterparts, but far more than newspapers in the Arab world.

Foreign reporters have access to other sources of information about the West Bank as well. One of the most popular is the nightly English-language television news broadcast
of Jordan, which is easily picked up in Jerusalem. Another,
amazingly, is the Palestine Press Service, a kind of "ministry
of information" for the PLO that operates in East Jerusalem. The PPS provides foreign correspondents with translations from the Arabic press, conducts tours of the West
Bank for visiting reporters, and serves as tipster, guide, and
spokesman for the PLO. There must be few examples in
history of an irredentist movement running its own information office in the "enemy capital."

The content of foreign reporting from Israel is largely
supplied by one of the most lively and accessible political
debates in the world. Politicians of all parties are constantly
prepared to reveal and denounce the sins and failures of their
rivals; the opposition keeps up a drum beat of criticism of
the government, and the government replies in kind. The
main problem for the foreign correspondent is often to sift
through the cornucopia of information and opinion and to
determine what is reliable and important.

In many countries, foreign journalists are treated with
indifference, but in Israel, which depends on the support of
American public opinion and whose politicians and political
parties are often supported financially and politically by Jews
from abroad, foreign correspondents can be an important
conduit. Many foreign reporters have been surprised to find
that they cannot only reach cabinet ministers and opposition leaders on the telephone, but that important public figures sometimes seek them out. A new correspondent in Israel
once told me disbelievingly, "In France you have to write a
letter to get a meeting with the prime minister's spokesman.
I was just over at the Knesset dining room and was invited
to tea with the prime minister."

Some Israeli leaders, notably Golda Meir and Menachem Begin, have been extremely sensitive to what is written about them in the world press. Golda once called in a
senior foreign reporter and demanded to know why he had
referred to her as "dumpy" in one of his dispatches. "I may

be prime minister," the seventyish Golda reprimanded him, "but I'm still a woman." Begin, who got into the habit of listening to the BBC during the prestate period when he was in the underground and the British had a price on his head, read widely in the world press every day. In his first years in office, he occasionally surprised foreign journalists by calling them on the telephone to express disagreement with something they had written.

On one occasion, shortly after Israel bombed the Iraqi atomic reactor, Begin attended a garden party at the British Embassy, where he was surrounded by foreign reporters. To one, Patrick Massey of Reuters, he confided that the Israeli attack had destroyed a secret installation forty meters underground. Massey filed the scoop, which was featured around the world. The following day, he learned that the installation was not forty meters below the earth, but four. He was still mulling over this embarrassing error and wondering how he could have made it when he received a telephone call from Begin, who had seen the report and realized that he had unintentionally misled the reporter. "First time in my life I've ever been apologized to by a prime minister," Massey recalled later.

Israel is a country in which virtually everyone has strong political opinions and is more than willing to share them with the world. During the Lebanese war, for example, a few of the public information officers in the army spokesmen's corps—reservists from all walks of civilian life who are supposed to explain army policy—bitterly criticized the government and its conduct of the war in the presence of foreign reporters. This kind of freedom of speech is taken for granted in Israel but often amazes foreign correspondents.

Friends of foreign correspondents can be important sources of information, a fact that sometimes leads to misconceptions, since most correspondents tend to socialize with college-educated, English-speaking Israelis. Often they mistake their friends' views for those of the country as a whole; and for years the foreign press had a tendency to underrate Menachem Begin's political popularity for precisely this reason.

Then, there are the neighbors. During the Sadat visit to Jerusalem, William Farrell, Jerusalem correspondent of *The New York Times* at the time, did a story on Israeli reaction to the Egyptian president. One of the people he spoke with was the elderly Bucharian-Jewish tailor whose shop is half a floor down from the *Times*'s Jerusalem office and close to the Israeli Government Press Office. The tailor predicted that Sadat would be warmly received which is, in fact, what happened. Other journalists read Farrell's article and began to drop in on the tailor for man-in-the-street comments on various issues. After a week or so, he hung up a bulletin board on the wall of his shop, with the heading "Dear Journalist: I am busy. Here are my opinions for the day," and listed his thoughts on various political matters.

The freedom of foreign correspondents is, of course, a function of Israel's open society. There is, however, a limitation on reportorial freedom—the existence of military censorship, which requires all reporters, local and foreign, to submit stories related to security matters for the approval of the military censors in Jerusalem or Tel Aviv.

Like much else about Israel, military press censorship is rooted in the country's security situation. Israel has been in a state of war with its Arab neighbors since 1948. Full-scale hostilities have taken place in 1948–49, 1956, 1967, 1973, and 1982, and in between there have been intermittent border clashes, acts of terrorism, and wars of attrition. Israel has thus been locked into what is essentially a perpetual state of war—while at the same time creating and maintaining an open society. The usual suspension of civil rights and liberties that has characterized modern Western democracies during wartime cannot be employed for the simple reason that for Israel it is always wartime. Military censorship, in its present form, is an attempt to strike a balance between a free press and the government's need to protect sensitive military information.

Before the 1982 war in Lebanon, Israel's military censorship had attracted press attention from time to time. *The New York Times* and some other American publications and

networks routinely labeled material passed by the censor as
such, but most journalists accepted it as a necessary evil.
During the summer of 1982, however, Israeli censorship was
transformed into an important issue by the American press,
particularly by the networks.

At the very beginning of the war, reports from Israel,
which were of course checked by the authorities, appeared
on American television with the caption CLEARED BY THE IS-
RAELI MILITARY CENSOR. The press also loudly complained
about Israel's policy of excluding foreign correspondents
from the battlefield for the first five days of the war. This
criticism was, for the most part, harsher than that directed
at the far more draconian exclusion and censorship practiced by the British during the almost simultaneous Falkland Campaign, but under the circumstances, it was
understandable.

These protests became exaggerated and unreasonable,
however, when a complicated set of circumstances put Israel in the position of censoring material gathered on the
PLO side of the battlefield. During the first week of fighting, the satellite facility in Beirut became inoperable and
television journalists there were unable to transmit their
material to New York. The networks approached the Israeli
military authorities and requested permission to send their
reports by way of the Israeli transmitter. In what was to prove
an example of misplaced liberality, Israel said yes, provided
only that the networks accept the same rules of censorship
as applied to the film being shot on the Israeli side of the
lines. The networks agreed, and for a few days Israel became the conduit for the televised reports of the Beirut press
corps.

It didn't take long for Israel to understand the absurdity
of the arrangement. In modern warfare, access to public
opinion is a weapon, and nations fight to isolate their enemies and cut them off from international exposure. Israel
was doing just the opposite; day after day it was helping to
transmit interviews with the PLO leadership, pictures of
Yasser Arafat kissing babies, and a good deal of tendentious
and sensational reporting on the war. Moreover, the Israeli

censor had no clear criteria for dealing with this material; after all, no arrangement like this had ever existed in the history of warfare. Things came to a head on June 21, when the censor refused to approve an ABC interview with Yasser Arafat.

Despite the ruling of the censor, ABC decided to send the material anyway. Such a deliberate violation of military censorship during wartime is an extremely serious offense, and in past American wars, correspondents had been expelled for less. Israel's response was almost laughably lenient—it suspended ABC's satellite privileges for forty-eight hours, but allowed its correspondents to continue covering the war.

ABC's reaction was brutal. It announced in its June 22 evening news broadcast that its satellite rights had been suspended, but didn't explain why. Over the next week it was joined by NBC and CBS in a dramatic campaign against Israeli military censorship; at one point CBS even blacked out its screen for twenty-two seconds in protest.[4] NBC's John Chancellor delivered a sermonette against wartime censorship and obliquely threatened Israel with a loss of American aid for practicing it.[5] ABC denounced the Israeli sanctions night after night.

There is a convention in American television news by which two sides to a dispute are both allowed to present their positions. That rule is often suspended, however, when the networks are themselves one of the parties. During June 1982, ABC, NBC, and CBS declined to allow Israel to explain the special circumstances that had led to the censorship of the material from Beirut. Israel was portrayed as practicing an almost uniquely harsh form of political censorship. Needless to say, none of the networks had ever given Israel public credit for its help in transmitting the Beirut material in the first place.

Wartime military censorship is by no means an Israeli invention. Every war fought by every democracy in this century, with the exception of Vietnam, has occasioned press restrictions, often of the harshest kind. During World War I, according to Phillip Knightley's excellent book *The First*

Casualty, Great Britain imposed censorship "so severe that
its legacy lingers today . . ."[6] In August 1914, for example, approximately 300,000 French soldiers died in the Battle of the Frontiers, the highest rate of casualties in the entire
war. The carnage was never reported in Great Britain until
after the war, and this despite the fact that a correspondent,
Gerald Fitzgerald Campbell of *The Times* of London was with
the French army at the time.[7] American reporters found that
everything they wrote was subject to censorship, much of it
aimed at protecting the army and the Wilson administration
from political embarrassment. Knightley tells of an incident
in which some reporters tried to send a story about cases of
wine presented to the Americans by the French as a gesture
of goodwill. The censors vetoed it on the ground that "it
suggests bibulous indulgence by American soldiers which
might offend temperance forces in the United States."*[8]

During World War II, Allied censorship was, if anything, even more demanding. The French, until they quit
the war, maintained a stringent system for checking and ap-
proving the copy of war correspondents. In England, all outgoing communications—mail, cable, or telephone—were
subject to censorship. Everyone, including newspaper editors, was prohibited from "obtaining, recording, communicating to any other person or publishing information which
might be useful to the enemy."[9] Throughout the war, censorship was routinely employed to repress unpleasant information, such as British loses in the Battle of the Atlantic.

The United States began military censorship in World
War II with the attack on Pearl Harbor. After the first dispatch by the United Press, the military censors managed to
prevent further independent reports for four days and
published their own highly misleading accounts of American losses. For the duration, America applied censorship both

---

*These acts of censorship during World War I were accompanied by a great
deal of voluntary "patriotic" self-censorship on the part of the press itself. *The Times*
of London, for example, defended its censorship of the casualties in the Battle of
the Frontiers as a contribution to British war morale; while on the other side of
the Atlantic, H. L. Mencken, perhaps America's greatest newsman, was forced, in
1915, to abandon his "Freelance" column in the *Baltimore Sun* because of his pro-
German views.

at home and abroad. An office of censorship was established in order to determine that the press was following the Code of Wartime Practices while in the field, all correspondents were required to submit their copy to military censors.

U.S. press restrictions were especially heavy in the Pacific theater, where General MacArthur informed soldiers that they would be court-martialed for talking without permission to correspondents.[10] Following the surrender of Japan, MacArthur placed southern Japan off limits to correspondents. It was a month after the atomic bomb attacks on Hiroshima and Nagasaki before a Western reporter was able to give an eye-witness account of the devastation they had caused.[11]

Allied censors were careful to mask the excesses committed by their forces, and Knightley claims not to have been able to find a single report of an atrocity committed by an Allied soldier.[12] Entire battles went unreported, and clearly nonmilitary subjects, such as the cooperation between Allied commanders and Vichy French officials after the capture of North Africa, were subject to what amounted to political censorship.[13]

The list goes on. During the Korean War correspondents came under the jurisdiction of the army and censorship both of military information and of "derogatory comments" about Allied forces or military leaders was strictly enforced.[14]

During the Algerian civil war, the French, whose notion of press freedom is rather undemanding by American standards, used censorship and the suppression of newspapers and magazines to control information about the fighting, sometime seizing foreign publications whose reports did not coincide with the French view of the war. Foreign correspondents whose coverage displeased French authorities, such as John Rich of NBC, were not permitted to enter (or reenter) Algeria.[15]

During the 1982 Falkland crisis, the British carefully screened the correspondents allowed to join the expeditionary force and then strictly censored all of their dispatches, reports, and photos. Journalists other than those taken to the scene by the British (who were thus under total control) were not allowed to approach the area of the fighting; indeed in one instance, the British informed a group of American journalists that they might be attacked if they attempted to hire a ship to follow the British fleet.[16]

Those few reporters who were able to land with the British troops on the Falklands were allowed a narrow, tightly supervised view of the fighting and were subject to very tough censorship. Nor were the British prepared to take any chances with foreign correspondents. All the reporters allowed to accompany the British forces were from British news organizations.

Most recently, in October 1983, the U.S. invasion force at Grenada excluded correspondents during the early stages of the operation—a censorship-by-exclusion that was loudly protested by the press—and generally applauded by the public.

In the perspective of this Western tradition of wartime censorship Israel's military restrictions are benign indeed. So much so, in fact, that following the Falkland Island's Campaign and the 1982 war in Lebanon, representatives of both Great Britain's television networks—BBC and ITN—officially praised the Israeli system and recommended to a parliamentary commission that it be adopted by the British authorities.[17]

During "normal" times, Israel's military censorship is little more than an occasional annoyance for journalists. The censor is forbidden to interfere with copy dealing with matters outside a clearly defined group of security subjects, and most resident foreign correspondents don't even bother to submit copy to the censor unless they themselves feel that there might be something censorable in it. Often, when they do, they are agreeably surprised to find him willing to negotiate over terminology rather than using his blue pencil.

David Shipler of *The New York Times*, who, like almost all journalists, is opposed to censorship on principle, puts it this way: "Censorship in Israel is usually very finely focused. It almost never strays into political areas; even its military dimensions are rather narrow. In most cases the censor doesn't even attempt to interfere with the content of the story—just with military details, such as the names of officers or the number of troops and types of weapons." One area in which military censorship might have been abused—the administration of the West Bank, which is under the technical control of the army—is not treated as censorable at all. "I've never even submitted a story on the West Bank to the military censor," Shipler says.[18]

Tim McNulty, who has been the *Chicago Tribune* bureau chief in Israel since 1982, is even more outspoken. "Mostly we just ignore censorship," he says. "It doesn't usually affect print journalists at all."[19]

One of the main reasons for this liberality on the part of the military censor is that in most cases he cannot enforce his rulings. In the era of direct-dial international calls and Telex, it is almost impossible to monitor communications between journalists in an open society and their offices abroad; a reporter with information he believes will not pass the censor can simply call his editor abroad and ask that the information be attributed to "defense analysts in Washington" or "observers in the Middle East." It can't be proved that this information actually originated with the reporter in Israel. Because of the extreme Israeli sensitivity to the issue of press freedom, it has been policy to accept these deceptions rather than challenge them. When, for example, the now defunct *Washington Star* printed the name of the head of the Shin Bet (Israel's equivalent of the FBI), which is subject to official secrecy, the *Star* claimed that the information had been obtained in Washington. Despite a strong suspicion that this was not the case, the government decided to drop the matter.

Only once in the past decade has Israel suspended a foreign correspondent's credentials for a violation of censorship. In February 1980, CBS correspondent Dan Raviv flew to Rome, where he broadcast a report on an alleged Israeli nuclear test. Raviv had obtained the information (whose accuracy Israel denied) in Tel Aviv and by reporting it in his own name, he made it impossible to ignore the violation of censorship. Raviv's press credentials were suspended, but he was allowed to remain in the country (as a Jew, he was even eligible to become an Israeli citizen under the Law of Return) and he continued to work as a reporter without credentials for some time, until he was posted to London. During the 1982 war, Israeli authorities agreed to reinstate Raviv's accreditation.

Israel is a very different country from its Arab neighbors, and its attitude toward the press is one of the most striking differences. The nature of its society leaves Israel open to the scrutiny of its citizens and outsiders alike, while its Arab adversaries, untroubled by prying reporters or free debate, hide their activities and ambitions from the rest of the world.

As always, when an open society comes into conflict with dictatorships it is at a great disadvantage. Its inevitable imperfections are magnified because they are both accessible and exceptional—and thus newsworthy; while the ugly realities of military regimes and feudal monarchies go unreported for lack of opportunity or interest. This asymmetry leads to a distorted perception—the dictatorship appears to the casual observer to do little wrong, while the democracy seems to do little else. In the case of a small, vulnerable nation like Israel, dependent on support of public opinion in the free world, such an optical illusion is exceptionally dangerous.

The natural antidote for this distortion is the respect and affection that journalists instinctively feel for open societies. The open society is the natural ally of the journalist, just as the dictatorship is his natural enemy. Given a choice between the two the reporter will normally prefer the former, a preference that will cause him to attempt to correct the distortion without sacrificing the integrity of his work. He does this not by repressing or softening negative news about the open society but by seeking ways to inform the public of the dissimilar ground rules that force him to protect the dictatorship.

There was a time in the Middle East when American reporters and editorial writers instinctively preferred Israel to the Arab states, not out of philo-Semitism or anti-Arab racism, not out of guilt for the Holocaust, not even out of solidarity with an American ally—but simply because Israel was an open society.

Today, for many in the American press corps, that attitude is passé, or worse. It is now fashionable for reporters to be "neutral," and "even-handed," as if a journalist's neutrality in a contest between open and closed societies is not incongruous. Such "neutrality" is, in fact, partiality, for it robs Israel of its natural antidote—not the unquestioning approbation of the Western press nor its support for every Israeli action and policy, but its good wishes and affection, and the benefit of the doubt.

11

THE WORLD FROM WASHINGTON

More than sixty years ago Walter Lippmann addressed the question of who and what determines what will make "news." Lippmann pointed out that human activity is so varied and complex, and the space for news so limited, that only a tiny fraction of each day's events can possibly be selected and reported. He likened the process of selection to the beam of a searchlight that moves "relentlessly about, bringing one episode and then another out of the darkness into vision."[1]

Lippmann wrote these words at a time when the United States was just awakening to its international role and the need for information about the rest of the world which such a role entails. Today, given America's global interests, that need has become a vital necessity; and it is Lippmann's searchlight—illuminating some places and leaving others in obscurity—that largely determines how it will be satisfied.

No one person controls the searchlight. The American media are far too varied and heterogeneous for that. But of all the factors that influence the selection and approach to foreign news in the United States, none is more important than the policies and attitudes of the American govern-

ment. Today, twenty years into the era of adversary journalism brought about by Vietnam and Watergate, for much
of the American press, much of the time, foreign news is
still essentially what the U.S. government says it is.

It is not surprising that this is so, for in most cases foreign developments usually need an American angle to become important news in America. Sometimes the angle is
provided by human interest: feature stories of the "Soviet
Teens Go Wild for Michael Jackson" or "Burt Reynolds Voted
Most Popular Film Star in Pakistan" variety, the point of
which is to show the influence of American trends or personalities on the rest of the world. (The search for such an
angle once prompted Ned Temko of the *Christian Science
Monitor* to ask Mahmud Labadi for the PLO's reaction to the
death of Elvis Presley).[2] Sometimes, in the case of "spot news,"
it comes from the involvement of Americans in some foreign event—ST. LOUIS RESIDENT DIES IN LISBON FIRE; TWO
HUNDRED AND TWENTY PORTUGUESE ALSO PERISH—a parochialism typical of, but by no means exclusive to, the American
press. But for most serious international developments—wars,
revolutions, international relations, and the internal affairs
of foreign countries—it is the interest of the U.S. government that most often provides the American angle.

There are, of course, exceptions. Some international
events are so compelling and dramatic that they are inherently newsworthy. The British invasion of the Falklands, the
Israeli rescue mission at Entebbe, the attempted assassination of the Pope or the ongoing confrontation between Solidarity and the Polish government all fall into the category
of cardinal news, that is, developments of intrinsic news value.
Such events are relatively rare, however. It usually requires
some perceived American interest to elevate far-off developments from the level of the esoteric to the status of important news. This dimension is most often provided by the
American government which gives institutional expression
to American interests and concerns around the world. Revolution in Central America, Libyan aggression in Africa, or
human rights violations in Argentina go on more or less all
the time; they become important to Americans only when

the U.S. government chooses to address them from the perspective of its policy and interests. In doing so, the government puts the issue on the press's agenda of international coverage, and it also uses its credibility and resources to influence the tone and content of that coverage.

This agenda-setting ability is not absolute, but it is considerable. Howard Simons, managing editor of *The Washington Post*, puts it this way: "The administration commands the high ground. Any time the President of the United States wants to get headlines or air time, all he has to do is call a press conference. He can say, 'I have a very important statement to make,' and he captures our front page. And so, in a sense, he controls the agenda [of foreign coverage]. But the whole administration does that. Of course we work very hard at trying to find out what's happening behind what we're told, and we've gotten much better at it, but you can devote just so many people and so much time."[3]

Leslie Gelb, diplomatic correspondent for *The New York Times*, agrees. Gelb, who served as a senior official in the Carter administration, has been a part of the process from both sides. "In the stories that make impact," he says, "you've got to report what power says and does, which is basically the government's position."[4]

Many journalists are aware of the government's capacity to influence the foreign news agenda and some, like Seth Lipsky of *The Wall Street Journal*, consider it natural. "We cover the news. The government says, 'Here is what we're going to do,' and then the press sits back and decides if it's news or not. I don't think that's a terribly sinister arrangement in itself."[5]

Others take a less sanguine view of the process. In early 1982, ABC's Ted Koppel asked rhetorically: "Why is it that twelve months ago, when the administration mentioned El Salvador, we all jumped down to El Salvador. There were a dozen television crews in El Salvador within a week. When the administration stopped talking about El Salvador, a month later there were practically no television crews down there— occasionally one might go down for a special assignment. The administration started talking about El Salvador again, and there they are, another dozen television crews down there. If that isn't manipulation, I don't know what is."[6]

Koppel is, of course, right. In the case of El Salvador, the Reagan administration took a previously obscure nation and by focusing attention on it, brought it center stage in the American press—an example of agenda setting par excellence. But many journalists would agree with Seth Lipsky that while the U.S. government may often be able to determine *what* the press covers, it has no control over *how*.

"OK, take the case of El Salvador," says *The New York Times*'s Craig Whitney. "All of a sudden in Washington they said that the place is falling apart [in March 1983], that they're about to run out of ammunition. Well, what you want to do in a case like that is to go down to the area. You say, 'Wait a minute, how does it look from El Salvador? What's happening down there, what do the people there say—are they really going to run out of ammunition? . . . The administration may provoke coverage that it really doesn't want."[7]

There have, indeed, been cases in which the U.S. government has encountered this boomerang effect, cases in which most of the press has been critical of official policy and doctrine. Vietnam was one example, and more recently Central America and Lebanon have been others. On close inspection, however, these boomerangs have two common characteristics that are absent in most foreign stories. First, they are all situations in which there is direct American involvement (or the potential for such involvement), and when American troops are committed, or American lives are in danger, the story ceases to be foreign news and becomes a domestic issue, subject to all the self-confident skepticism that the press brings to bear on such issues. Second, and just as important, they have all taken place in areas to which the American or other Western media have had access. Whatever the U.S. government claimed about the progress of the war in Vietnam, for example, was scrutinized by an army of American journalists on the scene. Similarly, when the Reagan administration insisted that the government of El Salvador was in trouble, Craig Whitney and the nation's other foreign editors could dispatch reporters to see for themselves. In Beirut, in 1983 and 1984, too, American journalists were able to observe the situation there firsthand and to form their own assessments about the future of the Gemayel government and its relations with the United States. When these two conditions are present—direct American involvement and media access—the press has both the motive and the opportunity to practice independent journalism. But usually they are not present, at least not simultaneously, and when they are not the government has an exceedingly good chance of setting the news agenda—and of successfully arguing its case, as well.

There are several reasons for this, not the least of which is the disparity between the number of American reporters stationed abroad, concentrated in a comparatively few cities, and the vastly greater number of American diplomats and officials overseas. As a result of this imbalance, when the American government *does* decide to turn its searchlight on some distant land, or to illuminate a previously obscure situation, it enjoys a great advantage, both in terms of the quantity of information at its disposal and of the quality of its expertise.

"They outnumber us hundreds to one," says Howard Simons. "While we have three State Department correspondents, they have hundreds of people involved in grinding out press releases, holding meetings and briefings. The administration commands the high ground."[8] This numerical superiority is even greater overseas, where one, two, or at most three correspondents may be charged with reporting on an entire continent where the United States has hundreds of professional diplomats.

The American government enjoys other advantages in its dealings with the press on foreign affairs issues. One is the close relationship—professional and sometimes personal—between many government officials and the journalists who cover international news in Washington. This relationship springs from a mutuality of need and a concert of interest which often exists between reporters and their sources. Over the course of time, journalists come to depend on government officials for information and guidance; they spend a good deal of time together, inhabit the same intellectual climate, and often arrive at common perceptions based on shared information.

These Washington-based reporters often dominate the coverage of foreign affairs, including events in nations where they have never been. This situation is especially true of newspapers with Washington bureaus but no foreign correspondents, but it also confronts (and often confounds) foreign correspondents as well. The Associated Press's Mort Rosenblum describes the problems that this can create: "When the two work at cross-purposes the foreign correspondents—closest to the action—are usually overshadowed. Washington reporters outnumber them, and they are closer to their editors."[9]

The ability of the American government to influence not only the subject but the content of foreign coverage is especially great in the case of closed societies. Even dictatorships that allow foreign journalists to live and work there, such as the Soviet Union or China, drastically restrict freedom of movement and contact with local citizens. Reporters are generally not allowed to travel outside a limited geographical area without the explicit permission of the government; usually journalists are required to live in official government housing under the watchful eyes of superintendents, guards, and other informers, and to employ government-approved local assistants. And always, reporters in closed societies suffer from the chronic lack of information that typifies modern totalitarian nations.

Given these limitations, the U.S. government often has a great deal more information—gathered by diplomats and intelligence agents in the field, or by technological means—than the press can ever hope to get independently. As a result, much of what appears to be news coverage is, in fact, information provided to the media by the government in briefings, leaks, and interviews. This near monopoly on news about many closed societies provides the administration in Washington with a powerful tool for dealing with the foreign-policy reporters in the capital; both a carrot—giving a journalist needed information—and a stick—giving it to the competition.

In the Middle East, where access for the press is especially limited and the appetite for news especially great, the American government has a particularly great leverage which is brought to bear both in Washington and in the field. As Douglas Watson of *U.S. News and World Report* puts it, "The main source for American reporters in most Middle Eastern countries are American diplomats."[10] The truth of this remark becomes obvious to anyone who carefully examines the reportage from places like Saudi Arabia, Syria, or Iraq, which tends to be heavy on "diplomats here believe" and very light on contacts with local officials and citizens.

The dependence of journalists on American officials in these countries has a kind of Catch-22 effect. The American administration begins to advocate some new policy or warn of an impending danger to American interests, and conscientious editors dispatch reporters to the scene for a firsthand look. They may or may not be able to obtain a visa, but those who do will usually find that they cannot pierce the curtain of secrecy that veils the subject they are trying to investigate. Lacking an alternative, they turn to the best available source of information—the local U.S. Embassy or Interest Section. Since these diplomats are American State Department employees, however, it is unlikely that they will deviate too much from the assessments that the reporters have come to check. Indeed, in many cases these diplomats are the *source* of the assessments, and are thus in the happy position of being both author and critic.

This process has been at least partially responsible for some of the more notable failures of the American press in the Middle East. Over the past decade much of the American media uncritically accepted (and transmitted) official assurances about the invulnerability of the Shah of Iran; the military superiority of Saddam Hussein's Iraq over neighboring Iran; the willingness of King Hussein of Jordan to accept the Reagan Plan in the winter and early spring of 1983; and the premise that Saudi Arabia would be prepared to support the United States' Middle East policy, including Camp David, in return for the sale of AWACs and other sophisticated military hardware. These notions, whether the wishful thinking by American policy makers and diplomats, or the ax-grinding insights of State Department "Arabists," have, when translated into journalism, done little to help the American public understand the complexities of the Middle East.

If the American government is at its most potent in affecting press coverage of dictatorships, it is also far from without resources for influencing the media's agenda and perceptions about open societies as well. These resources are normally brought to bear in support of American policy in disputes with otherwise friendly nations. This is what happened when, during the Carter administration, the U.S. government decided to use its prestige and influence to focus American media coverage on Israeli settlements on the West Bank.

Ever since Israel captured the West Bank in the June 1967 Six Day War, American policy has consistently opposed permanent Israeli control over the area. During the decade that followed the war, Israeli governments led by Golda Meir and Itzhak Rabin sought a territorial compromise based on the Allon Plan, that would leave between forty and fifty percent of the territory in Israeli hands while returning the rest to Jordan. During these years Jordan's King Hussein constantly refused to accept the idea of compromise and insisted that the entire region be turned over to him (or, after the Rabat Arab summit in 1974, to the PLO). Faced with an impasse, the Meir and Rabin governments proceeded to "create facts" by establishing Jewish settlements in areas that the Allon Plan envisioned as remaining in Israeli hands—the Jordan Valley, the Hebron district, and greater Jerusalem. The U.S. government did not support the establishment of these settlements, but it was not too upset about them, either.

In his memoirs, Henry Kissinger, who supervised American foreign policy between 1969 and 1977, dealt extensively with the Middle East and the Arab-Israel conflict, but hardly mentioned the West Bank at all. Even more surprising, he made virtually no mention of Israeli settlements despite the fact that dozens of Jewish collectives and villages were established during this period. Kissinger's lack of interest in these settlements is an expression of the general attitude of benign neglect toward Jewish settlement activities in the West Bank during the Nixon and Ford administrations.*

Since the act of Jewish settlement in the West Bank was not a *cardinal* news story of the Falkland invasion or Entebbe rescue mission variety, the American media paid it little attention during the years of official American apathy under Nixon and Ford. Typical of their approach was this wire-service dispatch, carried far back in *The New York Times,* on January 2, 1970—one of the slowest news days of the year.

"Tel Aviv (Reuters): Israel today established its fourth settlement in the occupied Jordan Valley.

"The settlement at the foot of Mt. Sartaba was named Messua, which means "beacon." It will be populated by members of Jewish religious youth movements serving in Nahal, an army corps that combines military service with agricultural settlement. The collective will raise vegetables on a twenty acre tract on the west bank of the valley which Israel seized from Jordan in the Six Day War."[12]

This was the ordinary tone of American press coverage of Israeli settlement throughout the mid-1970s. Even the announcement, in 1970, of the establishment of Kiriat Arba, a Jewish neighborhood in the all-Arab town of Hebron, attracted only moderate attention in the nation's press. The American government did not choose to deal in any serious way with the issue of West Bank settlements, and lacking an American angle, the nation's editors displayed little interest in the story.

All this contrasts dramatically with the Carter adminis-

---

*In *Years of Upheaval,* Kissinger makes twelve specific references to the West Bank in the course of twelve hundred pages, and most of these are cursory comments in the context of Israeli-Jordanian relations. In contrast, former National Security Adviser Dr. Zbigniew Brzezinski devotes a large section of his book to the question of the West Bank and Jewish settlement there.[11]

tration's virtual obsession with the West Bank and Jewish settlements there. Carter's approach was based on a 1975 report by a study group at the Brookings Institution, whose members included Zbigniew Brzezinski and William Quant. The report was grounded in the notion that Middle Eastern stability (and by extension, Western oil supplies) was primarily threatened by the Arab-Israeli conflict, and that the heart of the conflict was not the Arab world's rejection of Israel, but the Palestine question. It followed that a resolution of the Palestinian problem would lead to a solution of the broader Arab-Israeli dispute, and to regional peace and tranquillity.

Jimmy Carter and his advisers believed that the solution of the Palestinian problem would be the creation of an entity or "homeland" in the West Bank and Gaza Strip. This reasoning led them to oppose any Israeli effort, especially the creation of Israeli settlements, that might foreclose the option of placing the entire territory at the disposal of the Palestinians. Settlements became, in the Carter lexicon, "illegal" and "an obstacle to peace."

When Prime Minister Itzhak Rabin visited Washington in March 1977, he was dismayed to discover that Jimmy Carter intended to press this policy, and the two men had an acrimonious series of meetings. Their disagreements were an idyllic honeymoon, however, compared to the dispute that followed the May 1977 election of Menachem Begin, whose Likud party came to office committed to securing Israel's permanent control over the West Bank and Gaza Strip.

From the very beginning, the clash between the two leaders was an uneven contest—a battle between the immovable object of Begin's resolve to keep the West Bank, and the ultimately resistible force of Carter's determination to prevent it. Both men saw Jewish settlement as a crucial factor in determining the future of the area; and when President Carter realized that quiet persuasion and diplomacy could not dissuade Begin from his settlement program, he went public, as a means both of bringing pressure on Israel and of establishing his credentials as an "even-handed" broker with the Arabs.

It was Jimmy Carter's intention to take a hitherto relatively obscure issue—Jewish settlement in the West Bank—and turn the searchlight of American national interest on it. He had a number of means at his disposal—from his famous March 1977 "Palestinian homeland" speech to briefings and off-the-record discussions with American pundits, reporters, and editors. Of all the techniques, none was as public, or as effective, as the daily State Department briefings.

To illustrate the process, consider a hypothetical settlement not too different from Messua, whose establishment had attracted so little attention back in 1970. The hypothetical settlement has been authorized by the Israeli government and founded by a group of Jewish teen-agers and young adults. Its establishment has been reported by the wire services from Jerusalem, and these reports have appeared, if at all, far back in the American newspapers. The next day, however, at the State Department briefing, one of the reporters, having been prompted in advance by the department's spokesman, asks him about the wire-service dispatch.

"Yes, we've seen that report," the spokesman answers.

"Well, does the State Department have any reaction?"

The spokesman consults his notes, and then informs the assembled journalists that the United States is unalterably opposed to such settlements, and considers them to be provocative and illegal.

"Does the government intend to convey its position to the Israelis?"

"Yes, we do. In fact, the President has already directed the Secretary of State to contact his counterpart in Israel and make our position perfectly clear. We are calling on the government of Israel to cease all settlement activity in the interests of arriving at a regional peace that will be comprehensive, fair, and provide security to all the peoples and states of the Middle East."

The settlement is now an important story, the focus of a major disagreement between the United States and an important Middle East friend. The dispute will be featured that night on American television news broadcasts.

The following morning the settlement issue will gain new impetus when it is taken up by *The New York Times*. The *Times* is America's newspaper of record, and it considers the declarations and attitudes of the U.S. government to be news by definition. No less important, the *Times* very likely has the largest Jewish readership of any newspaper in the world, including the Israeli newspapers. No one at the *Times* knows what percentage of its readers are Jewish, but it is generally assumed that it could be as many as half, and some guess more. Newspapers are usually interested in what interests their readers. The *Chicago Tribune* has plenty of news from Poland, the *Miami Herald* specializes in Central America, the *Houston Chronicle* has a great many stories about Mexico. *The New York Times* is very aware of issues concerning the Jewish state and gives them considerable prominence. Naturally, any conflict between the U.S. government and Israel will be of special interest and concern to hundreds of thousands of *Times* readers. It will appear on the front page, in the right-hand column at the top. The placement means: Major Story.

That morning the *Times* will be spread across the breakfast tables of countless readers for whom it is both a national institution and their hometown newspaper. Among them will be the senior editors and executives of ABC, NBC, CBS, AP, *Time, Newsweek, The Wall Street Journal*—all of whom are headquartered in New York—as well as the intellectuals, writers, and academics who form the little world of communications in New York City and beyond. By the time they finish their breakfasts, they will be aware that the small wire-service report they saw yesterday, and half listened to on the evening news, is no longer a small story but an important development.

Within hours, rockets will begin to fly. Reporters in Israel will be asked to visit the settlement, by now the center of a U.S.-Israeli controversy, to expand on the story, and to give it a human face by interviewing local Arab residents and Israeli settlers. Their articles will appear alongside background reports on the history of Jewish settlement in the West Bank, reports from the State Department on the growing anger of the U.S. administration toward Israel, and editorials and columns, most of which will condemn the obstacles that Israel's intransigence is putting in the way of peace. *Time* magazine will be preparing a cover story called, ISRAEL VS. AMERICA: THE CRUNCH FINALLY COMES.*

Within a week, the small Jewish village on the West Bank will be as famous as Tel Aviv and, in some quarters, as infamous as Jonestown. Each thrust by Washington will be parried by the Israeli government, tempers in the two capitals will flare, and the press will record and comment on the controversy in detail. Somewhere, in the back room of one of the networks, someone is planning a special.

Does this mean that the American government has artificially manipulated the news? Not quite. American-Israeli relations are an important issue, and any major irritant or disagreement is a matter of valid concern. Certainly an open dispute between Washington and Jerusalem falls well within the conventions of American news judgment.

At the same time, the extensive coverage of the settlement's establishment has been dictated not by its intrinsic news value, or by the independent news judgment of American journalists, but by U.S. government policy, which includes not merely opposition to the settlement, but the decision to make that opposition public. The story of the settlement was thus not *necessarily* big news. Consider:

The same Israeli youngsters set up their tents on the West Bank; the same wire-service correspondent files the same story describing the settlement; the next day, at the State Department briefing, the same question about the settlement is asked. Only this time the spokesman responds differently:

"Well, yes, we've seen the reports," he says.

"What's the department's reaction?"

"We're studying it."

"That's all?"

"Well, as you know, the United States has a point of view

---

*Every news organization has its pet subjects, which it uses repeatedly. *Time*, whose outrage at Israel's West Bank policy is only slightly greater than that of Yasser Arafat's, has a passion for the "long-awaited crunch in Israeli-American relations."

on various developments in the Middle East, including those which affect Israel and other friendly nations. At the moment, however, urgent regional business is taking precedence over this and other less pressing developments."

"What urgent regional business?"

"Glad you asked. We're especially concerned about recent developments in the Persian Gulf. Now . . ."

And, of course, there will be no settlement story that day, no report on the evening news, no *New York Times*-inspired rocket that will send reporters and photographers out to the West Bank. *Time* magazine may even refrain from doing a cover story.

During the Carter administration, Israeli officials in Washington and Jerusalem were well aware of the U.S. government's efforts to influence American public opinion as a means of pressuring Israel over the settlement issue. In those days I often discussed this aim, and the techniques used to achieve it, with American reporters in Israel, many of whom were aghast at the suggestion that the demand for news about the West Bank and settlements was influenced in any way by Washington, and one or two of the less polite made it clear that they considered the very idea to be a proof of my incipient paranoia. I was, therefore, gratified when some of these same journalists began to complain in private, shortly after the Reagan administration took office, that their editors were no longer interested in important West Bank stories, and could they please find out something about this terrorism business that Haig kept mentioning.

Which did not mean that there were *no* articles about settlements and the West Bank, or that interest died altogether; it simply meant that the administration was swinging its searchlight in other directions. When the Reagan Plan was published in September 1982 it occasioned a spate of articles about the West Bank, and so too did the possibility of a PLO-Jordanian acceptance of the plan. These were, however, sporadic flashes of interest, and nothing like the sustained attention America's elite news organizations focused on the area during the Carter-Begin period.

Nor was the Carter administration's influence limited to agenda setting. Virtually the entire American press supported the administration's view of the settlements as an illegal and negative phenomenon. To a certain extent this would have happened in any case—there were American commentators, editors, and reporters whose own opposition to the settlements predated Jimmy Carter. But among the less ideological members of the Washington press corps there was a strong inclination to accept the American position in the dispute, and indeed, "illegal West Bank settlements" became a kind of journalistic stock phrase, like "war-torn Lebanon" or "rock-ribbed Republican."* As Barbara Newman once remarked, it was difficult for most American journalists to conceive of a positive story about Israel's West Bank policies during those years.[13]

The issue of West Bank settlements is a complex one, and it is not my intention to maintain that the press attention it received, and still receives, is entirely a function of the U.S. government's searchlight. The Likud's West Bank policy is a matter of extreme controversy in Israel itself, and many prominent Israelis regard it as misguided or even disastrous. This controversy has engendered an internal Israeli debate which is itself newsworthy. But the fluctuations in American media interest in the question, which correspond roughly to the rise and fall of official U.S. concern, illustrate the influence that the U.S. government has on the press agenda for foreign coverage; while the near unanimity of the press in support of the U.S. government's position in the controversy demonstrates the truth of Leslie Gelb's observation: "Whatever skepticism there is about one's own government we in [the Washington] press corps, with very few exceptions, would take the word of the American government over that of a foreign government."[14]

This predisposition was graphically demonstrated during President Carter's visit to Israel in March 1979. Carter

---

*In fact the legal status of the West Bank settlements was not as clear as the Carter administration contended. Some leading international experts have argued that they are not illegal—and this has been the position of the Reagan administration as well.

arrived in Jerusalem accompanied by the White House press corps and reporters and pundits from virtually every important American news organization. Altogether more than two hundred traveling news personnel joined the already large Israel-based press corps to report on the visit, the purpose of which was to bring about a conclusion of the stalled Israeli-Egyptian peace talks.

As it does for all state visits, the Israeli government established a press center with communications equipment, briefing rooms, and other technical requirements. We were informed by the White House advance party, however, that "its" reporters would not use the center; the American officials insisted upon a separate press facility for members of the Carter press contingent. The reason for this rather perplexing demand was not immediately apparent, but it later emerged that press secretary Jody Powell was conducting misleading briefings on the talks for the American reporters. These briefings were apparently given as a means of pressuring the Israeli government and, incidentally, of providing an alibi for any possible failure of the Carter mission.

On the last night of the Carter visit, Powell informed the traveling press at their exclusive briefing that the talks had broken down due to the intransigence of Prime Minister Begin. At about the same time the Israeli spokesman, Dan Pattir, was telling journalists at the Israeli press center that the talks were far from deadlocked, and that, in fact, there was a good chance that they would succeed. Pattir was telling the truth, and the Israeli, European, and a few Jerusalem-based American correspondents who attended his briefing got it right; those who attended Powell's did not. They were angry and embarrassed when their pessimistic reports of Israeli-inspired deadlock were published the following day—at about the same time that President Sadat announced his acceptance of the deal worked out in Jerusalem between Begin and Carter. A number of correspondents publicly denounced White House perfidy in the use of the press, but many of the most vocal were reporters who had scarcely left the Hilton Hotel, and the American press center there, during the course of the presidential visit.

Thus the American government is a powerful, sometimes decisive factor in determining the agenda, and often the content, of much of America's foreign news coverage. The tools at its disposal make it the most important single hand on the searchlight. But it is by no means the only hand, and its power is far from unlimited. A number of other factors contribute to the "what" and the "how" of foreign news coverage. Perhaps the most important is an intangible—the attitudes and intellectual fashions current among the people who work for, and control, the media. This is a diverse group, ranging from multimillionaire press barons to the reporters in the field, and by nature they tend to have varying, often opposing views of the subjects they deal with. This creates a system of checks and balances on most issues and prevents the American press from becoming uniform in its judgments. But occasionally, the majority of media executives and journalists find themselves on the same side of an issue— a rare occurrence that upsets the delicate balance of forces at play in the press. Such a consensus developed regarding the Middle East during the decade following the October 1973 war.

12

STRANGE BEDFELLOWS

Nothing upsets American journalists more than the suggestion that news judgments are influenced in any way by the interests of ownership. For many, the thought that the individuals and corporations who control media companies might use this control to affect the news process in any way is simply inconceivable. One reporter recently reacted to such a suggestion by calling it "the Marxist conspiracy theory of American news management."

In one sense he is right, of course. The traditional Soviet accusation that a few big businessmen control the American media for their own nefarious ends, manipulating news and opinion in the pursuit of private profit, is a ridiculous distortion. The American media are vast and varied; they reflect liberal and conservative points of view and include a large number of anti-establishment organs. Individual news organizations are made up. of different departments and employ a heterogeneous mix of reporters, editors, and executives. Moreover, there are a variety of powerful factors that influence the end product of journalism—developments in the public arena, the perceptions of individual reporters (each of whom brings a personal perspective to his

255

work), the public's interest, budgetary considerations, chance, competition, and luck. *And* the attitude of those who own the media.

One needn't be a Marxist, however, to acknowledge two elementary facts—that the American press, with very few exceptions, is privately owned, and that its owners are not exempt from the normal impulses that affect human behavior. This does not mean that they are necessarily a rapacious group of self-interested manipulators. Some, especially those for whom ownership is a matter of family tradition or personal prestige, are prepared to sacrifice both profit and personal predilection for integrity. The fact remains, however, that they can, if they choose, greatly affect the attitudes and output of their companies. Sometimes this is done through overt intervention, but more often it is accomplished by simply setting a tone. Even this happens rarely—most owners have little stake in most subjects—but on issues that concern their economic or other interests, it does sometimes happen.

Critics of the American press have long been aware of, and concerned about, the potential influence of business on journalism. Fifty years ago William Allen White of the *Emporia Gazette* fulminated about the state of American journalism which, he felt, had degenerated from "a noble calling," to "an eight percent investment and an industry."[1] A generation later, in 1958, Edward R. Murrow addressed the question in a controversial speech before the Radio-Television News Directors Association in Chicago. According to Murrow, perhaps the greatest broadcast journalist of all time, "The top management of the networks, with a few notable exceptions, has been trained in advertising, research, sales, or show business. But by the nature of the corporate structure, they also make the final and crucial decisions having to do with news and public affairs.

"Upon occasion," he concluded, "economics and editorial judgment are in conflict. And there is no law which says that dollars will be defeated by duty."[2]

In 1966, *The New York Times*'s James Reston made almost the same observation. ". . . owners and managers of newspapers and radio and television stations are not likely to spend more time thinking about their duty than about their economic security," he said.[3]

Many of today's newspeople concede that, back in the bad old days, when tyrants ruled the press and professional standards were less exacting, news organizations were often subjected to crude pressure to conform to the economic interests or personal idiosyncracies of their publishers. It isn't so very long ago that Colonel Robert Rutherford McCormick ran the *Chicago Tribune* from his atomic-bomb-proof tower with an imperious and somewhat cracked elan, or that Henry Luce operated *Time,* in the phrase of the late governor of Louisiana Earl Long, "like a man who owns a shoestore and stocks all the shoes to fit hisself."[4] In those days, the word of the owner could be enough to kill a story or inspire a puff piece. But, today's journalists argue, such things no longer happen. There is a complete separation between the owner and the staff. No one from the business side tells editorial personnel what to do, and if someone were to try, he would be exposed and condemned by his own employees. Most journalists are so convinced of this that they view as paranoia, or worse, suspicions that their organization's output sometimes reflects the essential beliefs or interests of its owners.

As evidence of their independence, journalists usually offer two basic arguments: that publishers and owners have rarely (or never) given them explicit instructions on what or how to report, and that their organization has sometimes published news inimical to the interests of its advertisers or even the owners themselves.

To evaluate these claims it is necessary to briefly examine two questions. How do modern corporate-owned news bureaucracies actually function; and what are the real economic interests of the people who control them?

News organizations are just that—organizations—and the larger ones employ many hundreds of editorial personnel, ranging from senior editors to junior desk people. At the top of the news pyramid there is a chief editor (the title varies from place to place), who is responsible to the publisher.

The publisher in turn is usually accountable to a board of directors. The degree of influence that the publisher and his corporate associates have varies greatly, depending on the personalities of the people involved. Some are activists; others leave their editors in relative peace. Certainly, few publishers or owners intervene in the daily affairs and administration of their media properties. It is not necessary, however, for them to act often or speak loudly in order to make their wishes known. As press critic Leon V. Sigal put it: "Even a whisper from the publisher resounds throughout the newspaper."[5] Editors usually try to insulate their reporters from direct management influence, but they themselves must be aware of a simple fact: It is the publisher, along with the board of directors, who has the power to hire and fire.

Senior editors are expected to be intelligent and subtle, certainly subtle enough to understand the ground rules of their employment. These do not normally include agreeing with every position and opinion of the owners. A good editor must, almost as a matter of personal integrity, depart from the wishes of his corporate superiors from time to time, and a wise management allows this leeway. Still, on cardinal issues, there will usually be an essential harmony of views. Some owners achieve this by hiring senior editorial people whose views on such issues already conform to theirs; others intervene on occasion to ensure that there is no deviation from the basic principles and interests of the organization.

Whatever the quality and intensity of communication on this level, it takes place far above the heads of the ordinary journalist. Senior editors, like senior executives in any large organization, have the job of communicating the overall "spirit" of the organization to their employees. As media critic and former Washington Post correspondent Peter Braestrup has put it, "Reporters and subeditors, the myths of the craft not withstanding, are highly responsive to firm managerial direction, either implicit or explicit. Particularly in newspapers and newsmagazines, 'operational' policies are what the top editor and his senior editors say they are."[6]

Good editors know that today's newspeople are mostly

college educated, insistent on their own professional prerogatives, and not likely to respond well to the kind of bul-
lying that typified the editor-reporter relationship in earlier
times. Direction is therefore accomplished in more sophisticated ways. Reporters with unacceptable views are not customarily assigned to beats where these views might clash with
the general atmosphere and essential policies of the organization. Sometimes when stories that displease editors are
used, the journalist is made to feel that his superiors are less
than satisfied, while reporters who consistently choose the
"right" subject and approach come in for commendation.
Journalists, most of whom have at least the normal amount
of ambition and ego usually understand this intuitively—but
they often deny, even to themselves, the existence of such
obvious corporate limitations on their personal autonomy.
A reporter who argues that he has never experienced inter-
ference from a publisher is like a biologist who denies the
theory of evolution on the grounds that he, personally, has
never seen a monkey turn into a man.

One newsman who became aware of the subtle corporate influences on his work was NBC correspondent Sander
Vanocur, who resigned from the network and described his
reasons in an article in *Esquire* in 1972. Vanocur saw the
network as Big Mother, a maternalistic organization that
promoted conformity to its standards and views. "You find
that your journalistic behavior pattern tends more and more
to be shaped towards an expression not of what you believe
but rather towards what Big Mother will find acceptable,"
he claimed. Vanocur found that he was taking on the psy-
chological trappings and perspective of the network executives, and described a chain of influence by which "the
commentators became subordinate to the producers, who in
turn were being continually second-guessed by management." The result of all this, according to the correspondent, was the development of a kind of management-inspired
group-think: ". . . I realized the process was so subtle that
for years I had taken on their institutionalized fears and in-
hibitions and had institutionalized them into myself."[7]

Astute editors and executives try to insulate their reporters from management pressure, not always successfully. Turner Catledge, former editor of *The New York Times,* recalled, "I wanted our reporters and editors to do their work without feeling that the publisher was looking over their shoulders. In truth, however, he was."[8] But even when the senior editors of a news organization are successful in shielding their personnel from corporate influences, they themselves can never be unmindful of the fact that they continue to serve at the pleasure of the publisher and his corporate associates.

Not surprisingly, owners of news organizations vehemently deny that they would ever use their control selfishly. There is a long tradition in America of corporations asserting that their actions are motivated solely by altruism, and an equally long tradition of treating such declarations with considerable skepticism. Normally this skepticism embraces journalists, whose experience and training predispose them to view all protestations of altruism with a jaundiced eye. Reporters often suspend disbelief, however, when it comes to their own profession. Most newspeople seem convinced that fundamental laws of business and human nature—including the principle that major corporations will not willingly work against their basic interests—simply do not apply to journalism.

Corporate interventions are rarely overt. Often it is enough for those in charge of the editorial side to be aware of the basic philosophy of ownership, and very little more need be said. Media critic Ben Bagdikian's observation is so obvious as to be almost self-evident: "Many corporations claim to permit great freedom to the journalists, producers and writers they employ. Some do grant great freedom. But when their most sensitive economic interests are at stake, the parent corporations seldom refrain from using their power over public information."[9]

And what are these "most sensitive economic interests"? To answer that question, and the related problem of how it bears on America's international press coverage, it is necessary to understand the structure of contemporary media ownership in the United States. In his book *The Media Mo-*

nopoly, Bagdikian, a former national editor of *The Washington Post,* examined this question and emerged with some fascinating conclusions.

In the past most American newspapers and broadcasting outlets were in individual hands, but today they are concentrated into the ownership of a few companies. Twenty giant corporations control more than half of all daily newspaper sales in the United States; another twenty control over half the magazine sales; the three networks and Cable News Network preside over most national television news, and ten corporations control well over half the AM and FM commercial markets in America.[10]

Most of the huge media-owning corporations have holdings and interests far beyond the news business. Bagdikian found that twenty-one major press owners, including *The New York Times, The Washington Post,* and the three networks, were among the five hundred largest corporations in the United States. The leaders of these corporations are typically involved in management decisions that affect not only their news properties, but other corporate interests as well.

Bagdikian pointed out that many corporations with media interests have now entered Louis Brandeis's "endless chain" of interlocking directorates. Directors of non-media-owning interests (such as oil companies, major banks, and other financial institutions) also serve as directors of media-owning corporations, and vice versa. For example, in 1979 RCA, which owned NBC, had directors who were simultaneously on the boards of Cities Service, Atlantic Richfield, and the American Petroleum Institute. *The New York Times* had interlocking directorships with Sun Oil, Charter Oil, Morgan Guaranty, Bethlehem Steel, IBM, and others; *The Washington Post,* with IBM, Allied Chemical, and Wells Fargo Bank; ABC, with executives from the petroleum industry; and *Time,* with the heads of Mobil Oil, the American Petroleum Institute, and others.[11]

All of this raises a problem, which Bagdikian summed up this way:

"Most of the fifty biggest [media] firms have a direct stake in foreign investments, and therefore in the foreign policy

of the United States. There is almost no country in the world
in which a subsidiary of the fifty media companies does not
have a significant investment. . . . Conflicts of interest, real
and potential, are infinitely greater because the large media
companies exchange directors, and therefore have common
policy views with other non-media corporations. . . . A dozen
of the country's largest multinational banks hold significant
voting shares in many of the fifty largest media companies,
control their debts, or exchange directors with them."[12]

It is obvious that media companies owned by such corporate giants define their economic interests on a national
and global scale. In one sense this is a positive development,
because it liberates news organizations from their traditional reluctance to offend major advertisers. This is especially true of the television networks which have a virtual
monopoly on national advertising space. On the other hand,
these giant corporations have, in Bagdikian's phrase, "a direct interest in foreign investments, and therefore in the
foreign policy of the United States."[13] In other words, media owners are no longer obliged to worry about the sensitivities of the local department store or of any other individual
advertiser, but they are vitally affected by the forces at play
in the national and international economy. And since 1973,
none of these forces has been more dramatic, and more influential, than the economic and financial power of the Arab
world.

This does not mean, I hasten to add, that American
businessmen who control media companies have been
"bought out" by the Arabs, or have capitulated to their demands. It does mean, though, that corporate heads in the
media field, like their counterparts in other giant American
industries, are far more sensitive to the financial clout of the
Arab world—and its potential consequences to the American economy—than they were before the 1973 Arab oil boycott. This sensitivity has, for many members of the American
economic establishment, been translated into a heightened
appreciation of the Arab point of view, and a fear that un-
satisfied political grievances—such as the Palestinian question—might lead to Arab actions that could threaten Western

economic stability, or that an excessively pro-Israel policy might limit America's (and their own) economic interests and opportunities in the Arab world.

This heightened sensitivity to the Arab point of view has been a constant factor in the thinking of the American economic establishment since 1973. It has found expression in a number of ways: the pro-Arab advertising campaign of Mobil and other major oil companies, the lobbying of the business community on behalf of the sale of AWACs to Saudi Arabia, and public and private support by many for a more "even-handed" American policy in the Middle East.

Not coincidentally, many of the media companies owned by the giants of the communications industry have themselves adopted a more "even-handed" approach to the region since 1973. How much of this is due to direct intervention of the owners, and how much the result of anticipatory sensitivity on the part of editors, is a moot point.

Naturally enough, the members of the press—owners, editors, and journalists—deny that the post-1973 economic power of the Arab world and its potential effect on the corporate well-being of the media-owning conglomerates have any connection with their new, more sympathetic approach to the Arab world. The Arabs, they contend, are a major force in the world's economic and political equation, and it is only good journalism to look more closely at their concerns and perceptions. And if in the course of that closer look, it appears that the Arabs have been treated unfairly by the media, or that the Israelis have been unduly favored, then what could be more equitable than to attempt to correct the imbalance?

Back in 1947, A. J. Leibling wrote: "I am delighted that I do not have to insinuate that they [newspaper owners] consciously allow their output to be shaped by their personal interests. Psychoanalytical after dinner talk has furnished us with a lovely word for what they do: they 'rationalize.' And once a man has convinced himself that what is good for him is good for the herd of his inferiors, he enjoys the best of both worlds simultaneously . . ."[14]

* * *

Thus, the events of 1973 transformed the attitude of America's economic establishment (including that part of it that owns media companies) toward the Middle East; but 1973 was also a watershed year for the American New Left's view of the region. For almost a decade the left, both old and new, had concentrated its attention and energies on ending American participation in the war in Vietnam and, indeed, had made opposition to the war a virtual litmus test of American liberalism. By the end of 1973, however, America had withdrawn from the conflict and the left was faced with a foreign-policy void. The Middle East had become the most important arena of international concern, and so it was to that region, and especially to the Palestinian issue, that it now turned in search of a compelling new cause.

The decade-long preoccupation with Vietnam transformed the American left. To a large extent, its traditional East-West orientation was replaced by a preoccupation with the Third World. The problems of Vietnam, and what was seen as America's ignoble motives for intervention there, sensitized many to the difficulties of the developing nations of Asia, Africa, and Latin America. The United States was perceived as a brutal exploiter, a superpower cynically pursuing its own economic and geopolitical interests at the expense of the world's downtrodden masses. The New Left, driven by guilt and compassion as well as by ideology, saw itself as the advocate for the Third World; it called for a reorientation of American policy and restitution for past "imperialist" outrages against the peoples of the developing countries.

In the Middle East, this attitude found expression in support for the cause of Palestinian national liberation, whose superficial resemblance to Vietnam gave it a reassuringly familiar feel. As in Vietnam, revolutionaries armed with Kalashnikov rifles were pitting themselves against American-supplied troops; and as in Vietnam, the struggle was being carried out under the banner of "national liberation and self-determination," a slogan to which many responded with Pavlovian alacrity.

These apparent similarities obscured the very real differences between Vietnam and the Arab-Israel conflict, however. Israel was (and is) a democracy, not a corrupt dictatorship. The Palestinian "revolutionaries" were, for the most part, not dedicated guerrilla fighters, but terrorists stationed outside the country who concentrated their fire on civilian targets in Israel and the West Bank or against noncombatant supporters of Israel abroad. Perhaps most significantly, the PLO, as the representative of the Palestinian cause, was intent not on merely creating a state for itself, but on destroying Israel. It eluded some PLO enthusiasts, and did not matter to others, that supporting the PLO meant implicitly supporting the organization's ultimate aim—the replacement of Israel by an Arab Palestinian state in which most Jews would have no place.

The enthusiasm of many American leftists for the PLO, and their concomitant hostility to Israel, is fraught with a number of ironies, among them the fact that Israel was founded with the support and blessing of much of the international left. Intellectuals such as Sartre and Einstein were among Israel's most vocal advocates. The Social Democratic parties in Europe were, for the most part, staunch friends of the Jewish state, as were many American labor leaders, intellectuals and artists. Some of this support came as a result of guilt feelings over the mass murder of Jews during World War II, but the Holocaust was by no means its only source. Israel was perceived as an island of enlightened, progressive values in a sea of regressive, reactionary, even feudal, Arab regimes. Israel had strong trade unions, a commitment to social welfare, and a system of parliamentary democracy. Its symbol was the kibbutz, the uniquely successful experiment in practical socialism whose influence extended far beyond the communal settlements themselves and permeated the thinking of Israel's national political and intellectual elite.

Nor did the left forget the enthusiasm which much of the Arab world, and notably, the leadership of the Palestinian Arab community, had displayed for Nazi Germany during World War II. The Mufti of Jerusalem, Haj Amin Al Husseni—Yasser Arafat's mentor and the leader of militant

Palestinian nationalism in the 1930s and '40s actively collaborated with Hitler; while it was the Palestinian establishment's obstinate opposition to Jewish immigration in the late 1930s that forced the British to close the country's gates to Jewish refugees, thus foreclosing their last option. Judged by the criteria and values of the postwar American left, the Palestinian leadership was not a shining exemplar of progressivism.

There was an even greater irony in the post-Vietnam tendency of the New Left to label Israel a "Western nation." The Vietnam generation knew little about Jews as victims; for them, Israel was an established nation, a fixture in the world they grew up in. Moreover, many identified the country with the Jews with whom they were most familiar—the comfortably middle-class Jews of the United States. Comedian Dick Gregory used to say that he knew the Jews would always beat the Arabs because "a camel can't outrun a Cadillac." It was a joke that Israelis couldn't understand—in the Middle East it is the Arabs, not the Jews, who have the Cadillacs.

In truth, despite Israel's Western cultural aspirations, parliamentary government, and pro-American orientation, it is a grotesque distortion of modern history to label Israel a "Western nation" in the exploitive sense that the New Left used the term. Most Israelis were born in Africa or Asia or are the children of refugees from Arab nations; and irony of ironies, the "Western" Jews of Israel, the "Ashkenazim," are in fact the remnants of the European Jewish community who were murdered by the Germans precisely because they were considered racially non-European and hence inferior.

Despite all this, once Israel had become identified by the New Left as a part of the Western establishment, it became the target for increasingly harsh criticism. Israeli policies and attitudes that had been admired by the progressives of an earlier generation were now sources of friction. The trauma of the Holocaust drew not sympathy but sneering accusations of paranoia; Israel's staunch anti-communism came to be regarded as provocative and perhaps even dangerous; while Israeli pride in being a friend and ally of the United

States and the free world was scorned by those Americans whose alienation and moral relativism led them to view America as just another superpower, and not necessarily the best one. Most of all, the Israeli opposition to the creation of an irredentist Palestinian state within artillery range of its main cities was seen not as a prudent concern for self-defense, but as an arrogant attempt to deprive a developing people of its inalienable right to nationhood.

In the mid-1970s, the attitudes of the New Left toward Israel began to influence a large number of America's elite journalists. It has always been a feature of American journalism that its owners and corporate executives tend to be conservative while its employees—reporters, editors, and producers—are measurably more liberal. A generation ago this distinction was expressed by the axiom that "publishers are Republicans; reporters, Democrats." In today's more highly charged ideological climate, it is fair to say that a majority of journalists in the elite media organizations are somewhat left of center in their political outlook. Three American academics who studied this question, put it this way: "Like other privileged Americans, the media elite . . . hold the cosmopolitan and anti-establishment social views fashionable since the 1960s." They found that in the election of 1972, while more than sixty percent of the voters supported Richard Nixon, eighty-one percent of the journalists surveyed voted for George McGovern.[15]

Most American journalists are not fervently ideological, but a good many were and are affected by a kind of left-wing trickle-down effect, including an acceptance of the left's Third World orientation. In 1979–80, Professor S. Robert Lichter measured the attitudes of elite journalists toward the developing world and found that three quarters of those surveyed disagreed with the statement "The West has helped the Third World"; fifty-five percent agreed that "American exploitation adds to Third World poverty"; and a similar proportion held the notion that "U.S. use of resources is immoral." Lichter concluded that "these findings should not be especially surprising because it is known that journalists tend toward liberal attitudes in many areas of life . . ."[16] From

the mid-1970s onward, one of the tenets of this kind of liberalism was that Israel is one of the exploiters rather than
one of the exploited.

Few American reporters who deal with Middle East affairs for prestigious news orgánizations would dispute the
overall "liberalism" of the elite press corps; but many would
argue that the ideology or opinions of a good reporter does
not necessarily affect his or her work. By this they usually
mean that a competent, ethical journalist is prepared to report news that is at variance with his own positions or may
harm some favorite cause. And it is true that most American journalists play it straight when it comes to reporting
"hard news." This, however, does not mean that their work
is unaffected by their personal opinions.

First, modern American journalism expects a reporter not
only to relate facts, but to make judgments. Sometimes this
is done in the body of a news story, but often it takes the
form of analysis articles in which the reporter is expected,
indeed required, to give his own opinion.

Another, less obvious way in which opinion comes to bear
is in the selection of subjects. Both editors at home and correspondents in the field customarily take part in the selection process, and their opinions, attitudes, and prejudices
have a significant, sometimes decisive influence on what is
and is not considered newsworthy. Moreover, many correspondents become subject to a kind of "group-think," which
translates into pack journalism. Once a consensus emerges
among a press corps—that the PLO really wants to recognize Israel, for example, or that Israeli settlements in the West
Bank are an obstacle to peace—then these perceptions take
on a life of their own. Newly arrived colleagues ask, "What's
the story?" and are filled in by the more veteran reporters,
and this provides a continuity of the collective perception.

An additional factor in the change in liberal media climate toward Israel is the inherent iconoclasm of journalists.
For a generation the Jewish state had been treated with kid
gloves in the American press. Once it became trendy to
"reevaluate" Israel, many reporters and editors with little or
no ideological bent found the opportunity to debunk some

"myths" about the Jewish state to be irresistible. In doing so, they responded to one of the oldest impulses of their profession—the need for novelty. Arabs biting Jews had long since ceased to be news; but Jews biting Arabs—*that* was a story.

No consideration of the shift in liberal sentiment toward Israel would be complete without a look at the impact of Menachem Begin and his Likud coalition. Many analysts have tied the decline of Israel's image among liberals in general, and liberal journalists in particular, to the emergence of Begin and his right-wing government. To a certain extent this is true, but it is also oversimplified. For the trend toward Israel-bashing in the Western press predates the rise of Begin.

In the aftermath of the October 1973 War, the Israeli government under Golda Meir was shocked by the lack of support for Israel in much of the West's media. Israel had clearly been the victim in that war; in fact, the decision to refrain from launching pre-emptive airstrikes on the massing Egyptian and Syrian armies was at least partly the result of Mrs. Meir's desire to demonstrate to international public opinion that the Arabs, and not Israel, were the aggressors. And yet despite this, many liberal commentators and editorial writers blamed *Israel,* and its occupation of the territories taken in 1967, for the Arab attack. The Israeli government was so concerned by this trend that it took the unprecedented step of establishing a Ministry of Information to improve the country's faltering image.

The ministry lasted only briefly, the victim of Israeli political infighting, but the problem remained and deepened. In June 1974, CBS presented a documentary entitled "The Palestinians," produced by Howard Stringer. "The Palestinians" was perhaps the first truly sympathetic look at the PLO and its goals ever shown on national television, and it presented the Middle East conflict largely through Palestinian eyes. The documentary came in for extravagant praise from supporters of the Arab cause in America and for an equal amount of criticism from Israel's friends. Far from being an isolated program, however, "The Palestinians" was a harbinger of a new approach to the Middle East, and particularly to the Palestinian question, by much of America's media.

At about the same time "The Palestinians" was aired by CBS, Henry Kissinger was warning the Israeli government that a failure to be more flexible on the future of the West Bank would result in a loss of support among American intellectuals and other liberal groups. This warning, however, fell on deaf ears in Jerusalem because, as Kissinger recorded, "a new Israeli government was being formed, including a party that opposed any territorial change on the West Bank."[17]

Kissinger was not mistaken. By 1975, a number of liberal American pundits such as Anthony Lewis had joined conservatives such as Evans and Novak as constant detractors of Israel. Even in denouncing the UN resolution equating Zionism with racism, Lewis could not refrain from noting that Israel's policy regarding occupied territory was, in some part, responsible for bringing it about. Israel, he said, "has persistently refused to make a real commitment to return the Arab territories won in the 1967 War. Her policy, instead, has been to rely on American support and huge amounts of American arms, playing for time on the ultimate territorial issue—time that I think is making life progressively harder for Israel, not easier."[18]

Nineteen seventy-five was also the year that the Brookings Institution, a bastion of liberal orthodoxy, placed the Palestine question squarely at the center of Middle Eastern instability and urged an Israeli withdrawal from virtually all of the West Bank and Gaza. This view was decisively rejected by the Israeli government, and when, following Carter's election, it became American policy, it led to a clash between Itzhak Rabin and the new American president.

In March 1977, Prime Minister Rabin visited Washington for talks with the newly elected Carter. The talks were not a success. Rabin saw that the American president was advocating the Brookings formula, including its suggestion that the PLO be included in the Middle East political process, an advocacy Rabin characterized as "extremely grave."[19] Rabin's behavior during the talks was later described by Carter as unresponsive, distrustful, and inflexible (surprisingly, the same terms that came to be applied almost reflexively to Menachem Begin by the American press), and the American president called their meeting "an unpleasant surprise."[20] The Israeli prime minister returned to Israel with the knowledge that the administration was now committed to the fashionable notion that a resolution of the Palestinian issue, and not an end to Arab hostility toward Israel, was the key to settling the Middle East conflict and that this resolution required the creation of a Palestinian entity in the West Bank—ideas that were wholly unacceptable to Rabin's government and party.

In the inevitable clash between Israel and the United States under Carter, the liberal American press was firmly on the side of the American president. When Jimmy Carter proposed a Palestinian "homeland," *The New York Times* called it a "wise policy,"[21] *The Washington Post* praised his courage,[22] and liberal press opinion generally supported the move, criticizing Israel's intransigence, insensitivity, and unfairness in not recognizing the "legitimate rights" of the Palestinians.

Significantly, all this occurred *before* Menachem Begin became prime minister of Israel. Nor is it likely that a Labor Party victory in 1977 would have stopped the erosion of Israel's image in the United States. The Carter administration, and with it, American liberal opinion, opposed Jewish settlements in the West Bank and Gaza—but it was under the Labor Party that the first of these settlements, including some near the large Arab population center of Hebron, had been first established. The Americans wanted to include the PLO in the negotiations for a regional settlement, but the Rabin government was determined to hold America to its commitment not to deal with the PLO until it recognized Israel's right to exist. The need for Israeli withdrawal from virtually all of the occupied territories was a matter of liberal and administration orthodoxy after 1977—but Labor was committed to the Allon Plan for the West Bank, which spoke of territorial compromise with Jordan and not the creation of a Palestinian homeland. Nor was the Labor Party prepared to relinquish Israeli control of the Golan Heights, or to compromise on the issue of Jerusalem.

But of course Labor lost in 1977, and Menachem Begin became Israel's prime minister. His election was pictured by the American press as a disaster, the victory of a right-wing extremist. In fact, in his first term, Begin's policies (as distinct from his rationale for those policies) were not too different from Labor's. But Begin had a genius for antagonizing his opponents and a habit of expressing even the most rational aims in irrational language. He made an inviting target for liberal critics whose anti-Israel animus, or sympathy for the Arabs, had been inhibited in the past by the fact that Israel was so palpably more enlightened and liberal than its adversaries. Now, with Begin, there was an Israeli leader who, whatever his actual policies, sounded (or could be made to sound) as inflexible and fanatic as his enemies. Many of the more timid liberal American journalists had been waiting for this chance—the opportunity to bring their public view of Israel in line with their privately held disapproval. Their means of doing so was to make a distinction between Begin (or the Begin government) and Israel. Many critics simply ignored the fact that Begin had been *elected* prime minister (and reelected, in 1981) and that his positions were not only official Israeli policy, but represented the views of at least a plurality of Israelis (and on many of the outstanding issues between Jerusalem and Washington, a clear majority). The Israeli prime minister became a man whom the American liberal establishment loved to hate, but the hostility directed against him was also at least partly a reflection of the general distaste that many left-of-center journalists had come to feel for Israel in the decade after the Vietnam war.

So it was that 1973 became the seminal year for the creation of a new, Palestinian-oriented coalition embracing the two most unlikely intellectual bedfellows in American journalism—the economic giants of management and the Third World enthusiasts in the press corps.* Moreover, this media

*It is interesting that this convergence of views was reflected in the wider sphere of American public life by the bizarre anti-Israel wall-to-wall Grand Coalition which included the radically chic (Jesse Jackson, Vanessa Redgrave, and Alexander

coalition was in essential agreement with the Middle Eastern policies of the Carter administration, themselves an amalgam of American economic self-interest and support for Palestinian "self-determination."

Given this essential concert of approach among the most powerful influences on the American press, it is not surprising that Palestinian media critic Morad Asi was able to write in 1979 that according to surveys, "media coverage of the Middle East (especially coverage in the printed media) became less pro-Israel and more neutral" in recent years; and that his own research on U.S. television news coverage indicated "increased recognition and less hostility towards the Palestinians and the PLO."[23]

Cockburn) and the reactionary right (Jesse Helms, Mobil Oil, and Spiro T. Agnew).

13

THE PURIM SPIEL OF ABDULLAH SCHLEIFER

In his novel *The Canfield Decision,* former Vice-President Spiro T. Agnew described "Operation Torch," the action wing of a cabal of powerful Jewish press barons determined to use their control over the media to promote Zionism in America. Agnew's novel, and his defense of it in a number of television appearances in 1976, sent shock waves through the journalistic community. For years dark mutterings about "Jewish control" of the media had been a staple of the anti-Semites; now, for the first time a major, if disgraced, political figure had expressed them publicly.

Agnew's thesis—that "The Jews" had gained control of the American media and were using their power to further their own parochial interests—echoed similar accusations from other times and other places. During the 1920s, the idea that the Jews were sapping the morale and subverting the morality of Germany through their ownership of newspapers and magazines was a central motif of Nazi propaganda. More recently, the Soviet Union has repeatedly charged that the American media are under the influence of the Zionists. Not long ago, Dr. Howard Spier of the London-based Institute of Jewish Affairs, discovered a vintage example: an article entitled, "How the Tail Wags the Dog" by Soviet media critic V. Gan which "exposes" the Zionist domination of such pro-Israel publications as *The Washington Post, Time* magazine, the *St. Louis Post Dispatch, Vogue,* and *Glamour.*[1]

The Arab world, too, has traditionally contended that the large number of Jews in the American press constitute a conspiracy aimed at preventing their point of view from getting a fair hearing in the United States. This accusation has stemmed at least in part from their mistaken assumption that all Jews in the media support Israeli policies and, given the opportunity, will act like journalists in the Arab world and lie for the cause. In recent years the Arabs have become more sophisticated about the workings of the American press, but they still make such charges, perhaps on the theory that they constitute an effective form of preemptive pressure.

It is a curious fact that some American Jews also act as though there was a Jewish media conspiracy—against Israel. They point to the many Jewish journalists who are prominent critics of Israel and accuse them of bending over backward to prove their objectivity. Some even condemn them as "self-hating" Jews whose anti-Israel animus is a function of their neurotic rejection of their own identities. Just as the Arabs claim that the Jews in the American press give Israel an unfair advantage, many American supporters of Israel contend that these same Jewish journalists are an asset to the Arab cause.

The raw material for all these dark suspicions is the greatly disproportionate number of Jews in the American press. At one time all three major television networks were run by Jews, and ABC, headed by Leonard Goldenson, still is (CBS founder William Paley resigned as chairman of CBS, Inc., in April 1983, but remains the company's largest shareholder). *The New York Times,* America's most influential newspaper, is owned by the Sulzberger family, while *The Washington Post* and *Newsweek* are controlled by the Grahams (Katherine Graham's father, Eugene Meyer, was Jewish). One of America's largest newspaper chains was founded by S. I. Newhouse, and other Jewish media owners include Walter Annenberg of Triangle Publications (*TV Guide* and several newspapers), Martin Peretz of *New Republic,* and Mortimer Zuckerman of *The Atlantic.*

Many of America's leading editors are Jewish, including A. M. Rosenthal of *The New York Times,* Howard Simons, managing editor of *The Washington Post,* Henry Grunwald of *Time,* Marvin Stone of *U.S. News and World Report,* William Shawn of *The New Yorker,* and Edward Kosner of *New York* magazine. Recently Norman Pearlstine was appointed editor of *The Wall Street Journal.*

There are a great many Jews who are prominent at all three major networks. Until recently Reuven Frank was NBC's president for news, and both he and his successor, Lawrence Grossman, are Jewish. So, too, are ABC vice-president Richard Wald and *20/20* executive producer Av Westin. Well-known Jewish newscasters include Mike Wallace, Morley Safer, Ted Koppel, Geraldo Rivera (his mother is Jewish), Marvin and Bernard Kalb, Barbara Walters, Jeff Greenfield, Martin Agronsky, and Cable News Network's Daniel Shorr. In his famous study of television news in 1973, Edward Jay Epstein interviewed thirty-six network news producers and editors—twenty-one of whom turned out to be Jews.[2]

There are a number of Jews among America's most prominent syndicated columnists, including Anthony Lewis, Flora Lewis, and William Safire of *The New York Times;* Meg Greenfield, Steven Rosenfeld, and Richard Cohen of *The Washington Post;* Joseph Kraft, Ben Wattenberg, and Roger Simon. And among the elite Washington press corps a recent study indicates that about twenty-five percent are Jews.*[3]

The list of Jewish journalists who have covered the Middle East in recent years includes Ned Temko of the *Christian*

---

*In this and other studies cited in this chapter, the term "elite press corps" refers to journalists working for *The New York Times, The Wall Street Journal, Time, Newsweek, U.S. News and World Report,* the three major networks and the News and Public Affairs Department of PBS, and three local public broadcasting stations— WNET in New York, WGBH in Boston, and WETA in Washington, D.C. Elsewhere in this book the term "elite media" refers to news organizations which have full-time correspondents stationed abroad.

Science Monitor, Thomas Friedman of *The New York Times,* Abdullah (Mark) Schleifer of NBC, Robert Simon and Bruno Wassertheil of CBS, Jay Bushinsky and Jane Friedman of CNN, Brooke Kroeger and Mel Laytner of UPI, Marcus Eliason and Art Max of AP, Jonathan Broder of the *Chicago Tribune,* and Charlie Weiss and Ron Pemstein of the Voice of America.

This long (and by no means exhaustive) roster of American Jewish media figures is impressive, but it is not likely to be mistaken for a conspiracy by anyone with much sophistication about the American press or the American Jewish community. For while there is indeed a disproportionate number of Jews in the media, "The Jews" are unrepresented. Far from being a disciplined cadre of pro-Zionist propagandists, the great majority of American Jewish journalists—from millionaire press barons to reporters—have only the most tenuous connections with the organized Jewish community in the United States. They tend to be much more representative of the attitudes and concerns of their professional peers than of their co-religionists, and on every issue of public policy, including Israel and the Middle East, there are Jewish-owned news organizations and Jewish journalists on all parts of the ideological and political spectrum.

Dorothy Schiff, the late publisher of the *New York Post,* once summed up her own Jewish identity, and that of her fellow Jewish media magnates by quoting C. P. Snow's observation: "Once you reach a certain financial level, people don't think of you as being anything but rich."[4] The men and women who own great media organizations usually live in the rarified circles of the American economic aristocracy, belong to exclusive clubs, educate their children at WASP private schools, and generally share the activities and attitudes of their class. Almost none belong to Jewish institutions or are otherwise involved in organized Jewish life in the United States, and most would be lost in an orthodox synagogue, or on an Israeli kibbutz.* The idea that such as-

*There are, of course, exceptions. Mortimer Zuckerman of *The Atlantic* and Martin Peretz of *New Republic* are involved members of the Jewish community and supporters of Israel, although not necessarily of recent Israeli policy.

similated and unaffiliated Jews might participate in a pro-Israeli cabal, or indeed that they have, as Jews, any particular pro-Israeli sympathies, is, to put it mildly, hilarious.

Nor are most American Jewish reporters candidates for an "Elders of Zion" press conspiracy. Wolf Blitzer, *The Jerusalem Post*'s Washington bureau chief, once remarked that in matters of Jewish identity, the Jews in the Washington press corps can be divided into two groups—those who work on Yom Kippur (the holiest day of the Jewish year) and those who don't; and it was Blitzer's observation that most of his colleagues fall into the first category. This impression got some empirical support from a survey conducted recently among members of the elite press corps in Washington. Of the survey's 238 respondents, 33 identified themselves as religiously affiliated Jews. This figure more than doubled, however, when the journalists were asked to give their *parents'* religion. In this secular outlook, as in much else, the Jews in the media are typical of their Gentile colleagues; according to the same survey, fifty-two percent of all journalists interviewed claimed no religious affiliation.[5]

Yet it would be misleading to suppose that even the secular, unaffiliated Jews in the American press have *no* special feelings about Israel, or that these feelings do not affect the way Israel is presented in the American media. In a study undertaken in the winter of 1979–80, Professor S. Robert Lichter found that fully ninety-one percent of the Jewish journalists he surveyed agreed with the statement "The United States has a moral obligation to prevent the destruction of Israel." This figure contrasts with the substantially lower level of agreement among Catholic journalists (sixty-five percent) and Protestants (seventy-two percent). It indicates that far from being self-hating enemies of Israel, most American Jewish media figures have positive feelings, at least insofar as the basic issue of Israel's survival is concerned.[6]

Many prominent American Jewish journalists contend that any conflict of interest between these feelings and the performance of their professional duties is more apparent than real. They point out that many American journalists have a personal connection with the issues they cover—Blacks dealing with civil rights, for example, or women reporting on feminist affairs—but that it is the essence of professionalism to recognize and neutralize any potential biases. "I have no trouble dealing with Israel," one senior editor who is Jewish told me. "I treat it just like any other country."

This is excellent theory, but it is rarely that simple in practice. Journalists' personal feelings *do* affect their work, especially in the areas of news judgment and editorial analysis. Most know this, and the fair-minded try to correct for any possible distortions. Michael Robinson studied this question and concluded: ". . . one might consider the relationship of news coverage of the Middle East and the religion or heritage of the correspondents. In this instance, the potential connection between the background and story is so apparent that journalists would almost certainly be sensitive to potential bias. In a Middle East analysis, Jewish correspondents, recognizing the circumstances, would probably work hard to correct any attitudinal influences on their stories."[7] Or, in other words, bend over backward to be fair to the other side.

To complicate matters further, most Jewish journalists in the elite American media are, like their non-Jewish colleagues, liberals, and they tend to share the liberal unease with many of Israel's recent policies, especially in regard to Palestinian nationalism and the future of the West Bank. Sometimes the combination of their identification with Israel and disapproval of its policies leads to a more personal, and thus harsher, criticism of Israel than the American press customarily accords foreign countries.

Nor is it easy for Jewish journalists to escape this sense of personal identification. Even those who feel no special connection with the Jewish state are often identified with it in the minds of their Gentile colleagues. During the war in Lebanon, for example, *The Washington Post*'s ombudsman sought to deflect charges of anti-Israel bias by noting the large number of Jews who work for the *Post*.[8] At about the same time a group of prominent Washington, D.C., Jews met with *Post* editor Ben Bradlee to discuss their critique of the paper's coverage of Israel. They offered a number of examples of what they considered unfair reporting, and Bradlee responded, according to Nathan Lewin, president of the Jewish Community Council of Washington, by noting ruefully that "the Jews on my own staff don't warn me about these things," as if it was their job, as Jews, to do so. It is very unlikely that the Jews on Bradlee's staff, or elsewhere in American journalism, are unmindful of the fact that they are often identified by their colleagues with Israel.*

As a result of all these contradictory influences and pressures, many American Jewish journalists feel considerable ambiguity toward Israel. They find themselves caught in the middle between their instinctive support for Israel and the need to be scrupulously fair to the other side. They must also be sensitive to the fact that what Israel is and does reflects on them as Jews—and to the danger that this sensitivity might lead them to overly harsh treatment of the Jewish state. Finally they must be aware that whatever they do they are likely to be accused of favoritism and personal bias.

All this leads to self-consciousness and ambivalence, qualities that have been especially evident at *The New York Times.* During the 1930s the *Times,* controlled by the German-Jewish descendents of Adolph Ochs, was editorially opposed to the creation of a Jewish state in Palestine, and although the paper's editorial policy is no longer anti-Zionist, it is often hypercritical. As Gay Talese in his book *The Kingdom and the Power* notes: "Veteran reporters in the *Times* newsroom have long been aware of higher management's sensitivity to things Jewish. The editing and handling of stories that are about Jews or of special interest to Jews is a bit more delicate and cautious, if such is possible to perceive— and even if it is not, the reporters' mere supposition sus-

---

*The presence of Jews in a news organization is not necessarily a guarantee against anti-Semitism. In 1979, for example, *Newsweek* informed its readers, "With the help of American Jews in and out of the government, Mossad [Israel's intelligence agency] looks for any softening in U.S. support and tries to get technical intelligence the Administration is unwilling to give Israel."

The editor of *Newsweek* later admitted that *Newsweek*'s insinuation that American Jews are disloyal to the United States "reflects an anti-Semitic stereotype" and informed the Anti-Defamation League that "we have engaged in some consciousness raising on this subject and I do not expect a recurrence." The letter to the ADL was signed by the magazine's editor-in-chief—Lester Bernstein.[9]

tains some of the past consciousness of George Ochs-Oakes."[10]

One example of that sensitivity has been the *Times*'s traditional reluctance to appoint a Jewish reporter as bureau chief in Israel. In 1979, Executive Editor A. M. Rosenthal apparently decided to end this taboo. He proudly announced at an editors' meeting that the paper had assigned a new man to Jerusalem and said he was glad that the *Times* had grown mature enough to appoint a Jew without a lot of soul searching. Joseph Lelyveld, at that time deputy foreign editor, turned to Rosenthal and said, "I thought we were sending David Shipler."

"We are," replied Rosenthal, and the two men stared at each other in confusion until Lelyveld, who knew Shipler well, said, "Sorry Abe, but he's not Jewish." Shipler, a WASP, was greatly amused by the story.*

For most American news organizations the suitability of Jewish reporters working in Israel has long since ceased to be an issue, and Jewish journalists are routinely assigned to Israel by the networks, the wire services, and many major newspapers. They are augmented by a seemingly endless stream of Jewish editors and senior personnel who visit Jerusalem ("I sure am glad I work for a WASP newspaper," the late Dial Torgerson used to say when he was Jerusalem bureau chief of the *Los Angeles Times*. "*My* editors never get east of London"). During my years at the Press Office I made it a rule not to raise the question of the religious or ethnic identity of visiting journalists but often Jewish correspondents did so themselves. Sometimes it was done in a transparent attempt to gain trust and cooperation, sometimes in the off-hand way in which an American reporter of Italian ancestry might mention his grandparents' origins to a government official in Rome; but usually it signaled that the journalist felt personally connected to the country.

The responses of these Jewish journalists to Israel varied widely. Some were struck by a brief proprietary concern for the country and a desire to make a contribution—which

---

*Early in 1984 the *Times* announced that Shipler's replacement in Jerusalem would be Thomas Friedman. Friedman is Jewish.

usually came in the form of unsolicited advice. Others were visibly disconcerted by their lack of familiarity with life as it is lived in a Jewish state and the absence of cherished Jewish symbols such as the corned beef sandwich and the bagel. Reactions ranged from admiration to hostility, from flashes of recognition ("I know that letter; it's an *aleph*, isn't it?") to bewilderment and disorientation. For most, however, being in Israel was clearly a personal experience that transcended simply visiting another foreign country.

During those years I witnessed a number of fascinating reactions to Israel by Jewish journalists, but none could match that of one of the Middle East's most bizarre newsmen—Abdullah Schleifer. Abdullah was born Mark Schleifer in New York, but as a young man he left the United States for the Middle East, converted from Judaism to Islam and changed his name. He also developed a fanatic's hatred of the Jewish state. When the Six Day War broke out he was living in East Jerusalem and working as the editor of the Jordanian English-language newspaper, the *Jerusalem Star,* and he was appalled when Israel conquered East Jerusalem and re-united the city. In 1972 he published a book on the war, *The Fall of Jerusalem,* a paean to the nobility of Jerusalem's Arabic culture, now despoiled by the jackbooted Zionist invaders. *The Fall of Jerusalem* was well received in anti-Jewish circles and has since become a classic of contemporary anti-Israel literature in the grand tradition of Rabbi Elmer Berger and Professor Noam Chomsky.

Despite the book, and his anti-Zionist articles for New Left publications in the seventies, Schleifer was somehow appointed NBC's Cairo bureau chief in the days when Egypt was as far from Israel as the moon. He was, it is safe to say, disagreeably surprised by President Sadat's 1977 mission to Jerusalem, for he soon found himself in contact with his former coreligionists both in Cairo and in Jerusalem. Despite his past anti-Israeli activities, we treated him like any other American journalist when he visited the country; but I can't deny that I longed for the opportunity to show him that he hadn't been forgotten.

That opportunity came in Cairo, in March 1980. I was

in the Egyptian capital with Israel's newly appointed ambassador, Eliahu Ben-Elissar, who was scheduled to make his first public appearance at the synagogue on Adlei Street, where Cairo's tiny Jewish community was to celebrate the holiday of Purim. The appearance drew a full complement of American journalists, including Schleifer, a towering man wearing a white knit Muslim skullcap. I took the reporters aside one by one and told them that the ambassador would speak after the reading of the Purim Megillah. "What's a megillah?" they wanted to know. "When is it read?" "How much time will we have to set up our equipment?"

"Just ask Abdullah," I told them. "He knows this stuff cold," and I was gratified to see his obvious indignation as his colleagues came up, one after the other, to consult with him on the significance and ritual of Purim.

The "Jewish component" in the American media coverage of the Middle East is both substantial and unpredictable. On any particular issue there may be Jewish journalists bending over backward to be fair to the Arabs, others bending over frontward to prevent their high expectations of Israel from turning into an overly harsh double standard, and still others looking sideways to see how their performance is being judged by their non-Jewish colleagues. Similarly, non-Jewish journalists may be doing their own bending in response to the real or presumed sensibilities of Jewish "higher management" in Gay Talese's phrase. All this bending and glancing leads to some distorted coverage, but its extent is largely immeasurable and often undetected; the public, after all, has no way of knowing which editorials, news decisions, and articles are the work of Jews, or what type of Jews they may be.

The exceptions to this anonymity are the comparatively few commentators who explicitly identify themselves as Jews and approach Israel from the standpoint of their own Jewish values and expectations. Perhaps the best known of these is Anthony Lewis, a man whom Menachem Begin once singled out as "no friend of Israel" during a national television interview. Lewis takes exception to Begin's designation. He has long been critical of Israel as it is but claims that he supports Israel as he would like it to be. An affable, somewhat donnish man of considerable intellect, Lewis is very proud of his Judaism ("I give a rather good Seder," he often boasts, and it is easy to envision the tweedy columnist pouring a glass of dry sherry for Elijah the Prophet on Passover eve). He and a few fellow Jewish commentators such as Milton Viorst, Nat Hentoff, and I. F. Stone sometimes speak to their readers, Jew and Gentile alike, specifically as Jews.

Back in 1980, for example, in a column emphasizing the religious meaning of Passover, Anthony Lewis wrote: "American supporters of Israel have a heavy responsibility. I believe most of them, in particular the leaders of Jewish organizations, are deeply troubled by the [West Bank settlements] policy. . . . But Israel's friends owe it to her to speak the truth about this self-destructive policy."[11] Two months after that, he denounced Theodore Mann, then chairman of the Conference of the Presidents of Major Jewish Organizations, for, of all things, supporting Israeli policy *against Mr. Lewis's better judgment.* "Mr. Mann very likely understands all this, or so I suspect," wrote Anthony Lewis, "all this" being Mr. Lewis's own evaluation of the Palestinian question. "But he [Mann] operates within a tradition that evidently demands solidarity above all."[12] Then, a month later, Mr. Lewis, in a column entitled A FATEFUL SILENCE, began this way: "Should American Jews speak out when they believe that Israeli government policies endanger the future of Israel?" Mr. Lewis's answer—"History will not forgive silence."[13]

The Lebanese war evoked a number of "Jewish" responses from American pundits. I. F. Stone, in *The New York Times,* in an appeal for a Palestinian state, asked, "Can we Jews not recognize the image in our mirrors?"[14] Nat Hentoff, the eminent jazz critic, treated his readers in the *Village Voice* to a reminiscence of his Zionist boyhood, then denounced Israel for war crimes and noted, ". . . What their [the Israeli government's] critics in Israel need, desperately, is some sense of solidarity from Jews in the United States who share their fear that Israel is losing its soul."[15]

Following the massacre at the Sabra and Shatilla refugee camps in Lebanon, Anthony Lewis, having mobilized Passover in his campaign to end Jewish settlement in Hebron, now turned to Yom Kippur for assistance in removing Menachem Begin from office.[16] Three days later, in *The Washington Post,* Richard Cohen summed up *his* Jewish problem in an article entitled WHEN JEWS LOSE THEIR TOLERANCE FOR DISSENT: "A whole lot of American Jews seem to view criticism of Israel as the ethnic-cum-religious equivalent of treason. . . . If personal experience is any guide, the tag is affixed with special vehemence when it comes to Jews. And I don't mind telling you, it hurts."[17] Mr. Cohen, however, misstated the situation. His columns on Israel were not "Jewish" criticism made by one member of the community and directed to others. On the contrary, Mr. Cohen wrote as an American journalist for *The Washington Post.* Some of his readers are Jews, but most are not. His was not "Jewish dissent" but liberal, *Washington Post*-style orthodoxy. On Lebanon, the only difference between him and fellow *Post* columnists Phillip Geylin, William Raspberry, or Mary McGrory was that Cohen sought to authenticate his critique of Israeli policy by playing up his Jewish background.

Similarly, the positions taken by liberal commentators who explicitly identify themselves as Jewish, such as I. F. Stone, Hentoff, Lewis, and others—that Israel should cease Jewish settlement in the West Bank and turn it over to the Palestinians for the establishment of a state, or that its foreign and defense policies are morally and politically objectionable—are often no different than the views of fellow left-of-center pundits such as Nicholas Von Hoffman or Carl Rowan. But by cloaking them in Jewish terms, they are meant to take on an additional weight. They are offered as a real expression of the Jewish spirit (perverted by Israel) or insider information on how the Jews really feel (as opposed to the lip service American Jewish leaders pay to Israel). When the columnist is sincere, as I believe Lewis and some of the others are, he uses his position in the general press to pursue an essentially internal Jewish agenda of his own; while if he is disingenuous, he simply drafts his "Jewishness" into the service of his personal opinions. In either case, Israel is placed in a uniquely difficult position, for these Jewish critics would be incensed (and properly so) by any Israeli attempt tò enlist their support on a "we're all in this together" basis. They would protest that they are *American* journalists, with no special loyalty to the Jewish state; and that the mere suggestion that they might agree to deal with Israel on such a basis is offensive.

Nor have I ever seen a column by an American Jewish columnist explaining why, as a Jew, he is compelled to support or approve of some unpopular Israeli action or policy. Columns written from the "Jewish perspective" in the general press are almost universally critical of Israel, often on moral grounds.

The tendency of some liberal Jewish columnists to take a dim view of Israeli policy is noticeable from 1975 onward. But like so much emotion surrounding Israel, it was greatly intensified by the election of Menachem Begin in 1977. Nor were the columnists the only Jewish journalists affected by the change. In the United States, Jewish newspeople with only a passing interest in Israel who had basked in the reflected glory of Israel's very popular leaders—Ben-Gurion, Golda, Abba Eban, and especially the heroic Moshe Dayan—found themselves identified with Begin ("rhymes with Fagin," *Time* magazine informed its readers [18]), a throwback to the ghetto Jew. "He reminds me of my Uncle Louie" was the reaction of many American Jewish journalists, who wouldn't necessarily want to be seen with the old man.

Objections to Begin were, however, far deeper than mere snobbery. He was the antithesis of the liberal Jewish ideal, a man who sought confrontation, proclaimed Jewish particularism, and framed his positions and policies in the language of the Bible and the Jewish world of Eastern Europe. Moreover, if Begin was unpopular with Jewish journalists abroad, he was positively anathema to many liberal Israeli journalists at home, and it was *they* who led the assault on his government during the next six years.

* * *

It was the night of May 17, 1977—election night in Israel—and hundreds of Likud supporters were gathered in the party headquarters on King George Street in Tel Aviv to follow the returns. At exactly 11:00 P.M., television anchorman Haim Yavin came on the screen with the projected results. Yavin deadpanned one of the most incredible announcements of his career—that after twenty-nine years of continuous rule, the Labor Party, the party of Ben-Gurion and Golda, had been defeated and the Likud's Menachem Begin would be the next prime minister of Israel.

As pandemonium broke out at Likud headquarters, dozens of foreign correspondents who had gathered for the Labor Party victory celebration realized that they were in the wrong place. As they rushed into the street, it occurred to many of them that they had no idea where the Likud headquarters *was*. For despite all the signs, no one had been expecting a Likud victory. The American Embassy in Tel Aviv had predicted a close win for Labor, and this assessment was accepted by Washington. Jimmy Carter later recalled in his memoirs that Begin was known to him as "a right wing radical leader" and that upon hearing of his election, "Israeli citizens, the American Jewish community and I were shocked. None of us knew what to expect."[19]

Most of the Israeli press greeted Begin's victory as a disastrous aberration and set up a tattoo of denunciation and vitriolic comment which, throughout his six years in office, never really ceased. Prestigious Israeli columnists such as Ze'ev Shiff, Yoel Marcus, Dan Margalit, Matti Golan and Amos Elon of *Ha'aretz*, Nahum Barnea of *Davar*, and most of their colleagues were bitterly opposed to the Begin government, its policies, and its rhetorical style. In addition Begin received little editorial support from the Israeli newspapers, and in the 1981 election, only *Hatzofe*, a tiny daily owned by the National Religious Party, endorsed his reelection.

Begin's unpopularity with the Israeli press was nothing new. Throughout his public career he had been regarded as the arch-villain of the Israeli establishment (including much of the press), which, divided in its preferences within the

Labor Party, was united in its opposition to the Likud leader. For years, as leader of the opposition, Begin had had a bi-weekly column in *Ma'ariv,* a right-wing newspaper which Begin, as prime minister, managed to alienate, and he would sometimes refuse to talk to journalists on the grounds that if he had something to say, he would write it himself. Begin's animosity toward the Israeli press was magnified by the fact that until the mid-1960s, the Israeli national radio had been under the control of the prime minister's office, and Begin's point of view had gone largely unarticulated. Even fifteen years later, he continued to believe that Israel's electronic media, especially television, were staffed primarily by journalists with a strong anti-Begin bias.

At the beginning of his first administration, Begin did make some overtures to the Israeli press, but they were quickly ended by what he saw as its immutable hostility. Throughout his term of office, he scrupulously respected free speech and the prerogatives of the Israeli media, but he often fulminated against their bias and usually limited his contacts to a few friendly journalists such as Yosef Harif of *Ma'ariv* and Shlomo Nakdimon of *Yediot Achronot.* Begin also discontinued the tradition by which the prime minister meets periodically with the senior editors of Israel's media in order to brief them on current developments. His decision to end this clubby arrangement did little to endear him to the editors, most of whom had, in any event, disliked him intensely for years.

Much of the Israeli press criticism of Begin, especially during his first term, concentrated on the distinction between him and his government on the one hand and the "real Israel" on the other. Begin was cast as an interloper whose election had been a protest against the Labor Party rather than a mandate for his own policies. It was widely believed that a brief period of "Beginism" would bring the country to its senses and that the natural order of things would be restored by a new, chastened Labor government.

It is difficult to overestimate the influence of the Israeli press and its view of Menachem Begin on foreign journalists stationed in Jerusalem, as well as on visiting newspeople.

It played a major role in setting the terms of reference by which Begin came to be judged; and its immediate post-election assessment of him as a reactionary, a nationalist extremist, and an aberration came to be the accepted wisdom of foreign journalists who had never met the man and had never heard of him until his election.

This process was exacerbated by a curious fact—more than half the resident "foreign correspondents" in Israel are actually Israelis (or long-time residents) who work for foreign publications. Many had, quite logically, been chosen for their contacts and familiarity with the Israeli scene, and in the pre-Begin period, that meant close ties with the perennially governing Labor Party. Some of them, like David Halevy of *Time* were former Labor Party functionaries; others were close to Labor Party circles and thinking. They did not need to be influenced by the local press to oppose Begin; their opposition flowed naturally out of their own Israeli political orientation and experience. The "Israeli" foreign correspondents became extremely influential, along with the local Israeli journalists, in helping form the attitudes of the "foreigners" in the foreign press corps.

Another powerful factor in the anti-Begin mood that infected the foreign correspondents in Israel was the fact that *The Jerusalem Post,* Israel's only English-language daily, was violently opposed to him and his policies. For many years the *Post* was a Labor Party organ, so much so that during the late 1960s, Labor Party politicians installed what one of the *Post*'s senior editors describes as "a political commissar" to prevent the newspaper from losing its pro-Mapai orthodoxy. In recent years the *Post* has become more independent, but it has retained its strong Labor Party orientation (and some Labor Party ownership, by way of the Histadrut Labor federation).

Following Begin's election, editors and columnists in the U.S., many of whom had long-standing relationships with Labor personalities such as Abba Eban, Itzhak Rabin, and others who had served as ambassadors to the U.S. or the UN, were at a loss to understand the upheaval in Israel. They heard the bitter criticism of Israel's new government by revered Israeli figures such as Golda Meir or Eban, noted the disconcerted and unenthusiastic reaction of the American Jewish establishment, as well as the alarmed assessments of the American government, and concluded that Begin was a disaster. The conventional wisdom was formed early: A week after his election, *Time* ran a cover with Begin's picture headlined TROUBLE IN THE PROMISED LAND, and *Newsweek* had an equally dramatic cover—ISRAEL: DAY OF THE HAWKS. Taking their cue from the Israeli press, Begin was depicted as a warmonger, a former terrorist, and a religious zealot. Nothing in his future activities—not the peace treaty he concluded with Egypt, not his broad national coalition which included such moderate and secular figures as Moshe Dayan, Ezer Weizmann, Yigael Yadin, not even his Nobel Prize for Peace—ever really changed the initial image of Begin as a fanatic and crypto-fascist.*

In America many Jewish journalists were attracted to the idea that Menachem Begin did not represent the "real Israel." To the extent that they identified with the country or were identified with it, they preferred a more moderate and modern figure. Many of them resented or scoffed at what they saw as Begin's "fixation" with the dark side of the Jewish experience, his rhetorical style, and his determination to pursue his policies without apparent concern for Israel's image abroad.

Often Jewish journalists who met with the prime minister took the opportunity to argue with him about the country's policies. They in turn were usually treated to a long and seemingly irrelevant lecture on Jewish history. After one such meeting early in Begin's first term, in which the prime min-

---

*In this regard, it is instructive to compare Begin's reception to that of Yuri Andropov. Of course Andropov and Begin were judged by different yardsticks— Andropov as a supposed *relative* liberal in a dictatorship, Begin as a presumptive *relative* extremist in a democracy. Still, it is interesting that Begin, who had been a parliamentarian for twenty-nine years and whose underground activities were, at the very least, mitigated by the Holocaust and British colonialism, was generally excoriated; while Andropov, the former head of the KGB, was often presented as a kind of liberal. *The Washington Post*, especially, found the ex-KGB leader to its liking. *Post* correspondent Charles Fenyvesi, wrote that he had made the KGB a "safe place for closet liberals" and that "once in power he could prove the paradox of a secret police chief being more reform-minded than the party he was to protect from reformers."[20]

ister went on at great length about the heroism of Judah
Macabee, a befuddled newsman confided to friends that Begin was crazy and disoriented. Begin, for his part, later told
an aide that the journalist's opening remarks had indicated
that he had come to argue, not interview, and Begin knew
that it would be futile to try to convince him about the justice of Israeli claims to the West Bank. "Still," Begin said,
"the man is a Jew, and Chanuka is coming up, and I thought
that learning something about our history might be good for
him."*

Sometimes Jewish reporters and editors who visited Israel acted as though Labor, and not the Likud, was in power.
They went for their assessments and briefings to Labor personalities and "balanced" them with an obligatory meeting
or two with Likud MKs or ministers. Sometimes they didn't
even want to do that. When *Time* magazine's editor Henry
Grunwald visited Israel in November 1981, for example, his
schedule included appointments with Shimon Peres, Teddy
Kollek, and a number of other opposition figures—but no
meetings with anyone in the government. Embarrassed *Time*
employees in Jerusalem sought at the last minute to arrange
a meeting with Israeli Defense Minister Ariel Sharon, but
Grunwald vetoed a suggestion that he meet with Menachem
Begin—surely one of the few times that a newsman has
turned down a meeting with a national leader.

The tendency to view the Begin government as unrepre-
sentative of "the real Israel" led to a practice, in reporting
on Israel, of giving equal weight to government and opposition positions. Any discussion of the West Bank settle-

*Anwar Sadat, whose press in America was as good as Begin's was bad, had a
different technique for dealing with hostile journalists. During a state visit to Israel
the Egyptian president was interviewed on *Meet the Press*. One of the panelists was
a Cairo-based *L.A. Times* correspondent, Don Schanche. Schanche had been stationed in Egypt for years, and Sadat knew him well. The Egyptian president, who
hadn't liked Schanche's question about some recent political arrests, squinted at
the nameplate in front of the reporter as if he were trying to make out the name
of a total stranger. "Well, Mr. ah, ah, Schanch—ee," he mispronounced the name,
"you probably have never been to Egypt. You must visit our country and see it for
yourself." "My God," said Schanche later, "the editors at home are going to think
I've been making up all those interviews."

ments, for example, was likely to include not two but three spokesmen—one for the Israeli government, one for the Palestinians in the West Bank, and one for Israeli opponents of settlement. This often created the impression that the Israeli government did not necessarily articulate the view of the majority—a misleading suggestion that caused considerable confusion in the United States about what Israeli policy actually was. A good part of the unwillingness of the American media to present Likud decisions as official came from a sense that "they couldn't mean it" and that anything Abba Eban was against couldn't really be legitimate.

I do not mean to imply that the subjectivity of some Jewish journalists, American or Israeli, was the sole, or even the primary, reason for Israel's diminished stature in the American press in the decade following the Yom Kippur War. Much of the decline would have taken place even if Menachem Begin had never come to power, or if there were no Jews in the media. The main factors that brought about Israel's bad press—the influence of Arab economic power and America's determination to appease it; liberal sentiment in favor of "self-determination" for the Palestinians and Israel's refusal to agree to a Palestinian West Bank entity; and Israeli defense policies such as the destruction of the Iraqi reactor or the 1982 invasion of Lebanon—all existed independently of any Jewish component in American press coverage. Moreover, most American Jewish journalists were (and are) far more influenced by the assumptions, conventions, and values of their non-Jewish peers and the ideas current in their professional milieu than by any parochial Jewish feelings.

On the other hand, it is idle to deny that some Jewish American journalists do take Israel's policies and postures personally and that this fact contributes to a greater degree of coverage, a sharper edge of reporting, and a more strident and moralistic tone of editorial commentary than is usually applied to other foreign nations, and certainly to other democracies. By and large, most American Jewish report-

ers, editors, producers, and columnists have bent over
backward to be fair and evenhanded—a worthy intellectual
and professional exercise, but one that has led to some con-
torted press coverage of the Arab-Israel conflict

14

THE VOICE OF
THE BEAST

Early in the war in Lebanon some of the members of the Commodore Battalion began referring to Israel's English-language radio newscast as "The Voice of the Beast."[1] Ten years of cumulative hostility to Israel were wrapped up in that phrase, along with enough venom to shock some of the uninitiated reporters who arrived in the Lebanese capital to cover the war. Several who later came to Israel repeated the phrase to their Jerusalem-based colleagues or to Israeli journalists with evident disapproval for the open partisanship it revealed.

When I first heard about "The Voice of the Beast," I couldn't help thinking that I had seen that phrase—or one very much like it—someplace before. It was only much later, looking through some old press clips from *The Washington Post*, that I remembered where. Back in March 1981, *Post* correspondents Jonathan Randal and William Claiborne had written about south Lebanon and described a small radio station run by American and Canadian evangelical Christians: "It is fondly known in the Christian enclave of southern Lebanon as 'The Voice of Hope,' " they wrote, "but north of the Litani River, in the rest of Lebanon, they called it 'The

Voice of Death.' "[2] Yes, indeed. North of the Litani River
and all the way to the bar of the Commodore Hotel, some
of whose patrons were about to write a new page in the history of modern war coverage.

The War in Lebanon began on June 6, 1982, almost fifteen years to the day after the start of the Six Day War. Israeli forces struck across the northern border in what was
originally presented as a limited action against the PLO terrorists who had menaced the Galilee for a decade. At first
the operation won the support of the Israeli public, and
considerable applause in the United States as well. But as
days turned into weeks, and then months, "Operation Peace
for Galilee" became the focus of an acrimonious debate both
at home and abroad. It was the first Israeli war ever fought
without a domestic consensus, a fact that meant continuous
political and press criticism within Israel and overseas. It was
also the first Arab-Israeli war whose coverage by the foreign
press became, in itself, a kind of battlefield.

Few wars in modern history have excited the media attention that Israel's invasion of Lebanon received. Millions
of words were written and thousands of feet of television
footage shown; the war became the subject of television documentaries, *Time* and *Newsweek* cover stories, and a considerable number of books and retrospective articles by journalists who covered it. This attention contrasted starkly with
the virtual privacy in which other recent Middle East conflicts have been fought. The war in the Persian Gulf, almost
two years old when Israeli troops entered Lebanon, was by
all odds as bloody and important a conflict, but it had been
all but forgotten by much of the American press. Nor had
the civil war in Lebanon in 1975–76 commanded anything
like the attention given to Israel's campaign there.

The war also highlighted the technological advances that
the electronic news media have made and their impact on
battlefield coverage. Vietnam is often called the first television war, but in Vietnam the cameras were only on one
side. In Lebanon, for the first time there were television
crews, armed with electronic news-gathering equipment and

the ability to satellite material, on both sides of the line and they provided a first—televised warfare almost in "real time." Previous Israeli-Arab wars had been the testing ground for new military technology; the invasion of Lebanon became a laboratory and showcase for advances in electronic war coverage.

The devastatingly bad press Israel received during the war was the product not only of technology, but of a number of trends and attitudes that had been ripening for years. A decade of sympathy for Palestinian nationalism and declining Israeli popularity and credibility combined to make Israel the target of a melodramatic and sometimes vitriolic press campaign, which was aided and abetted by Israel's own conduct, both of the war and its press relations.

Israel made a number of errors in its dealings with the media. In retrospect, it was a mistake to have banned foreign correspondents from the battlefield during the first five days of fighting, especially since this restriction was used by some reporters as an excuse for their grossly exaggerated accounts of Israeli destruction in the coastal cities of Tyre and Sidon ("How did you expect us to report it correctly if we couldn't get there to see it?"). This defense was largely disingenuous—the exaggerations continued well after the areas were open for inspection—but the presence of foreign journalists with the Israeli forces in the first days of the war might have promoted greater accuracy. As it was, Israel's decision left the story in the hands of the Beirut-based correspondents during these first few days—with predictable results.

It was also a mistake to allow American television to send its reports from Beirut via the Israeli satellite facilities after the Beirut transmitter became inoperative. No one could quarrel with the efforts of the PLO leadership to make its case on American television; but it should have been equally clear that Israel was under no obligation to assist that effort by allowing interviews with Yasser Arafat to be broadcast from *its* facilities. The unbalanced and unprincipled reaction of the three networks to Israel's censorship of material gathered on the PLO side—material which Israel was, after all, under no obligation to transmit—was reminiscent of the child who kills his parents and begs for mercy on the grounds that he is an orphan. Israel should have simply told the networks that processing and transmitting material gathered on the "enemy side" was not its concern.

Jerusalem's greatest self-inflicted wounds, however, were a result of the way the war was fought and the way it was explained. The prolonged shelling of Beirut may or may not have been a good military tactic (and in retrospect, it seems very doubtful that it was), but it created an insuperable public relations difficulty. No one can shell a city day after day and expect to be seen in a positive light.

To make matters worse it often seemed that Israel had no explanation, either for its tactics or for the strategic aims of the operation. It had; but the nation's political leadership largely failed to articulate them. In his book *Big Story,* which analyzes the press coverage of the Tet Offensive in 1968, Peter Braestrup argued that Tet, which was presented by the press as a major American defeat was, on the contrary, a disaster for the Viet Cong. He laid the blame for the press's "distortion of reality" at the feet of President Lyndon Johnson, who chose to remain silent.

"Particularly during a foreign policy crisis, the Chief Executive plays a special role with respect to the practical needs of the press and television. . . . Braestrup wrote: "Faced with the competitive task of providing instant reportage and prompt explanation, [newsmen] are ill equipped to tolerate lingering uncertainty or ambiguity. . . . If the man in the White House, however beleaguered, does not soon satisfy this need, newsmen look elsewhere."[3]

Like Lyndon Johnson, Israel's chief executive, Menachem Begin, stood mute throughout most of the campaign, while often the cabinet ministers who did appear before the press were, to put it charitably, inadequate. Ya'akov Meridor, the minister in charge of the Lebanese refugee problem, presented confused and contradictory figures on the number of civilian casualties in Lebanon, a failure that caused grave damage to Israel's credibility; while Defense Minister Ariel Sharon's reputation for honesty and credibility, never high, sank to new lows as the war progressed.

Begin's silence was largely a function of his frustrated conviction that the press was hostile and that no matter what explanations he offered, it would continue to be. This represented the full circle for the Israeli prime minister, who had come to office convinced of his ability to explain and justify his policies to Western public opinion. In his televised pre-election debate with candidate Shimon Peres in May 1977, Begin had dwelled on Israel's poor image in the international press and had maintained that it was largely a function of Labor's inability to communicate; now, after five years of what he regarded as a calculated bias against Israel by much of the world press, the Israeli prime minister simply chose to ignore it. This decision cost Israel the opportunity to effectively present its side of the story.

Another factor in the negative media reaction to the war was the fierce domestic opposition that it excited. The Labor Party initially supported the operation's declared goal of driving the PLO out of artillery range of the Galilee, but this support began to dissolve as the war and its aims expanded. More and more Israelis publicly criticized the campaign, and their criticism, unprecedented during wartime in Israel, was duly noted by the foreign press. Whatever the merits of their arguments (and in retrospect, much of what they feared was correct), it was a major blunder for Menachem Begin and his government to attempt such an ambitious policy without first securing a firm national consensus.

Israeli ineptitude had a parallel in the incompetence displayed by many foreign journalists and editors whose work graphically exhibited the uneven quality of Middle East reporting. Expert journalists worked side by side with neophyte reporters, who lost their poise in the confusion and destruction; old Middle East hands' by-lines appeared alongside those of correspondents who couldn't tell Druze from Druids. Many misreported the destruction of the town of Damur—caused by the PLO years before—as the result of the Israeli incursion. *The Washington Post* repeatedly referred to the Ein Hilwe refugee camp as "razed" when, in fact, it was damaged badly but far from totally destroyed (it's still there, and open for inspection). The destruction wrought by Israel's thrust into Lebanon was greatly overstated; this was acknowledged by many, including ABC anchorman Peter Jennings: "I recall driving from Beirut down to Jerusalem early in August . . ." Jennings said, "driving through Sidon and Tyre and finding, at least to my own satisfaction, that the damage that had been reported in Sidon and Tyre had indeed been exaggerated."[4] Jennings went on to categorize much of the reporting from Lebanon as "sloppy."[5]

The ABC anchorman may well have been referring to reports such as ABC's Mike McCourt's on June 28, in which he described (but had no pictures of) "two square miles of West Beirut [that are] now dust and mortar. The rest of the city, nearly all of it, resembles some ancient ruin. . . . The total in human terms has been appalling. Ten thousand dead, up to twenty-five thousand wounded, and more than half a million people, mainly Lebanese, left homeless."[6] The kindest thing that can be said about this description is that it was untrue in every detail.

McCourt and his colleagues in Beirut were under considerable pressure, and it is perhaps understandable that some of them panicked. Many newcomers to the area were apparently unaware that Beirut was a badly scarred city even before the first Israeli shell fell (tens of thousands of Lebanese had died in the civil war of the preceding few years in the Lebanese capital, and whole areas of the city were blasted). Of course factual errors in such a pressurized situation are inevitable, but the war in Lebanon spawned some memorable ones. Two in particular stand out as examples of the poor quality of much of the reporting from Beirut.

The first had to do with casualty reports during the first three weeks of the fighting. On June 10, the Palestine Red Crescent floated the figure of 10,000 killed during the first four days of the war, and at about the same time Francesco Noseda, the representative of the International Committee of the Red Cross (ICRC) in Beirut, said that there were an estimated 600,000 refugees.

The figures were first reported (and accurately attributed) by the BBC, and then picked up and repeated throughout the West. Israel claimed that both were wildly inaccurate. It had no exact figures of its own (indeed, such figures during the midst of battle are impossible to calculate), but it appealed to the common sense of the press corps. It pointed out that the Palestine Red Crescent, far from being "the Lebanese equivalent of the Red Cross," as it was often called, was in fact an adjunct of the PLO run by Yasser Arafat's brother, Dr. Fathi Arafat, and that its assessments were, at the very least, suspect. Moreover, the casualty figures related to south Lebanon, but the PLO was no longer in the area, and thus had no means of arriving at any accurate figure. Finally, Israel reminded the Beirut press corps that even during the relatively less frenzied period of the Lebanese civil war, the journalists in Beirut themselves had often written about the unreliability of "official" casualty figures and the impossibility of getting accurate statistics.

The prima facie evidence against the ICRC refugee figure was, if anything, more obvious. Simply put, there hadn't been 600,000 civilians—Lebanese and Palestinians—in the entire area before the war.

Despite the improbability of both the 10,000 and 600,000 figures, they were given wide currency in the American press. On June 10, NBC's Roger Mudd stated, "Neither side has even estimated its loss of life, but the Red Crescent, which is Lebanon's Red Cross, is quoted as estimating that ten thousand civilians have been killed or wounded since Friday"[7]—as if the Red Crescent were not a side in the dispute. The casualty figure was echoed, without qualification, by ABC's Barrie Dunsmore[8] and NBC's Steve Mallory (who spoke of 9,000 killed) on June 14.[9] They attributed these estimates to the "Lebanese police" or "Lebanese government," although they must have known that neither existed, nor had they existed in south Lebanon since the PLO had taken over that part of the country in the mid-1970s.

As for the refugee figure, it was so absurdly high that the Red Cross took the almost unprecedented step of recalling its representative, Francesco Noseda, after Noseda himself repudiated his earlier exaggerated estimate on June 15. Despite this, NBC's Jessica Savitch said, four days later,

"It is now estimated that 600,000 refugees in south Lebanon are without sufficient food and medical supplies."[10]

Print journalists were somewhat more careful than the television reporters, but they too made use of the exaggerated and obviously politically motivated statistics without sufficient explanation or caution. *The New York Times, The Washington Post,* and other major American newspapers used the Red Crescent number without properly explaining that it was in fact a PLO statistic, and quoted the Red Cross refugee assessment without wondering how so many refugees could have come from a region with so few people.

Israel later published official casualty figures for south Lebanon—265 dead in Sidon, 50 to 60 in Tyre, and 10 in Nabatiyah. These figures were flawed by the fact that they included only Lebanese civilians and not Palestinians in the camps, a piece of intellectual dishonesty that cost Israel considerable credibility. Despite this, however, the Israeli figures were much closer to reality than the PLO and Red Cross inventions of early June 1982. As David Shipler of *The New York Times* later put it, "It is clear to anyone who has traveled in southern Lebanon, as have many journalists and relief workers, that the original figures of 10,000 dead and 600,000 homeless reported by correspondents quoting the representatives of the International Committee of the Red Cross during the first week of the war were extreme exaggerations."[11]

If the early exaggeration by most of the American press of civilian casualties was the major factual lapse of the war, a small incident involving UPI was perhaps no less significant. On August 2, UPI distributed a picture of a Lebanese baby girl with a caption saying that her arms had been blown off and her body severely damaged and burned, as the result of Israeli bombardment. This photo received prominent play; President Reagan apparently saw it in *The Washington Post,* clipped it out of the paper, and put it on his desk, as a symbol. *Time* magazine quoted an aide to the president: "That picture of the baby with arms burnt had more impact on him than fifty position papers."[12]

The photo of the baby was real, but the caption wasn't.

Israeli physicians who saw the photograph in the newspaper realized that no infant whose arms had been recently amputated would be bandaged and displayed by a nurse as this one was. The Israeli Ministry of Health conducted a search and found that the baby (a boy, not a girl, named Eli Masco) had not lost any limbs. He had a broken arm, from which he was recovering. UPI, after some initial dithering, published a correction, but by this time millions had seen the photo and had been impressed by its dramatic caption; and many of the newspapers and television stations that had carried the story did not bother to publish the correction.

There were, of course, other babies who were maimed and killed during the war, unintentionally but inevitably; and this fact was amply documented by American journalists in Beirut. In that regard the photo was not "symbolically" untrue. But of course the job of the press is to report things that actually happen, not things that *could* have happened. From an example of Israeli cruelty, the UPI photo became a different kind of symbol—of the slipshod quality of much of the coverage that came out of Lebanon during the war and of the gullibility of editors who used it.*

The exaggerated casualty reports from south Lebanon, the attribution of damage caused during the Lebanese civil war to the Israelis, and the UPI baby photo were the most glaring factual reportorial errors of the war. To a certain extent such errors were inevitable, the by-product of confusion, excitement, and the pressure of deadlines. But they also had a common theme—the inhumanity of Israel's attack against innocent civilians. These reports from Lebanon were the raw material with which American opinion makers fashioned a picture of cruel and unusual behavior by the Israeli army. Indeed, even without embroidery, the war was grisly enough. Innocent civilians *were* caught up in the fighting, and many were killed, wounded, or made homeless; and

*There is a bizarre footnote to this incident. Three years earlier, following the recapture of the Grand Mosque in Mecca in 1979, the Saudi news agency published and distributed photos of one of the rebel leaders taken into custody, seated with his hands tied behind his back. UPI mistakenly captioned the photo as that of a rebel whose arms had been cut off as a punishment. The editor who made the error that time was fired.

the fact that they were put into the line of fire by the PLO, which placed its positions among civilians for protection, in no way ameliorated their suffering. The television footage of death and destruction—the unavoidable consequences of any war—dismayed and shocked Israeli viewers quite as much as it did the American public.

Coverage of major events such as the war in Lebanon tends to start with a premise and develop from there. In this case, much of the media took for their point of departure the idea that Israel had, for insufficient reason, invaded its neighbor and was acting in an unnecessarily brutal way. This was the "big picture." Reports, no matter how improbable, that tended to confirm this idea were accepted without sufficient scrutiny. Some editors were motivated by sensationalism, some by a desire to match the competition, and some by simple herd instinct. Others may have been moved by ideological or political motives. But whatever its origin, the fact is that the American press was accident prone against Israel during the war.

The thematic treatment of the war also led to a lack of journalistic proportion. The PLO *was,* after all, Israel's declared arch-enemy. It *had* used Lebanon as a staging ground to menace the Israeli north for more than a decade. There *was* no sovereign government in Beirut to put a stop to these activities. Previous limited Israeli actions, such as the 1978 Litani Operation, had failed to assure a tranquil life for the citizens of the Galilee and to guarantee them immunity from PLO rocket and artillery attacks; and Israel now resorted to full-scale military action in an attempt to drive the PLO out of the south, help establish a strong government in Beirut, and restore the peaceful ambience that had characterized the Israeli-Lebanese border until the arrival of the PLO. Whatever the practicality or wisdom of such a plan, it certainly was not the unprovoked attack on civilians that much of the media portrayed it as being.

In fact, during the campaign, Israel made considerable efforts to minimize civilian casualties; far greater, certainly, than any similar effort made during the barbarous inter-Arab fighting in Lebanon over the previous decade. Despite this, some journalists portrayed the Israeli invasion as an uninhibited and almost unprecedented act of savagery. The best known was NBC's John Chancellor, who visited Lebanon briefly and on August 2 told his viewers, "What will stick in the mind about yesterday's savage Israeli attack on Beirut is its size and scope. . . . Nothing like it has ever happened in this part of the world." Media critic Joshua Muravchik responded to Mr. Chancellor (not on national television with millions of viewers, of course) this way: "Ever? Surely Mr. Chancellor has heard of the Bible, the Roman Empire, the Crusades? But even taking him not to have meant 'ever,' his assertion certainly must have come as good news to the survivors of Hama, Syria . . . or to those of Khoramsharr, Iran, which was reported destroyed in the Iran-Iraq war. Both cities once had populations near 200,000."[13] In fact, during the Hama massacre Mr. Chancellor had been NBC's anchorman, and he had reported the mass murders at Hama with a dry indifference.

For some time Israel had been charging that many of the American journalists in Beirut had ceased to be dispassionate observers of the Middle East conflict and had in fact become advocates for the Palestinian point of view. These charges were often rejected by editors in the United States as so much Israeli paranoia or as a tendency to blame the messenger for bearing ill tidings. One positive result of the war in Lebanon was that it brought a number of PLO sympathizers out of the closet. In July 1982, for example, Jonathan Randal wrote quite seriously that "since the 1967 Arab-Israeli war, Israel has habituated the Arab world . . . to a rising level of violence in this region."[14] Given the regional tradition of intramural butchery—massacres by Arab dictators of their own populations, the Lebanese civil war, the Iran-Iraq war, the adventures of Libya in Chad, not to mention the PLO's attacks on civilians, and the 1973 war launched by Syria and Egypt against Israel—it was clear that Mr. Randal was speaking as a polemicist and not as a reporter.

Nor was Jonathan Randal the only correspondent whose emotions overcame normal professional reserve. *The Wash-*

ington Post's Edward Cody wrote movingly of his admiration for the man who had helped plan the massacre of thirty-five Israeli women and children on the Haifa-Tel Aviv road in 1978.[15] Another *Post* correspondent, Loren Jenkins, published an article in *Rolling Stone* that made several comparisons between the Israelis and the Nazis and elegantly argued the Arab version of history—that Zionism is illegitimate because the Jews stole their land.[16] Jenkins was especially indignant about the Holocaust: "They [the Israelis] think they're owed something because of what happened [in World War II]," he fumed in an interview with the *Aspen Times*.[17]

Public anti-Israel animus and pro-PLO sentiments were by no means limited to the journalists of *The Washington Post*. Tony Clifton, for example, who covered Lebanon for the *Post*'s sister publication *Newsweek,* wrote a book following the war, called *God Cried,* whose theme was Israeli responsibility for the Middle East conflict. He confided to Mustapha Karkouti of *The Middle East* magazine, "I have always been sympathetic to the Palestinian cause," and went on to explain, "It has always seemed to me that there is no hope for peace in the Middle East unless the Palestinians have their own state. I believe the PLO does represent the Palestinians, and that Yasser Arafat is a good leader." Clifton also expressed his outrage at the lack of interest in the Palestinian plight, which he equated with that of the Jews under the Nazis. Clifton, perhaps unaware that six million Jews had been murdered while the nations of the world had refused to accept Jewish refugees, said, quite baldly, "It seems that history is repeating itself with the Palestinians. People don't seem to be reacting in the same degree as they did in the forties with the Jews." Clifton, whose book was published by Palestinian Naim Attalah, summarized his hope for the project by saying, "I would be disappointed if there were no reaction from Zionist groups."[18]

The open partisanship of Tony Clifton, Jonathan Randal, Loren Jenkins, Edward Cody, and other members of the Commodore Battalion put an end to the pretense that they were simply professionals doing their job, with no personal commitment to either side. It also contrasted pleasantly with the old American tradition in which Israel's bitterest detractors deny any anti-Israel bias. In an era in which even George Ball wants to punish Israel *"for its own good,"*[19] the outspoken opinions of journalists who believe that the Jews had it too soft in the 1940s and stole their country from the innocent Palestinians, or that PLO terrorists are "honorable officers" and Israel has habituated the Arab world to violence, are refreshingly candid.

Whether these partisans are also reliable correspondents is another matter. The Lebanese reality revealed by Israel's invasion had, in many cases, little resemblance to the country they had been reporting about, and it raised some embarrassing questions. One had to do with the near-collective cover-up by the Beirut press corps of the PLO's brutal ministate in south Lebanon. Another, related to the reasons for the often uncritical press coverage[20] afforded the PLO over a decade, an especially blatant example of which was provided when Congressman Pete McCloskey visited Yasser Arafat during the war. After their meeting, the two convened a press conference, attended by the Beirut press corps, in which the congressman claimed that the PLO chief was prepared to recognize Israel, while Arafat equivocated and avoided confirming the announcement. The reporters had seen this ploy used before, but apparently no one challenged it; on the contrary, they treated McCloskey's interpretation of Arafat's remarks as more significant than Arafat's own words.

Later, considering this curious misrepresentation, *The Washington Post*'s ombudsman wrote: "It remains inexplicable that these early reports did not take account of Arafat's double-talk. His comments were concurrent with McCloskey's and made in front of presumably seasoned journalists. All could see that Mr. Arafat was clearly aiming at correcting the impression that Mr. McCloskey was rendering [that the PLO was prepared to recognize Israel]. The fact that the PLO chairman said anything less or more than 'that's right' should have been the reporters' clue that they were hearing a conflict of views."[21] Nothing more damning than that—that the Beirut press corps "inexplicably" transmitted what they must have known to be a false account of PLO moderation—has been charged by any Israeli official about the Commodore Battalion.

Tim Llewelyn of the BBC once wrote that the Beirut-based correspondent's job was to compete with the reporters stationed in Israel, each side trying to tell "its" side of the story.[22] But in the War in Lebanon, as it had been in the Middle East for years, "symmetry" was a game with only one player. The Israel-based foreign correspondents reported the deep split in the country and reflected the critical spirit with which many Israelis viewed the campaign. In fact, a good deal of their reportage was derived from the Israeli press, which distinguished itself by exceptionally good reporting and, among columnists, a generally critical approach to the war. In December 1982, the International Press Institute of London commended Israel's journalists for a "heroic" and "victorious" performance in Lebanon. The institute noted that the Israeli government had tried censorship at the source during the first days of the war but that the press had successfully resisted it as the British press during the Falkland crisis had not (the institute also noted that there had been no effort made by the Israeli government to curb press criticism).[23] After the massacre at Sabra and Shatilla, Israeli journalists led the way in uncovering the details of the atrocity, and in fact, a good many "scoops" that appeared in the American press were little more than rewrites of Israeli investigative reports.

The Lebanese war demonstrated the "heads-I-win-tails-you-lose" advantage of the PLO's press coverage. Had there been an aggressive, adversarial press in Lebanon, as there is in Israel, it would have been impossible to protect the PLO as so many foreign correspondents did. But such a Lebanese press had long since ceased to exist. Had there been an active opposition among the Palestinians, voices critical of the PLO and its practices—including its tactic of hiding behind civilians—might have been raised. But of course there was no such opposition to the PLO; and most Beirut-based foreign correspondents, in the habit of ignoring the opinions of the Lebanese themselves, made little or no mention of *their* evident hatred of the PLO.

The war in Lebanon also demonstrated the double standard by which much of the Western press has, during the past few years, come to judge Israel. An Arab hunger strike in an Israeli prison in the summer of 1980 got more attention than the mass murder of political prisoners that took place in Syria at about the same time; riots in the West Bank came in for more coverage than the Iran-Iraq war; Israeli wartime press censorship was dramatically highlighted by the same news organizations that accepted the much harsher' British variety without undue complaint. During the Egyptian-Israeli peace process, the ultimative demands of Anwar Sadat were called "flexible," while the concessions of Menachem Begin were routinely labeled "intransigence." The intolerant language of Israeli settlers was widely reported as typifying Israeli extremism, while the bloodthirsty pronouncements of the official PLO leadership were dismissed by the press as "rhetoric." All this led to the suspicion that the Jewish state was being treated differently from other nations.

One of the strangest defenses of this double standard was offered by a long-time critic of Israel, syndicated columnist Nick Thimmisch. "The media employs high standards to measure Israel" he wrote, ". . . because Israel always claimed high standards for itself."[24] Or as *Washington Post* columnist Richard Cohen put it: "It [Israel] asked to be measured by a higher moral standard."[25] In other words, Israel *wants* to be judged differently than others.

There is a fundamental confusion here. Israel does not ask to be judged by a higher standard than its neighbors—it simply *has* higher standards of political morality than they do, at least by Western criteria. That is not an aspiration but a fact. This fact, however, does not mean that Israel, in fighting Middle Eastern dictatorships, must be limited to the tactics that, say, Mr. Cohen would use in a disagreement with his neighbors in suburban Maryland. It is an unfortunate fact

of life, for Israel more than for the American critics of Israeli morality, that it is engaged in a struggle for survival
with enemies who don't fight fair.

More to the point, the double standard that is applied to
Israel—and virtually no one disagrees that one is applied—
is a bit different than the one pundits such as Mr. Thimmisch or Mr. Cohen mention. It is not that the Jewish state
is expected to behave differently (and better) than its Arab
neighbors, but that it is subjected to more exacting standards than those applied to other democracies at war. It is
irrelevant to judge Israel, surrounded and beleaguered, by
the norms of peacetime America. Israel, after a generation
of stress, isolation, and provocation, has never approached,
much less exceeded, the kinds of behavior that Western democracies in similar circumstances have displayed. Arab-Israeli citizens have never been put in concentration camps,
as the U.S. did to the Japanese in World War II; Israel has
yet to carpet-bomb enemy cities on the British model or to
drop atomic bombs on civilian targets in the interests of
shortening a war. Richard Cohen and Nick Thimmisch (and
Reuven Frank, former president of NBC News, who told an
interviewer that Israel "is held to the same standards as the
U.S. and the West European countries")[26] expect Israel at
war to behave like other democracies at peace—in essence,
a *double* "double standard."

Indeed, the double standard, as it is applied to democracies, usually works just the other way around. Harsh measures and draconian policies adopted during wars against
dictatorships are forgiven, or at least mitigated, in the free-
world's view, by the presumed "good record" of the democratic nation. What is despicable in the totalitarian foe—the
bombing of British cities by the Germans, for example—is
regarded as understandable when it is done by democracies
(at Dresden, for instance) to bring about the prompt defeat
of the enemy. This principle is applied routinely in daily life.
The good citizen who breaks the law is treated more leni-
ently, and not more harshly, than the habitual criminal.
Somehow, in the case of Israel, all this has been stood on its
head.

In a now famous article, *Commentary* editor Norman Podhoretz identified the tendency to treat the Jewish state differently from other democracies in similar circumstances as anti-Semitism. He claimed that the essence of anti-Semitism, discrimination against Jews *as* Jews, was precisely expressed by the double standard applied to Israel.[27] Podhoretz's article occasioned an outraged reaction from Israel's critics, from William Buckley to *The Nation,* who counterattacked by accusing Podhoretz, and other supporters of Israel, of trying to prevent criticism of Israel by branding it as anti-Semitic.[28]

In fact, Podhoretz and most other American Jews were tip-toe careful to distinguish between most media criticism of Israel and the few exceptional cases of anti-Jewish bias. Some Jews, haunted by the specter of the Holocaust, did make irresponsible blanket accusations of anti-Semitism against the press, but this happened rather less than many journalists later claimed. Acting on the principle that a good offense is the best defense, some of Israel's critics even counterattacked and charged the American Jewish community with the crime of calling people anti-Semites—surely a new felony in the historic catalogue of Jewish maltreatment of the Gentile world.

The question of who is an anti-Semite is, in some ways, a semantic one. If one uses the Nazi criterion—hatred for all Jews without exception and the desire to murder them—then it must be conceded that there are very few, if any, in the American press. But there was anti-Semitism before Hitler and it took various forms, one of which, simply stated, was treating Jews or Jewish institutions unfairly. The double standard applied to Israel is precisely this kind of unfairness, even if the people who use it are unaware of it and even if they intend it as a compliment.

The War in Lebanon also brought into the open a kind of sadism not previously employed by responsible journalists against Israel—comparisons between the Jewish state and the Nazis. Until the war, this analogy had been the province of the Soviet Union, some Arab dictators, and a few Jew-baiters on the lunatic fringe. It is clearly an anti-Semite's device, one which Connor Cruise O'Brien, the former editor of the British *Observer,* called "anti-Jewism."

"I would suggest a pragmatic test for possible anti-Jewism, in discussion of Israel. If your interlocutor can't keep Hitler out of the conversation, if he is feverishly turning Jews into Nazis, and Arabs into Jews—why, then, I think you may well be talking to an anti-Jewist.

"And how, indeed, could they miss this golden opportunity of getting across the message: 'The Jews have no right to complain about the Holocaust. They're as bad as the Nazis themselves.'

"I am speaking of course of *mild* anti-Semites who sincerely deplore the Holocaust, and think that Hitler must have been provoked into over-reacting, just as Begin. . . ."[29]

The journalists who used the Israeli-Nazi analogy—who took the anguish of the Jewish people and turned it against them as a polemical tool, or sought to trivialize the Holocaust by casting it as just another by-product of conventional war, are a mixed bag. They include some "respectable" newsmen and women, along with the publications of the American Nazi Party, the Communist Party, and a few splinter racist groups. What is most disturbing is that there is very little difference between the sentiments expressed by the two.

Columnist Nicholas Von Hoffman, for example, wrote in the *Spectator,* "Incident by incident, atrocity by atrocity, Americans are coming to see the Israeli government as pounding the Star of David into a Swastika."[30] Columnist Georgie Ann Geyer described Israeli "atrocities" and asserted, "We do not have to replay forty years ago and keep silent."[31] The Liberty Lobby's newspaper, *Spotlight,* ran a headline US IS ISRAEL'S PARTNER IN GENOCIDE,[32] while syndicated seer Carl Rowan, in a column entitled "Begin and Sharon Are Imitating Hitler," told his readers: "In their zeal to ensure that the Jewish people never suffer another Holocaust, Israel's leaders are imitating Hitler."[33]

Author Pete Hamill, writing in the *Philadelphia Daily News,* quoted an Israeli friend who, looking at Israel, said, "Forgive me, but all I can think of is the Nazis."[34] Hamill's anonymous "friend" was not the only one who looked at the descendants of Hitler's victims and saw Nazis. *Thunderbolt,* the newspaper of the National States Rights Party, reported that "Jews continue to scream about the Holocaust and their treatment at the hands of the Germans in World War II. Many historians today say that no Holocaust ever took place in Germany. Yet today the Jews are acting like the "Holly-wood Nazis" they themselves have produced on numerous TV and movie shows."[35]

The *Chicago Tribune*'s Vernon Jarrett felt that Israel's conduct "seems designed to make civilized man forget or depreciate the Holocaust," a result he claimed to deplore, even though it resulted from "the conduct of those [such as the Israelis] who would perpetuate its spirit in the extermi-nation of other people."[36] The *Workers Vanguard,* the news-paper of the Workers World Party, said: "The Zionist state could only be carved out of the living body of the Palestin-ian people with Hitlerite methods."[37] *Washington Post* cor-respondent Loren Jenkins, writing in *Rolling Stone,* "quoted" unnamed Israelis as having spoken of a "final solution" to the problem of Palestinian terror, and found an unnamed Red Cross official who supposedly said of Ansar Prison that "there is no way to escape the fact that this is a concentra-tion camp." Jenkins himself endorsed the analogy by add-ing that "Ansar is not talked about much in Israel; it is a private embarrassment to people whose own days penned behind barbed wire are vividly branded on the mind."[38]

The "Jews are Nazis" analogy was especially common among political cartoonists. Artist Steve Benson, whose car-toons are distributed by the Washington Post Writers Group, compared Ariel Sharon with Nazi war criminal Klaus Bar-bie and showed goose-stepping Israeli storm-troopers guarding a death camp labeled BEIRUT[39]; Tony Auth de-picted the ghost of a Jewish inmate of Auschwitz looking at a bombed out site in Lebanon and, in horrified recognition, saying, "Oh, my God."[40] The *Louisville Courier-Journal* ran a picture of Begin looking into a hole where Lebanon had been, captioned "A final solution to the PLO problem,"[41] and the *Los Angeles Herald-Examiner* carried a Bill Shorr cartoon in which Begin said, "For every problem, there is a final solution."[42] The *Indianapolis Star* carried one cartoon by Oliphant of a wrecked city with a sign saying WARSAW GHETTO crossed out and the words WEST BEIRUT substituted[43] and another with Israeli soldiers saying, "We were only obeying orders."[44] *The Arizona Republic* ran a picture of Begin wearing a badge saying NEVER AGAIN, and an Arab standing next to him wearing a button saying UNTIL NOW.[45]

During the war, NBC's John Chancellor visited Beirut and informed his viewers, "I kept thinking yesterday of the bombing of Madrid during the Spanish Civil War," which was carried out by Nazi pilots, on Hitler's orders, in the service of international fascism. It, more than any air bombardment of the last fifty years—in World War II, Korea, or any of a dozen other modern wars—struck Chancellor as the most appropriate comparison to Israel's attack on the PLO in Beirut. Chancellor then looked up and asked rhetorically, "What in the world is going on?"[46]

It is difficult, in one sense, to answer that question. To refute the charge that Israel behaved in a way that might make a rational person think of Auschwitz, the Warsaw Ghetto, or Adolf Hitler is, in itself, to consider the proposition. As Jean-Paul Sartre once wrote, anti-Semites "like to play with discourse, for, by giving ridiculous reasons they discredit the seriousness of their interlocutors . . . it is their adversary who is obliged to use words responsibly, since he believes in words."[47] Beyond anything else, the Jews-are-Nazis analogy made it clear that there are American journalists who, in the case of the Jewish state, do not believe in words.

Whether they are also anti-Jewists is a moot point. If the twentieth century has given Jews anything, it is the right to assume that they have enemies and to decide for themselves who these enemies are. Each Jew will necessarily make the decision for himself, and none may automatically speak for his fellows. It is, in any event, beyond the competence of the Gentiles in this century to instruct Jews, individually or collectively, about who is or is not an anti-Semite.

There can be little doubt that the Israel-Nazi analogy (or the equally illogical, if less spectacularly offensive, comparison between Begin's Israel and Khomeini's Iran, made by *Washington Post* managing editor Jim Hoagland)[48] does not result from happenstance. It was arrived at, *in spite of* its manifest irrationality, precisely because it constituted the strongest possible statement that the Jewish state is an evil and illegitimate entity. Not better than its neighbors, not even as good (because they, after all, are not Nazis), but worse. And, of course, if the Jews are Nazis, then their supporters in the United States are Nazi collaborators. This kind of commentary, unlike other types of criticism of Israel, is extra-rational, but it is far from uncalculated. Its intent is to deprive the Jewish state of the affection with which it is widely regarded in the United States, and of its support. It is designed to destroy the basis on which Israel is objectively entitled to these benefits—its status as a member of the (admittedly imperfect) family of enlightened democratic nations.

AFTERWORD

The 1982 war in Lebanon marked the peak of the anti-Israel fever that had been building in the American press for a decade. Following the February 1982 publication of the Kahan Report on the massacres at Sabra and Shatilla, and the resignation of Ariel Sharon as Israel's defense minister, the fever began to subside. In mid-May 1983, when Israel concluded an American-sponsored agreement with the Lebanese government of Amin Gemayel, Israeli officials in Washington and Jerusalem began to detect a more friendly tone in the American press, and by the beginning of 1984 these same officials were speaking with relief about an "enormous improvement."

As usual there were a number of factors that combined to bring about this change of tone and focus. The resignations of Menachem Begin and Ariel Sharon and their replacement by the low-keyed Yitzhak Shamir and Moshe Arens, removed a major irritant from American-Israeli relations. Unlike their flamboyant predecessors, the new Israeli leaders spoke softly and couched their policies in moderate language. Confrontation gave way to consultation and cooperation, particularly after the United States and Israel agreed to undertake strategic coordination during Prime Minister Shamir's visit to Washington in November 1983.

This new bilateral harmony was promoted by the fact that late in 1983 America found itself in a low-grade shooting war with Syria and its allies in Lebanon. Secretary of Defense Caspar Weinberger flatly asserted that the government of Hafez Assad was linked to the terrorist murder of 241 marines in Beirut; Secretary of State George Shultz denounced Damascus as an ally and agent of the Soviet Union; and the Reagan administration generally focused its attention, and its media searchlight, on Syria's negative role in Lebanon and beyond.

Another major factor in the new attitude of the Reagan administration (and, not coincidentally, of the press) toward the region was the PLO's 1983 rejection of the Reagan Plan and its continued refusal to recognize Israel's right to exist. It became clear at the Palestine National Council meeting in Algiers in February 1983 that the PLO, even in its dispersed and demoralized state, had no intention of abandoning its National Covenant or its dreams of destroying Israel. Critical articles on the organization and the opulent life-style of its leaders began to appear in *The New York Times*,[1] *The Wall Street Journal*,[2] and other major American publications, a sure sign that the PLO had lost much of its revolutionary mystique. Exiled to North Africa, Arafat no longer had a captive press corps and his gunmen could no longer intimidate or scare away uncooperative journalists as they had in Beirut.

Late in 1983 the PLO chairman made an effort to reestablish a foothold in northern Lebanon, but it ended in fiasco. Arafat suffered an ignominious defeat at Tripoli at the hands of his former subordinates (including his one-time spokesman Mahmud Labadi). The organization was deeply split; once again PLO "fighters" flashed V-for-victory signs at the television cameras as they boarded the ships that had come to evacuate them.

All this had a decidedly off-putting effect on many of the PLO's supporters in and out of the press, who prefer their underdogs to be winners. In any event, Central America was rapidly becoming the fashionable issue for the 1980s, and it began to attract much of the attention that the media's Third World enthusiasts had lavished on the PLO during the previous decade. The Palestine Liberation Organization was not exactly passé, but it did appear a bit shopworn, and Chairman Arafat's two-day growth of beard and checkered *kaffieh* threatened to enter the museum of radical chic along with Mao's Little Red Book and the Nehru jacket.

Strangely, just as the left's awakened interest in the PLO had coincided with the post-1973 rise in Arab petro-power, so too did its decline in interest parallel the world oil glut. Despite the fact that two erstwhile OPEC giants, Iran and Iraq, were at each other's throats in the Persian Gulf, the price of oil continued to go down, and by 1983 there was a buyer's market for petroleum. Even Saudi Arabia was feeling the squeeze, and while there was no fear that *Time* magazine's favorite desert democracy was about to go bankrupt, it was clearly not the economic and political force it had once seemed. The pervasive fear of a Saudi oil embargo receded, and America's economic establishment, including the giant communications companies, were once again able to view Saudi political demands with a degree of perspective, not to say apathy. Not surprisingly, at about this time the American press began to "discover" that the Saudis were not quite the paragons of moderation, pro-American influence, and regional power that they had been cracked up to be, and articles with titles like ARAB "FRIENDS" MORE CRITICAL OF SAUDIS: OPENNESS OF COMPLAINTS SUGGESTS SAUDIS SWAY IN MIDEAST IS OVERRATED[3] and PIQUE IN WASHINGTON OVER THOSE "MODERATE SAUDIS"[4] began to appear in the national media.

Nineteen eighty-four began with a number of developments that seemed to symbolize the improvement in Israel's image, and the declining press fortunes of some of its adversaries. Early in the year, for example, Jacobo Timmerman announced his plans to leave Israel. Timmerman had lived in Israel for less than five years, couldn't speak or read Hebrew, had never served in the army, and knew almost nothing about the country, none of which prevented him from representing himself as an authentic (perhaps *the* authentic) voice of Israel's anguished conscience. A moral critic of the P. T. Barnum school, Timmerman did very well for himself duping the rubes at *The New Yorker* with his Israeli-impersonator act; but when the opportunity arose to go back to Argentina and sue the government, he abandoned the "oh my aching Israeli soul" scam, and skedaddled.

Another symbolic departure was that of *Village Voice* media critic Alexander Cockburn, who was caught taking money from a now-defunct Arab think tank and suspended indefinitely. Cockburn is a talented and amusing controversialist, one of the few genuine Israel haters capable of reading a sentence without moving his lips, much less writing one. At last word he was about to join the staff of *The Nation,* an acquisition that will almost certainly raise the left-wing magazine's circulation among the executives at Mobil Oil, who will presumably receive their copies in plain brown wrappers.

There was yet more symbolism in the assault on the Commodore Hotel that took place early in 1984. During the war in Lebanon, some of the more paranoid members of the Commodore Battalion had warned darkly that the Israelis might nuke the hotel, but when the attack came it was carried out by the vanguard of the Islamic revolution. One day in the midst of the house-to-house fighting in Beirut, a Shi'ite disciple of the Ayatollah Khomeini burst into the hotel, entered the sanctum sanctorum—the hotel's bar—and proceeded to trash every liquor bottle in sight, a punishment that even some of the Battalion's Israeli detractors found cruel and excessive.

All these symbolic events, along with Jerusalem's new-found popularity in Washington and the decline in PLO and Saudi prestige, combined to create a virtual second honeymoon between Israel and the American press. Like all such reconciliations, however, suspicions lingered that the basic causes of friction might reassert themselves. The disagreement between Israel and the United States over the future of the West Bank was dormant but far from resolved, just as the left's residual affection for the PLO and the economic establishment's atavistic fear of the Saudis were still there, ready to be reactivated by circumstances or the flash of the administration's searchlight.

In Israel the political debate—temporarily calmed by the laid-back style of the new leadership and the country's economic problems—began to reawaken in early 1984. That debate, over such cardinal matters of national policy as the future of the West Bank and the Israeli military presence in Lebanon, stirred interest abroad; as usual, it was Israel's own democratic institutions that furnished the raw materials for the American media. In February 1984, for example, the government-appointed Karp Committee reported on cases of anti-Arab brutality by Jewish West Bank settlers and criticized the failure of Israeli security forces to put a stop to them. The committee's findings made headlines in Israel and subsequently around the world, at about the same time that the Iranians, Iraqis, Libyans, Syrians, and Lebanese were busily slaughtering thousands of their own and each other's citizens in relative privacy.

The perceptible improvement in Israel's image in the American press, whatever its duration, was a welcome development, and it was reassuring to find the free press of the United States on the side of the region's only open society for a change. At the same time, this new appreciation of Israel did nothing to change the basic flaws in America's Middle East coverage.

The Middle East, perhaps more than any other region in the world, can be understood only if it is seen as an interrelated whole. The countries in the area are bound together by ancient rivalries, supernational religious revivalism, great-power competition, and above all, a tradition of suspicion and antagonism that each nation feels for almost all its neighbors. The policies and practices of these nations— Israel no less than the Arab states—are more often than not reactions to the perceived attitudes, actions, and ambitions of neighboring nations. Such reactions appear inexplicable when the actions that precipitate them are hidden from view. Yet with most of the Middle East off limits to the press, or unwilling to allow more than the most superficial inspection, that is precisely what happens.

Nor do things promise to get easier in the immediate future. The return of Syrian influence to West Beirut in February 1984 was an ominous development, for it means that once again the bulk of America's Middle East correspondents are within reach of the terrorists. How well these correspondents will withstand the pressures for self-censorship remains to be seen, but it is unlikely that the presence of Syrian-dominated hit teams in the Lebanese capital will improve the quality of American reporting from Lebanon and Syria.

There was a time when the question of Middle East press coverage was of no great consequence to the average American. That time has passed. Recent years have shown how deeply the United States is involved in the region, one of the last great arenas of superpower competition. A national debate on the wisdom of American involvement and the parameters of American policy in the Middle East depends upon the flow of reliable, comprehensive, and balanced information from the area. It is the job of the American press to provide that information. If it cannot do this, it must be candid with the public about the reasons why. Anything less will distort America's view of the region at a time when clarity is vital for making decisions that will critically affect the future of the Middle East and the United States.

NOTES

PERSONAL NOTE

1. A.J. Liebling, *Liebling Abroad* (New York: Wideview Books, 1981), p. 192.

INTRODUCTION

1. A.J. Liebling, *The Press* (New York: Pantheon Books, 1975), p. 120.
2. Ibid., p. 318.
3. Walter Lippmann, *Public Opinion* (London: The Free Press, 1965), p. 229.
4. In a letter to my assistant, Janice Ditchek (undated).

CHAPTER 1

1. From an interview with Peter Larkin, March 1983.
2. William Adams and Phillip Heyl, "From Cairo to Kabul with the Networks, 1972–1980," *Television Coverage of the Middle East,*

ed. William C. Adams (Norwood, N.J.: Ablex Publishing Company, 1981), pp. 1–35.

3. Barry Rubin, *International News and the Media* (Beverly Hills and London: Sage Publications, 1977), pp. 22–24.

4. Edward Said, *Covering Islam* (New York: Pantheon Books, 1981), pp. xi–xii.

5. Mort Rosenblum, *Coups and Earthquakes* (New York: Harper Colophon Books, 1979), p. 38.

6. From an interview with Michael Elkins, September 1983.

7. *World Press Encyclopedia* (New York: Facts on File, 1982), pp. 1100–1102; 781–784; 565–566; 1064; 1072–1074.

8. Ibid., p. 308.

9. Ibid., p. 311.

10. *Washington Post,* September 14, 1981.

11. *Washington Post,* November 27, 1978.

12. *The Arab Image in Western Mass Media: 1979 International Press Seminar* (London: Morris International, Ltd.), p. 80.

13. U.S. Congress, Senate, Committee on Foreign Relations, Subcommittee on International Operations, *International Communications and Information, The Media,* 1977, p. 193.

14. A.J. Liebling, *The Press* (New York: Pantheon Books, 1975), p. 257.

15. Andrew Heiskell, Testimony before the U.S. Senate.

16. U.S. Congress, Senate, Committee on Foreign Relations, Subcommittee on International Operations, *International Communications and Information, The Media,* 1977, p. 197.

17. Andrew Heiskell, Testimony before the U.S. Senate.

CHAPTER 2

1. *Report of Amnesty International* (London: Amnesty International, 1982), pp. 347–348.

2. *Washington Post,* June 25, 1981.

3. Ibid.

4. *New York Times,* February 22, 1982.

5. Mort Rosenblum, *Coups and Earthquakes* (New York: Harper Colophon Books, 1979), p. 95.

6. From an interview with Doyle McManus, March 1983.

7. *Report of Amnesty International,* 1982, p. 348; *International Herald Tribune,* August 5, 1980.

8. "Lebanese Press Freedom—Who Is Killing It?," *International Herald Tribune*, August 5, 1980.

9. Salim Lawzi, *Events*, September 24–30, 1976.

10. *Christian Science Monitor*, January 5, 1977.

11. From an interview with Doyle McManus.

12. "Shut Up," *New York Times*, January 4, 1977.

13. *The Economist*, December 25, 1976.

14. *Washington Post*, January 26, 1977.

15. *New York Times*, June 5, 1977, and July 5, 1977.

16. *Washington Post*, March 25, 1978.

17. Salim Lawzi, *Events*, September 24–30, 1976.

18. "Publish and Perish in Syria's Front Yard," *The Economist*, August 2, 1980.

19. *New York Times*, March 6, 1980.

20. *The World Press Encyclopedia*, 1982, p. 601.

21. *Washington Post*, July 24, 1980.

22. Ibid.

23. *International Herald Tribune*, August 5, 1980.

24. *Washington Post*, July 24, 1980.

25. From an interview with Doyle McManus.

26. *Jerusalem Post (Observer Service)*, March 17, 1982.

27. *New York Post*, June 6, 1980.

28. *International Herald Tribune*, August 5, 1980.

29. From an interview with Doyle McManus.

30. *The Listener*, August 21, 1980.

31. *New York Times*, February 22, 1982.

32. *International Herald Tribune*, August 5, 1980.

33. "Publish and Perish in Syria's Front Yard," *The Economist*, August 2, 1980.

34. *The Listener*, August 21, 1980.

35. From an interview with John Lane and Peter Larkin, March 1983.

36. *Jerusalem Post (Observer Service)*, March 17, 1982.

37. *Christian Science Monitor*, March 8, 1982.

38. Rosenblum, op. cit., p. 1.

CHAPTER 3

1. From an interview with Milt Fullerton, October 1982.

2. From an interview with William Farrell, October 1982.

3. From an interview with Nick Tatro, September 1983.

4. From an interview with Milan Kubic, September 1983.

5. From an interview with William Marmon, February 1983.

6. *Wall Street Journal,* November 3, 1975.

7. *Chicago Tribune,* May 20, 1973.

8. *New York Times,* October 27, 1975.

9. From an interview with Claude Salhani (conducted by Linda Reinbaum), January 1983.

10. *New York Times,* February 2, 1976.

11. Ibid.

12. *New York Times,* July 4, 1976.

13. "Beirut's Thin Green Line," *Newsweek,* August 23, 1976.

14. Ibid.

15. *Christian Science Monitor,* March 22, 1982.

16. "Who's Afraid of the PLO?," *Newsweek,* March 1, 1982.

17. *New York Times,* April 10, 1983.

18. From an interview with Doyle McManus, March 1983.

19. Peter M. Ranke, in a letter to the author dated November 26, 1982.

20. From an interview with Doyle McManus.

21. From an interview with Milt Fullerton.

22. *New York Times,* February 22, 1982.

23. From an interview with William Marmon.

24. Peter M. Ranke, in a letter to the author dated November 26, 1982.

25. Duane Thompson, "Protection Peddling," *Jerusalem Post,* August 21, 1981.

26. *The Listener,* August 21, 1980.

27. "Who's Afraid of the PLO?," *Newsweek,* March 1, 1982.

28. Robert I. Friedman, "Between the Lines in Beirut," *Columbia Journalism Review,* November/December 1983.

29. From an interview with Barbara Newman, February 1983.

30. From an interview with Geraldo Rivera, March 1983.

31. Peter M. Ranke, in a letter to the author dated February 15, 1982.

32. *Columbia Journalism Review,* November/December 1983.

33. From an interview with Jean Carlo DePalo (conducted by Herbert Krosney), December 1983.

34. From an interview with Hans Benedict, January 1983.

35. Peter M. Ranke, in a letter to the author dated November 26, 1982.

36. From an interview with Geraldo Rivera.

37. From an interview with William Farrell.

38. *New York Times,* February 22, 1982.

39. Jonathan Randal, in a letter to the author dated November 1, 1982.

40. From an interview with William Farrell.

41. Jonathan Randal in a letter to the author dated November 1, 1982.

42. "News Gathering Under the Gun," *Time,* March 1, 1982.

43. From an interview with William Farrell.

44. "News Gathering Under the Gun," *Time,* March 1, 1982.

CHAPTER 4

1. From an interview with William Marmon, February 1983.

2. "News Gathering Under the Gun," *Time,* March 1, 1982.

3. From an interview with William Marmon.

4. *Chicago Tribune,* May 20–25, 1973.

5. "Beirut's Thin Green Line," *Newsweek,* August 23, 1976.

6. *New York Post,* June 6, 1980.

7. *Guardian,* August 5, 1980.

8. "Publish and Perish in Syria's Front Yard," *The Economist,* August 2, 1980.

9. A.J. Liebling, *The Press* (New York: Pantheon Books, 1975), p. 36.

10. *International Herald Tribune,* February 10, 1982.

11. Ibid.

12. *New York Times,* February 18, 1982.

13. *New York Times,* May 29, 1979.

14. *New York Times Index,* 1981, "News."

15. From an interview with Craig Whitney, March 1983.

16. *Jerusalem Post,* March 17, 1982.

17. "Who's Afraid of the PLO?," *Newsweek,* March 1, 1982.

18. Martin Peretz, "A Journalistic Cover-Up," *New Republic,* February 26, 1982.

19. *Washington Post,* March 4, 1982.

20. *Washington Post,* April 17, 1982.

21. *Washington Post,* April 28, 1982.

22. *Washington Post,* June 13, 1980.

23. *Washington Post,* June 11, 1980.

24. *Washington Post,* August 22, 1981.

25. *Washington Post,* September 27, 1981.

26. *Washington Post,* October 1, 1981.
27. *Washington Post,* January 19, 1980.
28. *Washington Post,* September 6, 1981.
29. *Washington Post,* August 8, 1980.
30. *Washington Post,* October 27, 1975.

CHAPTER 5

1. "Under the Israeli Thumb," *20/20,* ABC News, February 4, 1982.
2. From an interview with Barbara Newman, February 1983.
3. From an interview with Barbara Newman.
4. From an interview with Geraldo Rivera, March 1983.
5. From an interview with Barbara Newman.
6. In a letter to the author from Jerry King, dated November 29, 1982.
7. John Weisman, "Israelis Say P.L.O. Controls TV News by Death Threats," *TV Guide,* March 6, 1982.
8. "Still Stonewalling," *New Republic,* March 17, 1982.
9. Associated Press, July 15, 1982; *Los Angeles Times,* July 15, 1982.
10. B.D. Johnson, "The New Perils for the Fourth Estate," *Maclean's Magazine,* May 17, 1982.
11. *Jerusalem Post,* August 21, 1981.
12. From an interview with Geraldo Rivera.
13. *Viewpoint,* ABC News, April 28, 1982.
14. *Chicago Sun-Times,* August 25, 1981; *Youngstown Jewish Times,* August 21, 1981.
15. *World News Tonight,* ABC News, September 8, 1981.
16. Ibid.
17. "*20/20*'s West Bank Program Subject of Controversy," *AAUG Newsletter,* February 1982.
18. From an interview with Geraldo Rivera.
19. From an interview with Geraldo Rivera.
20. From an interview with Geraldo Rivera.
21. As cited in a letter from Frieda Lewis, national president, Hadassah, to ABC chairman Leonard H. Goldenson, February 9, 1982.

CHAPTER 6

1. Peter Werner, "Han Klarade Det igen," 7 *Dagar*, December 9, 1983.

2. *New York Times,* April 10, 1983.

3. Y. Harkabi, *Palestinians and Israel* (Jerusalem: Keter Books, 1975), pp. 63–66.

4. "Voice of Palestine," Cairo, June 8, 1974, as quoted from the BBC monitoring service, June 11, 1974.

5. Ibid.

6. Ibid.

7. Zbigniew Brzezinski, *Power and Principle* (New York: Farrar, Straus & Giroux, 1983), p. 94.

8. *Washington Post,* March 7, 1977.

9. *Washington Post,* March 11, 1977.

10. *New York Times,* March 13, 1977.

11. *Washington Post,* March 15, 1977.

12. United Press International, March 15, 1977.

13. *Washington Post,* March 21, 1977.

14. Ibid.

15. *New York Times,* March 19, 1977.

16. "The PLO Still Hangs Tough," *Newsweek,* March 14, 1977.

17. *Washington Post,* August 9, 1977.

18. "Palestinians: A New Unity," *Time,* August 29, 1977.

19. "Sabbath of Terror: Al Fatah Attack," *Time,* March 8, 1978.

20. *New York Times,* May 2, 1978.

21. Ibid.

22. Reuters, January 17, 1979.

23. "Convention in Damascus," *Time,* January 29, 1979

24. "The PLO Gameplan," *Newsweek,* May 21, 1979.

25. *New York Times,* June 11, 1979.

26. *Jerusalem Post,* September 10, 1979.

27. *Washington Post,* June 2, 1980.

28. Ibid.

29. *New York Times,* June 5, 1980.

30. *Washington Post,* July 6, 1980.

31. *Washington Post,* August 2, 1980.

32. "Arafat Gets Tough Again," *Newsweek,* September 8, 1980.

33. *Jerusalem Post,* November 27, 1980.

34. Ibid.

35. *New York Times,* September 24, 1981.

36. *Washington Post,* July 21, 1982.
37. From an interview with Michael Elkins, January 1984.
38. *New York Times,* March 4–8, 1982.
39. "Under PLO Rule," *The Economist,* August 7, 1982.
40. *Washington Post,* June 25, 1982.
41. *Guardian,* June 22, 1980.
42. *Washington Post,* March 15–18, 1981.
43. *Washington Post,* March 16, 1981.
44. From an interview with David Shipler, October 1983.
45. *Jerusalem Post,* August 2, 1982.
46. *New York Times,* September 5, 1982.
47. *New York Times,* November 29, 1982.
48. *Jerusalem Post,* December 1, 1982.
49. *Wall Street Journal,* December 30, 1982.
50. *New York Times,* February 22, 1983.
51. *Washington Post,* February 23, 1983.
52. *New York Times,* February 23, 1983.
53. *Washington Post,* February 16, 1983.
54. *Washington Post,* February 17, 1983.
55. *Washington Post,* February 7, 1983.
56. *Washington Post,* February 14, 15, 17, 22, 1983.
57. *New York Times,* February 15, 1983.

CHAPTER 7

1. *Middle East Contemporary Survey,* Vol. 4, 1979–80 (New York: Holmes & Meier, 1981), pp. 682–697.
2. *New York Times,* November 25, 1979; *Washington Post,* November 24, 1979.
3. From an interview with Milt Fullerton, October 1982.
4. *NBC Nightly News,* November 21, 1979.
5. A.J. Liebling, *The Press* (New York: Pantheon Books, 1975), p. 318.
6. Ibid., p. 222.
7. *Washington Star,* December 6, 1979; *New York Times,* December 17, 1979.
8. *Washington Post,* December 5, 1979; *Washington Star,* December 6, 1979.
9. *Middle East Contemporary Survey,* Vol. 4, p. 688.
10. *Washington Post,* January 28, 1980.
11. *Washington Post,* March 14, 1978.

12. Robert Lacy, "How Stable Are the Saudis?," *New York Times Magazine*, November 8, 1981.

13. From an interview with Peter Larkin, March 1983.

14. *Washington Post*, March 14, 1978.

15. From an interview with Craig Whitney, March 1983.

16. From an interview with Doyle McManus, March 1983.

17. From an interview with Don Schanche, September 1982.

18. From an interview with Jaap Van Wessel, January 1983.

19. Henry Kissinger, *Years of Upheaval* (Boston: Little, Brown, 1982), p. 661.

20. From an interview with Doyle McManus.

21. From an interview with Craig Whitney.

22. Otis Chandler, Testimony before U.S. Senate Committee on Foreign Relations, Subcommittee on International Operations, June 9, 1977, pp. 199–200.

23. From an interview with Don Schanche.

24. From an interview with David Aikman, January 1983.

25. From an interview with Peter Larkin

26. Liebling, op. cit., p. 366.

27. Anti-Defamation League Research Report, "The U.S.-Saudi Relationship," spring 1982, pp. 30–32.

28. *Washington Post*, February 25, 1981, and March 10, 1981.

29. *Miami Herald*, April 15, 1982.

30. William Stewart, "Shoring Up the Kingdom," *Time*, March 16, 1981.

31. *New York Times*, May 13, 1981.

32. *New York Times*, August 9, 1981.

33. *Washington Post*, November 14, 1981; *New York Times*, November 17, 1981.

34. "A Bold New Plan by the Saudis," *Time*, August 24, 1981.

35. *New York Times*, November 17, 1981.

36. *Washington Post*, November 26, 1981.

CHAPTER 8

1. "The Horror of Hama," *The Economist*, May 15, 1982.

2. *Report of Amnesty International* (London: Amnesty International, 1982), p. 345.

3. *New York Times*, January 4, 1981.

4. *Washington Post*, June 25, 1981.

5. *Jerusalem Post*, August 18, 1981.

6. *New York Times*, September 4, 1981.

7. *New York Times*, December 1, 1981.

8. *Washington Post*, February 1, 1982.

9. *New York Times*, February 11, 1982.

10. From an interview with Seth Lipsky, March 1983.

11. *New York Times*, February 12, 1982.

12. *Baltimore Sun*, February 15, 1982.

13. *Philadelphia Inquirer*, February 16, 1982.

14. From an interview with Craig Whitney, March 1983.

15. *New York Times*, February 11, 1982.

16. *New York Times*, February 19, 1982.

17. From an interview with John Lane, March 1983.

18. *Christian Science Monitor*, April 1, 1982.

19. *Washington Post*, May 3, 1982.

20. *Wall Street Journal*, May 6, 1982.

21. "The Horror of Hama," *The Economist*, May 15, 1982.

22. *Los Angeles Times*, February 19, 1982.

23. *Washington Post*, March 4, 1982.

24. *Washington Post*, May 3, 1982.

25. *Washington Post*, June 29, 1983.

26. From an interview with Don Schanche, September 1982.

27. From an interview with Jonathan Broder, September 1982.

28. From an interview with Douglas Watson, October 1982.

29. From an interview with Jonathan Broder.

30. From an interview with Douglas Watson.

31. From an interview with Milt Fullerton, October 1982.

32. *Washington Post*, May 15, 1981.

33. *Washington Post*, December 6, 1981.

34. Bill Pierce, "Photographing Violence," *Popular Photography*, November 1983.

35. *New York Times*, January 6, 1984.

CHAPTER 9

1. *New York Times*, October 16, 1980.

2. From an interview with Jonathan Broder, October 1982.

3. From an interview with Craig Whitney, March 1983.

4. From a conversation with Anwar Sadat, September 6, 1979.

5. From an interview with Jonathan Broder.

6. From an interview with Ted Stanger, September 1982.

7. *Christian Science Monitor*, February 2, 1982.

8. *Jerusalem Post,* June 27, 1980.

9. Ibid.

10. Jimmy Carter, *Keeping Faith* (New York: Bantam Books, 1982), p. 506.

11. *New York Times,* April 13, 1980.

12. *Washington Post,* April 19, 1980.

13. *Washington Post,* June 21, 1980.

14. *Wall Street Journal,* June 13, 1980.

15. *Washington Post,* April 26, 1981.

16. "War in the Persian Gulf," *Time,* October 6, 1980.

17. *New York Times,* September 23, 1980.

18. From an interview with Jonathan Broder.

19. *Washington Post,* October 11, 1980.

20. *New York Times,* October 16, 1980.

21. Ibid.

22. Ibid.

23. *New York Times,* September 23, 1980.

24. *Washington Post,* September 24, 1980.

25. *New York Times,* September 28, 1980.

26. Mort Rosenblum, *Coups and Earthquakes* (New York: Harper Colophon Books, 1979), p. 49.

27. "War in the Persian Gulf," *Time,* October 6, 1980.

28. *Wall Street Journal,* October 7, 1980.

29. *New York Times,* October 21, 1980.

30. *New York Times,* October 16, 1980.

31. *New York Times,* September 26, 1980.

32. *Washington Post,* September 30, 1980.

33. *Wall Street Journal,* October 7, 1980.

34. *Wall Street Journal,* September 29, 1980.

35. *Washington Post,* October 5, 1980.

36. *Washington Post,* September 28, 1980.

37. *Washington Post,* May 30, 1982.

38. *Christian Science Monitor,* September 29, 1980.

39. *Lincoln* (Neb.) *Sunday Journal and Star,* October 12, 1980.

40. *Washington Post,* September 20, 1981.

41. *Christian Science Monitor,* May 20, 1981.

42. *NBC News Update,* November 20, 1983.

43. *Jerusalem Post,* January 27, 1984.

44. "A Hot and Holy War," *Time,* March 22, 1982.

45. The World Service of the BBC, February 20, 1984.

46. From an interview with Craig Whitney.

CHAPTER 10

1. James F. Larson, "International Affairs Coverage on U.S. Evening Network News, 1972–1979," *Television Coverage of International Affairs,* ed. William C. Adams (Norwood, N.J.: Ablex Publishing Co., 1982), pp. 15–39.
2. *Newsday,* September 22, 1982.
3. Jules Witcover, *Marathon* (New York: American Library, 1977), p. 122.
4. *CBS Evening News,* June 22, 1982.
5. *NBC Nightly News,* June 23, 1982.
6. Phillip Knightley, *The First Casualty* (New York: Harcourt Brace Jovanovich, 1975), p. 80.
7. Ibid., p. 92.
8. Ibid., p. 130.
9. Ibid., p. 218.
10. Ibid., p. 281.
11. Ibid., p. 300.
12. Ibid., p. 294.
13. A.J. Liebling, *Liebling Abroad* (New York: Wideview Books, 1981), p. 192.
14. Phillip Knightley, op. cit., p. 349.
15. Ibid., p. 370.
16. According to Independent Television Network correspondent Michael Nicholson, Davis Institute Press Seminar, Jerusalem, May 3, 1983.
17. Minutes of the Evidence Taken Before the Defense Committee, July 22, 1982, pp. 47 and 72.
18. From an interview with David Shipler, September 1983.
19. From an interview with Tim McNulty, September 1983.

CHAPTER 11

1. Walter Lippmann, *Public Opinion* (London: The Free Press, 1965), p. 229.
2. From an interview with Ned Temko, April 1983.
3. From an interview with Howard Simons, February 1983.
4. From an interview with Leslie Gelb, February 1983.
5. From an interview with Seth Lipsky, March 1983.

6. "The. Networks and Foreign News Coverage," *The Washington Quarterly*, spring 1982.

7. From an interview with Craig Whitney, March 1983.

8. From an interview with Howard Simons.

9. Mort Rosenblum, *Coups and Earthquakes* (New York: Harper Colophon Books, 1979), p. 162.

10. From an interview with Douglas Watson, October 1982.

11. Henry Kissinger, *Years of Upheaval* (Boston: Little, Brown, 1982), pp. 1267–1269; p. 1282; Zbigniew Brzezinski, *Power and Principle* (New York: Farrar, Straus & Giroux, 1983), pp. 85–89.

12. *New York Times*, January 2, 1970.

13. From an interview with Barbara Newman, February 1983.

14. From an interview with Leslie Gelb.

CHAPTER 12

1. George Seldes, *Freedom of the Press* (New York: Garden City Publishing Co., 1937), p. 110.

2. "Murrow's Indictment of Broadcasting," *Columbia Journalism Review*, summer 1965.

3. James Reston, *The Artillery of the Press* (New York: Harper & Row, 1966), p. 5.

4. A.J. Liebling, *The Press* (New York: Pantheon Books, 1975), p. 223.

5. Leon V. Sigal, *Reporters and Officials* (Lexington, Mass.: D.C. Heath, 1973), p. 32.

6. Peter Braestrup, *Big Story* (New Haven: Yale University Press, 1977), p. 526.

7. Sander Vanocur, "How the Media Massaged Me," *Esquire*, January 1972.

8. Turner Catledge, *My Life and Times* (New York: Harper & Row, 1971), p. 190.

9. Ben H. Bagdikian, *The Media Monopoly* (Boston: Beacon Press, 1983), p. xix.

10. Ibid., pp. 9–18.

11. Ibid., pp. 23–25.

12. Ibid., p. 5.

13. Ibid.

14. Liebling, op. cit., p. 18.

15. Linda Lichter, S. Robert Lichter, and Stanley Rothman,

"The Once and Future Journalists," *Washington Journalism Review,* December 1982.

16. S. Robert Lichter, "America and the Third World: A Survey of Leading Media and Business Leaders," *Television Coverage of International Affairs,* ed. William C. Adams (Norwood, N.J.: Ablex Publishing Co., 1982), pp. 67–78.

17. Henry Kissinger, *Years of Upheaval* (Boston: Little Brown, 1982), p. 848.

18. *New York Times,* November 13, 1973.

19. Itzhak Rabin, *Pinkas Sherut* (Tel Aviv: Sifriat Ma'ariv, 1979), Vol. 2, pp. 507–517.

20. Jimmy Carter, *Keeping Faith* (New York: Bantam Books, 1982), pp. 289–90.

21. *New York Times,* March 19, 1977.

22. *Washington Post,* March 11, 1977.

23. Morad Asi, "Arabs, Israelis and TV News: A Time-Series, Content Analysis," *Television Coverage of the Middle East,* ed. William C. Adams (Norwood, N.J.: Ablex Publishing Co., 1981), pp. 67–71.

CHAPTER 13

1. *Jerusalem Post,* August 21, 1983.

2. Edward Jay Epstein, *News from Nowhere* (New York: Vintage Books, 1973), pp. 222–223.

3. S. Robert Lichter, "Media Support for Israel: A Survey of Leading Journalists," *Television Coverage of the Middle East,* ed. William C. Adams (Norwood, N.J.: Ablex Publishing Co., 1981), p. 41.

4. Stephen Birmingham, "Do the Zionists Control the Media?," *More,* July/August 1976.

5. S. Robert Lichter, "Media Support for Israel: A Survey of Leading Journalists," loc. cit., p. 44.

6. Ibid., pp. 40–50.

7. Michael Robinson, "Future Television News Research: Beyond Edward Jay Epstein," *Television Network News: Issues and Content Research,* eds. William C. Adams and Fay Schreibman (Washington: George Washington University, 1978), p. 204.

8. *Washington Post,* September 21, 1982.

9. From a letter by Lester Bernstein to the Anti-Defamation League dated September 20, 1979.

10. Gay Talese, *The Kingdom and the Power* (New York: Bantam Books, 1970), p. 113.

11. *New York Times,* March 31, 1980.

12. *New York Times,* May 22, 1980.

13. *New York Times,* June 30, 1980.

14. *New York Times,* July 19, 1982.

15. *The Village Voice,* June 29, 1982.

16. *New York Times,* September 23, 1982.

17. *Washington Post,* September 26, 1982.

18. "Kind . . . Honest . . . Dangerous," *Time,* May 30, 1977.

19. Jimmy Carter, *Keeping Faith* (New York: Bantam Books, 1982), p. 284.

20. Tom DeFrank, "The Press Rolls Out the Red Carpet for Yuri Andropov," *Washington Journalism Review,* March 1983.

CHAPTER 14

1. "Mabat Sheni" ("Second Look"), Israel Television, October 17, 1982.

2. *Washington Post,* March 18, 1981.

3. Peter Braestrup, *Big Story* (New Haven: Yale University Press, 1977), p. xi.

4. *Viewpoint,* ABC News, October 19, 1982.

5. Ibid.

6. *ABC World News,* June 28, 1982.

7. *NBC Nightly News,* June 10, 1982.

8. *ABC World News,* June 14, 1982.

9. *NBC Nightly News,* June 14, 1982.

10. *NBC Nightly News,* June 19, 1982.

11. *New York Times,* July 14, 1982.

12. "When Push Comes to Shove," *Time,* August 16, 1982.

13. Joshua Muravchik, "Misreporting Lebanon," *Policy Review,* Winter 1983, p. 54.

14. *Washington Post,* July 18, 1982.

15. *Washington Post,* July 7, 1982.

16. Loren Jenkins, "Palestine, Exiled," *Rolling Stone,* June 9, 1983.

17. *The Aspen Times,* October 7, 1982.

18. Mustapha Karkouti, "God Cried: An Eyewitness in Beirut," *The Middle East,* June 1983.

19. *Jerusalem Post,* March 17, 1977.

20. *New York Times,* April 10, 1983.

21. *Washington Post,* August 2, 1982.

22. Tim Llewellyn, *The Listener,* August 21, 1980.

23. Associated Press, December 14, 1982.

24. *Boston Globe,* August 14, 1982.

25. *Washington Post,* June 10, 1982.

26. *Jerusalem Post,* August 2, 1982.

27. Norman Podhoretz, "J'accuse," *Commentary,* September 1982.

28. Christopher Hitchens, "On Anti-Semitism," *The Nation,* October 9, 1982; *New York Daily News,* August 19, 1982.

29. *Jerusalem Post,* July 6, 1982.

30. Nicholas Von Hoffman, "America on the Sidelines," *The Spectator,* June 19, 1982.

31. *West Palm Beach Evening Times,* June 28, 1982.

32. Abraham Foxman, "The Lebanon-Holocaust Analogy," *Anti-Defamation League Memorandum,* November 16, 1982.

33. *Cincinnati Enquirer,* July 6, 1982.

34. *Philadelphia Daily News,* June 24, 1982.

35. ADL Memorandum, November 16, 1982.

36. *Chicago Tribune,* August 22, 1982.

37. ADL Memorandum, November 16, 1982.

38. Loren Jenkins, "Palestine, Exiled," *Rolling Stone,* June 9, 1983.

39. *Arizona Republic,* September 21, 1982.

40. *Philadelphia Inquirer,* June 25, 1982.

41. *Louisville Courier-Journal,* July 1, 1982.

42. *Los Angeles Herald Examiner,* September 21, 1982.

43. *Indianapolis Star,* July 2, 1982.

44. *Indianapolis Star,* October 4, 1982.

45. *Arizona Republic,* September 30, 1982.

46. *NBC Nightly News,* August 2, 1982.

47. Jean-Paul Sartre, *Anti-Semite and Jew* (New York: Shocken Books, 1948), p. 20.

48. *Washington Post,* July 18, 1982.

AFTERWORD

1. *New York Times,* April 10, 1983.

2. *Wall Street Journal,* March 21, 1983.

3. *Wall Street Journal,* March 14, 1983.

4. *New York Times,* January 23, 1983.

INDEX

ABC:
  Arafat interviews:
    (Sept. 1979), 140
    (July 1981), 115–16
    (June 1982), 229
  coverage of massacre at Hama
    (1982), 184–85
  Jews prominent in, 277
  "Under the Israeli Thumb" (docu-
    mentary), 93–94, 111, 117,
    117n., 118–25
  "Unholy War" (documentary), 111–
    15
Agnew, Spiro T., 273n., 275
Aiken, Vic, 184
Aikman, David, 169
Ajami, Fouad, 212
Alexandre Hotel, Beirut, 80
Algeria:
  civil war, censorship in, 231
  control of local press in, 39–40
Aliagany, Gaafar M., 175
Allenby Bridge, 100, 101
Allon Plan (for West Bank), 244, 271
Amer, Ibrahim, 73n.
Andropov, Yuri, 291n.
anti-Semitism:
  at *Newsweek*, 281n.
  in press, 311
  in Saudi Arabian press, 170n.

AP:
  and Chafets interview (1982), 99
  Israeli operations of, 219–20
  on mustard gas in Iran-Iraq war,
    215
  operational pattern of, 35
  see also wire services
Arab-Israel conflict:
  "balance" in reporting of, 79, 81,
    147–48, 235, 263, 308
  differences of, from Vietnamese
    conflict, 264–65
  Kissinger on, 244–45
  and Middle East reporting, 22
  and oil embargo (1973), 30–31
  war in Lebanon (1982), 296–305
Arab nations:
  as closed societies, 18–19, 20, 45–
    46
  governments of, 29
  local press in, 38–40
  minorities in, 29
  news management by, *see* news man-
    agement: in closed societies
  summit meeting of (Rabat, 1973),
    131
  unity and division among, 28–29
  see also Egypt; Iran; Iraq; Jordan;
    Saudi Arabia; Syria
Arabs, 27, 28

339

P9-CDI-305

SPECIAL
PEOPLE

BY

Julie Nixon Eisenhower

Simon and Schuster   NEW YORK

Designed by Irving Perkins
Manufactured in the United States of America
1   2   3   4   5   6   7   8   9   10

Library of Congress Cataloging in Publication Data

Eisenhower, Julie Nixon.
Special people.

1.   Biography—20th century.   I.   Title.
CT120.E37   920'.02   77–2129

ISBN 0–671–22708–4

Acknowledgments

In the summer of 1976 I found myself writing a book, which in itself—given the number of authors today—is not unusual. But in an office two doors away, also working on a book, was my father, who predicted after finishing his memoirs in 1961 that he would never undertake another similar project; and across the continent in Pennsylvania my father-in-law was immersed in his third book—the very two members of my family who had advised me not to subject myself to the self-imposed task of writing.

Though I had much I wanted to say in my book, that summer and fall I often found myself remembering their advice. Writing was not easy for me and it would have been far more difficult without the encouragement of many.

I am particularly grateful to Michael Korda, editor-in-chief of Simon and Schuster, for his enthusiasm for the project and for the editorial assistance he and his associates provided.

Two friends in Washington, Cynthia Milligan and Bruce Herschensohn, read each chapter as I wrote it and offered ideas and words of cheer. My spirits were lifted innumerable times also by transcontinental telephone calls from my lifelong friend Helene Drown of Los Angeles.

To Tricia, who let me use her apartment so often while I was

5

writing the book, to my parents for their loving encouragement and constant support, and to David for his patience, help, and most of all his confidence that I could complete the job—heartfelt thanks.

And lastly, I want to express appreciation to all the Special People for generously sharing their time with me.

*For
my
family*

Contents

9

Introduction

In the spring of 1976, I walked from our apartment in Northwest Washington to the downtown shopping district, just a few blocks from the White House. I was not stopped once by anyone on the street. Nor, to my knowledge, was I recognized, something that had not happened since my father had become President in 1969. At that moment I realized a new period in my life had begun. David and I were no longer at the center. We could begin to pursue our lives with more freedom and objectivity than ever before. For the first time in a long time I felt like an observer.

I had frequently considered writing a book about my experiences during my father's years in public life, especially about some of the people I had met, many of them men and women who have shaped our lives, even shaped our world. I had observed some of them at close range and discovered that the image of the public person often did not reveal the inner, private person.

In *Special People* I describe six individuals who have affected my own thinking. Some have inspired me. Some have opened a new perspective to me. Others have taught me about love and patience. Each comes from a different world. Each represents a vastly different approach to life.

Golda Meir sacrificed her personal life to serve her ideal— the creation and preservation of Israel.

Ruth Graham has also lived for a cause. Her commitment has been to helping others develop their own faith in God.

11

Charles, Prince of Wales, was born to power. He is destined to exercise leadership in the future, a leadership which will be based on beliefs and values he has chosen to embrace despite the expectations and pressures of the publicists, courtiers and advisers who have surrounded him since birth.

Anne Morrow Lindbergh is a writer whose words have spoken directly to the concerns of millions—her perceptions have been shaped by a lifetime of public tragedy and success.

Mao was a revolutionary whose daring, intellect and tactical brilliance transformed China.

Mamie Eisenhower's existence has been one of complete devotion to her family. Her husband's credo, "Duty, Honor, Country," became her own.

In writing about these men and women, I explored questions which intrigued me. Above all, I learned that despite their diverse backgrounds, goals, and faiths, these six individuals share a passion: they love life. Life is an adventure, a challenge, to be lived to the fullest, to be made better for oneself and for others. Talking to these men and women and examining their lives helped me to learn more about my own life and attitudes. Perhaps in *Special People* the reader will find glimpses of himself and insights into his own life as well.

Golda Meir

"Don't become cynical. Don't give up hope. . . . There is idealism in this world. There is human brotherhood."

THE WOMAN WHO SAID, "I have no ambition to be somebody," is a legend already, great in her own lifetime— Golda *Shenayou* (our Golda). It is Israel, the dream and the state, that has given the world Golda Meir. For Israel's story is also her story.

Her eyes are full of pain and wisdom. But it is not unusual to see pain and the wisdom of many years in the eyes of a woman in her eighth decade. Nor is it surprising that those eyes are framed in deep smile lines. What was unexpected were the lightning changes from dark brooding to gentle concern.

And there was no fire in Golda Meir's eyes.

I had expected fire.

When Prime Minister Meir returned to her old elementary school in Milwaukee after more than sixty years, she told the children to get involved in "causes which are good for others, not only for yourselves." There has always been a cause for Golda. Her passionate belief in the concept of living for a cause or for duty has often made her a driven woman. But she has always been aware of the reasons for her struggles and her sacrifices. It is Israel's good fortune that the cause she embraced as a very young woman was that of a Jewish homeland.

She has seen her dream of a Jewish state come true, although

15

Israel is still not accepted by her Arab neighbors, and year after year Golda Meir's hopes of establishing a lasting peace have remained only that—hopes. Yet she does not give up. She has a cause and nothing can discourage her, neither chronic incapacitating migraines nor phlebitis, neither disappointment in people nor in nations, neither military disasters nor political defeat.

How is it that this woman who had "no ambition to be somebody" achieved greatness and power?

I visited Mrs. Meir in her temporary retirement office in Ramat Aviv, a fairly new area on the outskirts of Tel Aviv where few trees or shrubs soften the desert bleakness. She works in an austere two-room suite, just her office and a small anteroom staffed by one secretary, in an equally austere and utilitarian gray government building. I was struck by the grim ruggedness of the land as I drove out from Tel Aviv. In many ways Golda Meir is like this land. She is rough-hewn and solid, a presence. For years she has clung tenaciously to these rocks, this sand. And, like rock and sand, she can be undeniably forbidding.

She is known and loved for her warm-heartedness, but as we talked I began to understand all the stories of how her colleagues in the government approached their initial meetings with Mrs. Meir with as much fearful apprehension as eagerness. When I asked a question she did not like or broached a subject that she did not want to comment on, she became absolutely rock-like. She did not move her stocky body. She did not respond. She seemed rooted to her chair. Immobile. Silent. Her eyes cold and dark. If she chose to answer, she spoke briefly and there was finality in her voice, even an edge of severity. One could not pursue the question or the subject further. I became very aware that I was talking to a woman who had had to make many difficult decisions, and whose voice and views could never be dismissed.

Her appearance is as forbidding as her manner. Her hair is pulled back and shaped into a flat bun. No longer thick, it lies close to her head. Unnoticeable. She has worn her hair long all her life because her husband loved it that way. And so does her son. It has never been washed at a beauty parlor. Golda claims they cannot get it clean enough. Even when she was Prime Minister, she would often end her long days by washing her hair at two or three in the morning.

She wears no makeup. She came to this arid land as a young woman to work with her hands, to build a new land. Nothing so frivolous as makeup could be considered, and as the years of struggle succeeded each other, there was never time nor heart for Golda to consider her appearance or her clothes. Characteristically, when she flew to America in 1947 in a frantic, last-minute appeal for arms to protect Israel from Arab attack, she thought nothing of boarding the plane with no luggage other than her handbag. And as Prime Minister, she never seemed to give a second thought to climbing a ladder to an observation post, her unwieldy body and utilitarian underwear in view of the soldiers and officials clustered below.

The physical punishment of her life's work—the one-hundred-and-one-hour hunger strike she led when she was forty-eight years old to protest the British refusal to allow refugees to land in Palestine, for example, and the sixteen-hour days she works even now—all this has left its mark. Her legs are thick and swollen, encased in heavy gray support hose. She suffers from a circulatory condition which has been aggravated by her refusal to spare herself as well as by two injuries incurred during the course of duty: fragments from a bomb that exploded at a cabinet meeting lodged in her leg and had to be cut out; and on a fund-raising mission in New York City her leg was broken in a taxi accident. She now walks slowly and heavily. But her arms and hands are still strong and vital. Her hands are worn, a reminder of the hundreds of holes she dug in the hostile rocky land to plant trees when she lived in the kibbutz, of the desperately poor years in Jerusalem in the 1930s when she took in laundry to pay for her children's schooling, and of the dozens of coffee cups and plates she still washes every day. But as she gestured, I noticed a coat of clear polish on the short, neatly filed nails, a reminder that the pioneer and the former Prime Minister is also a woman.

I felt quite awed by her, but there were many moments during our talk when Mrs. Meir was even warmer and more caring than I had expected. Her first words to me, even before she had shown me into her office, had been "How is your dear mother?" And as we sat down, she pressed for more details on my mother's health. "But tell me more," she said with sincere concern. Several times during the course of the morning, she told me that she wished she had been able to ask me to her apartment instead of to the office, as if apologizing that the small cakes and nuts which accompanied our coffee and the two bouquets of pink sweetheart roses could not make up for the intimacy of her own home.

The night I arrived in Israel, I had driven from my hotel in Tel Aviv to Ramat Aviv to look at the building where Golda lives. Just a three-minute drive from her office, it is a drab, two-story apartment complex, resembling nothing so much as a squat concrete box. When she was Prime Minister, Golda had said, "I know about low wages. I live among the working people." She still lives among the working people. They are her friends and neighbors. But her experiences set her apart even from them. Golda's apartment was immediately identifiable, for instance, because of the sentry box outside. As a former Prime Minister, she is still guarded. Five or six packing boxes literally filled up her tiny yard. She was in the process of having her apartment painted, which was why our meeting took place in her office.

The office itself was unexpectedly impersonal. I had formed a mental picture of it beforehand. There would be her desk crowded with papers and memorabilia, a comfortable sofa and an easy chair, bookshelves crammed with books and photographs of family and colleagues on every surface. Just a week before, I had visited Clara Stern, Golda's younger sister who lives in Bridgeport, Connecticut, and Clara had told me of the fierce love and respect her sister had for books. Every once in a while Golda asks Clara to help her weed through the memorabilia that every public person seems to collect, but whenever Clara suggests that her sister get rid of a book, Golda is horror-struck. Even an outdated tome of statistics is held on to and treasured.

But there were no books evident in the office. It looked like a motel room, and the stiff little bouquets of sweetheart roses only accentuated the look. The furniture, completely nondescript, consisted of a coffee table in front of a small sofa flanked by the two chairs in which we sat, and, of course, her desk and desk chair. It was an anonymous room.

As we drank our coffee, I told Mrs. Meir about my visit to Israel ten years before with my parents and sister. Since none of us had ever been to Israel, Tel Aviv was the highlight of our family vacation through Europe that summer. We had been in the city for only two hours when an invitation came to visit David Ben-Gurion, the man who had led the fight to found the State of Israel, at his small house on the outskirts of the city. Tricia and I were rarely included in my parents' invitations, but this time we were, probably because in 1959 Ben-Gurion had visited our home while on an official trip to Washington. Tricia, then in the seventh grade, was studying Judaism in school and my parents arranged for her to meet him. She had a test the next morning and Ben-Gurion, with great patience, answered some of her questions, explaining the significance of the menorah and why the Jewish holy day is Saturday instead of Sunday. Tricia was excited to meet the country's first Prime Minister—and she got an "A" on her exam.

When we arrived at Ben-Gurion's home we went immediately upstairs to his tiny study. All four walls were solidly lined with books so that the room seemed even smaller. While my father and Ben-Gurion were talking, his wife took Tricia and me aside and told us how difficult it had been—she described it as "an ordeal"—to convince her husband, who had insisted his salary as Prime Minister be no higher than that of the average working man, that their children should have the luxury of music lessons. I asked if her husband played any instruments and Mrs. Ben-Gurion had answered, "No, he just plays on my nerves."

When Golda heard the story, her face lit up and she laughed, a low pleasant laugh. A smile lingered on her face. And at that moment I glimpsed beauty. Her smile is surprisingly sweet and it changes the expression in her eyes to a gentle softness. I had seen the same expression in an extraordinary photograph of Golda her sister had shown me the previous week. It was her favorite picture of Golda, Clara told me, and I could understand why. When Golda's eyes take on that softness, she is a beautiful woman.

But now, the smile faded. Her eyes suddenly became somber and all-knowing again. She was quiet. Perhaps thinking of the past. Of Ben-Gurion.

"He was a loner," she said slowly. "When he was not at work with people, he was always writing, writing, writing. He was one of the greatest men, not only in Israel, but in the world."

"What makes a great man?" I asked her.

Without hesitating, she replied, "You have to have an ideal. There is a difference between someone who has great financial success or great academic success and a great man. The great men gave their lives to an ideal which everyone thought was crazy—and which became a reality."

As she spoke, the "great men" suddenly became those men and women she had watched create a new country. The pioneering men and women who had come to this desolate land of sand and stones and scorching sun and slowly, painfully, had made the desert flower and had built a Jewish state.

"They were largely self-made individuals," she said, "who achieved much with very little. They had great minds and a lot of knowledge, some of which they acquired by themselves."

After a pause, she added, "And they had moral quality. This enabled them to influence even the young."

It was a revealing, if unintentional, self-portrait. Golda had known few advantages as a child, but she had had ideals and dreams. The ideal of becoming a teacher. Despite her parents' objections (they wanted her to stop school after the eighth grade and go to work), she insisted on acquiring an education. And she had had that other ideal, that daring dream, "which everyone thought was crazy," of a homeland for the Jews.

Golda has that moral quality which enables her to influence "even the young" even now, even as a woman in her seventies.

She has never been too busy to talk with young people. A typical Golda story is of the time during her first year as Prime Minister when she learned that a group of American students at the Hebrew University in Jerusalem, who were unhappy over her statements supporting the United States involvement in Vietnam, were planning a protest demonstration. She made a point of squeezing time out at the end of a busy day to meet with them in her official residence. The students talked with Golda for two hours. They ate her cake and drank her coffee. When she had to leave for an appointment, she invited them to stay on and watch television.

Ideals, determination, intelligence, character, the ability to influence the young—Golda has all the qualities of greatness that she had singled out for me. Her greatest strength of all, according to one of her oldest friends, may be her utter honesty about herself and about situations. Others have been impressed by the same quality.

When the Labor Party elected Golda as their nominee for Prime Minister in 1969, Moshe Dayan abstained from voting because he did not feel she was the best person for the job. But Golda won his respect almost immediately because she was "straightforward and direct." He found that "she did not resort to evasion."

It was Golda's clear perception of the world and the place of weak peoples or nations in it that made her dedicate her entire being to Jewish statehood. I asked her about the 1938 International Conference on Refugees which was called by Franklin D. Roosevelt at Evian-les-Bains, France, to discuss what to do with the Jews and other refugees fleeing from Hitler's Germany. Palestine was not even given full representation at the conference and so Golda was in the audience as "the Jewish observer from Palestine." Sitting in the midst of the luxury and beauty of the Hotel Royal overlooking Lake Geneva, Golda found it a searing experience to listen to the representatives of thirty-two countries say that they would like to take in substantial numbers of refugees but were unable to do so because it would be too great an economic burden. The conference was a turning point in Golda Meir's life.

"I realized then," she told me, "that a world which is not necessarily anti-Semitic—because Hitler was denounced at the conference and there was considerable pro-Jewish sentiment—could stand by and see others who were weaker victimized." Mrs. Meir, an old, gray woman now in a plain blue shirtdress, spoke without bitterness, but her voice was heavy and lifeless.

"We can't depend on any others," she said flatly. And there was a long pause. At that conference in 1938, Golda did not know what lay ahead in the Holocaust. How could she have conceived of the extermination of six million Jews? Or dreamed that one day she would listen to a Nazi Commandant testify at Adolf Eichmann's trial that "very frequently women would hide their children under their clothes, but of course, when we found them we would send the children in to be exterminated"?

Finally Golda said, "I remember at the end of that conference I said to the press—'I hope I live to see the day when Jews won't be pitied.' Today people are for us. People are against us. But no one pities us."

She has lived to see the day. The Jews may still be the object of hatred, but with their highly trained and disciplined army, they are not to be pitied.

I asked Mrs. Meir if, now that she is removed from the turmoil of being at the center of government, she has any greater understanding of the hatred that threatens Israel's survival. She replied, "The Arabs are not against Jews. They are against Israelis. And as for those who support the Palestinian terrorists," she shook her head and then went on, "in order to justify supporting terrorists, you must picture the object of your hate as something very terrible." Her knowledge of the Arabs' irrational fear of "something very terrible" is what compels Golda to be so adamant about Israel's need to be strong.

There was another question that I had to ask Golda Meir. But before I spoke, I could not help but think of the scorching sun outside and the sandy soil surrounding the concrete of her office building, of this inhospitable strip of land—only 8,000 square miles, not as large as our State of Maryland—that the Israelis have clung to and cultivated and slowly transformed into a modern nation. I asked my question.

"Mrs. Meir, fifty years from now will Israel still be in a virtual state of siege? When will peace come?"

"Peace depends upon two things," she answered without hesitation. "It depends on the Arabs and it depends on the world. But the world is giving in to terrorism. It is giving in to oil."

I reacted to this by describing the inability of the United Nations to counter the wave of terrorism as "a joke." But before I could finish my thought, Mrs. Meir interrupted me.

"A joke?" She spat the words out.

"It is a tragedy. Not a joke. The U.N. is a tragedy. There sits the world. The Arabs, the Moslems and the Communist bloc rule the world. They can pass anything they want to. And what shocks me most is that the free world just abstains."

She spoke bluntly of the lack of courage and moral conviction of the nations who abstain rather than protest each terrorist outrage. Her voice was low and dispassionate. She spoke slowly, so slowly that I could write her words down in longhand. But there was a look of disgust and frustration on her face. She could control her emotions when she talked of the reality of oil ruling the world, but that did not mean that her anger that the socialist nations of Europe had failed to support Israel, the only socialist democracy in the Middle East, had diminished or disappeared. The hearts of these nations may be with Israel, but their pragmatic heads are with the Arabs—they import three-fourths of their oil from the Middle East. As a lifelong idealist, Golda Meir finds their pragmatism a bitter pill to swallow.

She is also angry and outraged at the uses the Arabs put their oil revenues to—"All that money on the arms race!" she exclaimed. And she told me, indignant at the senselessness of it, that the infant mortality rate in the Arab countries is the highest in the world.

Golda, who has four grandsons and a granddaughter, has both

a world leader's and a woman's very personal interest in peace. Her eldest grandson has just entered the Army and the other three will follow soon; her granddaughter has already done her Army service. She is extremely proud of her grandchildren. Her voice becomes mellow and happy when she talks about them. And like any grandmother, she loves to talk about them.

With pride she told me that her youngest grandson was asked once how it felt to have a famous relative. "Well," he replied, "I tried to keep it a secret, but it leaked."

Her nineteen-year-old grandson who is in the Army is also having his difficulties keeping it quiet that his grandmother is the former Prime Minister. When he learned that his grandmother was going to visit his base, he telephoned her and begged, "Please, don't come." She canceled her visit. A few days later, he had an even closer call. With glee, Golda re-created the scene for me. Her grandson and some of his Army buddies were discussing fellow soldiers on the base. They had discovered that the son of the Ambassador to the United Nations and the son of the head of the Air Force as well as sons of other prominent government officials were in their company. And, rumor had it, so was Golda Meir's grandson. At this point, Mrs. Meir acted out the incident. "There he was. Sitting and shivering," she said with a smile. And she hunched her shoulders, pulled her elbows in and brought her arms close to her chest as she rubbed her hands in mock fright. "He was saved only because many are named Meir."

As Golda talked about her beloved grandchildren, she said—and it was obvious this was something that she and her family had often discussed—"We figured it out that for the next ten or twelve years the boys will be in the Army. There will be two at a time, all the time. Perhaps as many as three." Almost as an afterthought, she told me something her son Menachem had said only a few weeks before. " 'Mother, when I was a child, you never would buy me a play gun or any military toys—and yet I've lived with guns all my life.' " I could almost hear Golda ticking off the conflicts in her mind—World War II, the struggle for statehood when Menachem was a member of the Haganah (the underground Jewish self-defense organization), and the three wars since Independence: Suez, the Six-Day War, the Yom-Kippur War.

When one considers the anguish of watching and waiting that will be hers, the terrifying likelihood that one or all of her grandsons might be killed the next time war breaks out, it is difficult to question Mrs. Meir's call for a strong Israel. But her belief in that necessity goes deeper than love of family. It has to do with an elemental human right, the right to exist. Mrs. Meir belongs to that older generation who actually watched the survivors of the Holocaust land on the beaches of Israel. She can never forget that one million children—a whole generation—were annihilated.

Golda Meir is old. Older than her years. And she is weary. More weary than she likes to admit. During most of our conversation, she kept her body still as if glad of the chance to sit quietly. She did not gesture often. And she spoke slowly and tiredly. When she first sat down she took her butane lighter and white leatherette cigarette case out of her pocketbook so that they would be within easy reach on the coffee table. I knew that she was a chain-smoker, and I had heard the story of the most recent excuse she had given her doctor for not quitting. "At my age," she had asked, "what other pleasures do I have in life?" But while I was there, she smoked only occasionally. Almost as if the effort of lighting the cigarette was too much.

We spoke briefly of the plans to do a Broadway play based on her life and the possibility that she might come to New York for the premiere. "If I'm still around, I'll see it," she said, and went on to add that she can no longer stand the pace of a trip jammed with events and people as she has in the past.

"It's not just the events," she said heavily. "It's in between the events. It takes everything out of me." And, indeed, the major concession that Golda has made to old age is to cut down on her customary schedule of back-to-back visitors to seeing just four or five people or groups a day.

Golda is not only physically weary, but also she is weary of the endless interviews, the same questions over and over. She refuses to discuss personal matters, to answer questions about her marriage or to comment on her family's support or lack of support for her career. And now that she is no longer in government, she cannot, as she has for decades, fill her conversation with her views on the issues facing Israel and how they should be resolved. So there are silences. Her reluctance to discuss political matters indicated that she still wields a great deal of power. She scrupulously tries to refrain from commenting on the sensitive issues facing the two major political parties. It may be that my impression of her bone-deep weariness came in part from her inability to talk spiritedly and with purpose about actions and decisions that will affect the daily lives of Israelis. The role of elder stateswoman comes hard to this activist who has devoted her life to government.

Despite her weariness, however, and despite her non-official status, she maintains a pace that is only slightly less hectic than before her retirement. She continues to push herself to the edge of endurance, although she admits that quick retreats to the bathroom to splash cold water on her face no longer revive her as effectively as they did in the past. As she described her previous day's activities to me, she said, "It was a very big day. I was really dead tired."

She had given two television interviews the day before we met —one French, one American—discussing the impasse in Arab-Israeli negotiations. She had had several appointments with people in and out of government and dealt with the day's share of the five hundred or so letters she receives each week. She had gone to bed at ten. At eleven there was a telephone call from Washington, from the Israeli Ambassador to the United States, her old friend Simcha Dinitz. He told her the American interview would be shown in the United States later in the evening. Golda thanked him and went back to sleep. At one o'clock the Ambassador called again. The telecast had gone well.

Dinitz was Mrs. Meir's political aide when she was Prime Minister and they had a close relationship. He was the man who day after day had read all the cables to her. "Golda learns by listening," he told me. He knows her love of being at the center of things, in pace with events. And so the night he telephoned, he knew that no matter how late it was, Golda would want to know how things had gone. And besides, he knew she would fall back to sleep without any trouble. She herself told me that her ability to fall asleep anywhere at any time is "my strongest point."

Over the years she has trained herself to get along with no more than four hours of sleep a night for several days at a time. But at the end of a stretch of twenty-hour days, she simply collapses and will sleep for fourteen hours without waking. Her sister told me that one of their mother's greatest problems with "Goldie" used to be trying to get her to go to bed at night—and then trying to get her up again in the morning.

During the War of Attrition in 1971 and 1972, when the Arabs waged an undeclared war of sporadic nighttime attacks along the border, Golda left orders to be awakened each time an Israeli was killed. Clara was staying with her sister at the time and she told me, "The phone would ring all night long." And Golda's ability to fall asleep easily deserted her during those long nights. The tension was relieved only once. The phone rang at three in the morning. Golda picked it up and listened as the operator said, "I want to report that twenty-six sheep were killed."

The Prime Minister had ordered that she be told about all casualties, but *sheep*? She turned over and tried to go back to sleep.

Within a few minutes the phone rang again. "I'm sorry, Mrs. Meir," the operator apologized, "it was only twenty-five."

The story made me realize just how intense a leader Golda was, always deeply involved in every aspect of her job. She insisted on knowing exactly what was going on and when and where. "I never, never signed a letter as Prime Minister," she told me, "without reading it first. No matter who had prepared it for me." This kind of meticulous attention to detail meant that she constantly drove herself to her emotional and physical limits.

And her insistence that she be informed of every casualty testifies to her great heart and conscience. To her, each death was a personal loss. Golda is a truly rare woman, a woman of steel—and heart. The adversity and pain of her early years explain a great deal about why she is that kind of woman. And yet, when one understands what she has been through, it seems remarkable that she drew courage and strength from adversity and pain, rather than bitterness.

Ben-Gurion has been quoted as saying that Golda "had a difficult childhood," but difficult is much too mild a word to describe Golda's life as a daughter of a poor Jewish carpenter in Russia at the turn of the century. It is hard to imagine the poverty of such a childhood. Four brothers and a sister died in infancy from disease caused by poor living conditions and malnutrition. Golda remembers always being hungry as a child. Her sister Sheyna, nine years older, occasionally fainted from hunger at school. But even worse than hunger was being different. Being despised because she and her family were Jewish. One of Golda's first memories, when she was a little over three, was of her father barricading the entrance of their home in Kiev with wooden planks because of the fear of a pogrom. Her father took down the planks the next day—the attack did not come—but Golda could not forget that people filled with hate against the "Christ-killers" might surge through the streets, brandishing clubs any day in the future.

It was Sheyna who gave meaning to Golda's consciousness of being different. She made Golda proud to be a Jew. Sheyna, whom Golda says was the greatest influence on her life apart from her husband, was a Zionist, and Zionists believed that Jews not only had a right to exist, but also had an historic mission as well—to return to Zion and establish a land of their own. And Golda accepted this mission. When she was seventeen, Golda decided that she must live and work in Palestine, not just talk about it. It was a courageous decision. Palestine was still an uncharted frontier. It would be another two years before the British government announced that it favored the establishment· of "a national home for the Jewish people" there.

In her memoirs, Golda wrote of Sheyna: "I think of her constantly." I asked why Sheyna had had such an influence on her. "Was it that she was an idealist?" I ventured.

For a moment, she looked offended. And then, her voice incredulous, she repeated "An idealist?" as if questioning how it was possible I did not recognize instantly the extraordinary strength and courage of her older sister. "An idealist," she responded, "and strong!" she added with great emphasis. When I had asked Clara earlier to describe Sheyna, her first words—without the slightest hesitation—were, "She had lots of guts."

Golda went on to talk about Sheyna. With admiration in her eyes, she said, "Sheyna wouldn't budge left or right from her ideals." In 1903, just before her father emigrated to America, he moved the family to Pinsk. But in Pinsk, Sheyna, despite her mother's objections, became deeply involved with the forbidden Socialist-Zionist movement. The possible consequences of Sheyna's activities—torture, imprisonment—so terrified her mother that she was forced to take her three daughters (Clara was born in 1902) to America before her husband was earning enough money to support them adequately. In 1906, they made the long journey from Russia to the United States.

Golda Meir has written movingly of her conflicts with her family once they were settled in Milwaukee over her desire to make something of her life. Her sister Clara feels strongly that those who have read only Mrs. Meir's autobiography cannot have a full understanding of why their parents opposed Golda so often. Clara said, "My father was a really wonderful person but he simply was not successful." And so her mother's obsession was only the natural wish that her daughters marry "good providers," men who could spare them the poverty and, most of all, the terrifying insecurity which she had endured. That is why she simply could not tolerate the idea of her daughter signing a teacher's contract which forbade marriage. She wanted Golda to drop out of high school and go to work. At fifteen, Golda turned her back temporarily on her parents and fled to Denver to join Sheyna, who had gone there to recover from tuberculosis. In

Denver, Golda Mabovitch met Morris Meyerson, a quiet young man whose parents, like hers, were immigrants. She disappointed her parents again by marrying him on the eve of her nineteenth birthday.

Morris Meyerson gave Golda "so much I did not get from my home," an appreciation for art and music and literature. And a new kind of love, gentle and understanding. He was a man of unusual sensitivity. And yet the marriage eventually became a source of frustration, pain and conflict for Golda and Morris. Mrs. Meir (she took a Hebrew name at Ben-Gurion's insistence when she became a member of his cabinet) is a woman who, when faced with unfavorable odds or even the near-certainty of failure, always defied the odds and fought. But her marriage was one situation she could not salvage. It was not something she could deal with simply by gritting her teeth and fighting on.

Golda married Morris with the understanding that they would emigrate to Palestine, and he kept his promise, even though as Clara was to tell me so many years later, "Morris was never cut out to be a pioneer." He loved music and art. Palestine was a desert wasteland, where only the sturdiest of pioneers could survive.

At Merhavia, the kibbutz where they settled, the heat, the periodic infestations of flies, and the never-ending bouts of malaria reduced Morris to near-chronic illness. They left the kibbutz and moved to Jerusalem. It was not solely Morris' health that prompted the move. There was another very important reason. They both wanted a child. Morris was opposed to the collective child-rearing of the kibbutz. Golda wrote, "He refused to have children at all unless we left." The following November, their son Menachem was born in Jerusalem.

Golda had grown up in an environment in which the good daughter was the girl who grew up to be a good mother, but the four years in Jerusalem when Golda, at Morris' urging, tried to be a full-time mother and homemaker were the most miserable of her life. She had come to Palestine to help build a just and progressive society for the Jews and there were many times when she doubted, possibly even hated, herself for not being satisfied with less. When she was thirty, she talked of the anguish of the modern woman and posed a question for all working women—and most of all for herself—"Is there something wrong with me if my children don't fill up my life?"

During those years in Jerusalem when her son and, two years later, her daughter Sarah were born, Golda and Morris experienced fearful poverty and hunger like the hunger she remembered as a child in Pinsk. The thought of her children going hungry was agony. She wrote Sheyna about her despair when she was refused bread and margarine on credit. And in 1928, Golda the idealist, the woman with a cause, the activist, seized the opportunity to become secretary of the Women's Labor Council of the Histadrut (the General Federation of Jewish Labor). It meant that she had to move to Tel Aviv. She found an apartment in Tel Aviv for herself and the children. Morris stayed in Jerusalem and visited them on weekends. This move and this job marked the beginning of the road that led to the Prime Ministership; just as it signaled the disintegration of her marriage. "Although Morris and I remained married to each other and loving each other until the day he died in my house in 1951 (when, symbolically enough, I was away), I was not able to make a success of our marriage," she wrote in her memoirs.

Golda Meir has rarely displayed personal pride in the course of her long public career. And that is why I remember particularly a boastful remark she made at a State Dinner in her honor at the White House in 1973. After dessert was served, my father had given the traditional short welcoming speech and had toasted Mrs. Meir. In her responding toast, Golda told the assembled guests, "I can honestly say at least one thing, I never ran away from a difficult situation." Because she refuses to discuss her marriage and has written about it only sketchily, we will never know how much she agonized when she reached the point when compromise was impossible and she had to choose "duty" over husband and children.

There can be no doubt but that Golda Meir loved her family.

But she had to be part of the world. In Clara Stern's words, Golda simply "always had to have a cause." Yet it must have been hard for her as she traveled for the labor organization to endure Sheyna's accusations that she was trying to be "a public person, not a homebody." And equally hard for Golda to learn to live with the rejoicing of her children when she was stricken with migraine headaches and unable to go to work.

Lou Kaddar, the effervescent French woman whose admiration for Mrs. Meir has led her to sacrifice much of her own life over the past quarter of a century in order to act as Golda's assistant, says quite frankly, "Golda tried to be a devoted mother, but she was not." Today, Golda's daughter will rarely leave her family for a night unless there is an emergency. When her mother cannot visit the kibbutz where Sarah lives, two and a half hours from Tel Aviv, Sarah will make the trip to Tel Aviv, but she usually insists on returning on the same day.

There were too many times in those years when the life or death of the country struggling to be Israel seemed to depend upon Golda's being away from home for days, weeks, even months at a time. Golda always went, but reluctantly. It was not that she minded the staggering demands of a job. When, as Minister of Labor, she had to find ways to feed and clothe 680,000 Jews who had come to Palestine from seventy countries at the end of World War II, she accepted the challenge without hesitation. What caused her anguish was being away from home, losing contact with family and friends. Their lives went on while she was away and she had to fit herself back into their patterns each time she returned. And there was something more, something deep within her that disturbed her each time she had to leave the country. She could not bear to be separated from the soil of Israel. Mrs. Meir has said that heroic "is not a word that I use easily or often," but she used it to describe the women from the developing nations of Africa who were willing to travel to foreign lands to learn the skills their own countries needed.

Since Golda's family found her involvement in government difficult to accept, it is remarkable that she had the strength to continue her career, a word that Mrs. Meir assiduously avoids. She is not a feminist. She deplores the invention of that "unfortunate term, 'women's lib.' " As a young woman who chose the kibbutz life in 1921, she wanted only an equal share of the burden. When I asked if she still rejects the idea of describing her working life as a career, her brief replies indicated that she thought the whole subject irrelevant. In clipped sentences, she said, "Work I did. But I did not choose a career like a medical career. I did not choose a profession."

"The government service? Politics?" I asked. "It all just happened?"

She nodded.

She sees her life as that of a woman doing a job, just as everyone should do something with her or his life. She is uncomfortable with the very notion of being a seeker of power. Women's issues are not of primary interest, or even very important to Mrs. Meir.

I remember when she was at the White House in 1973. Coffee was served in the Blue Room after the State Dinner and the room was jammed with the powerful and the famous trying to edge closer to Mrs. Meir, trying to catch the eye of the Israeli Ambassador or of my parents or of an aide, of anyone who would introduce them to her. Those who had been at White House dinners before knew that time was limited. The coffee ritual lasted only ten minutes. But Mrs. Meir spent most of those minutes talking to some young female military aides. The aides were excited— and rather embarrassed since their main duty was to locate those guests whom the State Department or the Israeli Embassy felt Mrs. Meir should meet and bring them up to her. But Golda wanted to talk to them. She was interested to learn that for the first time military women had been given duty at the White House, not because this was a breakthrough for women, but because it was a parallel to Israel, where both men and women serve in the armed forces.

She was Prime Minister in a nation in which no woman can testify in a religious court, which means that divorce is impossible without the consent of the husband. A country where the Orthodox males thank God daily that they were not born women. A country where abortion is illegal. In her five years as leader of Israel, she never gave priority to women's issues. She handled most questions about her sex lightly, as when she was asked how it felt to be appointed the first woman Foreign Minister. She replied, "I don't know. I was never a man Minister."

Leaders of other nations came to regard Golda as simply Prime Minister, not as a woman. And that is what she wanted. My father told me, "She never wanted to be treated like a woman, but like a leader." Secretary of State William Rogers once commented to French President Georges Pompidou on how curious it was that the two trouble spots in the world at the moment, India and Israel, were both governed by women. Pompidou arched his eyebrows and said, "Are you sure?" It was meant as a witticism, but there was a serious undertone—a respect for women who were totally in control in what traditionally were men's jobs.

When Golda speaks of the great women of Israel, she does not single out the women in Parliament or in the Labor Movement, the movers and the doers, but the mothers who hate war and yet willingly watch their children go to Israel's defense. To Golda, these are the truly great women.

Golda Meir's friends and associates in government see her as a very feminine woman, despite her achievements, despite her strength and outspoken honesty. The picture they painted for me was of a tender, womanly figure which went far beyond the familiar grandmotherly image. They see her as a sensitive person whom one wants to protect from criticism, from overworking, from pushing herself too far.

She has suffered from severe migraine headaches for years, so severe that she is often incapacitated for hours during an attack. The woman who thought nothing of dawn-to-dusk work on a desert kibbutz or of taking on a job that required constant travel, entertaining and decision-making is defenseless when migraine strikes. It is then that the kind-hearted woman who worries over her friends is in turn cared for by them. The room is darkened, the phone turned off, a sedative given. There is always someone to sit by her bed and hold her hand until she falls asleep. Someone to be there when she wakes up.

Golda's indomitable sense of duty was never described to me as an obsession, but as an admirable, lovable quality. This gray-haired woman with the painful legs and the cruel migraines has proved time and again that she can out-read, out-talk, out-smoke and out-think many younger men and women. But those who know her have a chivalrous attitude toward her, a desire to serve and protect. Her sometime driver, Danny, who is assigned to the Foreign Ministry and who helped me during my visit said, "Golda! I would give my life for that woman. That's all!"

People love Golda because she loves them. Danny told me about the day she gave him a ride to work. She was Foreign Minister then. On her way to the office, Golda passed Danny on the road. Golda, who as usual was in the front seat beside the driver, ordered the car stopped. Danny hopped in the back seat and they proceeded to the foreign office. The driver told Danny later that Golda had scolded him. "What's wrong with you?" she had asked. "Why didn't you stop? Didn't you see Danny?"

All her life Golda Meir has established intimate contacts with her working associates, her household help—even the soldiers assigned to guard her as Prime Minister. And in their turn, these young men became very attached to the woman for whom they were expected to give their lives if it proved necessary. They came to know the woman behind the Prime Minister.

On Saturdays, a holy day during which no government business is conducted, no official receptions or meetings held, she would often be home alone. The soldiers knew Golda hated solitude. And when they saw that she was alone, they would call her personal assistant, Lou Kaddar.

At eight-thirty the phone would ring in Lou's third-floor walk-up, not far from the Prime Minister's residence in Jerusalem.

Lou would know what it was before she picked up the receiver.

"What time is it?" she would ask angrily, exhausted from a typical week of sixteen-hour days.

"Were you asleep, Lou?"

"Yes. Why are you calling me?" She knew perfectly well why they were calling.

"How would you like to spend the day with Golda?" All the soldiers called the Prime Minister "Golda."

"Go to hell," Lou would shout into the phone.

"How about nine-fifteen? We'll pick you up."

"No," Lou would say and hang up. But she would always be downstairs waiting at nine-fifteen. Lou spent many Saturdays in Golda's kitchen while Golda bustled about preparing good plain Jewish food for her. Despite the fact that French-born Lou does not care for anyone's good plain Jewish cooking, I got the impression that she enjoyed those Saturdays.

Golda has a gift for friendship. Although she is single-minded in her devotion to work and duty, she has had the ability to surround herself with people who are slightly irreverent and candid, like Lou Kaddar.

Before she became Prime Minister, Golda had never gone to a resort for a vacation, with the result that she found herself at a loss when her doctor ordered her to spend three days at a spa and get some rest. Lou Kaddar went with her, but every afternoon Lou would disappear for an hour or so. She told Golda she was going swimming. But Golda, who hated being alone possibly more than anything else and who could not imagine that anyone could want to go swimming alone, told Lou half-jokingly that she didn't believe she really spent all that time at the pool.

The last evening of her vacation Golda and Lou went for a walk, trailed as usual by security men. When they came to the pool, Golda said scornfully, "There's your dear swimming pool. If you like to swim so much, why don't you go in now?"

Lou, fully clothed, jumped into the pool.

"Come out. Come out, Lou. You'll get a cold," Golda called frantically. She ordered her bodyguards to go for towels. Lou, her clothes ruined, decided to make the most of the opportunity to tease Golda and swam around until she was ready to come out.

When one realizes how much Golda Meir depends on others for companionship and stimulation, it is sad to read in her memoirs the many references to the joys and satisfactions of the kibbutz and her regret that she "did not find the strength" to return to the life of a close community. She has never forgotten her pioneering days as one of the settlers of Merhavia or the excitement of transforming the land by one's labor. When she told me about the journey that led from the United States to Merhavia so many years ago, she became animated. "I took none of my appliances or furnishings. I thought, 'I'll live in a tent. What do I need curtains for?' Oh, I was deliberate." Golda made sweeping gestures in cadence with her words. "No water. No electricity. Just rocks and swamps." She exulted in her description of the land she had chosen.

She left Merhavia in an effort to save her marriage, but she has always retained an idealized view of kibbutz life and sees it as "the solution for how men should live most fruitfully." During World War II, for example, she suggested that Palestine should become a kibbutz-like society with a network of cooperative kitchens so that at least the children would get enough to eat, but the idea was turned down. When she served as Israel's first Ambassador to the Kremlin, she ran the embassy like a kibbutz. She even cooked communal meals in her hotel room on weekends and washed the dishes in the bathroom, in the days before the Russians allotted them permanent quarters.

The kibbutz way of life appeals to many women because they can work and raise their children at the same time. Mrs. Meir is convinced that kibbutz parents spend more time with their children than many parents who live more traditional lives. Certainly there are no neglected children in the kibbutzim.

Clara told me of visiting her niece, Golda's daughter, at Revivim, the kibbutz where she has lived since 1946. At the time, there were ten babies in the nursery. Instead of going to her own baby, Sarah picked up another infant first and played with it for a few minutes. During the hour that they were in the nursery, five other mothers came in. Each picked up the same infant and cuddled it rather than going to their own babies first.

"What's so special about that baby?" Clara asked finally.

"Her mother died a few weeks ago," Sarah told her. The other women had become substitute mothers.

I made the journey to Revivim to meet Sarah and her husband and their two children and to see the community where Golda now has a small retirement apartment and where she can be, at least for a few days now and then, part of a larger community.

For two and a half hours I drove through the miles and miles of sand that separate Revivim from Jerusalem. There were vegetable fields and fruit groves at intervals, desert miracles made possible by irrigation. Revivim, which is Hebrew for dewdrops, is in the very heart of the Negev and had once been considered barren and uncultivable. The kibbutz was founded by seven young men, one of them Sarah's future husband, in 1943. They lived in a cave for the first two years. Despite irrigation with salty water, they could get nothing but palm trees to grow in the beginning. When Sarah joined the kibbutz three years later, life was still harsh, as it was to be for years to come.

Lou Kaddar had told me the story of how in 1956 several wealthy Jews from abroad had come to visit Revivim with the idea of making a financial contribution. Asked if they cared for any refreshments, the visitors said that all they would like was ice water. When they were told that it was not available, the visitors were terribly insulted and left the kibbutz. No one had a chance to explain that it was assumed they would not want to drink salty water.

Even today life in the middle of the Negev is not easy. At least once a week a sandstorm whirls across the cultivated acres and around the apartments of the five hundred people who live and work in Revivim. Sarah's daughter Naomi, a tiny, slender girl with long black hair, who looked too young and frail for her job taking care of the eight-year-olds, described what it is like when a storm comes stealthily in the night. You are awakened not so much by the howling wind, but by the feeling of sand which seeps in under the doors and through the window cracks and steadily covers the objects—and the people—within. Although Naomi shrugged in a gesture of acceptance, of "what can one do," I knew that each time she experienced the suffocating sensation of sand on her face and in her nostrils, it was as frightening as the first time. Naomi has lived on the kibbutz all her life and now that she is married continues to live and work there. She is accustomed to hardship, but it was obvious that one never grows accustomed to sandstorms.

Sarah Meir Rehabi has succeeded in living quietly in Revivim, despite the frequent visits of her famous mother. I discovered just how quietly when I arrived at the kibbutz and tried to find her apartment. I had picked up two young hitchhikers, paratroopers who were going to Revivim on weekend passes to spend the Sabbath with their families. I asked them how to get to Sarah's apartment, but when I followed their directions, I was told that Sarah had moved several months before. It took two more tries before I found someone who could lead me to the row of new apartments on the very edge of the settlement where she lived.

Knowing what Sarah had endured as one of the pioneers of Revivim, I was eager to meet her. Sarah is a "sabra," the term used to describe a child born in Israel. In Hebrew it means prickly pear. Golda once said that one sees only the prickly exterior of the sabra, but that inside, like the pear, "they are juicy and sweet." The word seemed to apply particularly to Sarah, a self-controlled, quiet woman who seems to have great inner strength. She is as reserved as the descriptions of her father indicate he was and physically she resembles her father more than Golda. Her features are small. And her hair is black and curly like Naomi's.

She offered me fruit and a loaf cake that she had made the day before and we talked of kibbutz life; of the fresh challenge each day of trying to grow different fruits and vegetables, flowers, trees. There was no mention of my visit with her mother the previous day. And there were no photographs of her mother in the book-lined living room. But directly across the hall on the second floor of the four-family apartment unit in which Sarah lived was a door painted white like the others. This opened into Mrs. Meir's apartment, its three rooms the same size as her daughter's.

As I left I had a better understanding of why Golda Meir has said that children and grandchildren are the greatest blessing in life. And I was aware of the legacy she was leaving to Israel in the lives of Sarah and Menachem and their children and their children's children. To leave such a rich legacy to the future was sufficient personal ambition for Mrs. Meir.

It had been said that she became Prime Minister because she was without ambition. The men who had worked with her in building Israel knew that the woman they saw on the surface was the same woman underneath, not likely to change her goals because of new power. And her age placed her beyond long-term political plans. Looking back on her service as Prime Minister, Mrs. Meir confirmed what her colleagues had known all along. "I had no particular relish for the job," she said. "I never planned to be Prime Minister."

But she became Prime Minister, a Prime Minister who retained her down-to-earth manner and outlook. It is fascinating to read excerpts from the minutes of a Central Committee cabinet meeting. In the formal parliamentary language, the noting of "none opposed, four abstentions," it is refreshing to find the Prime Minister referred to as Golda. "The Central Committee earnestly appeals to Golda to retract . . ." Mrs. Meir had complete respect from her colleagues. It was just that she had always been Golda and Golda she would remain.

Her lifestyle remained practically unchanged despite the grandeur of the Prime Minister's residence. Her kitchen was still the center of her social life, the place where she enjoyed talking to friends and where she worked late into the night over briefing papers and documents once her friends had left. And almost inevitably it became the meeting place for other members of the government. Clara Stern, who frequently came to Jerusalem to stay with her sister, told me about a cabinet meeting that had lasted from eight at night to three the next morning. A Libyan jet pilot was flying over Israeli territory, asking for asylum. The cabinet members were summoned quickly. They sat around the dining-room table, the door to the kitchen open, and during the night-long discussions they wandered freely back and forth between the kitchen and dining room. Clara remembers that the Minister of Finance arrived without having had dinner. He went straight to the kitchen, opened the refrigerator door and stared helplessly at the contents until Clara suggested a tuna fish sandwich.

Golda usually had no help at night. The maid prepared the noonday meal, washed up and was gone by four. Fortunately, that particular evening Clara and Golda's eldest grandson were there to make the tea and coffee and serve the sandwiches and cakes. But one wonders how Golda managed to maintain her thread of thought and purpose on other similar occasions when there was no one to help her and, as hostess, she had to make the innumerable pots of coffee and set out the food.

Despite the informality of her kitchen "headquarters," Golda was in no way unprofessional about her job. When Clara visited her, the two sisters would always breakfast together. Clara, eager to learn as much as possible about what Golda was doing and about Israeli politics, would pepper her sister with questions. "But Golda never told me anything," she said when I visited her in Bridgeport. Clara worked out her own way of getting information from Golda. She would study the English-language *Jerusalem Post* over their breakfast of eggs and Arab flat bread and coffee, while Golda whipped through her own copy of the *Post* and the Tel Aviv newspapers, written in Hebrew. Clara would read an item from the *Post* out loud and then quickly glance up at Golda. "She wouldn't say a word," Clara told me, "but I would study her face. And then I'd know if something was going on."

Golda has never forgotten who she is or where she came from. Her first visit to Washington in 1969 when she had been Prime

Minister for only six months illustrates the enormous contrasts in the woman who could bargain so confidently for her country and at the same time be so excited and awed by the ceremony surrounding her new position. The main purpose of her visit was to ask for twenty-five Phantom jets and other military hardware to be paid for with low interest loans. Lou Kaddar told me that she had never seen Golda more nervous than just before they reached Washington. "We needed those Phantoms," Lou said, "and it was her job to get them."

Golda was driven to the White House in the long black Presidential limousine, impressive with the small Israeli and American flags flapping briskly on each side. The Chief of Protocol, Bus Mosbacher, sat beside her. As the car entered the White House grounds and Golda saw the men in Army, Navy, Marine and Air Force uniforms lining the driveway, saw the band on the lawn and the platform near the house loaded with photographers and television equipment, she took Mosbacher's hand and held it tight as she said nervously, "Don't let me make a mistake. Don't let me make a mistake." Yet in her talks with my father after the official arrival ceremony, Golda forcefully presented Israel's case, with no trace of nervousness. My father said later that Golda "used her emotions. They didn't use her." And although she said that she would have to go back to the Knesset, the Israeli Parliament, for approval, she left no doubt that she was the one making the decisions.

But at the social climax of the visit, the State Dinner that followed the formal talks, Golda once more became the excited, emotional woman. She had tears in her eyes and a tender smile on her face when the Marine band played first the Israeli and then the American anthems. In the receiving line, between my parents, she looked startlingly small. Golda had such a presence, one never thought of her as being physically small.

My mother had been able to arrange for Leonard Bernstein and Isaac Stern to play for the Prime Minister and other guests after dinner. In the huge gold and white East Room, Golda sat between my parents in the center of the first row. Six-foot-tall portraits of George and Martha Washington, the President and First Lady whom Golda had learned about as a Russian emigrant schoolgirl in Milwaukee, hung on the walls. Photographers and reporters stood shoulder-to-shoulder at the back of the room and in both doorways. Their eyes and those of most of the one hundred dinner guests were trained on Israel's first woman Prime Minister. But Golda was oblivious of the attention, completely absorbed in the music. At the end, she impulsively hugged both Isaac Stern and Leonard Bernstein, thanking them for having given so much beauty and pleasure.

She did not stay for the dancing, but went back to Blair House, the guesthouse for foreign visitors. Once in bed, she ordered coffee and then relived every detail of the evening with Lou Kaddar, who perched at the foot of the bed. Golda Meir rarely has had the opportunity or the inclination to pay attention to the small details of social events because her whole being is focused completely on the mission that prompted the parties and dinners. And so now, Lou, as she had so often in the past after other parties, described the flowers, the antiques, the portraits, told Golda who was there and what they had worn. And, excited as a girl after a dance, Golda would ask, "Did he really say that, Lou?" "Oh, Lou, what did she wear?" on and on into the night.

Golda Meir is not a complicated person. She is forthright, strong and dedicated. Her outlook is dominated by one consideration—what is best for Israel. She acknowledges readily that the Jews have had a tragic history. Yet she has been able to work to make life better for her people. To her way of thinking, the only way to deal with adversity is as clear as the contrast between black and white. You give in—or you fight. And Golda is in her element when she is faced with a situation in which she can fight. But the personal tragedies of life—the illness which strikes down a friend, the senseless suffering of another person, the sudden death of a colleague—are much more difficult to deal with than the problems of feeding or clothing a million people or coolly arguing across the negotiating table with an intransigent enemy.

Because she is an uncompromising idealist, she finds it difficult to accept imperfection and impossible to forgive. She has said she will never forgive the Germans, nor the Arabs for certain atrocities, not even Ben-Gurion for the positions he took in some of their political disputes. She is not forgiving of herself either. Whenever she refers to her failed marriage, she places the blame on herself. When one realizes that her lifelong philosophy has been that nothing is impossible, one understands how soul-shattering this personal failure above all others must be to her still.

She is an idealist who has never sought power or fame. Instead she has sought purpose and duty. She is an idealist who believes the spiritual strength of the Jews is "indestructible and eternal." An idealist who believes man is master of his fate. More than half a century ago, she wrote a friend in New York, "I was happy I saw a naked rock. You see, some day when there is a forest along this road, I will know and everyone will know that those trees were not planted for us. We did not find them. Those trees will be there because we planted them."

Even now as age and disappointment weigh heavily on her, Golda continues to be an idealist. And an optimist. She says that only the old in Israel are optimists, because only the old can really know how far the country has come since the first kibbutz settlements.

"How can one make the younger generation more optimistic?" I asked. "And how in this midst of increasing materialism can Israel keep alive the Zionist spirit of a just society?"

"There is no recipe," she answered simply. "But we are a young country. We can still see evidence of the pioneer spirit. That is important."

As we talked, I sensed that she had faith, not so much in the young, but in Israel, the land and what it stood for. Perhaps without her realizing it, Golda Meir is vitally important to any spark of optimism among the young. It was her idealism and spirit which first drew me to her and made me eager to know more about her beliefs and her life. I will never forget the remarks she made at the White House in 1969. After her talk with my father she declared that she would return home to Israel and tell her cabinet, her people, her children—"Don't become cynical. Don't give up hope. Don't believe that everything is judged only by expediency. There is idealism in this world. There is human brotherhood."

There was a great deal of suppressed emotion as we ended our visit together. It was the day after the third anniversary of Israel's third war since statehood, the war which compelled her to say, "I will never again be the same person I was before the Yom-Kippur War." Twenty-five hundred Israelis were killed in that war. Critics claim that she could have prevented the war if she had called for a general alert in the country. As I sat facing her that morning in her small office, I could only try to imagine the pain and rejection she must feel. The accusations and repercussions were the major cause of her resignation seven months later. It seemed cruel, after her long life of struggle and achievement, for Golda to have to sit out her retirement years in the shadow of the Yom-Kippur War.

When I asked if she could tell me anything about the war, she said, "We did not have the proper intelligence," and then her voice trailed off and she sat silent. It was obvious that she still was unable to reveal more than what she had written in her autobiography: "There is still a great deal which cannot be told." But it was not just her inability to divulge information that was still classified. Golda did not want to discuss this time in her life that had been so painful and often beyond her control; the months that had extinguished the fire I had once seen in her eyes.

It was equally difficult for me to talk about the man who had brought us together, who was the reason Golda Meir had agreed to see me. When she asked, "How is your father? Is he writing every day? What is he doing now?" I started to describe the progress of his autobiography. But other thoughts ran through my mind as I talked. The isolation and loneliness of San Clemente. How my father seemingly was condemned to a life of inaction. I thought of all Golda Meir and my father had done for what they hoped would be a lasting peace. Their efforts were a thing of the past now. They would never again work together.

Suddenly, though my words were still about his writing, my voice broke and there were tears in my eyes. I looked down at my notepad. But I made no pretense of turning the pages, of searching for some last question. I was silent. Golda was silent, too.

Later, after we had touched lightly on other topics and I had regained a steady voice, I asked her, "Why is it that some people seem to have fewer obstacles and tragedies in their lives than others?" She did not answer. Perhaps her answer came a few minutes later when she impulsively put her arms around me to kiss me good-bye. Her answer to the vicissitudes of life is compassion, not words.

Golda Meir had begun our visit with concerned questions about my mother's health. And her very last words were of my mother. Golda told me to take warm greetings back home. And then she shook her head as if the words were not enough. She wanted to say more. "Your mother is a wonderful person. Through all that period I kept asking, 'How did she endure it all? How did she endure it all?' "

I am surprised that Golda asked the question. For she knows the answer. "Nothing in life just happens," she said once. "You have to have the stamina to meet obstacles and overcome them. To struggle." And that is how Golda Meir has lived her life, working for Israel, struggling to make a dream come true.

Ruth
Bell
Graham

"Yea, I have loved thee with an everlasting love: therefore with lovingkindness have I drawn thee."
—JEREMIAH 31:3

H ER B IBLE is so worn and soft that Ruth Bell Graham can roll it like a magazine. She turns each page gently so it will not tear. And each page is familiar. She has read and reread it in moments of happiness, moments of pain, when she was seeking answers, and when she was merely expectant. The hundreds of underlined verses and the margins filled with tightly written notations, some in pencil, some in blue or black ink, attest to the extraordinary way in which Ruth Graham communicates with God.

The first time I saw Ruth's Bible was just before Christmas in 1973. The Grahams had spent Saturday night at the White House as guests of my parents, and on Sunday Billy Graham preached at the interdenominational church service in the East Room. After dinner on Saturday, I had asked Ruth if we could visit together before church the next morning.

I had always been fascinated by Ruth Graham. Her husband is a famous evangelist who has delivered the message of God to millions of people, yet Ruth seems most comfortable when sharing her faith in God quietly, face to face with another seeker. She is spiritual, but at the same time spirited and very much a part of this world. How many other grandmothers take up hang-gliding in their fifties? Ruth did. And the first time she jumped off Maggie Valley Mountain she had barely recovered from injuries caused by falling out of a tree when she was putting up a swing for her grandchildren, injuries so severe that it was a week before she regained consciousness. And how many grandmothers borrow their son's black leather jacket and go vrooming along mountain roads on a Harley-Davidson? A daring driver, Ruth (and her motorcycle) ended up in a ditch once, in a lake another time.

The Grahams had been friends of my parents for over twenty years and though I had talked to Ruth many times before, we had never discussed her faith. This time was different. I was very much aware of the quiet assurance she found in God. I envied it. I wanted to know how Ruth, a woman with spunk and a strong will, could yield her life so completely to God. What gave her the faith to pray about the small things in her life and the large? To pray and to believe that God listens? That God answers?

The third floor of the White House was very quiet that Sunday morning. The domestic staff was busy downstairs preparing the coffee and pastries that would be served after Dr. Graham's sermon. Ruth and I talked in the little sitting room next to their bedroom. It was dark and gloomy despite the bright December sunshine outside. The balustrade that circles the White House roof blocked the sun, and because of its columns the rays that did penetrate the room fell like bars across the furniture and rug. But Ruth seemed radiant, despite the dark room and the fact that she and Billy had stayed up late the night before talking with my mother and father. She laughed as she unbuckled the strap that held her Bible together and excused the worn appearance of the book. The thin black strap looked like a belt and Ruth said that was exactly what it was, a woman's belt that she had cut down for this very purpose. I was startled by her hands as she fingered the pages of her Bible. They were extremely lined and rough. The only touch of elegance was the wide gold wedding band. But Ruth's hands were capable, surely strong enough to guide a motorcycle or hang, high over the valley, on to her gliding kite.

My questions came rapidly, all at once:

"How do you study the Bible?"

"How do you learn from it?"

"Why all the seeming inconsistencies? Why so many instances of cruelty?"

"Why do you believe in it so deeply?"

Ruth listened quietly until I paused. Then with a smile she said, "I'll try the scatter-gun approach." She held the book in her lap and slowly turned the pages until she came to passages which had meaning for her. I was surprised by her casual, random search, this thumbing through pages, but Ruth explained, "God doesn't deal with people in a formulated way. We shouldn't either." And this was a message she reinforced several times. As I listened, I realized that she offered no easy answers. There were no three steps to comfort or a formula for faith in Ruth Graham's approach. There was nothing pat about her response to my questions.

"It's surprising that there aren't more inconsistencies in the Bible," Ruth said as she leafed through the pages. "So many different people wrote it. And from so many different points of view. It's the differences that make it valid. You know the old story about the four blind men and the elephant. One man held the tail and told his companions that it was a rope. Another ran his hands over the body of the elephant and insisted that it was a wall. The third put his arms around the elephant's leg and said it was a tree trunk. The fourth touched the elephant's trunk and believed it was a snake.

"But in the Bible, none of these differences between the people who wrote it affect the great doctrines."

She turned to the back of her Bible and stopped at Chapter Eight of Romans. She read out loud to me, "Who shall separate us from the love of Christ? shall tribulation, or distress, or persecution, or famine, or nakedness, or peril, or sword?" She paused for a moment and then said quietly, "Only sin, sin which touches every man and woman, separates us from God's love." Then she turned to an earlier verse in Romans and read, "For all have sinned, and come short of the glory of God."

As she spoke those words, Ruth was already eagerly turning back to Isaiah. She read the fifth verse of the Fifty-third Chapter, substituting her own name, "But he was wounded for Ruth's transgressions, he was bruised for Ruth's iniquities: the chastisement of our peace was upon him; and with his stripes, Ruth is healed." She read the words with emotion, her voice almost caressing each syllable, in a Southern accent so marked that it was almost unbelievable that Ruth, the daughter of missionary parents, spoke Chinese before she learned English. She wanted me to know and be assured of the gift of God's love.

"But let's look at the Psalms," Ruth said. "I always draw great help and comfort from them." As she turned page after page, it seemed as if every other verse were underlined. It was apparent that each of them had spoken to her in a special way. When she reached the Thirty-seventh Psalm, Ruth laughed softly. "I've set up camp in Psalm Thirty-seven." She ran her finger down the page and stopped at the fourth verse. "This is the one I think I love more than all others," and she read, "Delight thyself also in the Lord; and he shall give thee the desires of thine heart."

"My favorite translation is from the Septuagint Bible," she said. "It goes—'Indulge thyself also in the Lord.' I love that thought of indulging myself in the Lord. Really, the main thing in studying the Bible," she said, "is to get into it and enjoy it."

At ten-thirty, when Ruth and I had to stop to get ready for the service, I left her with two strong impressions after our hour and a half together. She was not at all a brittle, upbeat Christian who denied all doubts or questions. And she undeniably enjoyed great inner peace. She had not answered all my questions, but somehow that seemed less important now. I was eager to know more about the Bible, and about Ruth herself.

The next time I saw Ruth Graham's shabby, cherished Bible was at the San Diego Crusade in August, 1976. Ruth shared it with me during the scripture reading that preceded Dr. Graham's sermon. She had hesitated before moving it a few inches closer to me so that I, too, could follow the lesson, and so I tried to focus my eyes on the verses and not let them wander to her marginal notations. I understood that these were as personal as a diary, for her eyes alone. I was not surprised by her reluctance to reveal her spiritual journey. A few months earlier, she had tried to dissuade me from writing about her, warning me in a letter that, "I feel a bit like someone doing a striptease when there's really not that much to show."

We were seated in the third row of a section of the stadium slightly to the right of the speaker's platform, lost in the anonymity of the crowd. The people around us were unaware that Ruth Graham was in their midst. Five minutes before, Ruth and Billy had quietly walked across the grassy field. Billy Graham never makes a formal entrance and I did not know that he and Ruth were on the stadium grounds until she slipped into the seat next to me.

She was very detached from the huge apparatus that made the telecast of the crusade possible—the scores of team members milling about, the formidable rows of local ministers sitting on the platform, the choir of several hundred, the cameras and sophisticated lighting and sound equipment. While everyone else was still preparing for the event, Ruth was already well into it. She did not look around the audience for her friends and staff members. She gazed at her husband on the platform. And she was silent. I knew she and Billy had been praying for months for the success of the crusade. I was sure that she was praying then as well.

Despite Ruth's attempts to separate herself from the non-spiritual aspects of the crusade while in the city where it was held, her husband's lifestyle and, therefore her own, is similar to that of many important and powerful individuals whose time is precious, whose staff members are numerous and whose lives are in need of special protection. The atmosphere surrounding the Grahams that evening had reminded me strongly of a Presidential campaign. When I arrived at their motel, there was the familiar motorcade, the cars all lined up in readiness for the drive to the stadium. There was the police motorcycle escort, gloved and goggled, ready for the signal to start. A member of the

Graham team was in constant walkie-talkie communication with the evangelist's top-floor suite. Bunny Graham Dienert, my good friend, took me to her parents' rooms. Standing watch outside was T. W. Wilson, who has been a friend of Billy's ever since they were boys. I had a feeling I had been there before. Even their suite looked like a thousand other motel rooms I had walked into during my father's campaigns.

One difference, however, was Ruth's Bible, held together with the same thin belt, ready to take to the meeting that evening. Their eldest grandchild, Stephen, was with them. He is tall and dark with deepset eyes like his grandfather's. It was hard to realize that Ruth and Billy, who look as if they are in their early forties instead of their fifties, had a twelve-year-old grandson.

We made small talk for a few minutes. Bunny teased her mother by saying that she was surprised Ruth was on time for the crusade. Bunny had telephoned her early that morning to see if Ruth wanted to have breakfast with her, only to discover that her mother had already left for Mexico with a man she had never met, a former convict who had been in and out of prisons since he was eight years old. Ruth had started corresponding with him shortly after his release from San Quentin two years before. He had spent eleven years there as an incorrigible, leading an animal-like existence. Three times a day his food was deposited in his cell by a shovel device with a handle long enough to extend through the two security doors. Nevertheless, it was at San Quentin that he committed his life to God and to rehabilitation work among ex-convicts. That morning in Mexico he had shown Ruth some of the halfway houses he had established for prisoners.

We said very little after Ruth had described her trip. I felt the familiar air of tension, the waiting to get on with something important. I knew, too, that Billy Graham had spent most of the day alone, eating almost nothing, preparing for the evening. Finally, it was time to leave. It was a relief to have the waiting over.

There was a police checkpoint at the entrance to the stadium and we drove directly to an underground area. Several people were there waiting anxiously for Ruth. Some were strangers. Others, including a friend of Bunny's, an alcoholic who was then in her fourth marriage, had met with Ruth when she first arrived in San Diego. Ruth had counseled them and prayed for them all week. There was another small, insistent group of people clustered around Billy Graham's trailer. He disappeared inside to meet with those who needed to talk with him, to have "only one minute" of prayer, just like those people who insist on a minute of the political candidate's time even when he must gather his thoughts for the speech ahead.

But when Billy Graham emerged from his trailer and walked across the stadium field with his wife, the resemblance to a political campaign stopped. No one noticed him. There were no cheers. No laudatory introductions of the speaker. Dr. Graham was one of some forty ministers on the platform. As the time neared for the service to begin, people became subdued and contemplative. And, like Ruth, they became expectant.

When I had watched crusades on television, Billy Graham loomed large. He was inescapable on the television screen. His eyes very blue and penetrating, his lips moving very fast. But in San Diego he was a small figure dwarfed by the vast stadium. He was mostly a voice.

When he finished speaking, he asked people to come forward to acknowledge their belief in Christ as their personal Savior. Stillness fell over the stadium. The only sound was the soft organ music.

Then a handful of people started to walk across the field. I looked up and saw movement at the top of the bleachers. Tiny figures, far away, began the long journey down narrow aisles. There were hundreds of people moving forward now—the man in a three-piece suit holding his small son by the hand; an elderly couple, the woman with a cane, supporting each other as they walked slowly toward the platform; there were teenagers holding hands; people walking alone.

These people were not responding to a man. They certainly were not mesmerized by the small figure of Billy Graham standing at the edge of the platform. There was no fever pitch of emotion in the crowd. Something far greater was at work. I understood Ruth's words now. "It isn't a culture or a personality responding to a program or a man," she had told me before the crusade, "but the soul responding to the God who created it."

Everywhere Ruth goes she meets men and women whose lives have changed because of a crusade. When an earthquake devastated Guatemala in 1976, Ruth and Billy Graham flew there, carrying supplies for the survivors. An hour after their plane had taken off for the trip home, it received a radio communication from a tiny Cessna hundreds of feet below them. The pilot had attended a crusade ten years before and as a result had become a missionary. He was on his way to Guatemala, bringing food and medicine and clothing, to help pull bodies out of the rubble, and to try to nourish the souls and bodies of those who had survived.

The question Ruth Graham is asked most frequently is, "Do they last?" How many of those who come forward night after night, year after year at crusades really begin a study of the Bible and try to follow the teachings of Christ? It is impossible to cite statistics, but one thing is certain—while Billy Graham can deliver the "invitation," he must depend on others to encourage those who have been evangelized. That is why it takes a full year to prepare for a crusade. Counselors have to be trained to talk to people at the crusade. Leaders have to be found to conduct Bible study groups afterward. Local churches must be encouraged to offer various follow-up programs. Ruth corresponds with those who seek her spiritual help, and she prays for the others with all the urgency implied in Chapter Four of Ecclesiastes, verse ten—". . . if they fall, the one will lift up his fellow: but woe to him that is alone when he falleth; for he hath not another to help him up." That verse is particularly meaningful to Ruth because she realizes the new converts have little chance of maintaining their dedication without continuing personal guidance and encouragement to study the Bible.

Ruth does not pray solely for the people who have found

faith through a crusade. Her prayers go out in many directions. She told me that she has prayed for Eldridge Cleaver ever since she read his autobiography, *Soul on Ice*, in which he described how he had raped every white woman he could, because he was so filled with hate and bitterness over the injustice of his life as a black man. Today, Cleaver is a committed Christian. He has been appearing recently at Word of Life rallies, testifying to his deep and growing faith, but Ruth's hope is that he will allow himself a quiet period for spiritual growth, a chance "to get into the scriptures and memorize them." She thinks it is important that he resist pressure from those who want to push him into the limelight, speaking and writing about his faith.

Her concern is based upon experience. "Too often," Ruth says, "we Christians, and that includes those at the crusades, put up a brand-new Christian to share his faith. Shortly afterward, he becomes discouraged or has doubts. It's like a child learning to walk. They fall a lot and you help them up again and little by little they become confident." She is convinced that a quiet growing period is necessary. "Even St. Paul disappeared for several years," she points out, "while he grounded himself in his new faith."

As the wife of an evangelist, Ruth Graham is expected to be ready and willing to offer spiritual advice to those who write to her and to those who seek her out in person. But there are times when Ruth herself is spiritually bereft: she still believes in God, but finds that she can no longer pray easily and spontaneously. These episodes of what she calls "spiritual dryness" always follow very busy periods when she does not have time to study the Bible on a regular basis. "It is just as if Bill and I get so busy and go for several days and don't sit down and have a good talk," she explained. At that moment I realized how much Ruth has sacrificed to the demands of her husband's ministry. There were many years when she could not travel with her husband because of the children, times when weeks and sometimes months would go by without her having the opportunity for "a good talk" with Billy.

I visited the Grahams at their mountaintop home in Montreat in North Carolina a month after the San Diego Crusade. Ruth picked me up at the airport in Asheville after my "puddle-jump" flight from New York, which had made two stops before touching down in Asheville. Montreat is tucked away in the Black Mountains, not an easily accessible crossroads despite the fact that it is the home of one of the most sought-after men in the world.

As we approached the house, Ruth used the radio intercom to let her husband know we were almost there. As soon as she had finished transmitting, Billy came on. "I know," he said. "We've been hearing a very interesting conversation for the last five minutes." The microphone had rolled into a crack between the car seats in such a way that the intercom button was depressed. The result was that no one could reach us and inform us that our chatter was being overheard. It must have been an amusing five minutes. Ruth and I had talked about the weather, the merits of several crusade staff members, and the arthritic problems of a mutual friend which somehow had led to a discussion of hot flashes. When we learned that we had had an audience (the radio is also hooked up to aide T. W. Wilson's house) we laughed so hard that tears rolled out of the corners of my eyes. Ruth was doubled over the wheel and for a few seconds, despite the dizzying curves of the mountain road, she pumped the accelerator wildly because she could not stop laughing. We were still laughing when Ruth drove through the electronically controlled gate for the final climb up the steep, winding road to the house.

The Grahams' house is made of hand-hewn logs from old abandoned cabins. The world of commercialism and cynicism seemed remote in this corner of the Black Mountains. The kitchen is the heart of the house, a large room, its walls and ceilings, like those of all the other rooms, of exposed timber. A fire blazed on the open hearth. A colorful rag rug covered the brick floor and pewter jugs dented with years of use were hung on wooden pegs. It would be hard not to feel at home in the Grahams' kitchen.

But the whole house was equally simple and welcoming. A hall window was filled with glass bottles. When I admired an especially pretty dark blue bottle, Ruth told me it was a Milk of Magnesia bottle minus its label.

The room I liked almost as much as the kitchen was my own, the spare bedroom. It invited a guest to relax, to sleep late—to be at peace. Everything was simple, but designed for a guest's comfort. Ruth kept a coffeemaker on the closet shelf so that guests could have that first cup of coffee in the morning without having to dress and go to the kitchen. There was another braided rag rug on the wide-plank floor. And another fireplace with the logs laid ready for a match. On the chest of drawers beside the bed was a row of books including a history of China, several works by C. S. Lewis, and a *Daily Light*, which contains scripture verses for each day of the year. Surprisingly there was no Bible.

My bed was huge—and high. I had to use a two-step wooden stair to climb in. I hoped that I would not be restless during the night. It would be a hard landing if I were to roll out of bed. Underneath was a trundle bed for the grandchildren. A koala bear and a green stuffed walrus were tucked away in the closet for their visits.

Ruth Graham's parents had settled in Montreat when they returned from China at the beginning of World War II. And because Billy traveled so much, Ruth chose to raise her children in this beautiful and peaceful community. It is the place, Billy says, where he most often finds renewal because he has more time when he is home to study the Bible and to think.

Everything is geared to Billy when he is in Montreat. Ruth refuses to have a firm schedule when Billy is there. "Being married to Bill, I have to hang loose and play it by ear," she told me. And then she laughed, "I tell my friends I have become a very loose woman indeed!" The daily routine was carefully designed around her husband during my visit. On Saturday, we ate our large meal of the day at noon. Ruth and the caretaker's wife, who helps with the housework, did the cooking. But the rest of Saturday and all day Sunday we were completely alone enjoying the peace and privacy that Billy looks forward to so much on the weekends when he is home.

Their house in Montreat offers more than privacy to the Grahams. It offers physical security. They had to move out of the little town up to their mountaintop twenty years ago when it became impossible to cope with the tourists who would walk into the yard, take photographs of the children, even look in the windows. People often arrived at the front door demanding to see Billy and then were extremely unhappy, sometimes quite unpleasant, if, as was often the case, he was not at home. Their present property, which they bought for five dollars an acre, is surrounded by an eleven-foot-high fence, erected at the suggestion of the F.B.I. after the assassination of Martin Luther King, Jr., a time when there was an alarming increase in the number of threats on Billy Graham's life.

Yro, their German-trained German shepherd, is probably even better security than the fence. He is a very large, very powerful animal. I was quite wary of him at first because I could not communicate with him. Yro responds only to German commands. Around Ruth and Billy, however, he was an affectionate and happy house dog. Much too well-trained to beg and whine at the door, he would look at us with mournful eyes whenever he was not allowed to come into the house. Saturday night, when we were eating supper in the kitchen—Ruth's good homemade soup, cheese and crackers—Yro put his nose on the table to survey our meal better. Billy gruffly commanded him to *platz*, lie down, and Yro obeyed meekly.

The fence, the dog and the radio communications setup between car and home are all security precautions urged on the Grahams by concerned friends and staff. The Grahams themselves have a casual attitude toward it all. Ruth, in fact, jokes that her guardian angel is "highly insulted," especially by the fence. She and Billy tend to turn the security measures into toys, just as Yro has become a rather lazy, sleep-by-the-fire pet.

The morning after I arrived, Ruth and I went for a hike. With Yro and a marshmallow fork to protect us against copperheads and rattlesnakes, we climbed up the mountain behind their house. I had to concentrate so hard on the thorny blackberry bushes and the thick "touch-me-not" vines that became entangled around my feet and legs that I did not worry much about snakes. And anyway, Ruth had assured me that we would get a little warning—according to her mountain neighbor, Dad Roberts, snakes smell like cucumbers.

Ruth set a fast pace up an incline that seemed almost perpendicular to me. "Let me know when you want to stop to rest," she said. I was sure she would call a halt before I did, but finally, rather sheepishly, I suggested we sit for a while on a log in an opening that was just "too picturesque" to pass by. The aspens and maples still had their leaves and the thick branches created a private world in which we talked. Here on the mountain, we seemed to be able to see each other more clearly than before and to talk more freely.

I asked Ruth about those times when she had told me she felt separated from God, when the words "my soul cleaveth unto the dust" seemed to be vividly true.

"I think of the time Bill and I were in Lausanne for a conference on World Evangelism," she said. "I was constantly meeting new people. Most of them had asked to see me. They wanted spiritual advice. After a few days, I was exhausted. It became a real ordeal. My ability to pray almost disappeared while I was in Switzerland."

She had not had time for quiet daily study of the Bible for several weeks before the trip. And when she did turn to the Bible again, she said, "I hardly knew where to begin. I felt as dry as a bone. Finally I started to read the Psalms."

It was the One Hundred and Nineteenth Psalm that caught her attention. In her hotel room, she read and reread it from every perspective. She pondered on what the psalmist himself felt—his fears, his temptations, his despairs, his hopes. "My soul melteth for heaviness: strengthen thou me according unto thy word. . . . Teach me, O Lord, the way of thy statutes . . . Give me understanding, and I shall keep thy law . . . Incline my heart unto thy testimonies . . . Behold, I have longed after thy precepts: quicken me in thy righteousness."

And she thought long about what God was saying through the psalm, of His promise of shelter and nourishment. "Thy word is a lamp unto my feet, and a light unto my path." "How sweet are thy words unto my taste! yea, sweeter than honey to my mouth." And finally she thought about what God's word requires of man. "My lips shall utter praise . . . My tongue shall speak of thy word: for all thy commandments are righteousness . . . thy law is my delight." Slowly renewal came and Ruth felt grateful that she could open her Bible, despite the weeks of perfunctory reading, and find encouragement.

Experiences like this have made Ruth eager for others to find God and stay near Him by studying his word. She has long been aware of the urgency of those people seeking answers who have thronged to the crusades, but it is only recently that politicians and the press have discovered that the Evangelical Christians, estimated to number seventy-eight million Americans, are big news—and a potentially powerful political force when united in belief.

That evening both Ruth and Billy spoke of their concern that the present wave of newly "born again," people who have experienced a spiritual renewal, may be exploited by "road-show" ministers who promise miracles, or may be ridiculed by the media.

We were sitting in the kitchen and had pulled our easy chairs close to the fire blazing on the open hearth. I felt very much at home in this isolated log house. It seemed unbelievable that Billy Graham would be leaving Montreat on Monday to pick up the role of a visible public figure, a role that he more and more reluctantly accepts. The uncomplicated desire that Billy and Ruth first shared to proclaim the message of God's love and forgiveness has become inextricably linked to a public image forged in part by Billy's daily newspaper column and his books—almost a book a year. The burden of this public role is made even more complex by the numerous films and publications of the Billy Graham Evangelistic Association. Administrative decisions for the Association are made by an independent board, but ultimately Billy Graham shoulders the responsibility for what is done in his name.

The public relations and publicity that are necessary to proclaim the Gospel to the world are a source of tension in their lives. Twenty years ago at one of the first televised crusades when there was a great deal of interest in Billy and his family, Ruth wrote her parents, "I will be so glad when the press gets all its stories written and the publicity dies down so that we can get on with the message." They both believe that it is the message that is crucially important, not the man who brings the message. He is simply the instrument.

Ruth married a man whose glorious gift she believed was his ability to preach the news of salvation. They both wanted the message to reach as many people as possible. But neither Ruth nor Billy ever dreamed that his ministry would be larger than any man's in the history of Christianity. More than one hundred million people have heard Billy Graham preach. The growth of his ministry seems almost like a miracle to Ruth. As the child of medical missionary parents, she heard her mother and father pray daily to God, asking Him to send them more people to "save," people from beyond the boundaries of the small town of Tsingkiangpu, where they had built a hospital. Today, just three nights of a televised crusade result in more than half a million letters from those who watch and listen and sometimes kneel to pray by their television sets.

I asked Ruth if she had ever dreamed when she met Billy at Wheaton College in Illinois that his career would bring such power and fame. She smiled and answered, "No, I wouldn't have had the nerve to marry him." It was a flip answer, one that I knew she had given before. But Ruth did not stop there. She hesitated, her face became thoughtful and then she said, "God has the wisdom not to let us see ahead."

The couple whose one-week honeymoon at Blowing Rock, North Carolina, had cost seventeen dollars could not have foreseen the pinpricks that come with celebrity, such as the news accounts that imply they lead a rich life with Billy wearing three-hundred-dollar suits. In truth, he is a perfect size 42 long and Ruth buys his clothes at Sears. His newest suit, with two pairs of pants, cost seventy-five dollars. "I tell myself that since Bill is trying to do the Lord's work, it's the Lord's problem to handle the criticism," Ruth said. But it was obvious that the rumors about personal extravagances and hidden bank accounts in Switzerland and South America really hurt. They try to deflate such stories by publishing Dr. Graham's salary every year. It is $39,000. And he accepts no honorariums for speaking.

Billy told me, "I would give almost anything not to be recognized. I would not be on television for anything except God's work." The strain of the quarter century of crusades held all over the world has taken its toll. Billy has never recovered from the New York crusade in 1957 when for sixteen weeks he spoke, sometimes twice a night, to capacity crowds in Madison Square Garden. More than two and a quarter million people attended those meetings. Billy lost thirty-seven pounds. Even harder than the physical strain was the struggle to find the time and the quiet for meditation and studying the Bible so that his sermons would not become mechanical or unthinking. In recent years, although the crusades last only a week, Ruth says, "Bill is totally washed out after each one."

I had not known before that Ruth was concerned about her husband's health. He looks vigorous and strong, but they estimate that he will not have the physical stamina to continue the crusades for more than another six or seven years. He will then have to cut down and adopt a less grueling schedule. High blood pressure haunts him as it haunted his father, who died at age sixty-five. Billy takes medicine to help control the condition and tries to exercise regularly. He jogs a mile in the afternoon, rain or shine, whenever he can manage to find the time. At home in Montreat, he also swims in the small pool that Ruth had built for him a few years ago during one of his long absences. The pool, directly off the bedroom, is very small—four strokes long by two strokes wide—but when Billy returned home and discovered Ruth's surprise, he was provoked and unhappy. She handled the situation with her usual spirited teasing, telling him, "It's cheaper than a funeral."

Saturday afternoon when I saw him come back from his run, looking slim in his bright-red turtleneck and jeans, I never would have believed that he had to watch his health so carefully. He does not appear any older than he did ten years ago—and he is not at all enthusiastic about a grandmotherly image for Ruth. At his insistence, she colors her shoulder-length hair. Ruth is candid about her new look. She laughed as she showed me a snapshot taken outside their house the previous year. Billy is looking down at her hair and saying something. She is laughing.

"Bill is telling me for the tenth time that month that my hair would look a whole lot prettier in the sunshine if it were brown instead of gray." After a little more friendly persuasion, Ruth accepted her husband's suggestion. As I watched the two of them together—the zest of their relationship, the teasing, the quick understanding—I felt sad to think that they face the very real possibility of only a few more years of marriage.

I mentioned this—it is easy to talk to the Grahams about any subject, even their own mortality. Neither of them was troubled by the idea of death. Ruth told me frankly that she is glad that the number of evangelists is increasing every year. "If Bill dropped dead tomorrow, there would be many to take his place." The Grahams accept death. They believe God will call them "home" when He wants them and not a minute earlier.

When Billy does start cutting down, Ruth wants him to give up the crusades and concentrate on television. "You can reach people that way who would never set foot inside a crusade," she says urgently. She believes it is vitally important to reach the greatest number of people possible because "If God does not judge America, He will have to send a letter of apology to Sodom and Gomorrah." She is serious. She is firmly convinced that judgment of the United States has been delayed as long as it has only because Americans have sent so many missionaries around the world.

She is also convinced that more than anything else in life, we need a sense of forgiveness, whether it be for a sin against a friend or an overt crime, because no man is without sin. She smiled as she illustrated her point. "Years ago, Edward R. Murrow visited us to film a segment for his program *Person to Person*. I spent two days cleaning house and getting ready," Ruth said. "Then the television crew came and set up their lights. When they turned them on, it was awful. You have never seen more cobwebs and dust in your life." She ended her story saying, "We think we are pretty good because we have not yet stood in the light of God's glory."

She told another story, a moving one about meeting a young girl named Wendy during a month-long crusade in London. Wendy, a heavy drug user, came to the crusade night after night, but she was still not committed, still searching. Wendy and Ruth had many talks together. One evening before the service began, Ruth told the girl, "One day you will come to something difficult in your life. And then—you will either go back on drugs or go on with Christ."

A few days before the end of the crusade, Ruth was sitting in the stadium at Earls Court when someone passed her a note from Wendy. "I am on drugs," she read. "Come help me." When Ruth found Wendy by the stadium entrance, she was almost unconscious. A girl with her explained that Wendy's best friend had died from an overdose that afternoon. Ruth took a package of Kleenex from her handbag, the only paper she could find, and on its cardboard backing she quickly wrote,

"God loves me.

"Jesus died for me.

"No matter what I've done, if I confess to Him, He will forgive me."

She tucked the cardboard in Wendy's pocket and then one of the crusade staff members took the girl home. A year later, Ruth met Wendy again in London. Wendy asked Ruth about the note she had found in her pocket. She had no recollection whatsoever of having asked Ruth for help, but that message Ruth had left with her had been her lifeline to God, she said.

Ruth believes with all her heart in that simple message she gave Wendy. The act of confession and acceptance of God's love means that no man need suffer the cruel fate of hell. And hell is very real to Ruth. She describes it as "eternal separation from God."

Ruth was the main researcher for Billy's 1953 best seller, *Peace with God*, and she had combed the Bible for definitions of hell. They were frightening—"intense darkness," "rubbish and debris," "place of judgment and suffering." That is why Ruth says with great feeling, "I don't want Bill to be diverted from what God wants him to do. It's so easy to be diverted." And she spoke of there always being cornerstones to be laid, advertising clubs to be addressed and, most of all, politics and politicians.

"Don't advertising men and politicians need the news of salvation?" I asked.

"Bill's job is to reach the greatest number of people possible in the most direct way," she responded. "And the most direct way is a crusade. He should not let the message be obscured by political overtones or by those well-polished jokes speakers tell at luncheons."

Billy reminded her of the time they had a private dinner at the White House in 1964 with President Lyndon Johnson. The President asked Billy who would make a good Vice-Presidential candidate, at which point Ruth was able to give Billy a warning kick under the table in the family dining room, only to have him blurt out, "Why did you kick me?"

Ruth was embarrassed, but not too embarrassed to remind him, "You're supposed to limit your advice to spiritual matters." The conversation ended abruptly. After dessert, Lady Bird and Ruth preceded their husbands out of the dining room, but Ruth heard the President whisper, "Now that they're gone, what do you think?" Billy, perhaps remembering that kick, changed the subject. Politics dies hard.

Lobbying with politicians for spiritual matters is quite acceptable, however. At another dinner in the White House, in 1973 during the visit when Ruth and I had our private talk, she asked my father if there were any way of sending Bibles to all the Americans in foreign prisons. She was especially concerned by news stories about young men and women in foreign hell-holes on drug charges. As a result of her request, the State Department provided the information needed so that the Billy Graham Evangelistic Association could send Bibles to prisons around the world. They are sent in the hope that somehow the Bibles will be delivered to all the prisoners once they arrive.

Billy Graham has ministered to the sick, the poor, the forgotten—and also to the powerful. Every President since World War II has found occasion to call on him, as have many world leaders. Winston Churchill told Graham, "I am without hope for the world." The former Prime Minister was despondent, Billy said, because he believed the world has changed for the worse since he was a boy—with rape and murder, violence and vengeance rampant.

Since Billy Graham has strong ideas about world affairs and especially the course our country is taking I asked the Grahams if it were not a constant temptation for Billy to take an active role in political affairs. He would not be the first minister with a large national following to become involved in politics. Martin Luther King, Jr., had as much political impact as any other figure of the past decades. And despite the traditionalists who believe the primary task of the church is the spiritual salvation of the individual, more and more ministers are seeking public office each year and speaking out on political issues.

I knew that he had been approached several times about running for the Senate and that there were those who would like to see him consider the Presidency.

Ruth Graham, however, is steadfast in her opposition to her husband's involvement in politics. "If he becomes identified with one party or one group, the effort is diminished," she told me. And so Billy, at his wife's urging, has tried to observe a political neutrality.

I realize there are many people who feel that he was not neutral in his relationship with my father during his Presidency.

But the close friendship between our families, which dates from 1950, the year my father was elected to the Senate, made a more "correct" distance virtually impossible. It was largely due to my grandmother, Hannah Nixon, that our families became friends. Nana met Billy Graham in 1947 when he was an unknown minister with Youth of Christ. She remembered him and two years later attended the Los Angeles Crusade, which was his first major evangelical effort. A year or so later, my father and Billy were introduced in the Senate dining room by a Democratic senator. My grandmother was the chief subject of their first brief conversation.

Ruth reminds me of Nana more than any woman I have known, though they are quite different in some ways. Nana was shy and reserved; Ruth is sparkling, and can be outrageously funny. Nana was beautiful only to those who knew and loved her; Ruth is a strikingly attractive woman. It seems incongruous to compare Nana with a woman so strongly associated with public displays of belief. My grandmother was so private in her faith that she took the Biblical injunction "When thou prayest, enter into thy closet, and when thou hast shut thy door, pray to thy Father" literally. Except with her sisters, with whom she used the Quaker thee and thou, she rarely spoke about God. When something important was happening in our lives, Nana would say, "I'll be thinking about you," and we knew she meant "I'll be praying for you." But the reason I link Ruth Graham and my grandmother in my mind is that their faith in God—more important to them than anything else in their lives—had made me want to believe also. And like Nana's, Ruth's faith comes from her Bible.

We talked late that night in front of the kitchen fireplace, until the wood was burned down to white ashes. "Let's end the evening in prayer," Billy said. And Ruth, as lithe and quick as a young girl, slipped to her knees. She rested her elbows on the seat of her chair and bowed her head over clasped hands. Billy prayed for those of immediate concern to the three of us, our families and friends, and he prayed for other people, most of whom we would never know or meet—for the starving, the disillusioned, those in prison. As he repeated the familiar verse, "For I was a stranger, and ye took me not in . . . for I was in prison, and ye visited me not . . ." I realized that this was the first time outside of a church that I had ever prayed for someone in jail. Our petitions seemed so enormous I understood why Ruth had instinctively fallen to her knees.

But no matter how enormous the request, for Ruth Graham prayer is "like talking to your best friend," a friend who is by her side twenty-four hours a day. When I had asked Bunny who her mother's best friend was, she seemed puzzled for a moment. She mentioned several people and then said, "I'm not even sure you can say Mother has a best friend, because she doesn't confide in friends that much. Really, the Lord is her best friend." Then Bunny added, as if she felt she had to explain, "I know that is unusual, because most of us—and that includes me—feel we need a human set of ears we can cry or complain to. Even though the Bible teaches us to trust God and to lean on Him."

Ruth never gets very far away from God. When we talked about relaxing on vacations, she told me that she takes three kinds of books on trips—books to inform, books to relax, and a book to serve as a conversation opener "for when I meet someone on the beach." But she relaxes most easily when she reads a psalm or a chapter from the Bible and then, as she sunbathes, memorizes it.

She has always memorized scripture "for the pure joy of it." Her ability to draw on passages from the Bible has often helped her in moments of crisis. A year ago she fell out of a tree while trying to put up a swing and suffered a concussion. She was in pain and terribly confused about dates and events when she eventually regained consciousness. But her greatest distress was her inability to remember the Bible verses she had spent a lifetime learning. For a week, she prayed, "Lord, I can give up anything—but not my Bible verses." It was more than two weeks after her concussion that somewhere from deep within her mind came the words "Yea, I have loved thee with an everlasting love:

therefore with lovingkindness have I drawn thee." She could
not remember what part of the Bible this verse came from and,
to this day, she cannot remember when or why she learned this
verse from Jeremiah. But as she lay in bed, cherishing these
words that had come to her, she knew a sense of great comfort.
And she prayed. "Thank you, Lord."

Ruth almost always has a pen and an open notebook beside
her when she reads the Bible. Just holding the pen is an act of
faith—faith that there will be something new to learn or a passage that relates to what she is feeling or thinking about. She
records in her notebooks her reactions to the Bible passages she
has studied, and her prayers, too. She puts the date next to every
prayer and dates the answers—some immediate, some years
later—as well. Not all the answers to her prayers are ones that
she originally asked for, but she does not expect to receive everything she asks for. As she told me, quoting the words of the One
Hundred and Sixth Psalm, "He gave them their request; but sent
leanness into their soul."

Ruth has read and reread six Bibles in her lifetime, studying
them until they fell apart from her constant handling. During
my visit, she was busy transferring into her seventh King James
version some of the notations from the Bible she had studied
since 1959. There is a beautiful view of the mountains from the
bedroom, but Ruth's study corner there is arranged so that she
faces the wall when she works. Every existing English translation of the Bible is on a shelf above her desk. The desk itself is
covered with pens, pencils and Ruth's notebooks. I asked her
about a small stone on one corner. It seemed out of place. She
told me that she had picked it up through the fence that separates
Hong Kong from mainland China. It is a constant reminder to
her to pray for people living in the country where she was born.
Ruth would like to return to China, especially to visit her infant
brother's grave, but she has been unable to obtain a visa. She
believes there is a small, but strong, underground Christian
church in China and her greatest comfort is to know that off
North Korea, on Chedujo Island, the Bible is being transmitted

via radio to China. Verses are read at dictation speed so that those listening can copy the scripture and pass it on to others.

Whenever she stops her Bible reading or other work and looks up, the first thing her eyes rest on is a crown of thorns hanging from a nail pounded into the rough log wall. When she was in Jerusalem a few years ago, the Moslem policeman who was acting as her guide cut a branch from a thorny bush beside the dusty road and shaped it into a crown. Ruth believes that Christ's crown of thorns came from the same kind of bush.

Having time to spend in her study corner is a recent luxury for Ruth. When Dr. Graham learned we had been in her work corner, he told me, still starry-eyed in his praise of his wife after thirty-three years together, that for most of their married life Ruth would get up at five in the morning and study her Bible before the children were awake. Ruth, slightly embarrassed, corrected him gently. "Honey, you know how many nights I would be up three to six times with the kids and then I couldn't get up early the next morning." Those days, when all five children were still at home, when she was too tired to get up early and study, she would place her Bible on the kitchen counter and read a verse or two whenever she had a minute. And Bunny remembers going into Ruth's room many times late at night when she was a little girl after waking up from a bad dream and finding her mother on her knees, her elbows resting on the bed, her head bent down in prayer.

I asked Ruth how much time she spends praying every day. She did not answer for a moment, then she said, "It's just a continual conversation. And I'm so glad you don't have to be on your knees to pray. I'd be plain uncomfortable. My knees are knobby."

I understood what she meant by "continual conversation" later on Saturday afternoon when the three of us were sitting on the deck porch off their living room, Billy in a bright sky-blue rocking chair that matched the color of his eyes; Ruth in her favorite unpainted oak rocking chair. She belonged in that chair. Her fresh beauty was as natural as the wood of the chair, burnished from many years of use. Billy read to us from a book on prayer by E. Stanley Jones, Mahatma Gandhi's closest spiritual friend in the Western world. When he finished and we had discussed what he had read—and many other things—Billy offered a short prayer. Ruth bowed her head, but did not get up from her chair to kneel. In the presence of good friends, with the pine-covered valley stretching out below us, it was easy to feel grateful to God. Praying seemed as natural as our conversation had been.

Ruth's approach to her religion is very personal. She is close to God, close to the Bible. "I have learned that there is no keener suffering," she told me, "than to see your children suffer." And she went on to relate this to what God must have felt for his Son on the cross at Calvary. In the same way, she is convinced that "There is no problem a mother faces that Christ does not know already first-hand." Because Joseph is not mentioned after the incident at the temple in Jerusalem, Ruth believes that he died when Jesus was still a boy and that is why Christ postponed his public ministry until his late twenties. Mary needed Him to help care for His seven brothers and sisters. And so, Jesus knew the difficulties and pressures of rearing children—the squabbling, the bruised feelings, the frustrations.

Ruth has her own child-rearing philosophy—based on common sense and the Bible. To her way of thinking, the Book of Proverbs has more wisdom than any book on child care she has ever read.

"How can you do better than 'Train up a child in the way he should go: and when he is old, he will not depart from it'?" she asks.

She trusts God so completely that she can let go of her worries about her children and even resist the natural temptation to cling. If you cannot fulfill your own concept of perfection, she says, why try to make your children fit into a perfect mold. A friend of thirty years told me, "Ruth has cherished the freedom of being herself. She is allowed to be Ruth. And so she does not try to control or mold those she loves." And it is true. She is herself.

Ruth Bell Graham, not only Mrs. Billy Graham. In return, Ruth has allowed her children to be themselves whether their choice was fashion modeling or college dropout. Several of her children told me that they will always be grateful to their parents for never once telling them that "you can't do that or say that, because of the ministry." Not surprisingly, the five children are markedly independent and all three of her daughters made their own decisions about marriage at an early age.

The Grahams' elder son Franklin was the child who most tempted them to intervene. It took Franklin almost seven years to complete four years of college. There were always other things he wanted to do including helping build a hospital in Jerusalem. When he finally finished the two-year college in Montreat, his cousin graduated the same day with honors. But Ruth can laugh as she quotes her son, "I just graduated with relief."

Franklin grew up in the happy environment of the log house on top of the mountain, but he did not have an easy childhood. It may be even more difficult to be a minister's son than the child of a politician. Not only did Franklin have to establish his own identity, but also he faced enormous pressure to resolve his own spiritual questions as if he were a carbon copy of his father. Franklin was the only Graham child who, though he joined the family prayers, was silent about his own beliefs.

Shortly after Franklin was born, Ruth wrote, "Spiritual growth can't be forced without raising a little brood of hypocrites." The children prayed at least once a day with their parents, usually after breakfast. They were never taught specific prayers, but encouraged to "talk to God in their own way." Sunday was the special family day. There was always some kind of shared activity or outing in the afternoon and the children were given treats that were forbidden on other days, like candy or Cokes. It was the Lord's day, a day to rejoice and be grateful.

But Billy was not home most Sundays when the children were young. He was gone at least nine months of the year—in Hong Kong or Nairobi or Chicago. Both the Grahams now feel that his absences were especially difficult for their sons, even though

Ruth was strong and not a coddling or overprotective mother. She encouraged all her children to be independent and nurtured their sense of adventure.

Franklin started "camping out" by himself when he was five. Ruth told me the story of his first night out—on the front porch. In the morning she asked him if he hadn't been worried that the polecat might come around.

"No ma'am," Franklin answered.

"Why not?"

"I had my gun with me."

"Honey, that wasn't a real gun."

"Oh, Mom, the polecat didn't know that!"

The top floor of the house was the children's domain. Billy told me that he never entered any of the children's rooms without an invitation. The second floor was simply off limits for adults except when Ruth made an inspection tour. And that was not often. She is easy-going about house cleaning. During my visit, the Grahams' cat did not make a single appearance all weekend. He does not like Yro and dislikes company even more. Now that the children are gone the cat has claimed their floor as his own. Ruth told me she is fighting a losing battle with the cat hairs. But she did not seem concerned.

In those early years Ruth carried most of the burden of discipline and in retrospect feels that she was not strict enough. She worries that in compensating for the children missing their father so much she loved them "not wisely but too well." But she never hesitated to spank them. She believed the advice offered in Proverbs: "Foolishness is bound in the heart of a child; but the rod of correction shall drive it far from him." Often she would spank two or three times a day, if necessary. Gigi, her eldest daughter, whom Ruth describes as "a real humdinger," came in for the greatest number of spankings. The amount of attention Gigi was getting finally galvanized her five-year-old sister, Bunny, into action. She was naughty for three days in a row. In exasperation, Ruth finally spanked her. Bunny was very pleased with herself. "When you spank me it means you love me," she told Ruth.

Today, Gigi has five children. Recently she worried about how much of her day she spent yelling at her children. She asked her mother, "Why is it that you never screamed at us?" Ruth answered, "You just don't remember, I did all the time." She told Gigi that one night she was terribly discouraged because she had scolded them all day. In exhaustion, she turned to God and prayed, "Please don't let the children remember this." Perhaps her prayer has been answered. Three of the children told me that while they clearly remember the spankings, they have no memory of Ruth constantly screaming.

When the children reached age thirteen or so, Ruth tried to learn to listen rather than reprimand. "I found that sometimes when they shocked me the most, they were just using me as a sounding board." Ruth expressed strong opinions on moral issues only. Long hair, beards, jeans—all were familiar sights around the Graham house and no cause for lectures.

Her trust in her children and in God did not fail her, even with the son who seemed spiritually so far away. After his wedding ceremony held on the lawn at the Graham house, twenty-one-year-old Franklin surprised his parents and friends by announcing that he and his bride had decided to commit their lives to God's service. For Ruth and Billy, it had been a long journey.

Ruth Graham chose to have five children. Both the Grahams are convinced that a mother's job is the "hardest and most important job in the world." Ruth believes that the real liberation mothers need is to be freed from the burden of working outside the home. She does not believe motherhood can be a part-time job. "A mother, like God, must be a very present help in time of trouble," she told me. "Children do not wait until five-thirty in the afternoon to encounter a problem."

"But what about women who have to work?" I asked.

She had a ready answer. "Children are perceptive," she said, "They know if their mother is working for an extra color television or because the family cannot do without the money she earns."

"What about those women who feel they do not have the patience to stay home all day long with small children?"

Ruth unblinkingly said, "I believe one can learn to be patient."

One almost has to be sitting next to Ruth as I was when she expresses these opinions. Otherwise she sounds rigid and, given the aspirations of women today, unrealistic. But when she describes being a mother, she is so earnest. She does not feel she denied herself during the years she spent with her children. She looks at a woman's life as a matter of timing—with different roles at different stages. Today, now that her children are grown, she has time for the poetry, painting and sewing she enjoys. She has the freedom to travel with her husband. As she talked, I was more aware than I had been before that her tanned face, although still youthful, is deeply lined. The lines seemed evidence of the struggle of bearing and almost single-handedly raising five children. But it was a struggle that Ruth clearly gloried in. I sensed no hint of regret.

Ruth feels there is no institution more worth fighting for than the family. The fight is difficult because the parents, two completely different people, must try to function as a single unit. In the words of the Bible, man and wife become "one flesh." Ruth describes marriage as a triangle: God at the top, with husband and wife on the same plane on the bottom. While the husband has certain responsibilities in the home and, in Ruth's view, final authority, and the wife other responsibilities, marriage is not a question of lording it over each other, it is a question of giving in to each other.

Ruth and Billy Graham have not found marriage to be an easy merger. A different culture, a different outlook on the world and different challenges separated Ruth Bell from Billy Graham. She grew up as a missionary's child in China, he on a dairy farm in North Carolina. Only one thing brought them together—their faith in God.

Ruth's childhood was spent in the Chinese village of Tsingkiangpu, where her medical missionary parents had established a three-hundred-and-eighty-bed hospital. From the time she was a baby, Ruth was familiar with death and suffering. She remembers the day she saw a pack of dogs devouring a baby, abandoned because it was a girl. It was a harsh life. There were nights when

Ruth's mother would be awakened by her children's screams of terror—rats were crawling over their beds. Bubonic plague and other diseases were rampant. Death was a very real presence. Not only death from disease. They lived in bandit country and every night some three hundred people were captured—some tortured, some killed. "I don't believe I ever went to sleep without hearing the sound of gunshots," she said. During the conflict between the Japanese and Chinese in the late 1930s, Ruth became accustomed to Japanese bombers flying over the house— so low she could see the bombs in the bomb racks. Today her daughter Gigi says, "Mother just doesn't know what it means to be afraid."

Ruth grew up seeing the people she loved most—her parents and her Chinese nanny—read the Bible daily. The nanny, Wang Nai Nai, who took care of Ruth and her two sisters and brothers, had been a procuress before her conversion. As an old woman she had taught herself to read so that she could read her own Bible. Because Ruth lived among many Chinese like her nurse, whose lives had been changed as a result of their Christian conversion, her faith in God was unlimited, and, until she went away to boarding school in North Korea, untested.

She was only thirteen and so homesick for her family that she cried herself to sleep for three weeks. She felt lost spiritually as well. "I knew Christ had died for the whole world," Ruth told me, "but who was I among so many?" Finally, she was sent to the infirmary. "I lay there in bed and for an entire afternoon I read the Psalms. I just drank them in." Then she turned to the Book of John. In the sixteenth verse of the third chapter she read, "For God so loved the world, that he gave his only begotten Son, that whosoever believeth in him should not perish, but have everlasting life." Hundreds of times before she had read the words or heard her parents recite them, but for the first time she believed they applied to her. She wrote her name next to the verse and claimed it as a truth in her own life.

It is not surprising that what she remembers most about meeting Billy Graham when they were students at Wheaton College is that "he wanted to please God more than any man I'd ever met." Billy had sought Ruth out because he had heard there was a girl on campus so devout she got up at five every morning to pray. When he met Ruth, he learned that the campus gossip was true—give or take an hour depending upon whether or not Ruth had been out on a late date the night before. He also discovered that she was a beautiful girl, with eyes more gold than hazel, long dark lashes, and a good figure. "I fell in love with Ruth the minute I saw her," Billy told me.

But it took a year before Ruth agreed to marry him. The main stumbling block in Billy's courtship was his previous engagement. He had been deeply hurt when the girl he had loved and planned to marry changed her mind at the last minute and decided to marry someone else. He promised himself that he would never kiss a girl again unless he was engaged to her. "I guess I was guarding against getting hurt a second time," he said. But Ruth found his coolness disconcerting. "I wondered what the matter was with him!" she said.

They were married immediately after Ruth graduated. Their early years were a tremendous struggle financially. And then there were all the little differences to contend with. Both learned to appreciate Ruth's favorite saying—"A happy marriage is the union of two forgivers." Billy is consistently punctual; Ruth tries to be. Billy is well-organized; Ruth's desk is a happy disarray of notes and letters. Billy takes naps as a way of lessening the daily pressures of his life; Ruth never naps.

The most difficult adjustment for Ruth in the early years of their marriage was learning to live with a man who had grown up in a family where the women did not take much part in the conversation. "In my family, women were very outspoken," Ruth said. "I had to learn with Bill that when I spoke, I should speak with more wisdom."

"My home life was so different," she added. "We were missionaries so we had to depend upon each other for company. In the evenings we took turns reading through the classics. Bill was more of a country boy."

There was something else about Ruth that Billy would learn later. She not only was used to speaking up and joining in the conversation, but also she had the kind of steely will that enabled her to resist the pressure from his family and friends who insisted that the Graham children be raised as Baptists. "They were not raised as Baptists. Or Presbyterians," Ruth told me. "They were raised as Christians." She was strong enough to keep her own identity, even as Billy was becoming more and more famous and as her life became more and more entwined with the team members who surround her husband. Grady Wilson (the brother of another Graham aide, T. W. Wilson) is Billy's usual traveling companion. He loves to tease. He is also a compulsive organizer. Several years ago when the team was flying from Albuquerque, New Mexico, to Japan for a crusade, Grady announced that he would give everyone a sleeping pill so that they could sleep during the long flight. Ruth, seeing a golden opportunity to tease Grady—and possibly having had enough of being organized—bought some empty pill capsules and filled them with powdered mustard. She substituted her mustard pills for Grady's sleeping pills—warning everyone else of what she had done. The following morning Grady complained he had just spent "the worst night of my life." Despite a double dose of pills, he did not sleep all night. And had heartburn to boot.

Ruth and I were sitting in the living room after lunch on Sunday as she reminisced about her childhood and the early years of her marriage. It was a beautiful room with its hand-hewn log walls, the flowers and greenery from her garden which Ruth had arranged, the view of the mist-covered valley below. We were in front of the fire. It was raining and we needed the fire to take the damp chill off the room. Ruth apologized for the rain, but when I told her that I had always liked the sound of the rain and the feel of it on my face, she smiled and said, "I always associate rain with happy times. When I was little, we would read and play games on rainy days. But Bill hates the rain. It sends his blood pressure up at least ten points. The sun seems to help him." After a moment, she said, "Bill doesn't like it here in Montreat for more than a week or so at a time these days, because it rains so much."

I thought of how much Ruth loved this house where her children had grown up and of all the beauty she had created in it. I realized that Ruth was still making adjustments in her marriage and that even now she was learning to accept her husband's reluctance to live the quiet round-the-hearth retirement life that she perhaps once thought possible. A lifetime of travel, a constant succession of new faces and places, had made it difficult for Billy Graham to settle down peacefully.

We had gone to church that morning in the Presbyterian Chapel in Montreat where the Grahams had been married. In an effort to worship unnoticed, we sat in the last row of the crowded church. The mica in its stone walls gleams as if it were diamonds and gives this chapel, hidden away in the Black Mountains, a romantic beauty. The Grahams are famous now, their lives very different from anything they had dreamed of when they were married in the chapel, but the love between them is still as enduring as the mica in its walls. It was evident from the moment I arrived in Montreat until they drove me to the airport late Sunday afternoon. As we said good-bye, I was glad that the Grahams would have a few hours to themselves before Billy left for his next trip on Monday. They were planning to stop at a McDonald's on the way home for hamburgers and Billy had made an effort to disguise himself with a plaid hat and dark glasses.

Ten years after their wedding, Ruth wrote a poem about her husband. Not about the Billy Graham the public knows, but about the Bill (as she always calls him) she chose to share her life with:

> I met you years ago
> when
> of all the men
> I knew,
> you,

I hero-worshipped
then:
you are my husband now . . .
and from my home—
your arms—
I turn to look
down the long trail of years
to where I met you first
and hero-worshipped,
and I would smile;
. . . I know you better now:
the faults,
the odd preferments,
the differences
that make you *you*.

That other me—
so young,
so far away—
saw you
and hero-worshipped
but never *knew*,
while I,
grown wiser
with the closeness of these years,
hero-worship, too!

I thanked her for showing her poem to me. "I would write the same thing again today," she said.

Ruth's life has revolved around her husband. It is the life she has chosen for herself. Her marriage is based on a perceptive understanding of the limits of the institution and of human nature. Not too long ago, she wrote down her philosophy for her daughters and other women. "Don't expect your husband to be what only Jesus Himself can be. . . . Don't expect him to give you the security, the joy, the peace, the love that only God Himself can give you."

Ruth has practiced this particular preaching all her married life. Her daughter Bunny told me how, during a Christmas visit home a few years ago, she had stormed into her father's room, because she and her husband of a few weeks had had their first big fight. Her father was obviously reluctant to interfere and told Bunny that he really felt helpless when it came to giving advice. "Your mother and I had our differences when we were first married," he said, "but I learned early that she was married to the Lord first."

The truth is that Ruth never intended to marry. When she met Billy, she fell in love, but she still did not want to give up her dream of becoming a missionary like her parents. Years later, she wrote a poem that revealed the depth of her dilemma and how, after prayer, she resolved the problem of her conflicting desires.

> My heart will not give in.
> We gave in,
> My heart and I.

I found it difficult to understand her youthful desire to spend her life as "an old maid missionary or a martyr in Tibet or some frontier country." I was particularly curious about her desire for martyrdom. Ruth, quite openly and seriously, said, "When I was a girl, I was always in awe of those who offered the greatest gift of all, their lives, in their eagerness to serve God." She does not regret, however, her decision to marry. "I have come to realize there are other ways to serve Him, and I understand the words 'the long martyrdom of life' now.

"I couldn't have made it down through the years without the knowledge that the Lord Jesus was with me," she said simply.

She could not have endured the long separations from her husband, the nights she would go to bed with his old, rough sports coat because she missed him so desperately. Nor could she have learned to accept the chronic cough that has beset her for the last fifteen years. It is only recently that the Mayo Clinic arrived at a tentative diagnosis. The doctors there now believe that it is caused by raw nerve endings in her throat. Whatever the cause, the persistent hacking often kept Ruth—and Billy—awake until dawn. Finally she was forced to move into a bedroom which adjoins his. These days she teases Billy—and only half in jest—that the next gossip about the Grahams will be the "real" reason they sleep in separate bedrooms. And her faith has enabled Ruth to accept without bitterness the knowledge that few people will ever understand the strain of being a public person, or understand just how much her husband has given up by not seeing more of his children as they grew to maturity.

How many times over the years did the children kiss their father good-bye as he left on one of his trips? And how many times did they watch Ruth say good-bye to their father? It was always a brief farewell. Ruth would walk quickly out to the car in the driveway with Billy, help him load the last items into the trunk and give him a quick kiss—more of a peck than a kiss, as if any intimacy would make the moment even more difficult. She would go back into the house immediately after Billy had driven off. "Let's look forward to his coming back," she would tell the children, usually adding, "We have to learn to make the least of all that goes and the most of all that comes." And she would immediately begin a major project in preparation for Billy's homecoming—spring cleaning, refinishing furniture and, more often than not, studying something completely new. During one three-month absence, she read all the fiction of Dostoevsky and Tolstoy and their biographies so that she would have something new to share when Billy came home. And always, Ruth read her Bible and wrote poetry. Only in her poems and to God did she confide the moments of loneliness the children never saw.

It is the knowledge that she is a partner in her husband's ministry that has sustained Ruth Graham more than anything else. Her desire to serve God is unquenchable. Like the Biblical Ruth, it is the very essence of her life.

The words of Ruth's most beloved hymn promise, "Thou art coming to a King/Large petitions with thee bring/For His grace and power are such/None can ever ask too much." If, as the

Grahams devoutly believe, the Lord has given Billy the gift of evangelism, Ruth has been given the gift of faith. Like a quiet stream, it runs deliberately and very deep. It is the center of her life. It touches the lives of all those who cross her path.

Charles, Prince of Wales

"The older I get, the more alone I become."

"LET'S RUN down the stairs."

It was the end of the future King of England's first day in the United States, July 16, 1970, and we were at the top of the Washington Monument, the last stop on a sightseeing tour of Washington landmarks by night. The sultry miasma rising from the land that had once been swamp obscured the view and twenty-one-year-old Prince Charles, who had already devoted untold hundreds of hours of his life to monument inspections, turned away from the viewing rail after a courteous few moments and casually made his suggestion.

It was directed to no one in particular; certainly not to the press "pool" of four reporters who hovered near us to record the Prince's impressions of Washington. There was a stunned silence and then weak smiles at the thought of the hot, grimy stairwell only a few feet away. Princess Anne and I exchanged strained glances.

Charles confidently moved toward the door marked Exit. "Let's go," he said. And with that, the Prince of Wales started running down the 555 steps of the monument. My husband David, with the quick reflex action of a good host, was right behind him.

Without a word, the Princess, my sister Tricia and I stepped into the elevator. As we began our descent we could hear them pounding down the stairs. "Let's race them," I said in a weak attempt to enter into the spirit of the occasion. Through the narrow elevator window we caught glimpses of Prince Charles in his expensive suit that looked as if it had been sculpted to his body, his white cuffs gleaming and every strand of his rigidly parted hair still in place, streaking past. He kept pace with us almost all the way down and burst into the lobby seconds after we stepped out of the elevator. David was a full flight of stairs behind him. And then his fortyish equerry David Chequetts, his Scotland Yard detective, and the clutch of Secret Service agents who had fallen in behind the Prince and David came hurtling, red-faced and perspiring, down the last steps.

The agents looked distraught. I knew how meticulously they had surveyed all the monuments we were scheduled to visit that night, located every exit, determined how close the nearest hospital was and the fastest route to it, prepared for all eventualities except one—that our royal visitor would run down the stairs of the Washington Monument.

When we got back into the large black Presidential limousine, I glanced at the Prince. Apart from a slight pink glow, he appeared as cool and well-groomed as he had been before the race down the monument stairs.

The downstairs sprint was not to be forgotten easily. Every time David stepped off a curb, got out of the car or climbed stairs the next day, he winced. I discovered that there were many in the press corps—and in the official party as well—who wondered if the Prince's action was to show he could be unpredictable even in the midst of a rigidly programmed, international goodwill tour. The business of being a "royal" is a very serious business indeed, and the rigidities extend to the most minute details. For instance, each time we used the car during the three-day visit, we were positioned according to the seating chart that had been given us—the Prince on the right, the Princess on the left, Tricia in the middle and David and I on jump seats in front of them.

At times throughout the visit I was embarrassed to find myself in the ranks of royalty-watchers and second-guessers. My sister and I had been the object of a similar kind of scrutiny for several years at that point and we disliked it. We were uncomfortable having our private lives made so public. But Tricia and I could remind each other that our day in the public eye was limited. And the interest in us did not begin to compare with that in Charles. Every act, every opinion, indeed every emotion he had displayed from babyhood was and is and will be analyzed in view of his future as King of England.

For Charles is a prince in a kingdom that no longer needs princes—or kings. He is a media personality in a world so inundated by media personalities that despite all royal caution and precaution, the image of the Prince of Wales is almost inevitably tarnished by association. He has lived with merciless publicity all his life. It is part of his "job" as Prince of Wales, and much of the publicity is palace-authorized in an attempt to satisfy public interest. He must be seen, and his activities described. He must submit to press coverage and at the same time repel as best he can the grosser intrusions into his private life. But he is almost powerless to control the degree of exposure. So great was the interest in one "romance" that ten thousand people descended upon the village of Sandringham and crowded around the little church to see Charles and the young woman he was dating attend Sunday services.

Almost every day of his life Charles has to draw the line mentally on what he will allow to be quoted and what not. He must cope with such questions as, "Do you wear pajamas to bed?" And his very refusal to answer that inquiry became a story in itself. The amount of attention given even the most trivial of his public utterances frequently verges on the ridiculous. When he planted an oak, remarking that he was glad it was not "one of those ghastly spruces," the spruce-lovers of the nation raised their voices in protest. His comments on women's liberation, marriage, political protestors, on anything at all, tend all too often to come back to haunt him. This imposes tremendous pressures. He must always express the "correct" views because, as he has learned, "I'm then held to those views for the rest of my life virtually."

Because of this pressure from the world about him and equal pressure from within himself, Charles has come to tolerate—and probably accept—most of the realities of royal birth, including the periodic rumblings about the high cost of the monarchy. Charles lives in a 115-room mansion on an estate valued at one million pounds. His annual salary is half a million pounds, augmented by revenues from the Duchy of Cornwall that come to more than a million and a quarter pounds a year in addition to the Duchy's traditional payment of two greyhounds, a pound of pepper, a hunting bow, gilt spurs, firewood, a pound of herbs, a gray cloak, one hundred old shillings, a large salmon, and a pair of gloves, all of which are presented with appropriate pageantry each year. With such wealth Charles probably will never be free of the feeling that he is indebted to the public and therefore at their command.

"I am constantly feeling I have to justify myself and my existence," Charles has said. "I must set an example. I must show people I am prepared to do things that they are expected to do." Charles insists that the greatest compliment anyone can pay him is to say, "He's so ordinary." The poignance of this desire reveals a great deal about the young man who, for the rest of his life, must be forever conscious of his public image. Although he protests, "I couldn't care less about my image," the world will make him care. He cannot escape the truth of André Gide's observation that "We make a man become what we think of him."

Many images of Charles had floated through my mind as my mother and Tricia and I prepared for the royal visit. Charles as a solemn infant with sleepy eyes, almost hidden by the satin bows of the fragile, beautifully stitched christening gown with its long train in which generations of royal babies had been christened. Charles at three, dressed for his mother's coronation with a full-lace jabot at his throat. Charles at nine, a wispy figure in a doorway at Buckingham Palace, seeming to wear an eerily gigantic crown—the great chandelier in the reception room beyond. And Charles at nineteen, a dark-haired young man kneeling at his mother's feet at Caernarvon Castle in Wales as he swore, "I, Charles, do become your liege man of earthly worship, and faith and truth I will bear unto you to live and die against all manner of folks."

I found the solemn promise of his vow beautifully moving. As Prince of Wales, Charles has a purpose in life, a mission, a mystical obligation. Viewed in its most creative light, to be Prince of Wales can mean a lifetime of service for others. But it is his destiny, not his choice. And it is a life in which the way people perceive him and his efforts becomes much more important than what he actually accomplishes.

His three-day visit to the United States with his nineteen-year-old sister, Princess Anne, gave Americans an opportunity to see Charles in action, to observe the person who said with refreshing candor, "I used to be shy, but I got over it through the sheer fact of trying."

The visit was designed so he would not "miss anything," and the program that faced him was truly grueling. As the British Embassy kept adding new events, Tricia and I started to question some of the additions. Each time we were assured that "This is something their Royal Highnesses are particularly interested in." In its final form the schedule for the visit included:

A tour of the White House

A helicopter trip to Camp David to have dinner with twenty young people

A nighttime tour of the Washington Monument and the Lincoln and Jefferson Memorials

A ceremonial visit to the House of Representatives and to the Senate

An inspection of the space exhibit at the Smithsonian

A luncheon and boat trip to Mount Vernon followed by a tour of George Washington's home

A dinner dance at the White House for six hundred people

A tour of Georgetown
A tour of the Patuxent Wildlife Center
A baseball game
A visit to the Phillips Art Gallery
Tea at the British Embassy
A private conversation with the President
An intimate dinner—just family—at the White House

And all this within fifty-three hours. This heavy scheduling was not all that unusual, at least not for the British royal family. David's grandfather had commented indignantly on a similar brutal program arranged for Charles' parents thirteen years earlier. "I told Prime Minister Macmillan," President Eisenhower said, "that I would have fired any aide who dared to set up a program like theirs for me." But Prince Charles is forever fated to be in the position of "not missing anything" whenever and wherever he goes on a royal tour. I doubt that he will ever protest, because he is a conscientious person, extremely aware of his royal duties.

I had swallowed the assurances of the British Embassy that Prince Charles and Princess Anne were intensely interested in each scheduled event, even though I myself had been the victim in the past of overly ambitious scheduling. Consequently, my astonishment was painfully real when on the last day of their tour, after the Prince had been taken to observe birds in a wildlife sanctuary and after he had sweltered in ninety-three-degree weather at a baffling and boring baseball game, he whispered with some apprehension as we started our visit to the Phillips Gallery, "We aren't going to have a long tour here, are we?"

Tricia and I particularly had questioned this addition to the program. But we had been told that the Prince of Wales was very fond of the work of the French Impressionists and most eager to see paintings at the Phillips. My suspicions about the Prince's control of his schedule were doubly confirmed later when I came across an interview he had given some months before his visit, in which he had made a point of saying that he had absolutely no interest in baseball nor any particular desire to see a baseball game.

The royal visit became a major media event from the moment it was announced a full month before Charles and Anne were due to arrive in Washington. The press learned, for instance, that no reporters would be allowed to cover his visit with Speaker of the House John McCormack. There would be an opportunity to take photographs, but the writing press would be barred. Speaker McCormack had felt that the Prince would be more at ease in asking questions about the workings of the American government and that both could speak more freely if the press were not recording every word. But his thoughtfulness stirred up a hornet's nest.

At the White House briefing, the journalists told my mother's press secretary, Constance Stuart, "You ought not to put up with that. Little John Monihan [the Speaker's aide who had given notice of this restriction was the target of their anger] making a decision like that is ridiculous. We want to know what the Speaker says to him [Charles] and what he says to the Speaker." As if Constance Stuart, a member of the White House staff, could countermand Speaker McCormack's arrangements.

Because of a combination of the close press scrutiny, the painstaking precision planning that was necessary if the schedule was to work and, most of all, the prerequisite that everyone "have a good time," there was considerable tension before the Prince and Princess arrived. The attention paid to every detail was truly staggering. The British Embassy briefed us, for instance, that Her Royal Highness would wear a hat during the formal welcoming ceremony on the White House lawn, although we were not prepared for her three-quarter-length gloves nor for the soft felt hat that the Prince of Wales, who was dressed entirely in chocolate brown from his shoes to the hat, carried in the ninety-degree heat.

The ceremony that surrounded them—the curtsies, the "Your Royal Highnesses," the "Sirs" and the "Ma'ams" that accompanied every meeting and every conversation—was difficult to adjust to. It was strained for me and many of my friends to address someone our own age so formally as "Your Royal Highness." Fortunately I found that when I wanted to speak to Charles or Anne, I was always able to catch his or her eye, so that I succeeded in sidestepping the problem altogether.

I was not the only one to be slightly ill at ease with all the formality. Even the senior members of the White House domestic staff felt its effect, although many of them remembered Queen Elizabeth's 1957 visit. The third floor, where the six small guest rooms were and where David and I stayed when we visited the White House, was almost spookily quiet during the royal visit. There was none of the customary laughter and chatter in the red-carpeted halls. The staff seemed to be in awe of the Prince's valet and Princess Anne's personal maid, who were staying on the third floor. The Britishers did not mingle with the White House maids and ushers. All their meals were served to them in their own sitting rooms including, as one of the maids told me, with respectful wonder, tea, complete with toast and little cakes and pastries, twice a day.

There was no resentment of their requirements or of the air of decorum that had descended upon the third floor. Quite the opposite. The staff was intensely interested in every aspect of our visitors' lives. One morning the Princess's maid wanted to do some ironing, so the maid on duty excitedly set up the ironing board and even put some fresh flowers in the laundry room for her. The Princess's maid started ironing one of her own dresses. "Aren't you going to iron anything for the Princess?" the White House maid asked. "Oh no," was the reply. "My Princess gives me very little to do." The White House maid, who had thought she was going to watch one of the Princess's dresses being ironed, was crushed.

I felt the royal presence as well. Several times I caught myself starting down the back stairway to the second floor to see my parents or meet the Prince and Princess—and stopped just in time. For the duration of the visit that stairway and the East Hall it opened onto below were British territory. The East Hall's heavy oak sliding doors had been closed to provide a living room for our royal guests. I had to remember to take the elevator at the other end of the hall. It was not a major adjustment, just a reminder that even the White House is not so large that the presence of guests goes unnoticed.

Slightly more unsettling was the fact that the Prince's valet, an older man, very quiet and reserved, and quite tiny, almost like an extremely dignified gnome, was in the bedroom directly across the hall from David and me. In the morning I usually would turn off the alarm clock, roll out of bed, take three steps to the door, fling it open and pick up the newspapers. But after a startled, early-morning eye-to-eye confrontation with the valet, I resorted to the long-arm-around-the-door technique to retrieve the papers.

Prince Charles, despite all the formality with which he was surrounded, always managed to come through as a thoughtful human being, not a royal robot. He had a gift for putting people at ease. In the first few hours of his visit, he charmed twenty of our friends whom we had invited to join us at Camp David for an evening of sports followed by dinner on the terrace. It could have been an awkward occasion since they were all strangers to Charles and Anne, but, in fact, it was almost as if the Prince were the host. He approached everyone with an open friendliness and made an unobtrusive point of talking with each guest. One of our friends, a graduate of a one-room schoolhouse on a Maine island, had been nervous at the prospect of making conversation with the Prince of Wales. But when the two met, the talk was as easy and natural as if they had known each other for years.

The British Embassy had told us that the Prince likes to shoot skeet, so as soon as we arrived at Camp David we bicycled, with Prince Charles leading the way, to the skeet range. The Prince took the first turn and he was so skilled—he did not miss a shot —that no one wanted to follow him.

When we arrived back at the Lodge for supper, we could smell hamburgers and steaks being grilled on the terrace. But Charles took one look at the pool and supper was delayed while he swam a dozen or so laps of the Olympic-size pool in a strong, competent crawl. One girl whispered to me, "I'm used to people being good at some things, but he's good at everything."

Almost an hour later, we sat down to supper on the terrace. It was an informal meal with banana splits for dessert. Charles liked his so much that he asked for a second. By this time we were running very late, and there was still a tour of Washington monuments by night ahead of us. Charles' equerry suggested that we should leave shortly several times, but the Prince did not seem to hear him. Finally the equerry said firmly, "We've got to leave now, Your Royal Highness, or we're going to be too late to keep the schedule." Charles nodded and in minutes we were at the helicopter pad for the trip back to the White House. I think that everyone would have been in favor of canceling this last item on the master plan of events, but the itinerary had been announced and we knew that there would be crowds—and the press—waiting to see Prince Charles and Princess Anne at each stop.

Whatever else they were, Prince Charles and Princess Anne were true professionals as quick-change artists. I had made what I considered a very fast change from slacks to a dress and stockings and David was still putting on his suit jacket as we hurried down the third-floor hall to take the elevator to the second floor. But when the elevator door opened, Prince Charles and Princess Anne were standing there, waiting. Charles was beautifully groomed again, this time in a gray-blue suit, a fresh white handkerchief in his pocket. The Princess's hair was freshly teased higher than ever. Even with a valet and maid to help them, it was an impressive performance.

When we got home well after eleven that night, there was no question of staying up to talk. We were all tired, and the schedule for the next morning called for a nine-thirty departure for Capitol Hill. Tricia, David and I said good-night to our guests on the second floor, where Princess Anne was staying in the Queen's Bedroom suite and Prince Charles in the Lincoln Bedroom.

Normally the Prince and Princess would not have stayed at the

White House, but at Blair House, just one block away, where most important foreign visitors and their aides stay. The house, beautifully decorated with American antiques, is large and consequently there is more privacy—and comfort—for visitors there than in the White House. It is their home and their staff for as long as they are in Washington.

But Queen Elizabeth had sent a personal message to my father through Walter Annenberg, the United States Ambassador to the Court of St. James's. The Queen had asked—quite sentimentally—if her son and daughter could have the same quarters in the White House that she and the Duke of Edinburgh had occupied on their visit to the United States in 1957 and that her mother and father, Queen Elizabeth and King George VI, had occupied in 1939. Of course, the Queen's wish was granted.

I got a glimpse of how strong Charles' sense of history and continuity must be at the arrival ceremony on the South Lawn of the White House when he enthusiastically told my parents and the assembled crowd how much he was looking forward to his stay in the Lincoln Bedroom. "It is a peculiar honor, I think," the Prince said.

Charles, however, could not know that what he called "a peculiar honor" was making my mother quite nervous. He was the first state visitor to use the Lincoln Bedroom since she and my father had been in the White House. It is a rather gloomy room with its heavy, horsehair-covered Victorian furniture. But it does evoke the age of Lincoln and the spirit of the man. There is a copy of the Gettysburg Address in President Lincoln's own hand on the desk. And the eight-foot-one-inch-long bed is the one that Mrs. Lincoln bought for the President more than a century ago, although he never slept in it.

At the time of Prince Charles' visit, I had a feeling that the mattress was almost as old as the bed. It was lumpy and hard, and to me, felt like straw. For at least a year, I had told visitors whom I guided through the White House that it was indeed filled with straw. But when word of this detail of my tour reached the curator, he sent me a short, crisp note advising me formally that the historic bed had a horsehair mattress. My mother was concerned that Prince Charles would be uncomfortable, but since eight-foot-one-inch mattresses are not easy to obtain practically overnight, she had no choice but to leave the old mattress on the bed.

None of us could forget the story of Winston Churchill's stay at the White House during World War II when he was an unhappy occupant of the Lincoln Bedroom. Characteristically, he remedied the situation himself. Near midnight on the first day of his visit, one of the ushers was startled to see the Prime Minister, wearing absolutely nothing but his slippers, a suitcase in each hand, moving himself across the hall to the comforts of the Queen's suite.

The morning after Charles' first night my mother waited anxiously with Tricia, David and me to say hello to the Prince and, she hoped, find out if he had had a good night. As he came down the hall, we all felt relieved. He was swinging his arms briskly as if he were carrying a walking stick. He not only looked rested, but also there was no hint of any morning-after twinges from his run down the Washington Monument only ten hours earlier. Knowing how sore David was, I was amazed Charles showed no signs of stiffness. There was no need to ask his equerry how he felt, however. David Chequetts limped slightly and, no matter how nonchalant he tried to appear, he could not hide his discomfort during the rest of the visit. Charles' first words were to tell my mother what a comfortable night he had had. We were grateful he was such a good sport, but, nevertheless, several months later my mother retired the mattress to the White House archives.

The second day of the visit started off with the ceremonial tours of the House of Representatives and the Senate. After the long, hot climb under the blazing Washington sun to the top of the Capitol steps, escorted and surrounded by officials of the Congress, city police, Capitol police, Secret Service agents and what appeared to be the majority of the Washington press corps, their Royal Highnesses were welcomed by the seventy-nine-year-old Speaker of the House, John McCormack. As he held Princess Anne's arm in grandfatherly fashion, Anne jerked it away, an act that was caught by the television cameras and duly shown on the news later that day.

Charles noticed his sister's annoyance and whispered to her, "It's much easier coming down," trying to reassure her that the ordeal would soon be over and she would be back in the air-conditioned limousine. The limousine became our refuge as the visit wore on. It was a place to talk and relax. We found that we all shared an enthusiasm for movies. We talked about our travel experiences and quite a bit about conservation, in which Charles was very interested.

At times we fell silent. The strain of so many public appearances, so many introductions, so many conversations with strangers took its toll and we were glad for the peace and quiet of the limousine. Charles would ask, "Now where is it we're going next?" We would tell him and then sit there quietly. Someone might make an occasional remark, but most of the time there was a comfortable silence. Shortly before we were due to arrive, Charles often asked who would be there and then he would fall silent again, preparing himself, thinking about the people he was to meet and what he would say. He was hardworking and appeared to be genuinely interested in all the people he met and the places he visited, even when, as in the case of the Phillips Gallery, I knew that his interest was perfunctory.

This was not true of his sister. The young blond Princess was having an increasingly difficult time feigning interest in the city of Washington. Astronaut Neil Armstrong's description of the moon rock on display at the Smithsonian Institution seemed to interest her mildly, but during her visit to the United States Senate, the Princess, who had informed us that she did not like history when she studied it in school, assumed the "Look straight ahead. Notice nothing to left or right, and you'll be liberated sooner" attitude.

She seemed incapable of handling the interest of the media in her first impressions of Washington. When a reporter asked how she liked the Lincoln Memorial, she responded, "I do not give interviews." Thinking her question had been misunderstood, the reporter repeated it. Anne stonily replied, "I do not talk to the press." By the time Anne pulled her arm away from Speaker McCormack, the media were more than ready to publicize her lack of cooperation and report every observed detail of her distaste for her royal obligations.

Princess Anne's transparently indignant reaction to the American press made it obvious that she never before had been exposed to a situation in which the press could actually approach and ask questions. It was also clear that neither she nor her brother had been briefed on how to handle the American press.

Charles gradually and with good humor mastered this new wrinkle in the public relations aspect of being a prince. He did not unbend enough to give the press any human interest quotations or anecdotes, but he smiled frequently. Princess Anne on the other hand, who seemed to be torn between feeling a lack of attention and heartily disliking the informal attitude of the American reporters, became more and more withdrawn and unapproachable.

When the White House staff assembled to meet the Prince and Princess, Anne strode quickly past the maids and ushers and chefs, bestowing brief nods of recognition. But Charles stopped and said a few words to each one. At this moment, Anne was a classic example of the public figure who has reached her limits of tolerance and patience. She was tired of being nice to people whom she barely knew and whom she would never see again. Tired of forced smiles. Tired of being a ceremonial figure.

No matter what her mood, Charles was unfailingly supportive of his sister, calm and cheerful, even though occasionally she openly expressed her impatience with him as well. There were times when he would stop to talk with people and thus delay our departure for a few moments and Anne, by her comments, would let him know that it irritated her to have to wait for him. It was a typical sisterly reaction—and would have gone unnoticed with any other brother and sister. But this was the Prince of Wales, the future King, and this was his sister. And the whole of Washington seemed fascinated by their every expression, word and gesture.

During private moments in the course of the visit, however, the Prince and Princess sought out each other's company. Both mornings they requested breakfast together instead of alone in the private sitting rooms off their bedrooms. But as each hour of their stay passed, I wondered more and more why Charles and his sister had traveled to Washington together. She could not conceal her dislike for playing a supporting role, having more attention showered on her brother than on herself.

It was the Prince who spoke at the official welcome on the South Lawn of the White House. It was the Prince whose views and remarks were listened to almost reverently. It was the Prince who had a long private talk with my father in the Oval Office. And it was the Prince who was the more compelling character. He naturally and gracefully stepped to center stage at every stop, at every event, in every gathering.

After the tour of the Capitol, we were joined by another group of young friends for a cruise down the Potomac River to Mount Vernon on the Presidential yacht *Sequoia*. In the planning stages it had seemed like an inspired idea: a pleasant trip on the water, beautiful scenery, an historic destination, a chance to have lunch outdoors and talk informally with young Americans. In truth, it was a mini-disaster.

It was a hot and muggy day, even muggier on the river, and I have never before or since seen the Potomac a deeper shade of murky brown. Dead fish bobbed on its polluted surface. Twenty minutes before we were due to dock at George Washington's estate, Princess Anne disappeared. Suddenly we spotted her at the wheel of one of the Coast Guard speedboats that were escorting us. Her lady-in-waiting—teased and lacquered hairdo disintegrating in the spray—was huddled in the stern as the boat roared by. The Princess rejoined us at the Mount Vernon dock. She gave no explanation. We asked no questions.

There was a time when I felt the Princess was truly enjoying herself and that was the evening of the ball. The receiving line was headed by Tricia. Charles stood next to her and I stood between Charles and Anne so that I could introduce the guests to her. But many people, in the excitement of meeting the Prince of Wales and his sister, assumed that the girl next to the Prince must be the Princess. Curtsies and "Your Royal Highnesses" were generously bestowed upon me. Anne and I tried to suppress our laughter, but there were times when it was impossible. Finally I said, "We'd better change places." "Oh, no," Anne replied with a devilish smile, "I'm rather enjoying this." And she really was.

I, not Tricia, had the first dance with Prince Charles that evening. There was a reason. My sister was embarrassed by rumors and news stories of a romance between her and Prince Charles, especially since she and Edward Cox, whom she married a year later, were secretly engaged at the time. We thought that if Tricia had the first dance with Charles, it might increase the speculation. So while David danced with Princess Anne, I danced with Prince Charles—at arm's length. He was very pleasant, commented on the music, which was purposely slow and nondescript so that even those who could do only the two-step shuffle would be encouraged to join us on the floor for the first dance. But his attention was elsewhere. He seemed miles away. Actually, very guardedly, he was already looking for someone, somewhere on that crowded dance floor, to have fun with that evening. I hoped he was successful. Everything was so beautiful that night, it seemed as if all the guests, and especially the guest of honor, should have a good time. A tent formed by thousands of tiny glittering lights had been erected over the dance floor on the White House lawn. And one could look up through the lights and see the full July moon in the sky above.

But Charles need not have bothered to scan the pretty faces at the ball. During the third dance of the evening, his partner felt a tap on her shoulder—and suddenly the Prince was dancing with someone who had chosen him. He concealed his astonishment masterfully, but when he came back to where we were sit-

ting he could not resist telling us that it was the first time in his
life a woman had ever asked him to dance. It was not the last.
Charles kept finding his partners switched with the result that
he spent quite a bit of time at our table during the dance. He
would sit there talking to us and, as subtly as possible, crane
his neck as he looked around to choose his next partner. When
he saw someone who attracted him, he would go over and ask
her to dance.

When the midnight buffet supper was served, the Prince
looked up from our table and said, "Your parents are up there.
On that balcony." The White House balcony was dark, but he
had spotted them sitting on porch chairs watching us. They had
given a dinner party for a small group of friends including Washington's "Princess" Alice, the daughter of Theodore Roosevelt.
After dinner, my parents and their guests had come out on the
balcony to watch us dancing in the tent of lights.

It seems to be impossible to spend time with a public figure,
a man who can be expected to be increasingly prominent as the
decades pass, without remembering even the smallest details of
his appearance. I noted that Prince Charles wore a signet ring
on his fourth finger. His dancing shoes were elegant blue velvet
slippers embossed with the golden feathers of his crest as Prince
of Wales. He was always well groomed, as befits someone who
travels with a valet. He is of medium build, has rather long arms
and a soft, melodious voice. And he has very pink cheeks, his
most striking physical characteristic. At our first handshake, I
glanced at him several times in quick succession, I was so struck
by the inverted triangles of vivid pink on each cheekbone, which
were of a velvety texture one might expect on the cheeks of a
three-year-old who has been playing outdoors in the cold. It
looked as if the color had been painted on with a fine-point
brush, but it was completely natural.

I was not the only royalty watcher. Most of our guests studied
him more or less openly and I admired the Prince's serene ob-
liviousness of their scrutiny. I remembered reading about how,
as a fourteen-year-old, Charles and several of his classmates

from Gordonstoun, the Scottish boarding school he attended, had stopped at a small restaurant while they were on a school boat trip. "A lot of people were looking in the windows," young Charles said later, "and I thought 'I can't stand this any more' and went off." As it turned out the nearest place of escape from the noses pressed against the restaurant windows was the adjoining bar—where the Prince ordered a cherry brandy and thereby made headlines around the world. PRINCE CHARLES, A MINOR, ORDERS BRANDY IN BAR.

There had been scores of other excruciating journalistic invasions into his life as an adolescent. It must have been agony for a shy boy to have his academic progress publicized and even endure having his underpants publicly displayed. The latter happened in Australia when he spent six months of his junior year in high school at Timbertop School in the foothills of the Victorian Alps. His laundry was sent out with the rest of the school's—until one day his underpants were put on display in the laundry window. From then on, his weekly washing was done in the seclusion of the school lavatories.

Incidents like these helped to forge the steely self-confidence with which the Prince of Wales faces the world. I only once saw him even slightly disconcerted during his Washington visit. The Royal Family takes it for granted that crowds will gather to watch them launch a ship, plant a tree, or visit an infirmary. But the day of Prince Charles' well-publicized excursion to watch the lackluster Washington Senators play baseball at the Robert F. Kennedy Memorial Stadium, there were only 7,500 fans in the stadium, which can seat 45,000. At the first sight of those sun-scorched rows and rows of empty seats, Charles paled, then he flushed. But as I watched, I saw his attitude change rapidly from shock and disappointment to acceptance. And finally dismissal. He simply focused on other things. I very much doubt that he indulged in any late-night brooding.

It was only on the morning of Charles and Anne's last day in Washington that the source of many of the tensions I had felt during the visit became clear to me, and I began to appreciate the enormous achievement represented by the Prince of Wales' unfailing equanimity, his determined attempts to say a few words to as many people as he could, and his gift for putting people at ease. I also began to understand what lay behind so much of Princess Anne's discomfiture and aloofness during her stay—and to feel a very real sympathy for her.

Tricia and I had been waiting near the Queen's Bedroom for Princess Anne to join us for a tour of Georgetown. Her lady-in-waiting and friend, Lady Mary Dawnay, alerted us that the Princess was almost ready. Then we heard Anne close the door of her bedroom. We stood up and watched her come down the hall, an erect girl in a very short, sleeveless dress and sturdy walking shoes.

Lady Mary, who was at least ten years older than Anne, dropped her knee almost to the floor in a deep, reverent curtsy. In that moment, I realized what it meant to be of royal birth. The Prince and Princess are ever conscious that they are royalty —and they expect obeisance, a constant deference. For three days, I had tried to relate to Charles and Anne as young visitors to our country, as two individuals close to my own age who had experienced some of the same privileges and penalties that come with being a public person. I had closed my eyes to the barrier imposed by royal birth, the barrier that is always maintained between the Royal Family and the rest of the world, scrupulously maintained even with those persons whom they know intimately. In America, Princess Anne must have suffered an abrupt culture shock, thrown into an environment where a careful distance between herself and others was not maintained, where there were few signs of reverence for her position in life.

Prince Charles once said, "I think one can be normal if one starts being an international person right from the word go. There is only a problem when you are thrown into it." After watching Charles and Anne together for three days, it was apparent, however, that the Prince has an idealized view of what being royal means. He assumes that royalty is immune from flattery and not affected by the extraordinary social insulation that is the result of—among other things—traveling with a staff hierarchy, which includes, for example, a lady-in-waiting who, in turn, is attended by a woman with the title "maid to the lady-in-waiting." Charles himself has come to grips with his position in life and has faced it with a good deal of courage and grace. It is a considerable personal achievement. But other royal personages unable to conquer shyness, or perhaps ill at ease or demanding, find it difficult to adjust to the world outside the family circle.

Charles speaks almost mystically about the role of the monarchy. During the cruise on the Potomac, he told us that people have a strong desire for stability and that the monarchy supplies them with an anchor. When one guest suggested that it also filled a "fairy-tale need," Charles did not deny it. At the time he visited Washington, he seemed to believe that political heads of state appealed only to those who had voted for them. He had his belief slightly shaken the Friday morning of his visit when my father dropped in to say hello to the members of the band as they rehearsed for the dance that night. Charles was fascinated by the band leader's reaction and told me how the musician had described the encounter to him. "The President walked out," the band leader had said, "and goddamn—if he didn't shake my hand!" The Prince seemed astounded that members of a rock group could relate to a "conservative."

This did not, of course, shake his conviction that monarchy was a better form of government. Ours, he felt, was a less civilized system. He spoke of the common procedure of asking the President his views on every topic imaginable and the ensuing inevitable criticism of those views. "We aren't subject to that," Charles explained to the group that had gathered around him on the yacht. "Our views don't make a difference to people's everyday lives."

Yet, from reading the newspapers, it is clear that Charles' views on a wide range of subjects are being sought these days. And as for criticism, it has to be a matter of personal opinion which is the more demeaning—a cruel political cartoon of the

President or a newspaper photograph of Princess Anne on the back of a Land Rover at a review of troops with her skirt blown up around her waist and her underwear exposed.

Charles gave me the feeling that he had given more thought to his future marriage than to his future as King Charles or the relevancy of the monarchy in the space age. The night of the ball, the Prince talked briefly about what he wants in a wife. His desire that she come from a family background that "understands" the requirements of royalty narrowly limits his choices. Since that summer evening of the ball, the prospect of marriage has become somewhat of an obsession for the public and thus for Charles. He has no recent examples to follow: A Prince of Wales has not been married since 1863, when Queen Victoria's son Edward married Princess Alexandra of Denmark, the prettiest of the eligible princesses of the era. He does, however, have some clearcut guidelines. The Act of Succession prohibits him from marrying a Roman Catholic, and, as "Defender of the Faith," he would be in an uncomfortable position if he desired to marry a divorced woman.

He seems to have made his own rules. The head must rule the heart, he has said. Falling in love is not enough. His wife must also be his best friend. And his marriage will have to last forever. "Matrimony," he has stated, "is perhaps the biggest step one can take in life. A lot revolves around that decision . . . success or failure."

Success or failure, because the Prince's circle of friends will never be a large one. His wife's companionship will have to fulfill many needs. Charles' satisfaction and happiness in life will come more from the personal life that he and his wife will create within the confines of the royal residences than from the glittering pageantry and increasingly empty responsibilities of kingship.

Success or failure, because there is no room for error. No way out through divorce. His marriage will be subject to the same close scrutiny as everything else in his life. It will be watched closely for cracks and flaws. And it must survive the unusual

strain of constant surveillance by an entourage of live-in servants, secretaries, equerries and ladies-in-waiting.

Success or failure, because Charles has the added pressure of
being expected to produce a child to inherit his throne. And
fatherhood is a role that seems to make the Prince uncomfortable.
He has said that raising children is an "appalling" responsibility,
a demanding job that must be undertaken jointly by mother
and father, because "that is what marriage is all about. Creating
a home."

Charles places so much importance on the family that he finds
it difficult to understand women who believe they have missed
opportunities to fulfill their potential because they have stayed
at home and raised a family. He finds the stridency of the
women's rights movement "uncivilized." And he has little sympathy for or comprehension of the frustrations and inequities that
generated the movement. "There are quite a lot of things women
don't want to do or can't do," he explains, "which men can do
because we happen to be constructed differently in a physical
sense."

The Prince of Wales laments that "men today do not often
think of women as somewhat fragile characters who need caring
for." Charles' view that the women's liberation movement tends
to make men "less gallant" is appropriate for his future role as
king-in-shining-armor, a king who will need a docile, supportive
queen at his side. He is very much the product of upper-class
English society—all-male boarding schools, a predominantly
masculine university environment (women represent only fourteen percent of the enrollment at Cambridge), exclusive men's
clubs and the military. To a great extent he has spent his life in
a masculine world.

He has never known an existence without the constant shadow
of a male detective, and at most times, the presence of an equerry
as well. In fact, Charles says, "I was brought up mostly with
older people." It is a strange statement on the face of it for a boy
who was sent away to boarding school when he was only eight
years old, but the explanation lies in the long school holidays

in the royal household with the more than one hundred members of the Queen's court. His motto as Prince of Wales is *Ich dien* (I serve), but he is surrounded by people who serve him. His great-uncle, the Duke of Windsor, once tried to explain what an equerry was to Will Rogers, only to have Rogers respond, "I guess we have the same animal out in Oklahoma, only we call 'em hired hands." Charles will always have his staff, his equerries and his private secretaries to help him deal with people and circumstances in the outside world.

Because of the detectives, he has never experienced a "normal" degree of freedom, although he cannot be blind to the easier relationships that develop between his friends and the young women they date compared to his own encounters with dancing partners or weekend guests. Being forever protected by a bodyguard means there are very few spontaneous moments in his life. He cannot run out to buy a new record. Or take a walk late at night to clear his head. First of all, he must notify the detective, then allow him time to get his coat, keys, order a car or whatever. There must be occasions when the Prince questions whether the record or the walk is worth the effort.

I wonder if Charles, even though he has had Scotland Yard protection since the day he was born, is able to take for granted the constant presence of another person who—though it is an expected part of his job—may often have to wait for him hours on end in a drafty corridor or a cold car in winter or have to be away from his family on holidays. A President's child is not required to adjust completely to Secret Service surveillance because it is a temporary condition and ends once the term of office is over, so I cannot compare my feelings with those of Prince Charles, but I found that when my father was President I was never free from the realization that my every action involved another person.

The Prince has been aware that he is "different" from the time he was a toddler, but his school years heightened his sense of being apart more than any experience in his life. Charles had to resolve the schizophrenic tension of being a "normal," regular member of his school and then very much a prince on public occasions and within the palace walls. He had memories and experiences which his classmates could not relate to easily. One's early memory at age three of not being able to sleep at night because of the throngs of people who cheered Her Majesty Queen Elizabeth II on her coronation day is not the kind of experience one shares casually with friends.

It was difficult, he said, to make friends at school because the other boys were accused of "sucking up" to him. It is ironic that a prince, the symbol of privilege, must deal with the prejudice of those who make him feel that "I have to show people that I am a reasonable human being." It was the Prince who almost always had to make the effort to make a new friend. Charles has his own definition of true friends. "They are the ones," he says, "who never say anything to anybody about me, although they are always being asked about me and what I'm doing."

It is not surprising that at Cambridge University, Charles' major field of study was history. "I believe strongly one can learn a great deal from history," he said. "It enables us to interpret the present and the future." This may seem a belaboring of the obvious, but for Charles, history was a key to understanding his role and coping with the problems of being a public person for all of his life. "I still think there is an awful lot of rot which is written about people who existed two or three hundred years ago. But they were human beings," he said, "and they had feelings and sensitivities." It is not hard to hear an echo of his adolescent years when his own feelings and sensitivities were most acute and when the news stories and pronouncements about his appearance or his potential must have been embarrassing and often hurtful.

Even in the palace-authorized biography by the man who holds the title of Arundel Herald Extraordinary, the court biographer Dermot Morrah, the Prince of Wales was described as "intellectually rather young for his years." There were similar comments from teachers and friends that he was a "late bloomer," a safe term to use because the same had been said of the young Winston Churchill. It was as if they found it necessary to find excuses for the young Prince with average grades and a pronounced shyness. It can be considered a personal triumph that Charles was finally able to acknowledge, "I may have been slightly late in developing"—and put it all behind him.

Possibly the most revealing public comment Charles has ever made about himself—for anyone who admits loneliness is vulnerable—is "The older I get, the more alone I become." He spoke these words with matter-of-fact acceptance. This is, this will be his life. A life apart. A life of loneliness. And the cruelest form of loneliness may be to feel lonely in a crowd.

I had a small glimpse of how that loneliness pervades almost every facet of his life when Charles visited us in Washington. He is lonely because so rarely can he be honest and candid with others. In the course of three days our conversations were lively and wide-ranging, but superficial. I learned that he played the cello and the trumpet, that he likes to act in private theatricals, that he does watercolors. I learned that he is interested in preserving the natural resources of this planet. But I learned very little about his concerns or personal struggles as an individual or his views on the issues facing his country.

There were many questions that I wanted to ask him. Trivial ones, but ones that might reveal the person. When he spoke of his requirements for a future consort I wanted to ask him more about a statement I had read, in which he was quoted as saying that he would not marry before age thirty. David and I had been married for almost a year. I wondered what he thought about early marriages. I doubted that many of his young friends were married, since Englishmen of the upper classes marry quite late.

I had a dozen questions of this sort, but they went unasked, partly because I knew how difficult it was to be constantly subjected to personal questions, and partly because they seemed inappropriate. I was equally cautious when it came to political issues. Only six weeks earlier, Washington had been the scene of demonstrations against the war by 100,000 people, most of them our age. And there was the surprise victory in England of Edward Heath and the Conservative Party. All these issues existed, but like submerged icebergs, they were invisible and unmentionable in the company of the Prince, because Charles is at liberty to express opinions on a very limited number of topics not only in public but also in private gatherings as well. It is not just a matter of offending some segment of public opinion. He cannot appear to influence issues. Even with friends, he must think before he speaks, weigh whether or not something he says will be leaked.

The Prince of Wales spent an hour and fifteen minutes alone in the Oval Office with my father on the last afternoon of his visit. My father purposely had no aides present, so that the substance of their conversation would remain confidential. When I asked my father six years later about their conversation he told me that he had been impressed by Charles' ". . . extraordinary interest in and understanding of the entire world scene. Not just the problems of his own country. I found that he cared, he cared a great deal," my father said, "about building a world of peace and about the responsibilities that all nations have to try to achieve that goal." He also said that the Prince had been most interested in the problems of the emerging nations, the new African countries.

My father had been surprised by Charles. He found him assured, yet totally lacking in arrogance or self-importance. But he did not give the impression that he was an "ordinary" man. He was very conscious of the duties his birth had placed upon him. My father had not expected him to be so articulate and informed. He was a different person than he had been led to expect from press reports and briefing papers.

I was surprised, because I had spent the better part of three days with Charles and while he was certainly articulate, I had not been aware of great intelligence or an informed grasp of events. But it was different with my father. My father was a head of state. The Prince of Wales could talk to him substantively. The world at large, however, will never witness the Prince's interaction with another world leader nor learn the details of his dealings with his Prime Ministers when he does ascend the throne. Never perceive more than a hint of the depth of the man. Because Charles is almost literally muzzled by the nonpartisan nature of the monarchy.

The inevitable result is that there is little incentive for him to think deeply about political or social issues, for if one thinks deeply, one begins to care about the actions that are taken. Or not taken. He cannot support further nationalization of industry, neither can he oppose it. It is hardly surprising then that when Charles does express an opinion, he tends to sound shallow. He has been forced to become a master of the innocuous generality.

One subject Charles is free to comment on is his ancestry. Of all his ancestors, Charles has stated that King George III is the monarch he most admires. He believes that the King "had a very raw deal through the history books," and his litany of George's virtues—sense of humor, marvelously eccentric, great human being, and English country gentleman, well-liked, comfortable— is a jarring contrast to the more familiar textbook characterizations of this king whose reign was marked by the loss of the American colonies and who was considered by many of his contemporaries to be retarded as a child, neurotic, and ultimately insane as an adult.

Charles' fascination with and sympathy for George III is quite understandable though in light of the theory that the King suffered from porphyria, an hereditary metabolic disease. Two British physicians published a study in 1969 in which they concluded that this disorder in the body chemistry caused George III to experience delusion, hallucination and psychoses. The British doctors believe that porphyria has afflicted four centuries of royalty, beginning with Mary, Queen of Scots.

When Prince Charles visited us in Washington a year after the report was issued, he seemed fascinated by this explanation for George III's depression. The Prince discussed the disease at dinner with my family the evening of his return to England. The subject of the King's depression and madness seemed to spring from nowhere. We were gathered close around the small, dark mahogany table in the family dining room on the second floor of the White House. The only light was the soft glow of candles. The room was pleasantly cool and a fire in the fireplace added to the feeling of intimacy and relaxation. My father had put on a tape of classical music and the tension and fatigue of the visit dropped away as if by magic. There were no more people to meet, no more galleries to tour, no more monuments to admire. That scorchingly hot afternoon at the ball park seemed far away. Within hours, Charles and Anne would be home in their own rooms in their own beds.

Charles seemed to particularly enjoy my mother. He was sitting on her right and I was facing him across the table. They were talking absorbedly when I overheard the word "porphyria," and I listened as he told her about the study and the subsequent new perspective on George III's supposed madness. Ironically, we were literally surrounded by scenes on every inch of the papered walls of British soldiers battling the American revolutionists during George III's reign.

For the first time Charles was speaking to us with feeling. He was acutely aware that the hereditary disease could manifest itself in the present generation—in his sister, his brothers, in himself. The symptoms, including the periods of derangement, do not appear until the victim is adult, and there is no known way as yet of preventing or curing porphyria. As I listened and watched him, so earnest and yet so debonair, I realized that not only his entire life but also his lineage is scrutinized. There are so many eager to compare him to past monarchs and to predict what he is capable of, and what he will become.

From all that the "Charles watchers" in Britain and the world can discern, the Prince is an exceptionally balanced and confident individual. He projects a cool image. His careful, measured approach to life is part of his heritage from his mother, a woman whose face registers few emotions in all the millions of photographs that have been taken of her. His smooth, confident manner is the mark of an individual who has defined the outer reaches of his role as heir apparent with great precision. "The one thing

I cannot afford to do is get left miles behind," he explains. "Likewise you don't want to be too far ahead. You want to be just a little bit behind, but ready to adapt gently and slowly—and in some cases take the initiative."

The job for which he has spent his life preparing may not be his for decades to come. His ability and willingness to adapt may help him in the years ahead. And when he does ascend the throne, his adaptability will enable him to accept a role that has almost no power.

The totality of this lack of power has its ludicrous aspects. If Parliament were to pass a bill for the monarch's execution, the monarch would be forced to sign it—or abdicate. The Prince of Wales has lightheartedly commented, "In company with convicts, lunatics and peers of the realm, I am ineligible to vote." But at the same time he absolutely disagrees with those who say the throne is less powerful today than under Queen Victoria. He defines the monarch's power as an "influence which is unseen, often unfelt by the general public." His definition may remind some of the emperor's new clothes, but Charles has to believe in this power. Without it, his life would be frighteningly empty and purposeless.

He also seems to derive a sense of power from the mystical solemnity with which he invests the monarchy. In his memoirs, the Duke of Windsor vividly portrayed the reverence which is accorded the monarch in his description of the death of his father. Queen Mary was holding her husband's hand. As King George V drew his last breath, she gently withdrew her hand and took the hand of Edward, her eldest son, and kissed it. Prince Charles is heir to that kind of reverence. Much of his power will come from his ability to preserve this spiritual aura.

Prince Charles believes that influence, which is royalty's power, is "in direct ratio to the respect people have for you." Yet how, within the restraints of his princeship, can Charles earn the respect of his subjects? When he took his seat in the House of Lords in 1970, the *London Times* called it "a link to history without any pretense of political significance."

He knows that Britons no longer take the monarchy for granted. Some feel that it is an anachronism, affectionately tolerated at the moment, but nevertheless out of place in today's world. And many of her financially beleaguered subjects view the Queen more as head of a privileged establishment than as head of the country, a view supported by the fact that the palace entourage is drawn exclusively from the upper classes. Charles is eager to counter the criticism. "One has to be far more professional at it [the monarchy], I think, than you ever used to be," he states. For example, he has established a "Prince's Trust," with a committee dispensing the funds, designed to help young people find "adventure, excitement, and satisfaction" by undertaking their own self-help projects. The trust has provided immigrant youth with funds to pay for driving lessons; another group was given enough money to clear an abandoned lot and buy football equipment. Also, by granting occasional magazine, newspaper and television interviews, he is breaking new ground for the Royal Family.

As heir apparent, he has felt the need to justify his existence, but once he ascends the throne, he firmly believes he will be transformed into "one of the strongest factors in the continuance of stable government." He is convinced that Great Britain will never crumble as a nation unless she loses sight of her values and principles and, in his view, the monarchy is the safeguard against such a loss.

Charles is very sure of those values. He does not mind being called square. "I may be square today," he has said, "but not in ten years' time. . . . As far as I'm concerned, I'm going to go on believing to a certain extent in certain things that I consider to be true and right, decent and honorable." This conviction may explain the Prince's serene public face.

But a great many young Britons find the "certain things" he believes in as relevant as the Queen Mother's baroquely flowered hats. When Charles was invested as Prince of Wales in 1969, a fellow student at Cambridge wrote him an open letter: "We should like to have a king who is not afraid to speak out against hypocrisy and inhumanity," he wrote. "No doubt they will want to put you in the British Navy. . . . They will give you a smart blue uniform and a stiff upper lip; we would rather give you a girl, a grin and a purpose in life."

It may be that the future king will yet find a way to personify purpose and service, to win the respect of the younger generation that has inherited the complicated and humbling problems of adjusting from a global power to an island nation dependent upon mutual ties of trade with other countries. Charles and his generation face a crisis of spirit, characterized by an apathy about work and a feeling of helplessness about the economic and social problems that have weakened Great Britain. If Charles could create a new spirit of hope and idealism, encourage an ethic of work and achievement, he might at the same time invest the monarchy with more meaning than it has today.

If the skeptical younger Britons could know the Prince of Wales, they would discover a rare conversationalist, a trivia expert, a good judge of human nature, and a man with a sense of humor that helps him withstand his often tedious ceremonial duties. He has described the image in his mind as he launches a ship—"The champagne bottle hits the bow, tiny cracks appear on the surface of the ship, and two tons precisely and beautifully fall apart."

They might also discover that they had something in common with this Prince who, because he has been "different" from birth, has tried to understand the minds and hearts of "normal" people, just as he tries to strip away false assumptions about himself and asks people to accept him for what he is.

When asked, "Wouldn't you like to be free?" his answer is: "Being free isn't doing what other people like you to do, it's doing what you like to do." In whatever he does, Charles tries to project the image of a young man doing his job. But one cannot resist asking if a young man of his potential should be sentenced to a lifetime of more show than substance.

The Prince is accorded the sustained press, public interest and even homage that is reserved for heroes. It is the kind of attention that touches the celebrities of our television age only fleetingly. Yet the only heroic thing Charles has ever done was to be born a prince: an instant personage. His mother, then heiress presumptive to the throne, gave birth at 9:14 P.M. Three hours later, at a quarter past midnight, the enthusiasm of the celebrating crowds who had gathered in front of Buckingham Palace had to be subdued by police loudspeakers announcing: "The Palace has requested a little quiet, if you please." Yet Elizabeth welcomed the cheers as a sign of tribute to the throne. She was a mother—and a princess. The human symbol—and the mystical. Accessibility—and remoteness.

In almost three days of shared experiences, I never really felt close to Prince Charles. The lack of rapport was not simply due to the famous English reserve. There was something more. He held himself apart. It was the royal barrier. Charles was unspoiled, good-humored, concerned—and yet royal and aloof.

As we shook hands in farewell, he said cordially, "You must come over and visit us soon." But I knew I probably never would have contact with him again except through the lens of a camera or from the viewpoint of a reporter. The media will inform me if he gets a speeding ticket, has a son, or loses his hair.

With the rest of the world, I will watch Charles as he strikes the delicate balance between relating to others as a human being and accepting the fact of his royal birth, which destines him one day to be anointed with holy oil and hailed by the peers of the realm with the cry, "God Save the King! God Save the King! God Save the King!"

Anne Morrow Lindbergh

"Life is a gift, given in trust—like a child."

Anne Lindbergh loved to fly. It put a "glaze over life," she wrote. "There is no crack in the surface." Life was "somehow arrested and frozen into form." Ironically, it must often seem to Anne Lindbergh as if she herself had truly been "arrested and frozen into form," one March night many years ago, frozen into an unwanted and almost inescapable image. The image of a bereaved mother. The woman whose perceptive *Gift from the Sea* has solaced and encouraged generations of other women, whose diaries reveal a keen intellect, an unflinching candor and a tempestuously emotional soul, is still less real to many people than the decades-old image of a bereaved mother.

A year after the kidnapping and murder of her eighteen-month-old son, Charles Augustus Lindbergh, Jr., Anne Lindbergh wrote in her diary, "I think about it all the time—it never stops—I never meet it. It happens every night—every night of my life." She did learn how to meet it, but she has called that facing of truth the most difficult task of her life. The last sentence in her diary entry for that day in 1933, "I will never be through with it," was to be prophetic.

I visited Mrs. Lindbergh at her home in Darien, Connecticut, in the spring and fall of 1976, more than forty-three years after she wrote those words. As we sat in her living room during my second visit, drinking tea and looking out over the peaceful waters of Scott's Cove, I learned how truly she had foreseen the future. We were talking casually about the volume of mail she receives and she had told me how much she dislikes resorting to form letters, yet the hours that she spends on her correspondence eats into the time she wants to devote to her writing. I suggested that she try to ignore as much of the mail as possible for several days at a stretch and then answer it in one concentrated effort.

"But there are always letters I can't ignore," she said, and went over to her desk. She came back with a telegram, a request for her comment on a just-published book which argued that Bruno Richard Hauptmann, the man convicted of the kidnapping and murder of her baby, was innocent. Mrs. Lindbergh read the telegram to me quickly and then put it down on her lap and folded her hands over it. Her eyes were wide, distressed. I did not know what to say. She spoke first, "It just never ends."

She will never escape completely that image of the bereaved mother, but she has been able to overcome it to a great degree because of her intense desire to communicate with others. Communicating has not come easily to Anne Lindbergh. One of her greatest obstacles, she said, is that she has felt "separated" from life. As we talked she returned to the word "separated" again and again.

"I had to break through quite a lot to find myself. It's a perpetual process. I'm still learning."

"What is the barrier? What is it that you find so separating?" I asked.

Mrs. Lindbergh thought for perhaps half a minute before she could find the precise words. Then she answered, "It was a very polite and gentle world I lived in."

Her father, Dwight L. Morrow, was a senior partner of J. P. Morgan, the international bankers. Anne described a life to me that revolved around family. Her brother and two sisters were her playmates and together they invented many of their own games. They wrote poetry and short stories and shared them with one another. They attended private schools. Like many wealthy New York families, the Morrows traveled abroad frequently.

When her father became Ambassador to Mexico in 1927, "a whole new life" opened up for Anne Morrow, the life of diplomacy. But she found when she joined her family in Mexico City during her vacations from Smith College that "even official life is separating." The large garden parties, the teas, luncheons and dinners with a limited group of people and the often superficial conversation seemed to isolate her family and acquaintances from the world.

"Then I married Charles," Anne continued. "This seemed to be real life."

But she had married a hero.

Charles Lindbergh came from a world far removed from that of Anne Morrow. He was a Minnesota farm boy, more interested in cultivating the land and in all things mechanical—especially automobiles and airplanes—than he was in literature or art. His mother, a high-school chemistry teacher, encouraged his technical interests, and his father, who had served in Congress as a Progressive Republican from 1906 to 1917, showed Charles the excitement and adventure of the outdoors, but taught him very little about politics or world affairs. Unlike Anne, who was an honors graduate of Smith, Charles left the University of Wisconsin in 1922 after three semesters to become a barnstorming pilot. In 1926, he was flying mail between St. Louis and Chicago in his own plane. And in 1927, this unknown airmail pilot took off from Roosevelt Field on Long Island on his way to Paris and glory.

Lindbergh's nonstop flight across the Atlantic was already a legend when Anne met him a year later when he stayed with the Morrows at the American Embassy during his goodwill visit to Mexico. From the moment the *Spirit of St. Louis* had landed at Le Bourget in Paris, Charles was the golden young man of America and Europe. He was brave—he had flown alone. He was modest and upright—a refreshing contrast to the cheap commercialism and spiritual emptiness of the Roaring Twenties. The conservative *New York Times* devoted its first five pages to his flight. One hundred thousand school children sang "Hail the Conquering Hero Comes" to welcome him to New York, while a crowd of four and a half million people cheered and pelted him with confetti.

When Anne Morrow married Charles in May of 1929, he was a hero to her as well. What appealed most to Anne as she fell in love with her hero was his "clarity . . . never a false note." But the world would never know the Charles Lindbergh she loved, never see him with clarity. He, too, was trapped in an image—first that of the All-American hero, and later in another image, almost the reverse side of the coin, that of the racist and the man who was "wrong" about World War II.

Marriage did not prove to be the open door into "real life" that Anne had expected. "Fame separates you from life," she told me that afternoon in Darien. When she said this I immediately thought of her description in her book *Hour of Gold, Hour of Lead* of what had happened when she married her hero and became part of the legend herself. "Fame is a kind of death," she had written, "it arrests life around you." I remembered those words because I had agreed with them. It is more difficult for the person in the public eye to communicate with others. You become cautious and circumspect. It dampens your spirit. It is easy to lose one's perspective.

Anne Lindbergh found fame a high price to pay for love and adventure. From the very beginning she disliked being recognized. Shortly after the wedding, she wrote her mother, "I have no patience, no understanding, no sympathy with the people who stare and follow and giggle at us." Neither Anne nor her husband ever learned to accept the public's interest in them.

I had often wondered if Anne Lindbergh had realized how changed her life would be when she married Charles Lindbergh, and if part of Charles' attraction for her was that he was a hero.

The night before my graduation from The Chapin School in New York, there was a party for seniors. As part of the school tradition, each of us filled out a questionnaire about our plans and dreams for the future. What we wanted to do with our lives. Where we would like to live. Did we want to have children? And how many? When one senior protested, saying it was "silly," the headmistress smiled and said, "One day you will be very interested." She went on to tell us that Anne Lindbergh, a member of the class of 1924, had written in response to the question about the kind of man she wanted to marry, "I want to marry a hero."

I remembered this story the first time I saw Mrs. Lindbergh. It was during my senior year at Smith College. She had made a rare visit to her alma mater to speak on the environment. Standing alone on the huge stage facing the two thousand students who had come to hear her, she looked small and lost. It was easy to think of her as the helpless victim of an infamous crime, but once she began to speak, she was forceful and I was captured by her words.

Later that afternoon, David and I had tea with her at the home of the president of the college. Her sister and brother-in-law, Constance and Aubrey Morgan, President and Mrs. Mendenhall, and David and I were waiting around the fireplace in the living room when Anne slipped into the room like a shy schoolgirl. She had changed into a skirt and sweater. Her body was slight, almost fragile. And the slight pull of her lips to one side when she smiled gave her a vulnerable, sweet expression.

We talked for more than an hour, mostly about world population problems. As a woman who had given birth to six children, she was quick to acknowledge a certain irony in her present concern about overpopulation. It would have been easy to underestimate the delicate woman whose head barely reached the top of her wing chair, to overlook the strength beneath her quiet until she spoke. She was self-effacing and gentle, but she gave the impression that she truly wanted to exchange ideas. She listened to others, her face intent as she absorbed their words, and she made her own points without trying to impress or compete, skillfully interjecting fresh ideas, then generously allowing others to expand on them. When we said good-bye, she had dispelled all images. She was not the "wife of an American hero," not a "tragic figure," not a "famous author." She was her own woman, full of ideas and eager to share them with the world, receptive to the thoughts of others.

We met again six years later in Darien. Her simple five-room house reflects the philosophy of Charles Lindbergh's later years, a philosophy Anne shared, of preserving natural beauty and of simple living. There are no traces of her husband now, no photographs or memorabilia of the young flyer. The only photograph, a beautiful scene of a forest at dusk shrouded in mist, was taken by their son-in-law. There is little else in the living room to distract from the beauty of Scott's Cove outside the large picture windows. This isolated stretch of water that opens into Long Island Sound is a sanctuary for geese and swans and other wildlife. It has been a sanctuary for the Lindberghs too. "My husband found it so very, very painful to be stared at, to be recognized," she said. Here on Scott's Cove, they were freer than they had ever been from this recognition.

They built this little house in 1963, the year their daughter Reeve, their youngest child, entered college. In the winter, when the trees are bare, Anne can see their old home only a few hundred yards away at the edge of the cove, a big house with plenty of room for five children and their friends. This house is different—small, tidy, functional. The way Anne lines up her shoes on the bathroom floor is a key to the philosophy of the house—the well-worn tennis shoes, the walking shoes, even her slippers are lined up in a corner, edge touching edge, not a precious inch of space wasted.

The living room serves as study and dining room as well. Anne often eats on a tray in front of the fire or beside the corner window overlooking the cove. Old cardboard cartons and typing-paper boxes, full of letters and other papers, are lined up on her desk, the desk that belonged to her father, and cover the top of the file cabinet beside it.

It was at that desk that Charles Lindbergh helped Anne with the first two volumes of her letters and diaries. He helped put the letters into categories. He read galleys. And he gave her courage —especially when she was working on the difficult second volume that dealt with the kidnapping and death of their son. Some of the Lindbergh children have never been able to force themselves to read that second volume.

In their last years together, when they lived in this small house, they seemed to regain some of the camaraderie of the 1930s when Charles was pilot and Anne his radio operator and navigator and they charted new air routes around the world. But now Anne Lindbergh is alone in the house. Alone she must live with her memories and sort out the images that fame created of her and her husband.

Criticisms of her husband are no more easy to bear now than when he was alive. She cannot bring herself to read the latest biography which repeats the old charges of anti-Semitism and of his distrust of democracy. Her reluctance has nothing to do with cowardice or an avoidance of reality, it is rather that she cannot face what she believes to be a view so distorted that it is unreal. More than that, she cannot skim such a book that puts her own stubborn loyalties into question, because Anne Lindbergh does not approach anything casually. Even when she expresses an idea in an informal conversation, she does so thoughtfully, conscious of every word and its meaning. There were times when answering one of my questions, she still seemed to be thinking about the previous one, her dark blue eyes far away, her body slightly hunched.

We talked about her husband, what he was really like. "He was someone utterly opposed to me," she had confided in her diary when she first met him.

"We were totally different," she told me. "He felt living was more important than writing," but she smiled ruefully and added, "He expressed himself very well when he wrote. Even his crash landing reports when he was an airmail pilot were good."

At first, Anne immersed herself in the world of this man who was so different, the world that seemed to be real life. "I lived adventure," she told me, "but I am not sure I would do all that traveling again." Her comment surprised me, because I had been wedded to the romantic idea of Charles and Anne Lindbergh flying off together, meeting the challenge of long, grueling hours in the air, flying over the Alps, landing their seaplane in the Yangtze River in China. Always together. But in the prefaces to her four volumes of diaries, Anne Lindbergh warns constantly— beware of images; go beyond images; don't freeze someone in your mind; allow people to grow and to change.

I suspect that Charles Lindbergh realized early in their marriage, possibly even before she did, that the "real world" for Anne was her writing. Under his tutelage she had become the first woman to earn a glider pilot's license and she had qualified as a radio operator, yet even as she entered his world, he was encouraging her to write. And his encouragement was not just verbal. He helped her, including drawing the maps, with her first two books, *North to the Orient* and *Listen, the Wind*, which described their round-the-world flights in 1931 and 1933.

Reading her diaries between 1929 and 1939, it becomes clear that she was torn during the first ten years of her marriage between wanting to be part of his world of action and wanting time alone to write. She was angry with herself in 1934 for her reluctance to go on a long trip. "I should be grateful to Charles," she wrote, "for pulling me out of my rut where I would always stay in my timidity if it were not for him." And four years later, as they were about to leave for the Soviet Union, she wrote, "I must go. I must be part of Charles' life."

But she needed freedom, too. Anne and Charles Lindbergh needed different kinds of freedom. Their youngest child, Reeve Lindbergh Brown, says that her father needed the outer freedom to "get up and get going," and her mother needed the inner freedom of time alone to think and write.

Charles Lindbergh's overwhelming energy was matched by his power of concentration. He would sit down and write for three hours after a seven-mile hike. He was an exuberant man, overpraising those he loved ("Your mother is the greatest author of the twentieth century"), and giving his wife and children the feeling that they could do anything. When he was with Anne and their children or with friends, he was frequently the most talkative of the group—in contrast to his taciturnity with the press and strangers.

"My mother was calm and calming," Reeve told me, "although she did not think of herself that way. When my father was away, Mother was not so much a disciplinarian as she was an example." And when Charles Lindbergh came home, he was such a strong and absorbing person that, according to Reeve, "He seemed to demand more oxygen than there was air. He would fill up the house, and they would co-exist."

They co-existed throughout their marriage, because they respected each other so much, despite different working styles, different needs and different ideas. Fame separated them from the rest of the world and they became each other's confidants and best friends. Having to be guarded with casual acquaintances because something might be leaked to the press was one root of their feeling of separateness, especially in the early years. At her husband's suggestion, Anne was even careful about what she said in letters to her family and friends. On her own initiative, she stopped keeping her diaries. But the kidnapping changed that. Three days before the baby's body was found in the woods a few miles from their home, Anne returned to her journal to preserve her sanity.

Public interest in the tragedy was intense. After the baby was stolen from its second-floor bedroom in the Lindbergh's home, the general manager of the United Press stated, "I can't think of any story that would compare with it unless America should enter a war." There was ten weeks of incessant publicity as Charles Lindbergh negotiated with people who claimed—falsely —to have clues. Two years later, there was another six weeks in the spotlight and the private horror of reliving the crime when Hauptmann was brought to trial.

From the time their second son, Jon, was born in August, 1932, five months after the murder of his brother, the Lindbergh family lived under the protection of armed guards whom they hired to shield them from the curious, from the press, and from lunatics. In her diary, Anne revealed just how separated from the world she felt in those years. When she was trying to find a nursery school for Jon, she had "a dread," she wrote, "of sending Jon out into that strange world C and I are in, where we are 'different.' "

Finally, three days before Christmas in 1935, the Lindberghs fled the country. In the secret of night, they boarded a passenger-freighter bound for England—and what they hoped would be a new life. Many Americans could not understand why they left. They had showered Charles Lindbergh with honors and acclaim. They had wept with him and for him. Now they resented losing their hero. But no one, not even Charles Lindbergh, until years later, knew the desperation that Anne expressed in her journal in the weeks before the abrupt decision to leave.

"I must control my mind—I must control my body—I must control my emotions—I must finish the book—I must put up an appearance at least of calm for C . . . but last night lying in bed, shrinking over into my corner, trying not to cry . . . not to wake C, trying not to toss or turn, trying to be like a stone . . . I felt I could understand insanity and physical violence. I could understand anything."

I asked her if she had any regrets about the three and a half years they lived abroad, in England and France. Despite the party atmosphere of our English tea, she left no room for cordiality or discussion in answering. "No, we had to go away. I couldn't have a baby. It was worth it for that."

After a year of relative quiet and peace, her third child, Land, was born in a London hospital in 1937. He was five years younger than his brother Jon.

The kidnapping brought Anne and Charles even closer together, because they lost so much faith in others. But their later grief separated them. They reacted differently to grief.

"Charles entered a totally different and, for him, private world," Anne told me. He studied the effects of high-altitude flying on man with Nobel-Prize winner Dr. Alexis Carrel. "My way out," she told me, was writing in her diaries and completing her first book, *North to the Orient.*

In a rare personal comment, Charles Lindbergh revealed his lifelong attitude toward written expression in his 1941 wartime journal: "I can seldom, if ever, put my deepest feelings into words." And yet the woman he married wrote about everything —even her grief. I shrink when I think of Anne Lindbergh's honesty in recording the daily horrors of the kidnapping and its aftermath. Writing it down made it real. It was no longer possible for her to believe "this isn't really happening to me." It was happening. And at the end of each day she relived it all in her diary. And she cried. But secretly, so that her husband and mother, who were captives of what she has described as the "stoic tradition of hiding grief," would not know.

As the years have passed, Anne Lindbergh has become convinced that expressing emotion is part of facing tragedy. She knows now that the healing would have come faster if she had communicated more of her grief to her husband.

"My parents and their generation," she told me, "were very moral and upright. Yet they were dishonest in being so stoical and not expressing emotion—whether it was about love or death." Not expressing emotion was denying life in a way. It meant that one took on what Anne Lindbergh calls "protective shells." But she rejected such shells. She wanted life. All of life, including the hurt.

Much of the hurt she would face in the years following the kidnapping stemmed from her husband's lingering bitterness toward the press because of their often ghoulish reporting of the crime, and from his obsession with what he regarded as the media's unwillingness to distinguish between his private and public life. "Charles simply could not understand anyone being interested in one's private life," she told me. "He just couldn't bear it," she added, her voice very soft—and sad. Charles Lindbergh came to loathe the intrusions of the press and he lost faith in their ability to report factually what he did and said.

When the American press reported erroneously in 1938 that the Lindberghs planned to rent a house in Berlin owned by an evicted Jew, Anne was terribly upset, but as she recorded in her diary, "C is marvelously untouched by all of it. Their scorn does not touch him any more than their praise once did."

In reality, however, the family, if not Charles, was touched. The press resented Lindbergh's disdain, and they resented even more the stigma of being the cause of his flight abroad. Lindbergh's public opposition to the United States' entry into World War II made him a legitimate subject for criticism for those who disagreed with his position. And because he would not explain what he meant by certain statements or employ the usual political tact in his isolationist speeches, his opponents' attack on him was tragically devastating.

"We are all still reeling from it, though in general the public has forgotten the whole business," says Reeve Lindbergh Brown, who was not even born until after World War II ended. Reeve's awakening came as a teenager. "When I learned that because of my father's war speeches some people saw him as a bigot, I was dumbfounded," she wrote me. "Reading things that were said about him during the war; parents of certain of my friends acting a little oddly toward me; a roommate of one boy I went out with telling my friend, 'Well, I don't mind meeting her, but you'll never get me to shake hands with her father'; and all the time, nothing corresponded to *my* view of my father, so that each experience of this kind was a crazy kind of nightmare."

Charles Lindbergh had experienced a similar nightmare, although on a more limited scale, when his father was hanged in effigy and denounced for his opposition to World War I. It was a strange repeat of history that saw Charles Lindbergh become the most prominent isolationist of his generation.

In 1936 during several trips to Germany arranged by Truman Smith, military attaché of the American Embassy in Berlin, so that Lindbergh could gather intelligence on German aircraft production for the United States, he concluded that America was the only country in the world that could compete with German air power. At the same time, he became convinced that American participation in a European war would be a disaster. Consequently, when the war started in Europe, Lindbergh, for the first time in his life, welcomed the spotlight that followed him because he wanted to use the publicity to warn against the coming danger.

He joined the America First Committee, the most powerful isolationist pressure group, in 1940. And he spoke over and over again at America First rallies warning that if America came to England's aid, the war would be prolonged and lead to a greater devastation of Europe, especially Europe's democracies—and perhaps lead to the loss of freedoms in the United States as well. One of his greatest fears was that America would become a regimented, militaristic society.

Anne Lindbergh aligned herself with the movement against American entry into the war with her book *The Wave of the Future*, published in 1940. It was an emotional appeal from an intellectual who was more of an artist than a politician, an appeal for this country to reform itself, to reaffirm the spirit of sacrifice and democracy. "If we had really lived up to what we believed democracy was, would there ever have been any Nazism?" she asked a few weeks after the book was published.

More than thirty years later, she told me, "I am not at all a political person." I understood that. A politically conscious person would not have written *The Wave of the Future*. At the time she had naively described herself as "an average citizen attempting to state the problem clearly, not to offer a solution." But she was not an average citizen. She was a famous—and vulnerable—personality. Today she acknowledges that those who called her a "confused pacifist" did so "with some justification. I learned slowly, more slowly than most people, that there were worse things than war."

Anne and Charles Lindbergh were caught in a political world where they did not belong. In Anne's world of writing and Charles' world of adventure and science, they fortified and encouraged each other, but in this world of politics, they seemed unable to help each other. Lindbergh allowed his wife to read his speeches, but he rarely accepted her suggestions for change. He seemed blind to the implications of many of his statements.

The only speech Lindbergh gave during his appearances at America First rallies in which he mentioned Jews was in Des Moines, Iowa, on September 11, 1941—less than three months before Pearl Harbor. This speech would cause him to be labeled anti-Semitic, a label that would stick.

Anne told me that when she read the draft of his Des Moines speech, she warned her husband that it would be interpreted as a racist attack, but Lindbergh felt that it was not anti-Semitic, simply the truth as he viewed it. And in Des Moines, he called on the Jews of the United States to stop "agitating for war" and to oppose intervention, because the Jews would be the first to feel the consequences when war came.

"Tolerance is a virtue which depends upon peace and strength," Lindbergh warned. He spoke of the vast Jewish influence in the country, especially in the field of communications, and hoped that the Jews, "a race I admire," would not use their influence to "lead our people to destruction."

"I cannot blame people for misinterpreting," Anne Lindbergh told me. "I can understand why the Jews dislike him. There were many times when I wanted him to change his speeches. There were many things I wish Charles had not said." With great distaste, as if she hated the next thought she had to express, she added, "He was tactless. He made blunders."

Why was Charles Lindbergh so reluctant to compromise and change his speeches? His wife must have asked herself this repeatedly, not only in the weeks of public furor that followed the speech, but also in the years to come. When I asked her why her husband was so implacable in presenting his views, she talked about his childhood. His parents, although they did not divorce, lived apart from the time Charles was five. His father maintained a close relationship with his son, but because of his political career he spent much of his time in Washington. Consequently, Charles Lindbergh became unusally self-sufficient and independent when he was still a boy. He was the only "man" on the farm in Little Falls, Minnesota, where he lived with his mother. Nothing in later life would shake the self-confidence he developed then. When he was thirty-eight, he wrote in his diary, "I never trust logical conclusions unless they combine with an inner intuitive feeling, which I find to be really much more reliable. Unless I have this feeling I know with almost complete certainty that my logical reasoning is wrong."

"Charles was not bothered by criticism," Mrs. Lindbergh explained, "because he listened to himself." But in analyzing this truth about her husband, turning it over and over in her mind, Anne Lindbergh characteristically sees that there is another side. She admired her husband's self-confidence and self-awareness, she said. Yet she realized that because of these qualities, when he became convinced he was right, he did not care what others thought. The result was a kind of pride that blinded his perceptions.

Anne Lindbergh never dreamed that one day she would decide to publish her diaries, but the time came when this intensely private woman chose to bare her thoughts and reactions to the years of fame and tragedy—the years from her courtship to the outbreak of World War II; the years which led the Lindberghs, because of their move to Europe and subsequent friendships with pacifists like Lady Astor, to formulate their stand against intervention. She has exposed their naïveté and their idealism. The reader sees the Lindberghs, bright-eyed and enthusiastic, on their trip to Germany to assess Nazi air power; reads of their distress at the reactions of those members of the American press and public who misunderstood the trip; winces at their shortsightedness in not responding to the criticism and failing to explain that the mission was undertaken to provide the United States with needed military intelligence.

In the preface to her prewar diaries, Anne Lindbergh makes an uncharacteristically harsh statement. She claims that she and her husband became the "scapegoats for a generation of failed hopes for peace," when the United States finally entered the war after

Pearl Harbor. Just as she is able to see the light and dark sides of her husband's self-confidence, so she can see the positive and negative aspects of hero worship.

"There is tremendous hero worship and devil-baiting in this country," she told me during my second visit with her in Darien. "Devil-baiting is the other side of the coin of hero worship. But that kind of attitude is immature, because one abdicates a sense of responsibility. Something or someone becomes all good or all evil.

"Lots of people were against the war. It makes one despair," she said in obvious frustration, "not knowing how to make people aware of the circumstances, the facts of the controversy." But when I asked if she planned to publish her diaries covering the America First years, she shook her head. "Probably not," she said.

Anne Lindbergh, who is so consumed by the need for honest relations between people and for honest written expression, finds those years and that controversy particularly painful. There is something beyond pain though that prevents her from publishing those diaries: her loyalty to her husband. She is unwilling to air the disagreements she and her husband may have had on the wording of some of his speeches, or on his hasty reaction to Franklin Roosevelt's attack on his patriotism (Charles resigned his commission in the air reserves), or on his refusal to communicate with the media.

A few months before her husband died, a book entitled *Charles Lindbergh and the Battle Against American Intervention in World War II* was published. "It has taken thirty years for a book like this to be published," Mrs. Lindbergh said. "The author doesn't agree with my husband's stands, but he does not question his integrity." She referred to the book in checking a date for me, and I noticed there were at least twenty bits of paper in it, marking various passages. "It is the first objective historical account," she said. "I am grateful that my husband could read it before he died."

The matter of integrity is important to Anne Lindbergh. She

insists that her husband abhorred prejudice of any kind, including racial prejudice. She does not ask that people agree with him on everything he said or did, but simply that they do not question his integrity. But she is not a woman to spend her life tilting at windmills. She will not pursue the battle for her husband's honor until her own death. Her only part in the battle now is to hope for perspective. The final assessment of Charles Lindbergh's role before and during World War II is out of her hands and in the hands of historians.

She wrote a letter to me six weeks after my father's resignation which reveals something of her philosophy of dealing with controversy. "I feel I must say one thing to you. I hope you will remember always that you are and will be far into the future, a living witness for your father whether or not you are a speaking witness—just as I feel that our children are and will be living witnesses for my husband, long after his death and mine." She and her children need not take up the gauntlet at each challenge. Facing life and living it in the light of what they have learned from Charles Lindbergh is all that is required. All that matters.

The years have taught Anne Lindbergh to accept the concept of the "living witness" and to believe that perspective may come. But it was difficult for her to live through the months after Pearl Harbor. Charles Lindbergh's opposition to the war was not easily forgotten. Thirteen days after the attack on Pearl Harbor, he tried to enlist in the Army Air Corps, but Secretary of War Stimson refused to give him a commission. After that his civilian services were turned down by Pan American, United Aircraft and Curtiss-Wright. Finally, Lindbergh went to work for Henry Ford. Since the bombers Ford was turning out at the huge Willow Run plant were desperately needed, he had no fears that he would lose any government contracts by hiring Charles Lindbergh. The Lindberghs moved to Detroit in 1942.

Anne Lindbergh felt the effects of their prewar political stand in a different but equally harsh way. The critical reaction to *The Wave of the Future* shook her confidence as a writer. One of the questions uppermost in my mind had been why there was such a long gap between her 1944 novel, *The Steep Ascent,* and her best-selling *Gift from the Sea,* published in 1955. I said I assumed that it was because of the demands of raising five children, but Mrs. Lindbergh's answer was unexpected.

"Yes," she said, "I was busy with the children, but also I was very upset. So upset that I did not want to go on writing." *The Wave of the Future,* which she had thought of as her "confession of faith," had been branded pro-Nazi by many critics, even though she had called the Communists and Nazis "scum riding the waves of the future." Looking back, Anne sees her book as "a pacifist document, and I can understand why it was misinterpreted because it was not a clear document," she told me. "But my reaction at the time was that if I expressed myself so poorly, I should not continue writing."

She explained that while *The Steep Ascent* was published in 1944, she had written most of it before 1939, before *The Wave of the Future.* She described it as a "fictional account of an actual incident" in her own life. It is a sensitively written story of a woman who comes close to death on a flight across the Alps and, in the moment of greatest danger, rediscovers the joys of life. "In a way," she told me, "you would say it was a comeback book." Although she was still hurt by her failure to communicate in *The Wave of the Future,* she had wanted to prove to herself that she still could write. But the reviews were indifferent and the sales were disappointing. It would be another decade before she decided to publish again.

And so she turned to a different art—and a different group of people. While Charles Lindbergh tested bombers at high altitudes, she became involved with the professors and students at Cranbrook Academy of Art, where she studied sculpture. "It was wordless. It gave me another vision," she said. And she made lasting friends there, some of whom she still sees.

The years immediately after the war, she told me, were the most difficult of their marriage. Her husband had spent the last year of the war in the Pacific, testing fighter planes and flying over fifty combat missions. When peace came, like hundreds of thousands of other men, he had to adjust abruptly to civilian life. No longer was he living the high-intensity existence of sacrifice, adventure and duty. No longer was he poised close to death. And Anne had her own adjustments to make when they left Detroit and moved to Connecticut. She missed the stimulation of the artist colony at Cranbrook and her friends there.

They saw very few people in Connecticut. "My husband was very unsocial, really," Anne said. And he began to travel a great deal—alone. With five children ranging in age from one to thirteen, Anne was needed at home. "It was not easy when he was gone, but when he returned he brought a stimulus to the marriage," she said. "In those years I was learning to be a person on my own but it's a hard process."

We talked about marriage and the seemingly unavoidable mistake of expecting more of the one you love than of others, expecting them to meet your needs effortlessly, to share your goals. Reflecting on her own relationship, she told me, "I learned that the partners bring different things to a marriage." She believes that one must accept the loved one just as he is and that the pain two people experience and the mistakes they make when their lives are enmeshed are not defeats or failures to be erased and forgotten. "Only two real people can meet," she wrote in *Dearly Beloved*, more than thirty years after her wedding day. "It had taken years to strip away the illusions, the poses, the pretenses . . . and this was why . . . you could never regret the past, call it a waste or wipe it out."

She wrote most eloquently about honesty in relationships and of what she had learned in her own search for independence in *Gift from the Sea*. It was an immediate success. It spoke to millions of women. Her editors had been worried that it would not sell. They thought a livelier title might help and suggested the well-known quotation from Thoreau "The mass of men lead lives of quiet desperation." Anne Lindbergh agreed that her book does have a note of desperation, but she rejected the suggestion. *Gift from the Sea* is more than a chronicle of search and of occasional discouragement. Anne Lindbergh writes of the patience and faith in oneself that are required in the journey toward independence. She stressed independence because "we are all in the last analysis alone."

She argued that in order to be more complete and whole, men should learn to develop personal relationships and become more inward-looking, women should become more self-sufficient, and both learn to accept impermanence—in relationships with friends, with children, even in marriage. First love is not forever. There comes a time when one fails to note that "this is our fourteenth-month anniversary." A man and a woman move apart because of different needs.

Anne Lindbergh stresses the need for "lightness of touch" with those one loves. The phrase is part of the skillful web of images she has woven to describe love and marriage. But I have found that the "fluidity," the "evolution" and especially the "lightness of touch" she speaks of repeatedly often do not fit the realities of marriage.

"Can you really achieve lightness of touch in marriage?" I asked her.

"No, no, of course you can't," she answered eagerly, sympathetically. She thought for a moment and added, speaking more slowly, "Perhaps you shouldn't. Because you love and you care deeply."

Ever honest and willing to have someone question even a cherished concept, Anne Lindbergh agreed that lightness of touch was not always possible. Perhaps what she was trying to express with this phrase is better stated in her poem *Even.*

> Him that I love, I wish to be
> free . . .
> Even from me.

There is a small gray building in the back yard of her house in Darien that looks out of place. It is Anne Lindbergh's writing retreat, an old toolshed that she and her husband found years ago on Route 1. When the Lindberghs moved to Darien, Anne had no quiet place where she could write and think with five children in the house. The toolshed became her haven and an important part of her own journey toward independence.

It is here that she worked on *Gift from the Sea.* Driftwood that Anne picked up on the beach decorates the crossbeams of the little house. There is one long shelf of books, most of them full of bits of paper marking various sections, and above the shelf hangs a cross of unusually beautiful cork, another treasure from the sea. Mexican pottery and three small Indian rugs add color to the otherwise austere room. Her desk faces the wall. She can see the cove that she loves only when she leans back in her chair. I was surprised by the size of her desk. No more than two or three books and a sheet of paper can be spread out on it, but a small basket filled with pencils, every one of them worn down almost to the eraser, was evidence that it was a working area.

She seemed quiet, a bit wistful when she showed me her little house. There was a hot plate with a kettle on it and a curtained-off corner with a wash basin and toilet so that she could spend the entire day in her studio if she desired, but from the cobwebs and the film of dust over everything, including the top of the desk, it was clear that she had not been working there lately. When I asked her why, she replied that there had been just too many requests, too many details of her husband's estate to attend to, and plans for his posthumous "Book of Values" that demanded her attention. She had not been able to snatch more than fifteen or twenty minutes a day for herself. Not enough time to write. She had not even written in her diary for more than three months.

It was not until I had left Darien that I realized Anne Lindbergh does not need the little toolshed any more. There are no children at home in need of attention. No household pressures. No need to juggle her roles as mother, wife and writer. The small gray building serves no real purpose—except as a symbol of her journey toward independence—now that she is alone.

Charles Lindbergh died of lymphatic cancer in August, 1974, at their home in Maui, Hawaii. He had not been well since the autumn of 1973, but the doctors did not diagnose his illness as cancer until the following July. He prepared for his death naturally and calmly, with the precision and courage with which he undertook the dangerous pioneering flights of his youth. Eight days before he died, he asked to be flown to Maui. Once there, he put his personal papers in order, made arrangements for his coffin, and planned what he would wear for burial. "He was so human and natural about it," their daughter Reeve told me. "I was never prouder of him than in his death."

Anne Lindbergh did not want to talk about those last days in Hawaii, but she did tell me that she hopes eventually to write about widowhood and about "our unwillingness to face death, to meet it."

She is meeting it now. Meeting it every day as she drinks from the dark blue china mug with "Charles" on it. She meets it at night by reading philosophy. A favorite book is *How I Believe* by Catholic theologian Pierre Teilhard de Chardin. "I always carry books with me. I have to have them to get to sleep," she said. And she needs them because she is now embarked on "the final lesson of learning to be independent—widowhood." She told me that "it is the hardest lesson of all." It is the lesson of learning how to see and do familiar things without the familiar person by your side to react, to laugh with, to listen.

Anne Lindbergh and I took a walk across an open field near her house, a walk she and her husband took so often together, a walk she now takes by herself almost every afternoon. It was spring, almost summer, and just a few days before her seventieth birthday. She seemed young, however, in her pink blouse and wrap-around skirt and tennis shoes—field glasses slung around her neck to observe the birds. We followed a track across the field toward the trees and then a path through the woods that led to a small pond.

Despite the many times that she has walked through this field and along these paths, there was nothing ordinary about them to Anne Lindbergh. She pointed out each new growth, each change in color. Her scruffy-looking cairn terrier and a neighbor's German shepherd kept us company, racing ahead as if the field were an exciting new adventure for them as well.

The walk evoked memories of her husband and emotions that Anne Lindbergh wanted to share. "It is very difficult—so very difficult to be alone," she told me. As she said this, she seemed very self-contained, certainly not a fragile flower that could not survive if uprooted. And so I was slightly startled when she confided in a low voice, "I still feel married." She added quickly, "I feel marriage goes on. I don't say this in some Ouija-board sense, but in the way you approach things, see things, always aware of how your husband would approach them, see them." She spoke earnestly as if asking, "You *do* understand what I mean?"

The Lindberghs shared a delight in the beauty of nature and found it no matter where they lived—the New Jersey countryside, an island off the coast of Brittany, in Paris and in Detroit. "Invisible things (of nature) speak to him, cry out, as people's emotions do to me," Anne wrote in her diary a few years after they were married. "It is quite exciting and he teaches me to see."

That walk, even without Charles Lindbergh, was a release for Anne. For as long as she can remember, nature has comforted her. I asked her why. The question seemed to surprise her. After a moment she answered carefully, "I find the cycle of nature very comforting—death in winter, rebirth in spring." When she was depressed, she said, "I would go outside and sometimes just walk around and around and say, 'Just what is it that you love? New grass? A bird?' Even in college I would go off alone and sit on a stump and think."

A few days after our walk, Anne Lindbergh wrote me, "There were so many unfinished threads." She wanted me to know that nature is a constant flow in her life, not a resource to be drawn upon only when disheartened. "I do like to go out and sit under a tree," she wrote, "or on an overturned boat with my bird glasses. A moment of quiet before the day starts—to pray—to feel myself one with nature before the inevitable desk work and telephone calls. It helps me to decide which are the most important things to do that day. (And I do it in the evening as well, if I can, which helps me to accept the things I have not done!)"

Her relationship with her husband makes me think of the words to a song by Simon and Garfunkel—"The only truth I know is you." His death must leave an awful void in her life. Although she had spent years learning to be independent and seems to be facing widowhood squarely now, for most of her marriage and perhaps even to the end, the practical, purposeful aspects of life were centered in her husband. In a sense, Charles Lindbergh was the strongest grip she had on life. And she knew this. Ten years after they were married, she wrote that only her husband's "technical ability and the children fit me into this world." Her world was one of poetry and ideas. When one reads her diaries, she often seems not to be a creature of this world. She is too sensitive, too poetic, too caught up in search of what she has described as "different planes of existence . . . *La vie triviale, la vie tragique.*"

Her husband recognized this other-world quality in Anne. In his journals he described the birth of their fifth child. During labor, Anne had propped up on her bedside table a postcard reproduction of a centuries-old American Indian sculpture, a wooden deer head with seashell eyes. The postcard represented something to Anne "that is beyond life and beyond this world in a sense, just as Anne holds that same element herself," Charles wrote. "She uses it as a bridge and on it crosses into a world beyond our own—a world to which she belongs more than anyone I have ever known. Anne always seems to me to stand on life and, at the same time, touch something beyond it. Yet her ability to touch beyond does not cause her to relinquish life any more than her ability to live restricts the unlimited travels of her spirit."

She loved flying because from the air she felt outside of life. Magically, she could look in. And writing gave her similar power. She was alone, guiding her pen across a piece of paper. In control.

Her fears made it difficult for Anne Lindbergh to fit into this world. Something irreplaceable had been torn from her—her firstborn—and she feared loving too much, feared the unknown. The candor of her prose and poetry, her openness even about her fight against depression, is extraordinary—a vivid contrast to her apparent fear of interviewers and her reluctance to express her thoughts to them, as if only she could interpret her private world to the larger world outside.

She still needs time in her private world. When I visited her she mentioned that she cannot write, cannot think if she is inundated with visitors and telephone calls. She is incapable of working on correspondence with her part-time secretary unless she has had time beforehand to think about each letter and mull an answer over in her mind.

All her life she has fought an almost abnormal shyness, the kind that "can freeze your face and tongue, paralyze the muscles in your jaw, paralyze your limbs, too, so that you cannot walk into a room or speak or even smile." I had the feeling that she was still fighting that shyness, although she seems to genuinely enjoy contact with others. When she told me about the pioneer surveying flights with her husband in the first years of their marriage, one of the adjustments she mentioned having to make was, "I liked different things. I liked people. I was terribly interested in the people in those faraway places." Yet there were many times when she liked people, but liked her own world more.

During that terrible year of testing when she had to deal with the anguish caused by the Hauptmann trial as well as that caused by the death of her older sister Elisabeth, she wrote, "I realize I avoid people because people mean so much to me. They throw me off keel so easily." And she was married to a man who avoided contact with most people. Anne Lindbergh could easily have become reclusive and withdrawn into her own world. But she broke through her fears and shyness because, despite her fragile sensitivity, she wanted to "live consciously."

Reeve Lindbergh Brown by chance captured a vignette of her mother in a movie she was taking of her first child. It was not until Reeve viewed the developed film that she realized what a revealing and beautiful moment she had recorded. Reeve and her husband had been spending a few days with her parents at Scott's Cove. It was the end of the day, a cool fall evening. Reeve filmed her little girl playing with her grandfather. Then Charles Lindbergh, bundled up in a lumber jacket against the chill, started to walk toward the woods. He was a solitary figure, his head down. Reeve could not help thinking that her father seemed old and slightly stooped. She knew he was ill, but she could not know that this was the last year of his life.

Almost out of film, Reeve decided to finish the roll with a few scenes of Scott's Cove in the sunset. She found her mother standing at the water's edge throwing handfuls of cracked corn to the birds. Reeve simply let the film run until there was no more. In those moments as she filmed, she was acutely conscious of all the worries burdening her mother—the pain of seeing her husband's strength and spirit weakened by illness, the dismay and impotence she felt over a soon-to-be-published biography that would reinforce the old anti-democratic and pro-Nazi image of her husband.

"All these things were going on in her life," Reeve said, "and yet she was there, feeding the birds—always nourishing others, yet always alone and private. I wanted to help her, to say something. But I realized that although she was very much alone, there was something wonderful about her aloneness. It was not the aloneness of being wounded or not being able to communicate or touch others. But aloneness in the sense of being all right and intact.

"She always meets life. She faces everything. Even now I cry when I watch that film."

Reeve's portrait of her mother in the midst of pain, still able to give and to nourish, helped me understand more fully a theme that runs through Anne Lindbergh's writings: you have to let go of life and it is given back to you. "Life is a gift, given in trust—like a child." This perception of life as a gift has made it precious to Anne Lindbergh. It has given her the courage to try to live as the heroine of *The Steep Ascent*—"Not to be hurried, not to be afraid, not to be imprisoned in one's self. To be open, aware, vulnerable—even to fear, even to pain, even to death." And not to be imprisoned by images or futile battles against them.

When Anne Lindbergh drove me to the train station after my last visit with her, we sat in her brown Pinto station wagon as we waited the remaining few minutes for my 4:40 train back to New York City. We were talking about Charles Lindbergh and his most recent biographer's assessment of him as a totalitarian because of his views on World War II. "One must wait for perspective," she said. "They say it will come eventually, but I am not sure."

She spoke matter of factly, almost without expression. I felt that she could face the probability that her perception of her husband would never be widely shared. We spoke briefly of my own father and the question of perspective on his life. There was much more I wanted to say, but the train was coming into the station. I had to cross the parking area and go up the stairs to the platform. There was only time to say good-bye.

I wanted to give her a quick hug, but I did not. Even at that moment, she was very much a controlled, private person, a person of strength. So instead, I took her hand and squeezed it.

On the way back to New York as I went over my notes and filled in the gaps, I reread a letter Reeve had written me about her mother's adjustment to widowhood. "She weathers everything and comes out whole," she had written, "she is the strongest person I know. We all worry about her constantly but she is, in fact, invincible." As I read those words, I was especially glad that despite Anne's eleven years of publishing silence, she had weathered that battle as well. Grateful, too, that she had softened her 1936 judgment that "writing is taking . . . and not giving."

I knew she had spoken recently at the commencement of her eldest grandchild and had told the graduates that when she was in college, she had confided to a friend, "To me the most exciting thing in life is communication," and that looking back over her life, she still believed those words. Her belief enabled Anne Lindbergh to overcome her fears and the restricting images that prohibited growth. It enabled her to resist withdrawing too much into her other world.

There is a Benedictine monastery a few hours' drive from Darien. Anne and Charles Lindbergh first went there several years ago to attend a seminar on conservation. They returned for other visits. Now Anne occasionally makes the journey alone. She likes to go, because "I have no image there . . . I am a naked soul." Her words did not surprise me. The monastery offers privacy for a sensitive woman who values above all else honesty and truth.

And perhaps its peace strengthens her so that she can continue to give her children not happiness, for that is impossible, but clues to life—the clues she wrote about in *Dearly Beloved:* "A thread of perception, a crack of light, a key to the open door." For her children, for me, and for many of those who have read her books, these gifts have been sufficient.

Mao Tse-tung

"Ten thousand years is too long. Seize the day! Seize the hour!"

O N N E W Y E A R ' S E V E, 1975, my husband and I watched the clock pass twelve in the presence of Chairman Mao Tse-tung, the revolutionary leader of China's 800 million people. This was to be the last New Year of his life.* It was one of the most extraordinary moments of ours.

We sat in Mao's study, deep within the Forbidden City where he dwelt, as he had once told André Malraux, "alone with the masses." The Chairman was no remote, godlike figure, but an old man, his body humbled by illness, but still alert, unselfconscious and seemingly eager to talk with us. There were times that midnight when it was difficult to remember that this frail, elderly man, who enjoyed his interpreter's gentle teasing, had once been the young revolutionist who had exhorted his comrades to "trample the beds of rich men's daughters."

We were the second to last Americans to visit Mao Tse-tung. Our visit came about through an odd combination of circumstances, more by chance than by plan. In September of 1975, a friend of ours from the 1968 Presidential campaign days wrote

* Both the Chinese New Year, which falls in February, and the Western New Year are observed in the People's Republic of China. *The People's Daily*, the country's daily newspaper, customarily ran a full-page portrait of Chairman Mao on January 1 to mark the holiday.

from Peking, where he was visiting American Ambassador George Bush, about the four weeks he had just spent traveling in China. He reported that so many of the people he had met had mentioned my father's 1972 trip and his initiative in establishing relations with the People's Republic that he was certain the Chinese would welcome a visit from us.

It was out of the question, of course. But David would have three weeks off between his law school semesters at the end of the year, and the more we thought about the outlandish idea of taking those three weeks to fly 7,500 miles in the dead of winter to a country we had never dreamed of visiting, the more tempting it became. A week later I called my father in San Clemente and asked if he could help us obtain a visa by getting in touch with Ambassador Huang-chen, the head of the Chinese Liaison Office in Washington. I knew the Ambassador had paid a friendship call on my father only a month earlier. Less than twenty-four hours later, David and I received an invitation to visit China as the personal guests of the Ambassador.

The rest of that fall was busy, taken up with work, law school and several visits to the Chinese Liaison Office to arrange the details of our trip—where we would go, what we should see. We requested the opportunity to deliver personally letters of greeting from my father to Chairman Mao and, if his health permitted, Premier Chou En-lai, whom we had heard was suffering from cancer. We were told that all our inquiries were being forwarded to Peking. The officials at the Liaison Office in Washington were very correct and maintained a strict posture of reticence about our itinerary. Right up to the moment of our departure we were uncertain of where we would be going and what we would see—or whom we would meet.

In early December, soon after President Ford's return from Peking, the Chinese had inquired whether we had any objections to "meeting our leaders alone"—meaning without any members of the American Mission in Peking being present. This was a hint that our trip was regarded as more than a simple courtesy extended to us in acknowledgement of my father's 1972 initiative, but at the time we attached no significance to it, since we were going to China as private citizens and had had no contact with the State Department.

Not until we actually landed in Peking at one in the morning of December 29 did we suspect that there was a greater interest in our visit (and a greater power behind it) than that of the anonymous officials of the Chinese Foreign Ministry. As our plane taxied to a stop, we looked out the window and saw six or seven people walking toward the plane. It looked like a greeting party. I was surprised that so many people would come out to the airport at one in the morning. It was a bitterly cold night and they were all so bundled up that I could not tell if they were men or women. But as we came down the steps, I recognized Nancy Tang. She had appeared in many photographs of my father's trip to China three years earlier. Nancy was Mao's personal interpreter. Ambassador Huang-chen was there, too. He and his wife had flown from Washington to Peking earlier that month.

After brief introductions, the Ambassador escorted us to a luxurious government guesthouse instead of to a hotel as we had expected. I knew that only people on official business were honored with guesthouse accommodations. And ours were truly magnificent. The guesthouse was the former Austro-Hungarian Embassy, a columned mansion with bullet holes in the walls from the Boxer Rebellion—and bathrooms larger than the kitchen in our Washington apartment.

It was now clear to David and me that our trip was destined to be far from routine. But we still did not dream that forty-six hours after our arrival we would be summoned for a private visit with Chairman Mao Tse-tung.

"We don't want you to be alone on New Year's Eve," Ambassador and Madame Huang-chen had said as they invited us to a small dinner party in our honor in the guesthouse. Despite the Chinese custom of dining early, our New Year's Eve dinner did not start until nine. It was leisurely, and we lingered at the table until I was afraid that I would fall asleep. At eleven, explaining how tired I was, I ended the evening.

Ten minutes later, when we were back in our bedroom, there

was a knock at the door. Already in my nightgown, I hid behind the wardrobe while David went to see who it was. The Protocol Officer excitedly announced, "Chairman Mao would like to see you." It did not seem necessary to ask how soon the car would arrive. I changed as quickly as I could back into the dress I had worn to dinner, and as I put it on I was very grateful to my mother. David and I had spent Christmas at San Clemente and as I was packing for our trip to China, my mother asked if I had a long-sleeved dress to wear in the evening. "You need one," she said. "The Chinese dress very modestly." I had nothing suitable, so she let me borrow one of her dresses—a dark flowered print, long and very soft, one of those dresses you can roll up in a ball in the bottom of your suitcase and not have to worry about wrinkles. I remember looking for my watch so I could note the exact time of our meeting, and as we left our room, I carefully carried the manila envelope containing the letter from my father to Chairman Mao.

The night was freezing cold as David and I were driven through Peking, alone in the back seat of a black Chinese-made limousine very much like a Rolls-Royce. We were enclosed in the heavy tank-like car by a cocoon of black net curtains that covered all the windows except the driver's windshield. The only vehicles on the streets, apart from Ambassador Huang-chen's limousine, which followed us, were horse-drawn wooden carts filled with farm produce, and some military jeeps and trucks. We rode in silence through the labyrinth of streets in the old part of Peking. No lights shone in the dark and as we passed mile after mile of walled city, we were acutely aware of being very much on our own, cut off from everything familiar.

At a checkpoint, guarded by People's Liberation Army soldiers, the car swung through a gate into the Forbidden City. Suddenly out of the black, a huge, brilliantly lighted billboard loomed up in front of us. In Chairman Mao's calligraphy, it bore his injunction "Serve the people." We swerved left almost immediately onto the winding lakeside road that led to Mao's house. Later, when I saw a Chinese newsreel of our visit, I realized that the billboard was brightly lighted so that the television cameras could film the arrival of our car. The front of the Chairman's house was also lighted for television. The abrupt change from the darkness we had been driving through to the glare of the high-intensity lights almost blinded me. I was able to discern only the bare outline of the modest, one-story house we were entering.

But it was not only the late hour and the sudden burst of blinding light that disoriented me. It was also the strangeness of being in an alien world and my awe that we were about to meet the leader whom millions of people considered more god than man.

We realized later that there had been clues to our midnight visit, clues that we had failed to pick up. One of the Ambassador's aides had been called to the telephone four separate times during the dinner party earlier. And the night before, the Vice Foreign Minister had remarked rather pointedly, "I understand you want to meet our leaders." Then, too, the schedule of that day, our third in China, had read, "Evening of December 31, OPEN."

A single attendant, dressed in a Mao suit like all the other Chinese officials we met, opened the door. He took our coats and those of Ambassador Huang-chen and the Foreign Minister. There was no conversation. Another man came forward to welcome us formally to Mao's private home. I recognized him. He was China's Chief of Protocol, who had escorted us to our meeting with the Foreign Minister the day before. Now he hurriedly ushered us from the small reception area into a dark room, just large enough for the Ping-Pong table and three or four wooden chairs we could distinguish in the gloom. A door at the other end of the room opened onto a lighted room beyond.

We walked quickly through the dark Ping-Pong room, and, as we crossed the threshold into the light, I saw Mao Tse-tung. He was sunk into an enormous, slipcovered easy chair, one of six identical chairs arranged in a semicircle in his study. My first impression was of a tired old man with vacant eyes, his jaw slack.

The Chairman struggled to his feet with the help of two young women dressed alike in gray Mao suits. Once on his feet, he tottered for a moment, and then the women stepped back and he stood alone. I sensed a stir behind us. A television cameraman and an assistant holding lights had slipped into the room. The cameraman photographed the Chairman as he leaned forward and gave first me, and then David, a firm handshake. Then they were gone as quickly and silently as they had appeared.

The Chief of Protocol motioned for me to sit next to the Chairman. I sat well forward in the huge chair. If I had sat back, my feet would have been several inches off the floor. After two days of intensive, non-stop lectures from workers, soldiers, peasants, Party members and Foreign Ministry officials, I expected similar homilies from Chairman Mao. Consequently, while his attendants were helping him back into his chair, I relaxed and looked around the stark room. There was no luxury here—floor-to-ceiling shelves filled with loose-leaf books and scrolls, strange six-foot-high lamps with high-intensity bulbs for television, wooden tables between the armchairs with cylinder-shaped tins of Panda cigarettes (Mao had the reputation of being a chain-smoker, but he did not smoke during our visit), delicate porcelain cups of green tea, and small lacquered trays containing rolled-up washcloths—warm and wet—to wipe our fingers. Beneath each table, a white spittoon. I had discovered the day before that spitting was a socially acceptable custom when we met with a high official and, right in the middle of a sentence, he cleared his throat and used the spittoon between my chair and his.

Once Mao was settled into his chair, I found it difficult to look closely at him. Despite my eagerness to meet the Chairman, now that we were actually in his presence I felt it was somehow an intrusion to see him this way. His jaw hanging down—obviously the result of a stroke—gave him a vacant look. His yellow skin seemed almost translucent. It had a waxlike texture and was almost totally unlined. His immaculate Mao suit, gray just like those of his attendants, hung loosely on his body. His long arms and large hands seemed dead weights dangling at his sides. And when he spoke, the sounds emerged as grunts—harsh, primitive, labored.

Talking with Mrs. Meir in her retirement office in Ramat Aviv, one day after the third anniversary of the Yom-Kippur War, the war which caused Golda to say "I will never again be the same person . . ." I.P.P.A. LTD.

Clara Stern's favorite photograph of her famous sister.
REGINALD DAVIS

Israel's first woman Prime Minister is greeted by my father at the North
Portico of the White House in 1973. "She never wanted to be treated like
a woman, but like a leader," he told me.

Ruth and Billy Graham in Hong Kong in 1975, the closest point Ruth has been to mainland China since she left the land of her birth in 1937 to attend Wheaton College in Illinois. At Wheaton she met a fellow student named Billy Graham.

Ruth reading in the window seat of the big log cabin house in Montreat, North Carolina, she and Billy built in 1956. From the window Ruth has a view of the Blue Ridge. RUSS BUSBY

Motorcycling is one of Ruth Graham's favorite pastimes. Here she gets a lesson from her son Franklin's friend and his little boy.

The Grahams outside their house in Montreat. "Bill," Ruth said, "is telling me for the tenth time that month that my hair would look a whole lot prettier in the sunshine if it were brown instead of gray."

Anne Morrow Lindbergh at work in her writing studio, an old toolshed the Lindberghs found on Route 1 not far from their home in Darien, Connecticut. RICHARD BROWN

Anne with her youngest child, Reeve, and her granddaughter. Reeve told me, "We all worry about her constantly but she is, in fact, invincible."
RICHARD BROWN

Ike and Mamie in the yard of their son's home on their golden wedding anniversary, July 1, 1966. BRADFORD BACHRACH

Mamie, my mother and I on the inaugural platform shortly before my father took the oath of office for his second term. Behind us, left to right, Attorney General Richard Kleindienst, Secretary of the Treasury George Shultz and Secretary of State William Rogers. WHITE HOUSE PHOTO

My family in front of the White House on Inauguration Day, January 20, 1973. Since David was on Naval duty in the Mediterranean, Mamie told everyone, "I'm playing David." WHITE HOUSE PHOTO

Mamie and I celebrating her birthday, November 14, 1974, at a small inn in Gettysburg. The photograph was taken by one of her Secret Service agents.

A proud moment: Mamie christens the 95,000-ton aircraft carrier named in honor of her husband. UPI

The highlight of the three-day visit to Washington of 20-year-old Prince Charles and his 19-year-old sister Anne was the ball at the White House for 600 young people. WHITE HOUSE PHOTO

We danced on a platform erected on the South Lawn of the White House under a "tent" of thousands of tiny electric lights, and a full July moon.
WHITE HOUSE PHOTO

In sweltering 90-degree weather we tried to explain baseball to Prince Charles and Princess Anne.

A less than gregarious moment on board the Presidential yacht Sequoia *as we journeyed down the Potomac River to Mount Vernon for a tour of George Washington's estate. David and I are at the left; the Princess is second from right.*

At two minutes to midnight on New Year's Eve 1975 we met Chairman
Mao at his home deep within the Forbidden City. His niece Wang Hai-jung
watches as David grasps the Chairman's hand.

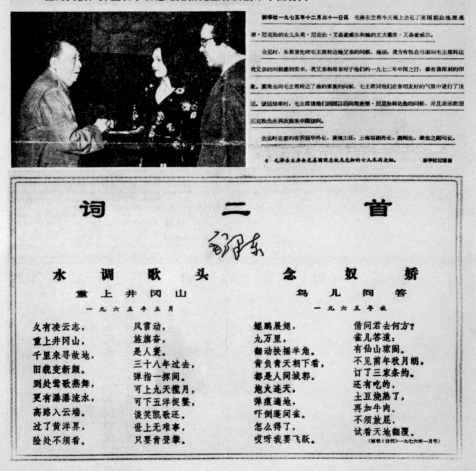

The People's Daily on New Year's Day 1976. Below the photograph of the Chairman greeting us are two poems by Mao in which he exhorts his people to continue the revolution and resist Soviet revisionism.

Dozens of smiling Chinese students were studying posters denouncing the Minister of Education when we visited Tsinghua University in Peking.

I took my father's letter out of the manila envelope that I had been carrying and gave it to Mao. He handed it to Nancy Tang, his interpreter, and she immediately set to work translating it for the Chairman.

During the three days she had spent with us since meeting us at the airport, we had found Brooklyn-born Nancy Tang to be a pleasant companion—and an unyielding Maoist. She had lived in New York until she was six years old, but she dismissed the United States as a country that "expects people to accept their lot in life." Nancy's hair was severely bobbed and she wore steel-rimmed glasses, but she looked young and seemed completely at ease as she sat next to the Chairman. When she translated Mao's words to us, she frequently consulted with the other two interpreters, who sat behind her on straight-backed chairs, to determine exactly what the Chairman had said. His speech was evidently unclear from time to time. After each quick conference, she would repeat Mao's words back to him before translating them for us. If she had not conveyed his thought precisely, Mao would grunt corrections and tap his fingers on Nancy's notebook. The interplay between Nancy and Mao was bantering at moments. She seemed almost playful as she submitted to his corrections. I sensed a hint of coquetry. There was a warm rapport between the aged revolutionary and his thirty-two-year-old interpreter, striking in this purposely and starkly asexual society.

It was not until my father's letter had been translated that I realized how very much in control and mentally alert Chairman Mao really was. He seemed pleased by my father's personal message and said very emphatically, "Mr. Nixon is welcome in China." (A month later my parents would meet with Mao Tse-tung in the Forbidden City.) Then he took my father's letter from Nancy's hand and, to my astonishment, distinctly and precisely read the date at the top of the letter, "December 23, 1975," out loud in English. It was an effective way of telling us that his physical handicap had not affected his mental agility.

Mao informed me that the chair I was sitting in was the same one my father had used during his visit almost four years earlier. I told the Chairman I would like to switch places with David so he could say that he too had occupied an historic seat. As we made the quick change, Mao laughed heartily. Then he asked, "How is Mr. Nixon's leg?" David launched into a description of the effects of phlebitis. When I saw that Mao was looking straight ahead and not at David or me, I uneasily thought that David might be telling the Chairman more than he wanted to know. But as our visit progressed, I discovered that he rarely looked in our direction, but instead concentrated his attention on the interpreters.

It was an extremely warm and friendly meeting. I showed the Chairman that I was wearing a small pin bearing his profile that the Ambassador's wife had given me. Though Mao had seen literally millions of men and women wearing similar tin medals, he reacted with a childlike delight and impulsively clasped my hand.

Mao had an unexpected gentleness—perhaps because of his age and the humbling dependence on others for basic needs which comes with illness. He did not posture. He spoke self-deprecatingly about a poem on struggle which would be published to mark the New Year. "It is nothing," he said, "I wrote it in 1965."

I found it impossible not to compare his attitude with that of other all-powerful dictators I had met. I thought especially of Brezhnev, who often spoke in a conspiratorial, melodramatic whisper so that his audience had to hang on to every word. Brezhnev enjoyed clapping his hands while people laughed and smiled on cue. And visiting Greece's Papadapoulos had seemed almost like a parody of an old movie. He received us, seated behind a huge fortress-like desk, in a room sixty by thirty feet. Visitors were given low chairs to assure they would listen in an attitude of proper respect. In contrast, within the Forbidden City, Mao and Nancy interacted as grandfather and granddaughter. Ambassador Huang-chen appeared relaxed and gazed casually around the room. I was surprised when he did not lean forward in his chair to catch every word the Chairman spoke.

Mao Tse-tung was the first person we had met in China who

dropped the pretense that the People's Republic is a utopian, perfect society. He actually sounded skeptical, almost disappointed in his people, especially the young. "Young people are soft," he said to us. "They have to be reminded of the need for struggle." At this he became animated, like a young man, for the first time during our visit. Vigorously, he jabbed his forefingers together to emphasize the need for struggle. Struggle was more than just a word for Mao, it was the underlying principle of his philosophy. "There will be struggle in the Party. There will be struggle between the classes. Nothing is certain except struggle," he told us.

Then suddenly he asked, "What do you think?"

His question was so unexpected that both David and I hesitated. Then we spoke at the same moment. "I agree . . ." Our voices were hollow echoes of each other. There was a silence as Mao waited for us to say more. Finally he spoke again, "It is quite possible the struggle will last for two or three hundred years."

It was very moving to witness the effort of this old man as he spoke of struggle. A whole country turned to the little red book of Mao's quotations whenever they felt in need of strength. But, I wondered to whom and to what did the Chairman turn in moments of doubt.

I was surprised that he made no effort to hide how keenly he sensed his mortality. When he spoke of the future, he spoke of a future out of his control. I remembered that he had once rated the chance of permanent success for his revolution at less than fifty percent.

The Long March, that now almost mythical 368 days, had tested and strengthened his generation, but now they were almost all dead. It worried him that he had to depend on this new generation, which had never experienced insurrection and war, to continue the struggle. Against the weight of history, he asked them to carry on the revolution to achieve a perfect classless society. "For thousands of years it was said that . . . it was wrong to rebel. Marxism changed that," Mao told Chinese youth.

As Mao spoke of struggle, I felt that in spite of the infirmities of age, he was more dedicated to struggle than the young Chinese we had met and talked with.

After this burst of energy, Mao was silent. Then, as if responding to a question he often posed to himself, he described how he had dealt with his opponents in the past. "We are not terrible. We recognize that people commit errors. And if they understand their errors, they are fully restored to their former positions." Then, defensively, as though seeking our approval, he said, "We don't shoot people." After a pause, he added, "We forgave several Nationalists the other day." He was referring to the release of some Nationalist soldiers who had fought the Communists during the civil war. It was clear that Mao was sincere in his fervent belief that man could be reformed. I wondered, however, if he was conscious also of the irony of his statement. There had been no attempt to reeducate all of those, some say as many as 26,000,000, who had perished in resisting the Red Chinese.

The time passed quickly, and around twelve-thirty the Foreign Minister started signaling us from across the room, tapping on his watch to remind us of the lateness of the hour. Twice during the next fifteen minutes, I got up from my chair. And twice the Chairman protested, motioning with both of his hands for us to remain in our seats. Finally we were allowed to say good-night.

Throughout our visit, I had been fascinated by the two young attendants who sat behind Mao and carefully, even tenderly, watched his every movement. They almost seemed to breathe with him. As we prepared to leave, Mao leaned forward to rise from his chair. One of the girls, swift and graceful despite her bulky Mao suit, ran a comb through his hair so that he would be ready for the television cameras again. She had an extraordinarily serene and beautiful face. And her hair—unlike that of any other woman I saw in China—was softly curled. Her gentle assistance was a reminder that the once physically powerful man was now dependent on a circle of attendants who jealously protected him from stress and helped soften his isolation.

When we said good-bye, there was a firmness and determination in the Chairman's voice as he told me, bringing his arms down heavily on the sides of his chair for emphasis: "When your father comes, I will be waiting." And there was bravado and an air of unreality in Ambassador Huang-chen's assurance as we departed through the Ping-Pong room that the Chairman did not just watch the game, but still enjoyed playing it. And there was a final sad silhouette of Mao in the doorway supported by his two nurses. He was a god to his people and yet a human man who ten years before had said: "Men do not like to bear the burden of the revolution throughout their lives."

Why were David and I given an audience with Chairman Mao on New Year's Eve? Was it because of the personal warmth of the relationship between him and my father? The Chinese speak of my father as a "man ahead of his time," because of his vision of Sino-American relations, and Acting Premier Teng Hsiao-ping told me on New Year's Day, "We have never attached much importance to the Watergate affair." David and I traveled to China on the wave of goodwill created by my father's 1972 trip and his effort to build a bridge across thousands of miles and decades of noncommunication. To the Chinese, the Shanghai Communiqué, which was jointly signed at the end of that trip, is insurance that the People's Republic will not be swallowed up by the Soviet Union.

The day after our meeting with Mao we saw a copy of the English-language news summary that the Chinese distribute to foreigners in Peking and read that the Agence France Presse correspondent George Bianni had written that David and I were accorded "astonishing" treatment, "unprecedented for people without high rank." The Chinese used our visit to send a message to Washington that they wanted the relationship symbolized by the Shanghai Communiqué to continue. At the same time, the Chinese felt that the current United States-Soviet détente was in reality a Soviet victory. Despite his years of diatribes against American "imperialism" in Vietnam, Mao feared that in the aftermath of Vietnam the United States was becoming isolationist. It was fascinating for us to learn as we talked with members of our party that conservative Ronald Reagan was popular in Peking because of his outspoken opposition to the "new isolationists" and to those who favored cuts in defense spending.

We were in China as private tourists without diplomatic passports. And yet the Chinese government was sending us home with an urgent message: Beware the grasping hand of Soviet imperialism. Perhaps they overestimated our ability to spread the word.

On New Year's Day at a luncheon given by Acting Premier Teng Hsiao-ping, David joked about entering politics. One of the hosts said, "We'll vote for you!" A quick calculation of voting-age Chinese meant David would carry the nation, with that kind of backing, by about 478,000,000 votes!

Whatever the reasons for the semi-official nature of our trip, there was a personal element that transcended cold political realities—Mao's attitude toward my father. We witnessed an emotional expression of this in the toast Ambassador Huang-chen gave at the small farewell banquet for David and me in Shanghai.

The Ambassador spoke bitterly of the broken promises of the Soviet Union, of how in 1960 the Soviets cynically abrogated the Sino-Soviet Pact, the pact which Mao had declared ten years earlier was "eternal and indestructible." "Our friendship was torn up like a piece of paper," Huang-chen said.

During the following decade, the rift widened and by the time my father became President in 1969, there was a real possibility that China and Russia would go to war. That was why the Chinese appreciated my father's stern opposition to Soviet "adventurism," whether against China or any other nation. I imagine that Mao also felt a rapport with a President who, despite the risk that the Soviets would cancel the scheduled Summit meeting in Moscow, went ahead with the May, 1972, bombing of Hanoi and the mining of Haiphong Harbor in response to the brutal North Vietnamese offensive, and in an attempt to end the war. Though Mao supported North Vietnam, there were indications later that he respected the determination of the United States to stand by its allies and friends despite Soviet pressure. The bombing was a bold action which won the respect, if not the approval, of a man who was known for his own daring in foreign policy.

The Ambassador ended his toast by recalling my father's words during his visit to San Clemente six months earlier. "When I left office I discovered who my friends really are." The Ambassador's aide had tears in his eyes as he translated Huang's final words for us—"The Chinese do not forget their friends."

The Ambassador's words were moving, but they were also jarring. Mao had liquidated many loyal friends: Kao Kang in 1953; Liu Shao-Ch'i in 1966; Lin Piao, who once extolled Mao as "China's greatest liberator, statesman, teacher, strategist, philosopher, poet laureate and national hero," in 1971. But perhaps this friendship with an American could be idealized because my father was no longer in office. His relationship with China was part of history, unchangeable.

At the end of the farewell banquet, we drank a toast to my father on the eve of his sixty-third birthday. Huang-chen asked that as soon as David and I returned to Washington, we telephone the Chinese Liaison Office to inform them of our safe arrival. "Chairman Mao has followed your trip," he said. "He considers you part of his family."

Despite every effort by Mao and our official hosts to make us feel at ease during our trip, most of the time David and I were in China we felt as if we were on another planet. Our isolation was complete. We did not know the language. We were insulated in government guesthouses or hotels where we ate all our meals with the Ambassador and the four other members of our party— the Ambassador's wife, his aide, a protocol man and the interpreter. The strain was greatest in Peking because the guesthouse there is still used by the Russians during the almost perpetual Sino-Soviet border talks, and we assumed that every inch of it was wired. As a result, we communicated through amateur sign language, facial contortions and double-talk.

In an attempt to maintain our perspective, we set aside what we called "the five minutes" at the end of each day. And we spent those five minutes reflecting on who and where we were—two Americans dropped down in an isolated, xenophobic and humorless society, cut off from the United States, even cut off from daily newspaper information after we left Peking. During those five minutes we would stand at a window at night and look out into a vast darkness, whether in Peking, Canton or Shanghai. By half-past nine, everyone was asleep, and cities the size of Chicago were as dark and quiet as an Appalachian farm except for the towering red neon signs proclaiming the slogans of Mao's revolution, the only steady light over a sleeping population which would arise, expressionless, within eight hours to resume the work of building New China.

There was little to remind us of life in the United States, with one memorable exception. At the zoo in Peking on New Year's Day we not only saw the pandas, but also ran into Representative Margaret Heckler, who was touring China with a group of Congresswomen. She had a copy of *The People's Daily* with the front-page photograph of David and me with the Chairman. "Wait until Bella* sees this!" she said, and rolled her eyes upward. For a moment we were back in Washington.

We were often surprised during those two weeks by the isolation that diplomacy, geography and ideology have imposed on the Chinese. Our host, Ambassador Huang-chen, had been China's representative to the United States since 1973, yet when I asked him what his favorite restaurant was in Washington, I discovered that he had never been in a Washington restaurant.

Our conversations were almost always one-way. The Chinese expressed little interest in America or the American way of life. They asked no questions about our life at home. This is not to say that they had not done a tremendous amount of research about us. They knew many details about our families and mentioned that General Eisenhower had visited Shanghai in 1938 with Mamie and their son John. I had brought a small album of snapshots of my family and David's, our vegetable garden in

---

* Representative Bella Abzug of New York.

San Clemente and our pets, thinking that these glimpses of our life might interest the Chinese, but they evoked only the mildest polite interest. The only photograph that drew any response was a snapshot of David with his grandfather—the devil incarnate to the Chinese, the man who had pulled the strings that activated the hated John Foster Dulles.

Mao's warmth and the reference to his considering us part of his family made me curious to know more about his personal life and especially about his children, but despite my efforts, I learned practically nothing. Mao was a one-dimensional god. His likes and dislikes, his loved ones and friends, were not discussed.

In his determination to supplant Confucian devotion to the family with loyalty to the state, Mao had made it clear that he was not creating a dynasty. There are conflicting accounts about the number of children he had fathered. Edgar Snow, the journalist who had several long interviews with Mao over the years, mentioned two sons born to Mao's second wife and two daughters by the fourth Madame Mao, Chiang Ch'ing. One biographer, Stuart Schram, writes that Mao's third wife, Ho Tzu-chen, bore him five children, including one born on the Long March.

I find it incredible that Mao divorced Ho while in exile in Yenan in order to marry Chiang Ch'ing, for Ho was one of the thirty-one women who survived the legendary six-thousand-mile Long March from southeast China to the mountain fastness of Yenan in the northwest. For one year and three days, the Red Army, 100,000 strong, retreated from Chiang Kai-shek's Nationalists. They crossed thirty-four rivers and eighteen mountain ranges, scrambling along mountain trails so narrow that men and animals fell off, struggling through mud so deep that many were swallowed up in the mire. Only 15,000 lived to reach Yenan.

The Long March became central to Mao's existence, the most important part of the image he created of his own greatness. He compared the Long March to the creation of the world, asking, "Since Pan Ku [the mythical creator of the world] divided the heaven from the earth . . . has history ever witnessed a Long

March such as ours?" And yet he eliminated from his life the woman who had shared this ordeal with him. It was as if he alone could comprehend the agony, he alone could be the ultimate symbol, the veteran of the Long March.

Even in his fourth marriage, Mao still cultivated the image of standing alone, godlike, with total focus on duty to the state. Chiang Ch'ing's identity was not tied to his. She became a public figure in her own right as the leader of the radical faction during the Cultural Revolution.

The other members of his family were invisible, with the exception of his niece, Wang Hai-jung, who at thirty-four was the Vice Foreign Minister. But she kept her identity separate from Mao's. Once we asked her how she was related to the Chairman. All she said, in cold dismissal, was, "Some people say that I am related." Every time I asked about Mao's family I met the same dismissal, the same closed door.

The only glimpses of the Chairman's human side come from his writings. Mao's early writings provide flashes of the man of flesh and blood. In 1919, after the suicide of a young woman whose parents had forced her into a traditional marriage, Mao wrote nine articles in thirteen days, passionately denouncing the old society and calling for the "great wave of the freedom to love." There are 57,000,000 copies of Mao's poetry in print, roughly equivalent to all the volumes of English-language poets in print since the invention of the printing press. His poem *Tapoti* gives the reader insight into a man who could describe sunlight and shadows on a mountain as

> Red, orange, yellow, green, blue, violet, indigo:
> Who is dancing with these rainbow colors in the sky?

and in the next lines stun—with hard revolutionary realism:

> Bullet holes in village walls.
> These mountain passes are decorated,
> Looking even more beautiful today.

Chinese rulers have always written poetry, but Mao's poetry seems more of a personal indulgence than a bow to tradition. He wrote in classical characters that the average Chinese could not understand. He had stated publicly that poetry, however revolutionary in theme, was not healthy for young minds. Yet he allowed "unproletarian" praise of his works. It seems evident that Mao wanted to believe his poetry was a useful vehicle for dramatizing political messages.

On New Year's Day, 1976, in full knowledge of his mortality, Mao used poetry to call for renewed struggle and to issue another warning against the Soviet Union. When we read *The People's Daily* only hours after our meeting with the Chairman, the impact of his words to us about struggle and revolution was dramatically reinforced by the poems that appeared beneath the large photograph of the Chairman greeting us (it was the first time in fifteen years that he had not appeared alone in his New Year's Day portrait). In one poem, *Two Birds, A Dialogue,* a big bird [China] rebukes the sparrow [Soviet revisionism] that is obsessed by such unspiritual things as

> Potatoes piping hot,
> with beef thrown in.

and tells him

> Stop your windy nonsense . . .
> The whole world is
> Turning upside down.

In the other poem, *Chinkiang Mountain,* the one Mao had referred to so modestly the previous midnight, he wrote exultantly of struggle.

> I have long aspired to reach for the clouds . . .

and concluded boldly,

Nothing is impossible,
If you dare to scale the heights.

We were told that the Chairman had taken great interest in
our trip, and it became clear to us that he had meant our midnight meeting as an introduction to understanding his country
and the forces at work in it. In the days that followed our meeting, I believe that we saw China almost through his eyes. He not
only dictated what we saw, but he was at the center of all we
saw. Mao was China.

Additionally, in the two days preceding our visit with the
Chairman, we had been shown the quintessential Maoist sights
—a restored portion of the 2,500-mile-long Great Wall; the
Great Hall of the People, where not surprisingly we were taken
to the Taiwan Room (which they referred to as "our beloved
province"), and the May 7 Cadre School in the East District of
Peking.

There are several hundred of these revolutionary schools created by Mao to "reeducate" the bureaucrats and professionals.
In Peking alone, where bureaucrats abound, there are forty May
7 schools. They exist to remind those potential élitists that in
Mao's words, "The masses are the real heroes, while we ourselves
are often childish and ignorant." The "students" at these schools
are sent to them alone, without their families, to work on the
land as the peasants do from six months to two years, and to
attend rigorous sessions of ideological criticism and self-criticism.

The school we visited seemed to be in the middle of nowhere,
the land around it was flat and winter-barren, a dead tan color.
The austere dormitories were like army barracks. We were
shown a topographical map of the fields that these educated men
and women cultivate. The visit was proof of Mao's determination that no sector of society should advance at the expense of
the peasants, who make up eighty percent of the population.

Mao knew the poverty and primitive backwardness of the
peasants well. He had lived in rural China for twenty-two years,
twelve of them in the caves of Yenan. And in his youth, as an

assistant librarian in Peking, he had experienced dire poverty. There was a time when he slept in a room with seven other men, so tightly packed that he had to warn the others when he wanted to turn over. The man who had lived intimately with peasants for two decades idealized them. To Mao, every peasant was a hero. In 1959 he wrote:

I love to look at the multiple waves of rice and beans,
While on every side the heroes return through the evening haze.

The most dramatic preparation for our meeting with the Chairman was being taken to look at the poster campaign at Tsinghua University on our very first day in China. A poster campaign at Tsinghua had signaled the beginning of the Cultural Revolution in 1966 when Mao successfully destroyed the existing Communist Party organization and replaced it with "revolutionary committees" of workers, peasants, and soldiers, all trained to bear arms in the event of Soviet attack, all reminded by Mao that "If no struggle goes on, it means the end of life for any people."

A decade later we were the first Westerners to witness what we were told was a continuation of this revolution. Our visit began with a long discussion with a group of students, peasants, soldiers and a few faculty members. They kept reiterating that the sole purpose of education was to transform the system so that it serves the peasants. Then to reinforce our new awareness that "it is a sin to despise physical labor," the student-peasant-soldier-teachers took us to see the posters. The poster area, merely a narrow alley with a brown, packed-dirt path, is ugly in its bareness. Groups of students, chunky-looking because of the layers of clothes beneath their trousers and Mao jackets, stood silently in front of the posters. The fierce caricatures of the Minister of Education, an alleged élitist, were illuminated by a naked light bulb in the gathering dusk of the late afternoon.

The existence of the sub-surface turmoil in the country became apparent to us very early in our visit, and it gave greater significance to Mao's words on the need for renewed struggle. In our conversations with Chinese officials in Peking, we became aware that there were elements within the Communist hierarchy, especially in the Foreign Ministry, that opposed Mao's relentless attacks against the Soviet Union. On the other hand, Mao's niece, Wang Hai-jung, openly devoted most of her conversation to the evils of the Soviet Union, which led us to believe that in the top echelons of government, Mao, though frail and weakened, was still firmly in control.

Wang Hai-jung's prominence and her anti-Soviet rhetoric reminded us of the harsh Chinese attacks only ten years earlier on American "imperialism." As a worker in the Foreign Ministry in 1966, Wang had been a leader of the Red Guards. During the Cultural Revolution, a conversation between her and Mao in which he told her, "Rebel, when you return to school," was given wide distribution.

Wang Hai-jung gave a luncheon for David and me that featured the famous Peking duck, but I was relieved when the meal was over because her extremely correct attitude toward us was unsettling. It was clear that she was our hostess only because it was her duty as Vice Foreign Minister. We must have reminded her of the hated American capitalists of her schooldays. (I was also relieved that she had waited until after lunch to show us through the hotel kitchen with its rows of greased ducks—all force-fed for four months—in various stages of being roasted.)

Cultural Revolutions are essentially an exercise in redirecting and reigniting hatred in order to unite the people more firmly. Mao used hate as a weapon and rekindled it whenever he felt the threat of revisionism or deviation from his line. It had been a vital force in the Cultural Revolution of 1966, and in 1976 Mao, knowing his death was imminent, was afraid once more that the bureaucracy had become élitist, that revolution was an abstract idea, not a fresh memory. He felt a need for renewed tension, for revitalized Communist fervor. This time the chief villain would be "the grasping hand of Soviet hegemony." And the villain's accomplices would be those in the Foreign Ministry who favored rapprochement with the Soviets.

We watched for signs of the political upheaval that the poster campaign at Tsinghua represented when we visited the four cities on our itinerary outside Peking—Canton, Kweilin, Hangchow and Shanghai. But we saw no evidence that life in these cities had been affected by the "continuing Cultural Revolution." And in the months between our visit and Mao's death, the poster campaign never equaled in intensity the Cultural Revolution of 1966. It seemed to be merely a last gasp by Chairman Mao to reaffirm the need for struggle.

The peasants went on their way to market with their produce as they have for centuries, and on the country roads outside the southern cities of Canton and Kweilin, we saw them toiling under huge loads of sticks and branches, twice as wide and half as tall as they were. The most sensitive political nerve we touched was when we commented on the small pyramid-like mounds that dotted the Kweilin landscape. Our hosts, rather embarrassed, explained that they were peasant graves, disapproved of by Chairman Mao because they were a focus for filial devotion and— perhaps more important—took precious land space. When my parents visited Kweilin six weeks later, we were unable to tell them anything of political importance about the city, which is famous for its beauty. The only valuable information we could offer was to alert them to a certain hardness in the guesthouse accommodations.

We spent a very cold night there in the only guesthouse we stayed in that did not have heat. We had a strange double bed, which I painfully discovered consisted of a wooden platform and a very thin cotton mattress, more mattress pad actually than mattress. After I had undressed for the night, I ran from the bathroom and made a flying leap into bed to get warm—and severely bruised my hip. David solved the rock-hard bed problem by sleeping on the pillows.

Even in the slow-moving, beautiful southern cities, there was always one place where the rigid discipline of revolutionary philosophy engendered by the Cultural Revolution was clear and ever present—the classroom. Repeating Mao's slogan "If the satellite goes up, the Red flag will fall down," the students and teachers emphasized that mass education and revolution were much more important than building satellites or trying to reach the moon. For our part, David and I wondered how much Mao's insistence on a revolutionary mass at the expense of an educated scientific or academic élite would hamper or deny the development of genius among young Chinese.

I remember our arrival at the Shanghai Middle School, timed to coincide with the daily military drill of its fifteen hundred students. Standing on a wooden platform in the bitter cold wind, we watched them drill using wooden sticks for rifles. Later we observed boys and girls at target practice—with real rifles. We received tightly suppressed smiles from the students if they were successful. We toured the factory run by the school, and then visited some of the classrooms—one where students were learning to read English, another where they were making radio parts.

In Chinese classrooms, where the main emphasis is on a new pride in country, ironically there are portraits of four Europeans: Marx, Engels, Lenin and Stalin. Mao viewed Stalin as a great Marxist-Leninist who committed "gross errors without realizing they were errors." Students read publications like *China Youth* that feature heroic descriptions of Mao, such as one of the Chairman at a ship launching, "a fatherly smile on his face, looking at us with saintly eyes that had the warmth of the sun." As a boy, Mao had thought he would be a teacher. Today millions of Chinese children are in Maoist classrooms.

We visited another kind of classroom, where Mao is the focus of life in a highly controlled situation, the commune. Ninety-nine percent of China's peasants, we were told, live in communes. Swedish anthropologist Jan Myrdal's description of a typical commune wedding illustrates how strongly life there is centered on Mao. The bride and groom stand in front of a table laden with sweets, Myrdal reports, and bow low before a portrait of the Chairman. They then answer questions from their family and friends about how they met and how their romance grew. That is the ceremony. The lesson is clear. Mao's philosophy is the only sacrament needed to give meaning to marriage.

A few days before we visited the Tali People's Commune in Canton, David had lightheartedly referred to some of the misconceptions Western observers had of the commune system when it was first established, especially the idea of segregated dormitories, and the eventual breakdown of the family. Because of this, we should have anticipated the kind of "typical house" we would be shown at Tali. It was shared by a husband and wife, their ten-year-old son, six-year-old daughter, their red rooster— and their newly married daughter and her husband. The bride eagerly pointed out every nook and cranny of her bridal bedroom to us—including the colored portrait of Chairman Mao on the bureau, her high-school group photograph, and her wooden hope chest.

We were overwhelmed by the bustling productivity and the atmosphere of self-sufficiency at the Tali People's Commune. The peasants seemed content with Mao's one major concession to their love for the land—private ownership of very small plots. Two "barefoot doctors"—a young man, and a girl about seventeen with thick bangs on her forehead and long braids—were called in from the fields to show us their medical kits, which contained bandages, antiseptics and a few bottles of pills. Their medical knowledge was limited to first aid. In the village the dispensary was stocked with five gallon jugs of snakebite medicine and glass jars of traditional Chinese medicines. An herb garden next to the dispensary provided the ingredients for the medicines. In the commune "hospital" we saw an ingenious incubator—a drawer with an improvised sliding glass top (open just a crack) that held three tiny infants wearing colorful knit caps.

One thing in particular baffled me during our first few days in China, the elaborate seven- and eight-course banquets we were served almost every night—and the inevitable waste of so much food. It made me feel uncomfortably "bourgeois" in that austere society. I was well aware that my hosts shared Mao's view that the workers and peasants, "though their hands were soiled and their feet smeared with cow dung . . . were cleaner than the bourgeois and petty bourgeois intellectuals." The Chinese considered us rich, soft capitalists, and we had to accept that role as we traveled in chauffeured limousines and stayed in comfortable guest quarters. But after several banquets, I realized that food is something the Chinese are allowed to enjoy and that our lavish dinners were in themselves a message—"the masses are eating well."

The food was always beautifully arranged. Twice the centerpiece was the mythical bird the phoenix, constructed of multicolored hors d'oeuvres. Soup was often served in intricately carved gourds, and the desserts were made of glutinous rice in the shapes of goldfish, pandas and other animals, and fruit. With all the rich food, I restricted myself to yogurt and hot, steamed bread for breakfast. I inadvertently endeared myself to our hosts when I told them that I preferred the soft round rolls to the toast the Chinese had thoughtfully prepared for our American-style fried egg breakfasts. I had not realized that steamed bread is what the peasants eat.

It was in the resort city of Hangchow, where the emphasis is on beauty rather than revolution, that I felt Mao's presence most vividly. Our visit to the pagoda-like guesthouse on the west lake in Hangchow was a clear indication that our journey had Mao's official blessing. Our hosts acted as if they were bestowing a great honor. They could hardly suppress their own excitement.

It was a pale-green house with a red-tiled roof in a setting of fairy-tale beauty on the edge of the lake. Graceful, curving branches were mirrored in still pools. Mist rising from the pools bathed the leaves and branches in a heavy dew. The only sounds were peaceful ones—geese honking on the lake and the gentle lapping of the water against the shore.

A sentry box surveyed the entrance and People's Liberation Army soldiers patrolled the grounds. At one point I opened a door onto the terrace and was startled to come face to face with two of the guards.

In the living room, Ambassador Huang-chen showed me the piano my father had played during his visit in 1972, and a movie screen concealed behind a beautiful scroll. Our hosts were avidly curious and whispered among themselves as we looked at the two main bedrooms and their large bathrooms. The rooms were nicely but not extravagantly furnished. There was no art on the walls. The warmth in the rooms came from the silk bed covers and rugs in the same color as the spreads. I was slightly embarrassed when the Chinese spent several minutes looking at the luxurious bathrooms, with their toilet seats completely covered in fuzzy cotton.

At the end of the tour, as we sat in the living room eating tangerines, I had the feeling that our Chinese friends did not want to leave. It was not until I learned that this house was the favorite retreat of Chairman Mao and Premier Chou En-lai that I understood the eagerness and reverence with which they absorbed every detail.

Our tour of China ended in Shanghai, a crowded, bleak city of 11,000,000, its streets filled with relentlessly purposeful people going to and from work. It was a startling contrast to Hangchow. In Shanghai there were constant reminders of Mao's demand that his people live selflessly for the state.

In a hospital so cold that the patients wore their coats in bed, the Chinese proudly described their pioneering work in restoring severed hands and feet, toes and fingers. One girl, whose fingers and half her palm had been cut off in an accident and sewn back on by the doctors, showed us how she could move her fingers ever so slightly twelve months after the accident. She was introduced to us as "an educated youth who went to the countryside to work with the peasants." Her tragic accident reminded David and me of the hazards that educated Chinese face when forced to do unfamiliar manual work.

A beautiful ballerina, a member of the district Revolutionary Committee, was one of our hosts at a dinner in Shanghai. Feathery wisps of hair fell across her forehead, the rest was pulled back in a sophisticated knot at the nape of her neck. She sat with her ankles gracefully crossed, and in a quiet, shy voice told us how she had spent the previous year working in the fields during the day and dancing on the ground at night for the peasants. There was no point in asking her how a year away from the discipline and structured life of a ballet troupe had affected her ability to perfect her art. It is not easy in China to question the idea of self-sacrifice.

Mao believed that the goal of art should be to enable the masses to understand what they see or hear; propaganda was essential. It was a cultural shock to see Chinese ballet and discover that the most difficult artistic feat the *Red Detachment of Women* dancers performed was to aim their rifles at the air above the heads of the audience as they did splits. Beautiful art work is still to be found in China, but most of it is for the export trade. For example, we saw one large exquisite ivory sculpture—priced at no less than 50,000 American dollars! The overwhelming emphasis in art is on revolutionary propaganda. The ceramics factory we visited in Canton was mass-producing black soldiers with clenched fists and upraised rifles for export to Africa.

It was impossible for us to forget the bitterness between the West and China. No day went by without a short lecture detailing Chinese grievances against the "running dogs of imperialism" and the "gangsters who would reverse the great gains of proletarian socialism." But the lectures were delivered with a kind of benign or diffident detachment, which seemed to indicate that either the words meant less now or that David and I had been set apart for the time being from the "hated gang of revanchist conspirators" because of our New Year's Eve visit with the Chairman. Except for these moments our trip was relatively carefree—until we arrived in Shanghai.

Three of the five Chinese who traveled with us had been born in Shanghai and were old enough to remember the era of the foreign economic and trade concessions and the presence of Western navies. Anti-Western feeling still runs deep in Shanghai. The local organization is radical. It was from Shanghai that Mao launched the Cultural Revolution.

When we arrived in the city, an undefined mood of uneasiness came over our official group. The interpreter, Mr. Ni, became "ill" and uncommunicative; the others became somber. Every remnant of the Western imperialist presence was pointed out to us as we drove through the city.

"On your left, we have the Cultural Hall, which, as you may recall reading, was once a British brothel."

There were no smiles. The spontaneity and sense of discovery we had shared had suddenly dissipated. For our Shanghai-born companions, the memories were strong and the associations bitter.

We spent the first night there at a banquet given by the Shanghai Revolutionary Committee. Our host, the Vice Chairman, was thoughtful, intellectual, and conversed freely regarding trends abroad. Unlike other Chinese we met, he seemed to take special pride in his appearance. His Mao suit fit well. His hair was skillfully trimmed. At his insistence, we tried to guess his age and were surprised to learn that he was over forty.

We played word games during dinner and described the current film rage at home, *Jaws*. Our host told us that "the people of Shanghai would not allow such a silly film. They would tear down the theater!" The conversation was pleasant and easy until Ambassador Huang-chen's wife interrupted with a seemingly random observation, "I read today in *The People's Daily* that the life expectancy in Shanghai is now seventy-three years."

Everyone nodded vigorous approval and our host leaned over to tell us, "Before liberation, people died on the streets. The life expectancy was only forty-nine years." And everyone nodded again.

The Vice Chairman pressed on. "I remember when I was a boy, about sixteen, I used to read an American publication called *Miller's Review*."

He paused. Were we supposed to have heard of *Miller's Review*? I glanced at Ni, our interpreter—Shanghai-born, bald, unkempt, a dedicated revolutionary with a genuine love for children. His gentle demeanor had hardened. He was perspiring and, quite uncharacteristically, staring directly at us as he translated. It was as though he, too, recalled reading *Miller's Review* as a boy and marveled that our faces did not register recognition when we heard the name.

"And I remember a particular story in *Miller's Review*." The words had now become Ni's. "There was a little item one day at the bottom of the back page. And do you know what it said?"

The Vice Chairman gazed off into space, but Ni's eyes were fixed on our faces as he translated.

"There was a wind in the northeast section of town last night. And in the morning, eight hundred bodies were picked up."

Ni stared at us, then shook his head.

Silence.

After this the conversation limped along until we left, tired and disturbed. The spell had been broken. Now we remembered who we were and they remembered who we were and what we stood for. It was Westerners who had callously dismissed eight hundred Chinese deaths with a small item on the back page of *Miller's Review*.

Mao had changed much in his country, but not the memories. Suddenly I saw his intense struggle against a legacy of thousands of years of grinding poverty more clearly and understood his constant exhortations that the peasants, once discounted and powerless, must be unified behind his cause.

One wonders if Mao exalted the masses and proclaimed the revolutionary power of the human will because few other options were open to him. During China's struggle for survival as a nation since 1949, there have been times when there were not enough guns, but there have always been enough men. In Korea in 1951, only the first line of men had guns. Wave after wave of young soldiers who followed behind picked up the guns of fallen comrades. When the Soviet Union abruptly cut off their aid in 1960, there was not enough gasoline, but there were always enough men to bear burdens, pull carts and walk or bicycle to work. In 1976, Mao, his country still lagging behind the West in developing nuclear capability, proclaimed that wars were not decided by nuclear weapons but by the courage and perseverance of the men who fight.

Mao's philosophy was a response to the economic realities of material poverty and an almost unlimited supply of manpower, but it was more than just a response; it was a design, a religion for daily life which applied to men whether or not they were impoverished. He believed "the strongest fort is our will." He believed in the capability of men to struggle and to succeed. He was a philosopher who never stopped trying to reform man, even though the realist in him told him it was impossible.

Mao Tse-tung wiped out almost all vestiges of Imperial China. His battle was against a deeply ingrained tradition of harmony and order. His victory represented a staggering reversal, destroying two thousand years of loyalty to Confucian culture and substituting it with the harsh concept of unending struggle.

When we met with Mao, he had been tempered by illness and by age. His philosophical self-confidence must have been shaken by the bitterness of the breach with the Soviet Union, which claims the same philosophy of revolution and brotherhood. Yet, I suspect that the words he wrote in 1949 to a friend of his revolutionary days in Canton are words he would have reaffirmed even as he faced death. "Do not let too much sorrow break your heart. Keep the whole world always in your far-sighted eyes."

In China, it was often difficult for David and me to follow that advice and keep the whole world in our eyes. Morning after morning we were mesmerized by the sight of thousands on foot, dressed alike, on their way to work, with the realization that in cities we never saw there were millions more, all delicately balanced on the edge of poverty. It was difficult not to be overwhelmed by the zeal with which they approached their bleak existence.

There were times when it seemed as if our long days in China would never come to an end, even though we were tightly scheduled with few free moments. It was inconceivable that we would soon return to the world of "you deserve a break today."

The weight and intensity of political thought was so great that one expected the slightest crack would destroy the whole structure. Yet on January 9, as we prepared to fly back home, China suffered a major blow that appeared to us to cause only a ripple of reaction—the death of Premier Chou En-lai.*

We received the news from an American journalist thousands of miles away in New York. His telephone call wakened us in Shanghai at seven-thirty, but the jolting news was not confirmed until Ambassador Huang-chen's aide came to our bedroom an hour later to advise us formally of the Premier's death. It was the morning of my father's sixty-third birthday.

I was surprised to hear the blare of martial music over loudspeakers, the same music we had heard the morning before. The hotel staff brought in a beautiful vanilla birthday cake with white and brown frosting, presumably for David and me to have with breakfast. And in a silk-covered box was an even larger cake, decorated with the Chinese characters for "Happy Birthday, Mr. Nixon," to take home to my father.

There was sorrow on the faces of the Chinese we saw that morning at the hotel, but everything else was the same. Despite the blow of Chou's death—and there would be emotional mass demonstrations after his funeral—our hosts made it clear to us that in the end, it is the masses who count, not the leaders. Chou's death would not change the course of history. Unspoken, but unavoidable, was the message that Mao's death would not change things either. In a sense, Mao had already passed into history. He was godlike, remote. China's strength would not be diminished by her god's physical demise.

I feel sure that in his declining years, Mao was aware of his place in history. He had always felt he was a man of destiny. As early as 1919, he had prophesied that "one day the reform of the Chinese people will be more profound than that of any other people . . . an age of glory and splendor lies before us." His words were always carefully chosen as if he were speaking for history. Even in those dark days of retreat in Yenan in the Thirties, when he was interviewed by Edgar Snow, he used to insist that after

---

* Soon after our arrival, we had been told that Premier Chou En-lai was too ill for us to deliver my father's letter to him personally, so I had given it to the Foreign Minister to transmit to the Premier.

Snow had written the interview in English it be translated back into Chinese. Then Mao would make corrections before giving his approval.

But the man who was realistic enough to see China's short-comings must have been realistic enough to see his own. He must have anticipated that his successors might come to find fault with him, just as Stalin's found fault with him, and Khrushchev's with him. Mao's legacy, while great, is flawed. He attained goals that had once seemed visionary, but at a fearful price. His life, perhaps above all others, gave rise to the violent and increasingly revolutionary demands of the world's poor. He advanced a global struggle that has and will continue to bring enormous dislocation and change—and death. From his early days in Canton through the years in Yenan and finally in Peking, death and violence were inextricably entwined with revolutionary idealism. Whatever history decides, Mao's life will stand as a testament to the power of the human will.

When we met with the Chairman in the middle of the night, we had an impression of a man restless in solitude. He was drawn and spent. Yet each time we started to leave, he ordered us to stay—almost as if he were clinging to visitors who possessed opportunities he may have wished were his again.

His painful physical vulnerability reminded David and me of the hours we had spent with President Eisenhower before he died. Sitting at his bedside at Walter Reed Army Hospital, we had been deeply conscious of our youth, of the opportunities ahead, and of the roads we had yet to travel. It was also a re-minder of how carelessly we live—and how much can be lost and wasted by living life casually.

We experienced the same emotions that New Year's Eve. When we finally got up to leave and the Foreign Minister led us to the door of the study, Mao had walked with us. We were told later that he had not made such a gesture for over two years. I felt sad when I shook his hand in farewell.

"You people are young," he said. "Come back to China. In ten years she will be great." He no longer smiled. The two nurses stood by his side supporting him. He waved twice as we disappeared into the darkness of the next room. I looked back for a moment. My last glimpse was of a weary old man, turning, attempting words with his nurses, then gently being led away to be alone again.

I like to think that Mao may have been tempted to give us advice, as the old advise the young, when we said good-bye. If he had, I believe it would have been those words that he repeated over and over for so many years, that were the very rhythm of his life:

"Ten thousand years is too long. Seize the day! Seize the hour!"

Mamie
Doud
Eisenhower

"Don't give them any of that prissy stuff. Give them a big wave. Really say hello."

MAMIE DOUD EISENHOWER has star quality. To a little girl, she outshone the President. I remember my first visit to the family quarters of the White House as if it were yesterday, not because I saw the intriguing upstairs home of the President, nor because of the historical significance of the day, but because of Mamie. I liked her because she laughed so much. It was on January 20, 1957. Because the 20th fell on a Sunday that inaugural year, there was a private inaugural ceremony at the White House in the morning so that Chief Justice Earl Warren could swear in President Eisenhower and my father for their second terms.

I had met Mrs. Eisenhower before, but only for the briefest of white-gloved handshakes. As my parents and my sister and I drove down Pennsylvania Avenue for the ceremony, I was excited because I was going to see where the President lived. I remember being surprised that we used an elevator to go from the ground floor to the East Room one floor above. To my mind, the visit was all too short. The swearing-in ceremony took less than fifteen minutes. Refreshments were served afterward but my Coke was gone in minutes, and we all just stood in the big room—which was empty except for a piano and several gold chairs—and talked. There was no opportunity to see anything— no bedrooms, no kitchen, no pets.

When we were escorted to the elevator to leave, I started to cry. Mamie and my mother bent down, very concerned. Through my tears I explained I wanted to play in the White House.

Mamie smiled and invited Tricia and me to stay for lunch with David and his sisters, Anne, who was seven, and Susie, five years old. There was creamed chicken mounded into a tall ring of white rice. I had never seen rice that "stood up" by itself before, and I was very impressed. We had peas and, to my dismay, tall glasses of milk. I hated milk. Afterward, David took us outdoors to play. We chased each other around the paved path that circles the magnolia tree planted by Andrew Jackson. All of a sudden, Mrs. Eisenhower appeared at the double-door entrance to the White House. "David, David! Come here!" she commanded.

Her grandchildren froze in their tracks. David was scolded for bringing his sisters and guests outside without coats. I do not remember much more about the visit except that I fell in love with Anne and Susie's four-story doll house and spent the rest of the visit playing dolls in the third-floor playroom.

In 1973, sixteen years after that visit upstairs at the White House, I drove down Pennsylvania Avenue again to another inaugural. Ike was no longer with us, but Mamie was in the car with me on the way to witness my father being sworn in to his second term as President. David was in the Navy then, on duty in the Mediterranean with the Sixth Fleet, and Mamie told everyone, "I'm playing David." The same self-assured, utterly natural quality that had impressed me as an eight-year-old was still very much in evidence.

During the ride down Pennsylvania Avenue to the Capitol, I gave an occasional timid wave to the crowds lining the streets. "Don't give them any of that prissy stuff," Mamie said. "Give them a big wave. Really say hello." And with that she stretched her arm out the window and, holding her hand high, waved it proudly like a flag.

The sight of Mamie waving must have been a flashback to the Eisenhower Administration for many people along the route. I could not help but feel disappointed that all they saw that day was her cheery smile and her big wave, little more than she had revealed during her eight years as First Lady. Mamie had seen her role as one of emotional support for her husband—and nothing else. That star quality she possessed could have catapulted her into a position of constant public attention and adulation. The country could have come to understand the strength, the endurance and the utter charm of Mamie Eisenhower. But public recognition could not have mattered less to her. She had no interest in promoting herself.

Up until the time of President Eisenhower's third heart attack in March, 1968, I had known Mamie only as a light-hearted, fun-loving future grandmother-in-law and a woman, as one of her friends put it, "with a whim of iron." My image of her was little more than "Smiles, Bangs and Jewelry," the subtitle of one of her biographies.

Tragedy showed me another side of her character and I came to have a great respect and admiration for Mamie as well as love. She had been tested many times. There had been the death of her firstborn son at age four and the uprooting strain of nearly three dozen moves before she and Ike finally retired to Gettysburg. There had been the long war years when Mamie was home alone with her Army wife's knowledge of the dangers her husband faced, along with rumors of romance. And later the anxiety of having her only son in the combat zone during the Korean War. But the supreme test must have been the eleven months at Walter Reed Army Hospital in Washington, D.C., when she lived in a small room just a few yards down the hospital corridor from her husband, the months of Ike's dying. Ike never saw her waver or weaken. Even the family rarely did. There were only a few times when her eyes, blue and round as a porcelain doll's, filled with tears. But she never cried in self-pity. Her tears came from the sorrowful knowledge of how little she could do for Ike, from the realization that he was ultimately alone in his suffering, alone in his dying.

It was a sadness we all shared. In my diary I wrote on June 16, the day after President Eisenhower suffered his fourth heart attack, "David is heartbroken because he pictures his grand-father as a maverick who would like to ride off into the hills and die with his boots on." That attack marked the beginning of the period when Mamie and her family had to stand by and watch as Ike, for the first time in his life, found that he no longer could control his destiny.

He fought his illness with courage, as he had fought all his battles. In August, he decided he was strong enough to address the Republican National Convention by television. His decision proved to be a fateful one. Mamie knew, even before the television cameras were set up in the living room of Ward Eight at Walter Reed, how much effort, how much emotion this speech represented for Ike. The next morning he suffered his fifth myocardial infarction. He never left his bed again. And Mamie knew that the strain of the speech was the main cause of this fifth heart attack.

Mamie had not tried to stop Ike from making the speech, nor did she resent this final devotion to duty. Ike's credo was her credo—duty, honor, country. Not that she did not put up a fight upon occasion for him to consider his own well-being and that of his family first. But that August, Mamie gave the impression in her every act and look that if Ike had to suffer one more cruel, breath-stopping heart attack, she was reconciled. Reconciled because Ike also knew the cost of this final act of duty—and accepted it as part of his service to the political party he had helped strengthen and in the cause of the country he loved.

From that day on, her life revolved almost completely around her husband. There were weeks and weeks when she never left the hospital. One exception was a surprise birthday party we gave for my mother. Mamie told us she could not accept the invitation until the last moment. It would have to depend on what kind of day Ike was having. She did come, but as soon as the cake was cut she left. "My beau is waiting up to hear all about the party," she explained to my mother. She told me later that Ike was awake when she arrived back at the hospital. She stood near his pillow in the darkened room and described the toasts, the piano playing, and how much he had been missed.

She guarded his energy jealously, allowing one old friend a ten-minute visit, another a stingy five minutes. I was touched by the way she denied herself the pleasure of seeing Ike with his grandchildren. She believed that more than two visitors at a time was too draining, so David and I would visit while she watched the clock in her room. When our time was up, the nurse would appear. "On Mrs. Eisenhower's orders, the time is up," she would say. Ike often insisted we stay longer, but within minutes, Mamie would come bouncing into the room, her wide, petticoated skirt swinging, and we would be cheerfully, but firmly, hustled out. Playing warden with people Ike wanted to see must have been a painful role for her at times. Another difficult task was censoring news that would excite or upset Ike. He was not told about the rioting at Columbia University in the spring of 1968 until the disturbances had quieted down, nor was he allowed to watch the annual Army-Navy game on television. Mamie filtered the progress of the game to the frustrated one-time Army football coach.

Mamie's efforts—strongly encouraged by the doctors—to regulate Ike's visiting hours resulted in what must rank as one of the classic Secret Service radio communications. David and I, who were both in college at that time, visited his grandfather as often as we could. One evening our trip from Northampton, Massachusetts, took longer than usual. We were in a Secret Service car, silent because we did not want to share our conversation with the agents, and they were as constrained as we were. Suddenly the silence was broken by a message crackling over the intercom. "Springtime advises you hurry. It is past Scoreboard's bedtime." Sunbonnet (Julie) and Sahara (David) had a good laugh, as did the agents in the front seat.

Mamie lived in a tiny sitting room and bedroom (complete with high hospital bed) just down the hall from Ike's suite. Apart from her hot pink telephone and the tins of cookies and boxes of fudge from friends, the room was surprisingly empty of personal belongings for a woman who loved to surround herself with knickknacks and family photographs. Perhaps her reluctance to bring personal objects to the hospital, like the tiny Coke bottle that was really a lighter and the miniature megaphone that contained a picture of Mamie, which had been on her bedside table as long as her grandchildren could remember, was an unconscious refusal to accept the gravity of Ike's illness. She was not blind to the deterioration in his condition—I remember the summer day when she was sad because "Ike will never be able to play golf again"—but she never gave up hope that one day the doctor would come in and tell her that Ike would be going home next week.

Mamie disliked closed doors and the sense of being shut in, so her door onto the hall was always slightly ajar, making it impossible to forget for one minute that she was in a hospital. There was a constant traffic of doctors and nurses up and down the stark white hall with its harsh fluorescent lighting. The windows of her rooms were sealed. The changing seasons outside did not touch those within. There were no scents of autumn leaves or the fresh smell after a rain.

She used to spend hours sewing facecloths together with long, looping stitches of thick yarn and stuffing them with foam to make pillows for her friends. And she politicked. She kept a bowl of Nixon buttons on the coffee table. I did not realize the extent to which she pushed my father's candidacy until one afternoon shortly before he won the Republican nomination, I met two soon-to-be relatives—Milton Eisenhower's daughter and son-in-law—who were visiting Ike. They were wearing Nixon buttons. I was elated and surprised since I knew the General's brother was not an avid Nixon campaigner. I learned much later that Mamie passed out buttons to everyone—visitors and doctors alike. Most found her "gift" difficult to refuse.

Despite the fact that she was in essence camping out at Walter Reed, she managed to create a happy atmosphere on special occasions. I remember particularly our Thanksgiving at the hospital in 1968. My parents, Tricia and I joined David and his family in the main dining room of Ward Eight. We had a traditional turkey dinner, the same Army fare being served throughout the hospital.

With the precision of an Army drill instructor, Mamie arranged for members of each family to share a course of the meal with Ike in his bedroom. Susie Eisenhower and Tricia had juice with him, David and I had fruit cup, and so on, until the pumpkin pie with my mother and David's mother. Mamie, at the head of the table, daintily but firmly orchestrated the entrances and exits of everyone from my father to David's twelve-year-old sister, Mary. As we went in and out of Ike's room that day, we had to pass the rows of monitors, a vivid reminder that this might be his last Thanksgiving.

Neither Ike nor Mamie lost their courage—or their humor. David and I visited him a month before the election. He was lying flat in bed, his head just slightly raised. He was so thin and wasted under the Army-issue sheet. The blueness of his eyes was startling in his dead-white face. When I kissed his cheek, I was surprised by the trace of beard stubble. Somehow I felt the lifeless skin could not produce a beard. As soon as we said hello, Ike gave us a huge grin and whipped open his hospital smock, exposing his Nixon "buttons." He had stuck Nixon decals on the electrodes attached to his chest.

When the morning came that the doctors told Mamie that her husband would not live through the day, she sat stoically in her chair by the window in the sitting room, a small figure, crumpled and silent, but a figure of dignity. Her sister, "Mike" Moore, Barbara Eisenhower and I did not try to offer words of comfort. There were none. Mamie, who had remained at Ike's side through so many months, had no interest in the deathwatch. Only at the very end, accompanied by John Eisenhower and David, did she slip into Ike's bedroom for one last look, to touch his hand one last time.

The thought of "what Ike would expect" sustained Mamie through the four days of state funeral ceremonies. She met privately with many of the world leaders who came to Washington to pay final tribute to President Eisenhower, including Charles de Gaulle. The family had been excited when they learned he was coming to see her, but Mamie, who had never been awed by the famous or the powerful, simply welcomed him as the old acquaintance that he was. De Gaulle had tears in his eyes when he bent over to kiss the hand of the frail woman who would carry on General Eisenhower's name and honor. Mamie was seated on a small sofa and she patted the cushion next to her in a motion for "Mr. Presidente" to join her. He did not blink an eye at the Spanish pronunciation of his title. Mamie sat calmly with the wartime leader of free Frenchmen everywhere. She vulnerable, and yet full of strength in her self-composure. He a hulking, tall figure, but gray—gray skin and hair, a gray film over his eyes, stooped and older now in his sorrow at Ike's death.

President Eisenhower's body was borne by train across the heartland of his country to his boyhood home, Abilene, Kansas. Mamie lay in her bed by the window and all through the night, as Ike would have wished, she waved to the little clusters of people standing beside the tracks. Before reaching Abilene, she ordered the train halted and a flag placed on the car bearing Ike so that his countrymen might know where he lay.

He was buried on David's twenty-first birthday. That night as the train returned to Washington, Mamie arranged for a birthday cake. She stood in the doorway of the dining car, her eyes glistening, holding on to her sister's arm as the train lurched, and sang "Happy Birthday" to Ike's namesake. The ceremonies were over. Mamie Eisenhower had to pick up the strands of her life. She had to go on.

As the wife of a great man, fame had touched Mamie Doud Eisenhower as well as her husband. Yet she remained remarkably unchanged. She was unconcerned with her public image, indifferent while at the eye of the storm of press attention, and indifferent now in retrospect. She does not pretend to be anything more than what one sees on the surface—a pleasantly rounded grandmother with a perky fringe of bangs beneath a flowered hat. A grandmother and an attractive woman with great feminine charm. Most of all, she was the woman behind the man, the woman who proudly proclaimed, "Ike was my career."

Mamie and Ike were plain folks, as common as cherry pie.

Mamie mirrored to an incredible degree the moods and mores of the Fifties. Happily, the emphasis on the old-fashioned virtues of wife and homemaker fit Mamie's natural lifestyle, because if one thing is certain about Mamie Doud Eisenhower, it is that she would not have changed herself to fit the Fifties.

She was nineteen when she first met Dwight Eisenhower, attracted to him because, as she told her grandson, she was sick of being courted by "all those lounge lizards with patent leather hair." Ike was different. "He was a bruiser," Mamie recalls proudly, well-built and handsome. Most intriguing of all to the flirtatious Mamie Doud, he had a reputation as a woman hater. She changed that. During their courtship, Ike often found himself sitting on the front porch with Papa Doud—waiting for Mamie to return from a date with another young man. She was irresistible. The newly commissioned Second Lieutenant inscribed his West Point photograph "to the dearest and sweetest girl in the world." It was a traditional inscription considering the quality that most caught his fancy—her sauciness. Mamie was charmingly saucy—and, as he learned later, as strong-willed as he.

She knew exactly what she liked and did not like right down to the colors she would wear and those she would not wear. The woman with the china-blue eyes rarely wore blue blouses because it did "terrible things" to her skin. Ike was to discover that often there was no logic behind her likes and dislikes or her reasoning. Some things in their marriage, including their bridge partnership, could not survive Mamie's carefree, "my way" attitude.

A typical scene at the bridge table:

Mamie bids.

Ike (making a valiant effort not to yell): "Why did you make that play?"

Mamie (with a pouting underlip and a shrug of her shoulders): "Oh, I don't know. Just 'cause I wanted to."

Ike throws his hand down, leaves bridge table in disgust, his face a flame color.

End of scene.

When Mamie talks about learning to live with Ike, she frequently contradicts herself. She never fails to remind me when I visit her in Gettysburg that, "There can be only one star in the heaven, sugar, and there is only one way to live with an Eisenhower. Let him have his own way." At other times, she pertly boasts, "Ike never told me what I should do, because he knew I'd go right out and do the exact opposite." Throughout their fifty-two years together, it was a sometimes tempestuous relationship which was least subject to strain when they had public roles to fulfill. The responsibility of being on view disciplined their lives and drew them together.

Mamie took a long time to grow up. "I was rotten spoiled," she says cheerfully. Her parents pampered her and Mamie adored them. She was unusually close to her mother. Fortunately, Ike and Mrs. Doud (he called her Min) became good friends at the very beginning. Min lived with them in the White House for months at a time, until 1958 when ill health forced her to return to her home in Denver.

Mamie's deep love for her family was to be a bond between my grandmother-in-law and me. I have never felt closer to her than on the evening of my parents' departure for their first Presidential trip to Asia in 1969. It was a sultry, rainy night. After we watched them board Air Force One, Mamie, Tricia, David and I sat in one of the limousines to watch the takeoff out of the rain. Tears welled up in my eyes. I could not repress the thought that something awful might happen—a crash, an assassin's bullet. It was one of those moments when you realize how uncertain life is and how precious parents are. Suddenly, I felt Mamie's hand, so small and fragile. She closed her fingers over mine. All she said was, "I understand." And I knew that she did.

When Mamie was married in 1916, it marked a wrenching break with her three sisters and her parents, to whom she had confided every emotion. She had to adjust to a husband who rarely verbalized affection and who had no use for small talk.

A slap on the back between the shoulder blades or a pinch was Ike's way of saying "I love you." His career as an Army man made Mamie's adjustment to marriage even more difficult. Before her wedding she had never spent a night alone. She knew little of the world beyond the comfortably well-to-do Doud household.

In making a home out of the two rooms that had been Ike's bachelor quarters at Fort Sam Houston outside San Antonio, Mamie added her own touches of elegance. With a twinkle she described to me how she rented a piano for five dollars a month and then to make room for it, she stashed all the "inessentials," like Ike's field equipment and revolver, behind it. But decorating was like playing house. What was harder for a sheltered girl was adjusting to the realities of Army existence—the abrupt orders to move, the hardship posts, the separations.

One month after the wedding, Ike had to leave on maneuvers. Mamie protested. Ike put his arms around her. "Mamie, there's one thing you must understand," he said. "My country comes first and always will. You come second." Mamie was nineteen then and it took her many years to learn to live with that statement. I suspect that it was not until Ike was President of the United States that she came to fully accept second place.

Ike had told Mamie that his country came first, but he might have phrased it differently after the birth of his son. He was on field assignment at Fort Oglethorpe in Georgia when Doud Dwight was born in San Antonio. Mamie makes the arrival of her baby sound like a slapstick comedy, but it must have been a frightening experience. A few days after Ike had left for Georgia, near eleven o'clock at night Mamie decided to mail a letter to him. Although barely able to drive—Ike had given her a few crash lessons before he departed—she took the car. When she came back she had a stomachache. She thought is was due to the nervous tension of driving alone in the dark. So she ate an orange in the hope that would make her feel better. Mamie told me, "Mama [Min Doud was staying with her] took an awful long time to explain about the stomachache!" Mamie spent most of that endless night sitting up in a rocking chair. In the morning, Mama Doud somehow arranged to have Mamie taken to the post infirmary—lying down in the back of a rickety, horse-drawn cart. To the surprise of the doctor, who had sent Mrs. Doud out for breakfast, the baby was born a half hour later.

Mamie and Ike loved Icky, as they called their baby, more than anything else in the world. They had never been closer than during Mamie's pregnancy. Ike had watched Mamie, who had no knowledge of sewing (it was he who had let out many of her dresses during pregnancy), lovingly stitch a long white christening gown. When Icky died four years later from scarlet fever, a deep sorrow separated his parents. Mamie had always expressed her emotions—every complaint, every thought, petty or important. Ike, to his dying day, found it difficult to express his feelings. Now they were tragically alone in their reactions to the death of their son. She grieved openly, he silently.

The depth of Ike's despair comes through even in his restrained account of Icky's death in his book *At Ease*. It was "the greatest disappointment and disaster in my life, the one I have never been able to forget completely," he wrote. Icky was buried in the Doud family plot in Denver, but when Ike made plans for his own burial in Abilene, he arranged for Icky to be re-interred there. On March 31, 1969, Mamie watched Ike's casket placed under a honey-colored marble slab. Another slab, as yet blank, lay beside him. At his feet was a tiny marble marker for Doud Dwight Eisenhower. Icky could not be left alone in Denver. To his parents, he was forever a child in need of nurture.

Half a century later, Mamie was still unwilling to say much about how Icky's death changed her relationship with Ike. The pain is too deep. But there is no doubt that the loss of their beloved son closed a chapter in the marriage. It could never again be unblemished first love. Ike was no longer an untried idealist, Mamie no longer a blithely romantic spirit. Now they regarded each other with open eyes.

When Mamie talks about her marriage, she paints no rosy, unrealistic pictures. "There were a lot of times when Ike broke my heart," she told me one rainy afternoon in Gettysburg. She was propped up in bed, where she spends more and more of her time, surrounded by books, photographs, boxes of candy, letter paper. "I wouldn't have stood it for a minute if I didn't respect him. It was the kind of thing where I respected him so much, I didn't want to do anything to disappoint him." Her face was uncharacteristically sad as if she were looking back on the times when she had disappointed him.

Mamie blames herself for many of the strains on their marriage, and says she would like to be able to go back and do some things differently.

John Eisenhower was born one year after his brother died and came to be the greatest source of happiness in their lives. Ike always wanted John to have brothers and sisters and Mamie now realizes it was hard for their son to be an only child. She explained, "I always felt there was plenty of time to have another child," but the years of constant uprooting rushed by. Ike was so convinced of the desirability of large families that later on he persistently—and insistently—tried to persuade his son and daughter-in-law to have a fifth child. Despite a healthy "bribe," they decided four children were sufficient.

More than anything else Mamie regrets that she gave in to the temptation to go "home" to Denver so often. The only times I ever felt Mamie was meddling in my marriage were when she strongly advised that I join David whenever we were separated by school or the Navy or campaign travels. I never resented this "meddling," because I sensed the reason for her urgency. Mamie had learned that there were always plenty of women waiting to bat their eyes at handsome young officers.

It is easier to understand her frequent, prolonged absences when one considers some of the homes she and Ike shared. In Laurel, Maryland, in 1919, the only place they could find was a rooming house several miles from the post, where the electricity was turned off at eight in the morning and did not go back on until after dark. Night after night, Mamie sat in their gloomy room with a two-and-a-half-year-old toddler waiting for Ike to come home—and the lights to go on. The only bathroom was down the hall. They ate at a boarding house around the corner. She lasted ten days there. Mamie's voice was anguished when she described the scene when she fled back home to Denver half a century before. "Ike begged me to stay," she said, "but I told him, 'Ike, I can't live my life this way.'" And Mamie took Icky and went to Denver.

In 1923, when she was pregnant with John, she sailed with Ike on a troop transport to his new station in Panama. Because of her severe claustrophobia, she refused to sleep on the bunks one on top of the other with only twelve inches between. Instead, she spent the nights on a short couch—so short she had to sleep in a jackknife position—for the week-and-a-half trip. And the Army post in Panama was not much improvement over the troop ship. It was all the nightmares of a gently-bred girl come true. Their first night in Panama, a rat gnawed at their bedroom door until daybreak. The cockroaches were "the size of mice." The legs of their bed stood in pans of kerosene to fend off the bedbugs. And, worst of all, a bat swooped down at them as they were getting ready for bed that first night. Mamie told me proudly how her hero, Ike, stood on the bed, unsheathed his sword and swung wildly at the bat, "just like Douglas Fairbanks." She laughed when she described that night, but at the time it was not at all amusing. In fact, life in Panama was as alien to Mamie as life on Mars. Within a few months, she was back in Denver again, where John Eisenhower was born.

Mamie's frequent retreats to the Doud home, whether because of inadequate housing or one of Ike's long absences on maneuvers or other duty, created tension in her marriage. She leaned on her parents for emotional support as she had before her marriage, and now they came to lean on her. When her older sister Eleanor died in 1918, Mamie spent six months with her family. She had been married only two years at the time. It was pleasant being home where family and servants cared for her and her child. It was impossible not to contrast how well her family provided for her, how comfortable she was at home, with the life Ike could give her on an Army salary, moving from base to base.

And yet the luxuries from Ike, like Mamie's silver tea service, were far sweeter, because they were so dearly bought, and a testament of his deep love. When the Eisenhowers lived in Washington from 1927 until 1935, Ike used to save as much of his five-dollars-a-week lunch and transportation allowance as he could—often walking several miles home from the old State-War-Navy Building. With this money and with his poker winnings, he bought Mamie the tea service—precious piece by precious piece.

Each time Mamie and Ike were reunited after a separation, she had to accept his decisions for their life, a change from the enforced independence she had had to assume when he went away, a change from the role of daughter that she enjoyed at home with her parents to that of a wife. Abruptly she was expected to fulfill Ike's needs in a wife—to be a woman, not a girl; someone to place on a pedestal, not a cute, volatile child to be coddled; someone to provide a haven from the pressures of his job. Mamie often said that Ike never brought his problems home with him and she never offered advice. "He didn't need that kind of help from me." The kind of help he needed was something Mamie seemed to have to learn how to give all over again after every retreat of hers to the family bosom. It is to the credit of both Mamie and Ike, and an example of their mutual respect, that despite the unusual strains created by Army life and their subsequent strong disagreements their son could write in his memoirs, "They never quarreled in front of me."

The Army Mamie knew was one of hardship for married couples, and yet she came to like this world that was so different from her own. When I asked her why, she told me of taking Icky's body to Denver for burial a few days before Christmas. Upon her return home to Camp Meade, Maryland, the men and women at the post had taken down their Christmas tree, put the red tricycle and other Christmas presents out of sight, packed up his clothes and toys. Mamie was to find comfort and support many times in the tightly knit Army family.

And so she endured thirty-four moves. Her furniture often

did not fare as well as she. During the transit from Washington to the Philippines in 1937, all her china was smashed and not a single chair came through undamaged. Ike was home for only one of those moves. At Fort Lewis, Washington, in 1939, he tried to help, but, as Mamie told me, he only "muddied the water." He randomly shoved boxes and unprotected furniture into the van. Did Mamie protest his "help"? "Good gravy, no! I never told him anything. He told me." She did, however, finally suggest that the movers were the experts in that situation.

And she endured a quarter century of short Army-ordered separations. And she endured the long, bleak years of separation during World War II. It was no easier for Mamie than for other Army wives to see her husband go off to war, even though the assignment in Europe was to be the greatest challenge of his life. She saw him only once between 1942 and 1945, years when she lost twenty-five pounds from anxiety and its accompanying insomnia.

When Ike came home after the war, he had, in Mamie's words, "changed terrifically." It may be closer to the truth that it was their relationship that had "changed terrifically." He had his own personal staff, his own routine. He was no longer dependent on Mamie for lunch money or carfare as in the prewar days. "He belonged to the world and not to me any more," Mamie told me. During the war, although Ike was a conscientious correspondent, he had been unable to share many of the details of his life. Most of the time his location and his actions were top secret. Mamie remembers that the closest he ever came to describing his location on a trip was to write, "I am someplace you would hate, way down under the ground." She learned months later that the "someplace" was Malta.

When in 1952, Ike chose a way of life that would mean permanent fame and entail constant press attention, for as he wrote in his memoirs, "Anyone who goes into politics becomes public property the day he does so," Mamie was not enthusiastic. She had never been an ambitious woman. She wanted only what was best for her husband and best did not necessarily mean the

Presidency. She understood, however, that despite all the aspects of political life that she and Ike would find uncomfortable, he was swayed by those who argued that it was his duty. Duty was a concept he could not ignore, and Mamie respected him for it.

Mamie Eisenhower sums up her years in the White House with the statement, "I never pretended to be anything but Ike's wife." She did not make a career out of the Presidential years and had a detached take-it-or-leave-it attitude about life in the Executive Mansion. After years as chatelaine of the large households that were part of Ike's position as Army Chief of Staff, President of Columbia University, and Supreme Commander of NATO in Paris, she was not over-awed by one hundred and thirty-two rooms and a staff of eighty. She had led the remarkable kind of life in which she could look back and declare, "Every job Ike ever undertook was a step up." Life went on almost as if her husband had not been elected to the most influential position in the postwar world. Mamie spent a great deal of her time in the White House planning for the life she would have with Ike in Gettysburg when they left Washington. She oversaw every detail of reconstruction and decoration for the farm they bought in 1948.

If Mamie Eisenhower were First Lady today, she would be a fish out of water, subject to pressure—which she would have resisted—to be involved in First Lady projects, to project a prescribed image. She predated the era of "the press secretary to the First Lady." Her social secretary, Mary Jane McCaffrey, handled all aspects of First Lady publicity. She rarely gave interviews. They were foreign to her come-sit-on-the-couch-and-chat-with-me nature; the kind of warm communication in which by the end of five minutes you are asking her to describe each charm on her bracelet.

Mamie set foot in the Oval Office only four times during Ike's Presidency. "And each time I was invited," she says. It was merely the continuation of the pattern Ike and Mamie had established in their first days of marriage in their two-room apartment in San Antonio. Ike never brought his business home with him, and Mamie frankly resented it if he did. When he was home, he belonged to her world, a world of light-hearted family life where there were no pressures.

In the 1300 pages of President Eisenhower's two-volume memoirs, there are only fifty references to his wife. A detailed account of the policies and history of his administration, it reveals little of the man who set those policies and made the history, and consequently Mamie figures hardly at all. Significantly, however, Ike confirms that more than any other person Mamie bolstered his spirit and will to continue when he lay flat on his back in a Denver hospital after his first heart attack in 1955. "She was convinced," Ike wrote, "that my job as President was not yet finished."

There was only one occasion when Ike sought Mamie's guidance on a Presidential decision—whether or not to seek a second term of office. Whenever Mamie is asked about that, she takes great care to point out that her advice was to urge Ike to do what he felt was best and to listen to his most trusted advisors. To Mamie, the White House represented the years of Ike's life that were most subject to strain and pressure. She had no sentimental attachment to the White House and often told me, "I don't miss that place at all." But she did not join her son John and her brother-in-law Milton Eisenhower in urging Ike to guard his health and not serve for four more years. "He still had a job to finish," she felt.

Everything Mamie undertook as First Lady was as Ike's wife. After his first heart attack, she signed every letter of acknowledgment and thanks for the 11,000 get-well messages, because she considered those who wrote as neighbors and friends. She entertained enthusiastically, enjoying the State Dinners and teas and all the other social duties that came with her husband's new position. Many women today view with wonder Mamie's preoccupation with perfectly planned parties and meticulous housekeeping while First Lady, but life was different then. There were long dissertations in the newspapers, for example, speculating on whether or not Mrs. Eisenhower would shake hands gloved or ungloved. Mrs. Truman and Mrs. Roosevelt had worn gloves, considering it "less fatiguing" to shake hands with them on, but Mamie, it was believed, would prefer the friendliness of the ungloved hand. (She wore gloves.) News accounts of Eisenhower era parties abounded with detailed descriptions of the ladies' dresses, the table decorations, and Mamie's costume jewelry. The fashion cry became, "If Mamie can wear junk jewelry, so can I."

Despite the seemingly fragile femininity of her two-inch-high heels and petticoated skirts, Mamie was a commanding figure within the White House. It was her home for eight years, and the staff did not make a move without consulting her first. She told me she regularly inspected every part of the house, including the coffee-break room in the basement used by the White House police, paying particular attention to the ashtrays.

She handled the financial budget—and it was often a struggle. When the Eisenhowers moved in, Mrs. Truman had left exactly $375 for redecorating. Mamie spent hours shopping for accessories that would fit the budget, including sheer curtains for the third-floor bedrooms that cost only a dollar a panel. And the staff learned to live with her major eccentricity—she could not tolerate footprints showing on the carpets before a party. Fortunately, very few of the mansion's rugs were without patterns and Mamie's favorite Bissel carpet-sweeper was not needed often. Despite her eagle eye, the staff came to love Mamie because she took such an interest in what they did and in their personal lives as well. I remember the great excitement that preceded each of Mamie's visits to her old home during my father's Presidency.

The Eisenhowers entertained more heads of state than any of their predecessors, and Mamie scrutinized every detail of the six-course State Dinners. Carnations were used on most occasions because she believed that people were not allergic to them. She delighted in dreaming up special decorations. The Easter luncheon for Senate wives in 1957 was her greatest triumph. It must have fulfilled every party fantasy Mamie ever had. Easter bunnies peeked out of robin's-egg-blue shells on the mantel of the state dining room. Butterflies of pastel net floated from the ceiling, and a birdcage was suspended from the center ring of the chandelier. The ladies wondered how two small birds could fill the room with chirps and trills until Mamie told one of the butlers to "turn down the birds."

In greeting foreign visitors, Mamie adopted the attitude that they were welcome guests in her home. When Elizabeth, the Queen Mother of Great Britain, visited Washington, my parents met her at the airport and escorted her to the White House where she would be the guest of President and Mrs. Eisenhower. Mamie warmly greeted Elizabeth as an old friend from postwar days in London. As she poured tea for Elizabeth in the West Hall sitting room, they settled down comfortably to nonstop girl talk, while my parents and Ike, who were sitting so that they could see the elevator, watched the ushers bring up trunk after trunk. My mother told me that Ike became more and more agitated as the luggage piled up. His face flushed and he rolled his eyes in disbelief as the trunks kept coming. Elizabeth and Mamie chatted on.

Creating a home for Ike was more important to Mamie than entertaining. She chose a small room on the second floor with the northern exposure painters need and turned it into a studio for Ike. It was next to the elevator so that he could slip over from the Oval Office for fifteen or twenty minutes whenever he had time. The President loved to cook and, because he could not putter around in the banquet-size kitchen in the White House without disturbing preparations for official entertaining, Mamie had a kitchen installed on the third floor, with the counters tailored to his height. Ike had done most of the cooking when they were newlyweds since, as Mamie likes to say, "I can only make two things: mayonnaise and fudge." Later on, cooking became one of his favorite ways to relieve tension. When my five-foot-three-inch sister started using the kitchen for entertaining boyfriends at the beginning of my father's administration, it was a struggle to work in "the General's kitchen," as the staff still called it. She could not reach the shelves without using a little stepladder.

Ike's health was Mamie's major concern. I remember the first time Mamie and I sat together on the second floor of the White House to watch my father address the nation. From the window we could see the brightly lighted Oval Office where technicians were testing cameras. As we waited for the speech to begin, it was unusually quiet on the second floor. No noise from behind the double doors of the family kitchen. No messages being delivered. No phone calls from the switchboard. The atmosphere of waiting and watching must have reminded Mamie of the times she had listened to Ike speak.

Mamie broke the silence. Her large blue eyes were opened wider than ever as she re-lived one of her biggest fears. "After 1955," she said, "whenever Ike gave a speech, I always sat there in utter dread that he would have a heart attack on the air." She did not need to say more for me to understand what the pressures of those last White House years must have been.

She was zealously protective of Ike. He had offered to make two campaign stops in southern Illinois for my father during the last crucial weeks of the campaign against John F. Kennedy in 1960. Two weeks before the election, however, Mamie called my mother. After Ike's last campaign trip on behalf of my father, his blood pressure had soared alarmingly. Mamie was near tears as she told my mother of her fear that if Ike tried to do too much, he would be stricken again. My father did not take the President up on his offer. On November 8, the election was decided by the closest popular vote margin in Presidential history. Kennedy carried Illinois by a mere 9,000 votes.

Although Mamie had never contemplated any role in the White House beyond that of the President's hostess and helpmeet, her activities as First Lady were determined to a great degree by her health. That she accomplished as much as she did is due largely to her great determination. Ever since a bout with rheumatic fever when she was seven years old severely damaged the valves of the left side of her heart, she has been acutely conscious of each heartbeat, and has not had a high energy level. When she is fatigued or troubled, the irregular heartbeat becomes frightening in its intensity.

By the time Mamie reached the White House, she had long

ago learned how to live with what doctors term a "cardiac injury." She knew how to pamper herself. Breakfast in bed and an hour or more of bed rest were part of her daily routine—despite the demands of being First Lady. And Mamie wholeheartedly believed what a skin specialist once told her—if women stayed in bed for at least one day a week, it would do more for their complexions than all the face cream in the world. Whether it is due to heredity or bed rest, at eighty, Mamie has a virtually unlined face.

She also suffers from Ménière's disease, a rare inner-ear syndrome, which was diagnosed at Walter Reed Army Hospital in 1953. The chief symptom is dizziness, and she has to hold on to someone when climbing stairs and when she is in crowds. Mamie's difficulties with her balance caused rumors that she drank heavily. Ike was so upset by the rumors about her drinking and the frequent sniping about her lack of activity that he forbade her to read *The Washington Post*. Typically, the dainty peaches-and-cream lady of iron will solved the problem by reading the *Post* secretly.

Mamie gave in to her health in only one respect. She was scared to death of flying. Ike wrote that she "never quite convinced herself that an airplane flies." But she did convince herself that her heart could not take easily altitudes over three thousand feet. Though she valiantly flew with Ike during most of his barnstorming campaign of 1953, she hated it. Characteristically, she did not try to understand or explain this fear. With a laugh and a shrug toward heaven, all she will say is, "I just don't like it."

Mamie became quite ill after a trip to the West Coast in the summer of 1971, and the doctors felt the best way to get her home to Gettysburg was by plane. My parents persuaded her to fly to Washington on board Air Force One. She agreed on the understanding that the plane would not fly much over three thousand feet. In the family sitting room on board the plane, my mother and I tried to keep Mamie diverted. We played gin rummy and chatted. Mamie was burrowed down in the large armchair by the window, her place of refuge in the treacherous air. Once in a while, she would boldly venture to peek out the window. As Air Force One soared to a cruising altitude of 32,000 feet, she remarked how beautiful the sky was from 3,000 feet. We agreed. And Mamie turned her attention back to our card game.

Considering the limitations of Mamie's physical strength, I admire the way she tried to fulfill what she felt were Ike's expectations of duty. Sadly, at the very moment when she most wanted to honor him—the state funeral in Washington—Mamie was not able to follow his casket up the forty-five steps to the rotunda of the Capitol. The small figure in black had to use the elevator.

Before Ike died, he and Mamie had decided that they would give the Gettysburg farm to the nation. Mamie had no intention of living there without Ike. She had once said, "Whenever Ike went away, the house sagged. When he came home, the house was alive again." But the only property that the Eisenhowers had ever owned in their fifty-two years of marriage was like a magnet. It drew her back. She is ambivalent about her life on the farm. She is often lonely and she is isolated from her family and most of her friends. Nor is she one to live in the past. "I'm not ready to die," she often tells her son and her grandchildren. "There are too many things I want to do yet." But part of her did die with Ike. "When Ike died," Mamie told me, "the light went out of my life." And that expresses it all.

Her happiest moments are when her son and daughter-in-law or her grandchildren come to visit her. But John and Barbara Eisenhower live in Valley Forge, Pennsylvania, a full three hours' drive from Gettysburg, and her grandchildren are even further away: David, Anne and Susan, all in New York, and Mary in Georgia. When we do go for a visit, I love to hear her voice—usually floating down from her bedroom—call out, "Sign in." The guest book in the entrance hall is a ritual at the farm and Mamie pores over it after her visitors have gone.

She is still a blithe spirit—on the surface. Widowhood has been a bitter experience in many ways. She has been hurt. Something precious has been taken from her. The public viewed Mamie as the one who had to be protected and shielded from the harshness of political life. Yet, in reality, it was Mamie who watched over Ike. Now the one she protected is gone.

For more than a year after Ike's death, his bedroom remained the same—as if he had gone out for nine holes of golf and would soon return for lunch in bed and a nap. But gradually, the little room, one-third the size of the one he shared with Mamie at night, has become a storage area. The scales have been pushed back into a corner. The narrow bed with the plain wooden headboard, which belonged to Mamie's grandparents, is covered with books and boxes. The personal items on his chest of drawers have been removed to make room for more books and boxes. But, despite the organized clutter, the room is still his, austere and masculine: an unframed round mirror above his bureau, the portrait he painted of David and Anne Eisenhower at the head of his bed.

He is there at every turn in the house. His gray velvet rocking chair still has the choice place in front of the television set. It has not been reupholstered, although there are bare spots on the arms where the nap has worn off. A pad by the telephone contains his handwritten phone numbers. The golf green on the lawn, now used as a sandpile for the great-grandchilden; the gone-to-seed vegetable garden; the skeet range at the end of the field in sight of Mamie's card table—all are reminders of Ike. His presence is so real that it is often painful for his grandchildren to visit the farm even now. And it is very real to Mamie. Sometimes as she lies in bed in the afternoon, she can see Ike's knobby hand, the knuckles broken so often when he was a semi-pro baseball player, grasping the railing at the top of the stairs.

Mamie needs many defenses against her memories and loneliness. She often does not come downstairs for several days at a time, but when she does come down and sit on the porch where she and Ike spent their evenings together, she fights the loneliness by playing complicated games of double-deck solitaire, while her radio or a television soap opera keeps her company.

"I don't file a fingernail without turning on the radio," she likes to say. She usually wears a dressing gown from her collection of fifty, many of them more than thirty years old. When she walks, it is a slow progress. She does not move fast because of her tendency to vertigo—and also because most of her dressing gowns are trailing affairs that more than touch the ground. But the house *does* seem to sag without Ike and at twilight, Mamie retreats to her bedroom again. She has covered the emptiness of Ike's side of their king-size bed with a protective wall of books stacked four or five volumes high, boxes of stationery and greeting cards and tins of sweets. The wall stretches from head to foot.

Mamie no longer has Ike to surprise with red-and-white "love-bug" undershorts on Valentine's Day, but she continues to lavish cards and small gifts on family and friends. Propped up against several pillows in bed, she will spend four hours at a time writing the month's birthday cards. Photographs of those she remembers on special occasions surround her. Her bureau alone holds thirty-eight. And she faithfully answers her mail from the public. Those who write announcing the birth of a child receive a "welcome to this world" letter from Mamie. She is proud of her distinctive, bold handwriting and each message is a work of art. She pays a great deal of attention to it and is distressed when it is not perfect. "I can't seem to get my M's right today," she told me once when I visited her at the farm.

Mamie tries valiantly not to be a possessive matriarch. Often we do not learn until it is too late how much she has counted on a visit or a phone call that never came. Mamie has seen five of the seven apartments David and I have lived in since our marriage, but in her effort not to cling, she has never spent the night. I understand why she made the trips to visit us in Virginia Beach and even in Atlanta Beach, Florida. She wanted to be able to visualize the rooms. "I sit up here in bed and think about you in your nest," she tells me. And whenever we talk on the telephone, her first question is "Where are you?" And I tell her that I am in the kitchen or the bedroom and know she is picturing it all in her mind.

She believes in family obligations and loyalty and uses her

telephone as a link with those she loves. Every other Sunday (she alternates with "Mike" Moore) she calls her Uncle Joel Carlson, now in his nineties, in Boone, Iowa, where he was born and where he has lived all his life. When Uncle Joel and Mamie spent Thanksgiving with my family in the White House in 1969, we discovered that Joel was not a docile character. He never was. When Mamie was born, Uncle Joel's first comment upon seeing the four-pound infant was that she looked like "a little picked chicken." During the Washington visit, Joel followed his own rigid schedule. Since Mamie was also accustomed to having schedules built around her wishes, there was a barely submerged conflict, although Mamie asked us to try to follow Joel's routine. It included a Coke at ten (Mamie has hers at eleven), dinner at six (Mamie usually dines at seven-thirty), bed at eight-thirty (Mamie retires two hours later).

A typical incident was the family movie party. We had a six o'clock dinner for Uncle Joel's sake and planned to watch a film afterward. In the theater, Joel settled into his chair, and promptly fell asleep. At precisely eight o'clock, the alarm clock inside Uncle Joel's head went off. He woke up, rose from his chair and announced, "Well, it's my bedtime. Good-night." Somehow the spell of the movie was broken when Uncle Joel's silhouette loomed on the screen as he slowly sauntered out. It was touching to see Mamie submit to orders from "Uncle," and slightly unnerving to hear him scold his seventy-three-year-old niece, who was as spunky and saucy as when Ike first met her on the parade ground at Fort Sam Houston so many years before.

Mamie rather enjoys racy novels. "To think—at my age—learning all about phonography," she says, taking pleasure in her conscious mispronunciation of the word. And she is a past master of the pointed remark. When I called her one Sunday, which happened to be Father's Day, she said, "Tell that beau of yours I'm sorry I couldn't send him a Father's Day card this year." It was a not-so-subtle expression of her desire for a fourth generation Eisenhower in the male line of the family. Her relations with family members are not always placid, but the disagreements are nothing more than skirmishes. Mamie says what she thinks and that is the end of the argument. She rarely sulks or holds grudges.

Because harboring hostility toward others is not part of her own personality, Mamie cannot understand it when she meets it in other people—and closes her eyes to it. If she reads something ugly about someone she cares for, she shrugs, "Oh, I don't believe that." Despite President Truman's belittlement of Ike in *Plain Speaking*, Mamie does not express any emotion other than puzzlement. In the tone of someone who is disappointed in a child she says, "Mr. Truman knew better." She prefers to focus on the happier aspects of the Truman-Eisenhower relationship, such as her Spanish lessons with Mrs. Truman. During the Truman Administration, a group of women met at the White House once a week for lessons and a luncheon. They rotated the shopping, cooking and serving duties. Did she learn any Spanish? "Heavens, no! We just talked."

Although Mamie loves to gossip in the sense of old-fashioned girl talk, she does not indulge in dissecting famous personalities. She is tight-lipped even about those she knew well, like General Douglas MacArthur. The most she has ever divulged about the seven years Ike served as MacArthur's aide in the Philippines is that the General was charming to women—and that he rouged his cheeks.

The woman who has met or entertained most of the great figures of the twentieth century is simply incapable of name dropping. Her idea of fun is well suited to the pace of life in Gettysburg. She turns down embassy and government invitations and finds more fascination in discovering the latest junk food in the grocery stores. She is always coming home with new things to try. She can tell you the most recent sugar prices and whether eggs are "as high as a cat's back." Thirty years of making ends meet on an Army salary have made Mamie vigilant about saving. Even today, despite the money earned by Ike's best seller, *Crusade in Europe*, Mamie watches every penny. And scrutinizes every bill, particularly the electric bills. One does not waste electricity in Mamie's house. Not long ago, a visiting family member could not sleep, so he decided to get up and read. Instead of ruining his eyes on the dimly lighted porch, he spent several hours reading in the hall bathroom. But he made one mistake. The next morning, Mamie's first order of business was to find out who had forgotten to turn off the light in the bathroom!

When Ike died, he left a huge wardrobe of suits. Mamie could not bear to see them go to waste, so I went through them and picked out five or six for David. Mamie was visiting us in the White House at the time and we arranged to have the tailor come when David got home from a golf game one afternoon. David dislikes shopping and dislikes having clothes fitted even more, but when he got home that day he could not escape our carefully laid trap. Mamie was ensconced on the blue sofa in the third-floor study with her cigarette case and ashtray next to her, and the tailor was there with the measuring tape around his neck and a big pincushion on his wrist. For the next hour and a half, David had to stand still while his grandfather's suits were being fitted to him. To this day, when Mamie is extolling my virtues to her friends, she will say, "Julie is so saving. She had Ike's suits remade for David." David is still wearing those suits today. They were very good suits.

Mamie is never happier than when I compliment her on a dress and she can say she bought it at Penney's for twelve dollars. She always pronounces the store's name as *Penné* with a mock French accent. It is Mamie's gentle way of spoofing those women who devote time and money to being the first to wear the latest high-fashion designer clothes. There is nothing pretentious about the farm, either. One is aware of this in the first few minutes. In the entrance hall, Mamie has two objects of equal value to her on display—a four-dollar ceramic elephant dressed in an Uncle Sam suit and an antique bronze-doré French clock.

Mamie is simply herself and she accepts others for what they are. She is intolerant only of those who "put on airs." Perhaps it is her Army background that makes her wary of social climbing and of those who pull rank. She is proud of Ike's cow-town origins. I once heard a cultured woman from New York, whose family sets great store by its social register status, tell Mamie the involved story of how her ancestors were among the early arrivals in the country and their great importance in the Colonial government, ad infinitum up to the Seventies. Mamie listened politely and then she chuckled, "Oh, yes, I know all about that. The Douds came over from Sweden in 1600." Since there were no Swedes in America in 1600, let alone Douds, her companion could hardly miss the point.

Part of Mamie's charm is that along with her unpretentiousness, she frequently enjoys being the center of attention. Because she has an engaging personality—she is fun, a flirt, one amusing contradiction after another—people have always been attracted to Mamie. And as Ike rose in the Army hierarchy, more and more people paid court to her. Yet she is blissfully unaware that she enjoys special attention. She likes to tell stories that illustrate just how much a part of the mainstream she really is. Her favorite is about spending Easter with us at Camp David. The Navy stewards dyed eggs with the names of each family member to serve as place cards at breakfast on Easter Day. Mamie relates that the eggs all bore formal titles—"The President," "Mrs. Nixon," but hers, to her delight, read just "Mamie."

I saw these two facets of Mamie's personality—on one hand desire for the simple life, on the other the focus of attention—during a jaunt to some of Gettysburg's tourist attractions. At the Electric Map, President Lincoln's Train, and the Wax Museum, Mamie was greeted excitedly by the managers and special tours were arranged for us. She enjoyed the recognition and would have been hurt if it had not been forthcoming. Yet we concluded our royal progress in a crowded Hardee's, nonchalantly eating hamburgers.

Mamie's attitude toward Secret Service protection is that those who claim they did not like it (i.e., granddaughter-in-law Julie) are pretending. "Everyone likes a little special attention." For a young person, however, being guarded is a nightmare. It means a complete lack of freedom to go anywhere or see anyone without a shadow. Former First Ladies are entitled to Secret Service protection until their death or remarriage. Mamie's agents are an important part of her life now. Without them, she could not travel as she does. And they are her friends. When she makes plans for the holidays, one of her major concerns is how they will affect the agents with small children. Ever since her first days in the White House, she has known each man personally, whether or not he enjoyed flying, liked fudge, how many children he had.

When she speaks of the agents to friends she calls them "my boys." They are held dear for different reasons. One is a survivor of David's childhood summers at camp, of the rattlesnakes in the showers and of the terrible food. Another, of impressive proportions, is affectionately referred to as "Twinkletoes." He breezes in to visit with Mamie, light on his feet despite his bulk, and lighter still in his comments. These men whose job it is to protect her have softened the devastating changes of widowhood. Yet even these friendships are susceptible to change. The agents serve on orders from the Department of the Treasury and at any moment they can be, and are, transferred. Mamie's family is still her center of gravity as it has been all her life.

Mamie Doud Eisenhower is the most sentimental woman I have ever known. Not long ago at the farm, I opened a drawer and found an old piece of paper folded into quarters. Tucked inside was a tooth, the string still attached. In pencil, John Eisenhower had written, "Dear fairy, please leave my tooth."

And she still believes in young love. It was Mamie who viewed the romance of her eighteen-year-old grandson with unabashed sentimentality and unquestioning acceptance. She grew starry-eyed when she talked to Ike about our college courtship. Ike, on the other hand, wrote David a freshman year "now that you are a college man" letter in which he outlined a plan for the future that, if the various educational degrees he suggested were earned, allowed for marriage when David was around thirty-three. When we were married our junior year in college, I wore the delicately thin garter of blue silk and lace Mamie had worn fifty-two years before. And on my finger was her mother's engagement ring.

Mamie cannot remember the date of the Geneva Summit meeting, but more than sixty years after she first set eyes on Dwight David Eisenhower she recalls every detail of their meeting down to the Sunday afternoon outfit she wore. Mamie must have been a vision in a pink cretonne skirt with an embroidered silk crêpe de chine blouse, a wide cummerbund with pink roses, and tiny rose-shaped coral earrings. The costume was completed by a chipped straw hat with a wide band of the same material as the cummerbund. Meeting Ike was the most significant event of her life.

Mamie lived for one man, and that man was dominated by the concept of service to his country. But she was not steam-rollered by his career or caught up in his crusades. Her concept of service was much narrower. She is a woman of tremendous self-confidence, a strong character who has obtained almost everything she wanted from life. It suited her to serve Ike because she loved him and admired him until he died in 1969. To most, ideal love is not belonging to someone, but it was for Mamie. She was Ike's wife, pure and simple, and happy about it.

Mamie Eisenhower has no interest in the immortality syndrome. She seems unconcerned about memorials to her husband or the necessity of reminding people of what he accomplished. She has a simple faith that what Ike was will shine through. What he was to her and to himself is what truly counts. When Ike was buried in Abilene, Dean Miller, the pastor of the church in Palm Desert where Ike and Mamie used to spend winters, captured the essence of Mamie Eisenhower's life: "Mrs. Eisenhower graciously shared her husband with the world, but he belonged uniquely to her."

920
Eis   Eisenhower, Julie
         Nixon
       Special people

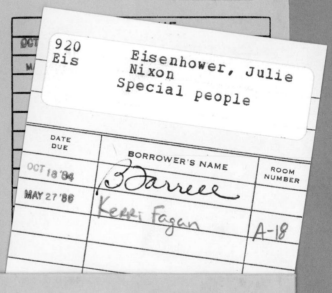

920
Eis   Eisenhower, Julie
         Nixon
       Special people

DATE DUE	BORROWER'S NAME	ROOM NUMBER
OCT 18 '84	Barrell	
MAY 27 '86	Kerri Fagan	A-18